Hallmarks of the Southwest

in cooperation with the Indian Arts and Crafts Association

Barton Wright

West Chester, Pennsylvania 19380

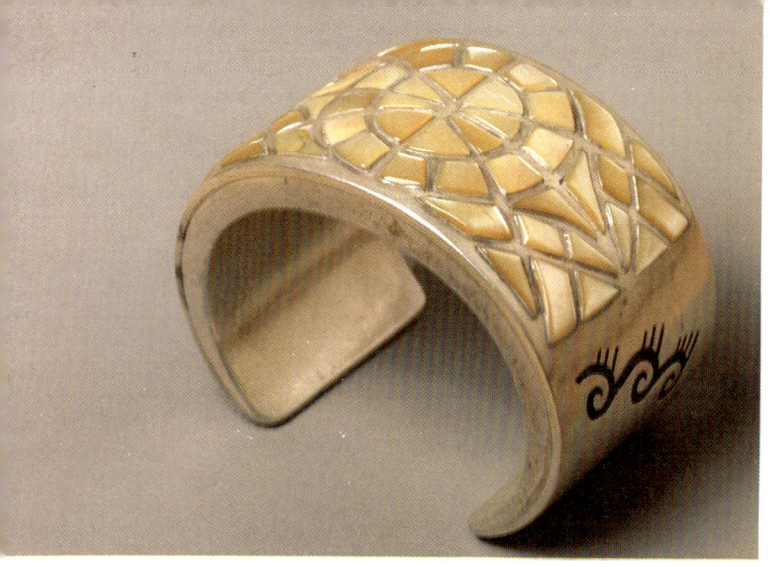
Joe Begay. Private Collection. Overlay with stones.

Paul Saufkie. Heard Museum (NA-SW-Ho-J-46). Sp. Silver overlay.

Hodson. Private Collection Channel inlay. Craftsmen is Anglo.

Lawrence Saufkie. Private Collection (MO-2OO).

Unknown maker. Heard Museum (NA-SW-Na-J-255). Channel inlay.

Silver overlay. C. Eldon James. Private Collection (MO-343).

R.C. Sr./Zuni. Private Collection (MO-626). Carved mosaic inlay.

Unknown maker. Private Collection (MO-521). Leekya style bracelet with stones.

Edaakie. Private Collection. Mosaic inlay.

Unknown maker. Private Collection (MO-529). Shadow box work.

Virgil and Shirley Benn. Private Collection. Channel and carved mosaic inlay.

Jackson. Private Collection (MO-559). Applique with stones.

Copyright © 1989 by Barton Wright.
Photographs copyright © 1989 by Stephen Miller.
Library of Congress Catalog Number: 89-84165

All rights reserved. No part of this work may be reproduced or used in any forms or by any means—graphic, electronic or mechanical, including photocopying or information storage and retrieval systems—without written permission from the copyright holder.

Printed in the United States of America.
ISBN: 0-88740-161-9

> Published by Schiffer Publishing, Ltd.
> 1469 Morstein Road
> West Chester, Pennsylania 19380
> Please write for a free catalog
> This book may be purchased from the publisher.
> Please include $2.00 postage.
> Try your bookstore first.

Contents

Preface 5
Introduction 7
Biographical Entries 9
Index I: Initials................153
Index II: Nicknames and
        Given Names 175
Index III: Symbols 177
Index IV: Shop Marks 197
Index V: Tribal Affiliations 199
Index VI: Unidentified Marks ...211
References 213

Kenneth Begay. White Hogan. 1950 Best of Show at Intertribal Ceremonial in Gallup. Flatware.

Kenneth Begay. White Hogan. Flatware.

Kenneth Begay and Ivan Kee. White Hogan. Flatware.

Unknown maker. Heard Museum (NA-SW-Na-J-323). Sandcast with stone.

Unknown maker. Private Collection. Hammered with stone.

Preston Monongye. Heard Museum (NA-Sw-Ho-J-40b). Centrifugally cast box with stones.

Preface

This listing of marks used by Southwestern Indian craftspeople is the result of a question asked by virtually everyone who encounters their work and that is, "Who made it?" The question was of importance to the Indian Arts and Crafts Association, a group of interested merchants, craftspeople, and collectors working to promote authenticity and ethical standards in the marketing of handmade American Indian arts and crafts. One of the avenues chosen by the organization to accomplish this was the preparation and distribution of booklets on various facets of native craftwork. These pamphlets were written by knowledgeable people whose interests coincided with the need. They were printed and used by members of the IACA for education and promotional purposes. Discussion of this question by the members produced an excellent commentary on how segmented the information was on the knowledge of craftsmen, of their numbers, and other data, and pointed out the need for a list of craftspeople's marks that was of greater extent than Margaret Wright's excellent work on Hopi silvermarks. Because of a long-standing interest in this field I volunteered to produce the needed booklet. However, the enthusiastic assistance received from both members of the IACA and non-members almost immediately converted the booklet to a book. Interest was expressed by advice, lists of marks offered, background and histories of the craftspeople, as well as leads to other artisans and lists. in addition a great deal of tolerance was shown for the length of time eventually required by the project.

It is almost impossible to thank each person who assisted because of the sheer numbers. Consequently I would like to thank the entire Indian Arts and Crafts Association, the Board of Directors, and the members, both merchants and craftspeople, who cheerfully let me ask questions and rummage through their goods while they were rushing to set up booths for exhibitions. I would like to thank Myles Libhart, the Director of Museums, Exhibitions, and Publications for the Indian Arts and Crafts Board for the assistance offered. I am particularly grateful to the trading families of Gallup whose members were so helpful, among these Ruth Cousins Hobbs who let me sort through her vault, Phil Woodard for his excellent records, Tom Woodard who shared his knowledge of craftsmen's histories and exhibition data, Bill Auble's backgrounds and John Kennedy's computer contents. Numerous merchants were of special assistance, Ed Youngs Inc., Atkinson Trading Co., Canyon Silver Company, Zach-Low Inc., Toh-Atin Gallery, Rocking Horse Ranch, White Hogan, Hill's Indian Jewelry Inc., Towayalane Trading Co., and the Heard Museum Shop are but a few of those who helped. Helen Turner, formerly with Don Watson's Indian Store, was of great value in both her comments and the list of trademarks she had accumulated and let me use. The superb photography is the result of Steve Miller's (Naval Ocean Systems Center) expertise and special interest. However, it is to the craftsmen themselves that I owe the most thanks for the objects of great beauty that afford so much pleasure and interest to so many.

It is hoped that those who use this reference will contribute their expertise and assist in the collection of additional trademarks and corrections of data contained here in. This can be accomplished by forwarding such information to the Indian Arts and Crafts Association at 4215 Lead, S.E. in Albuquerque, NM 87108 or by phoning (505) 265-9149.

Unknown maker. Heard Museum (NA-SW-Na-J-484) Squashblossom necklace, leaf pattern.

Victor M. Begay. Private Collection (MO-333). Squashblossom necklace, petit point cluster.

Ambrose Roanhorse. Heard Museum (NA-SW-Na-J-297) Squashblossom necklace, cast naja with wrought beads.

Unknown maker. Private Collection (MO-410) Wrought bracelet with stones.

Preston Monongye. Heard Museum (NA-SW-Na-J-39). Stone and wood inlay.

Kenneth Begay. Heard Museum (NA-SW-Na-J-119). Hammered stones.

Jesse Monongye. Heard Museum (NA-SW-Na-J-463). Mosaic inlay.

S.M. Bahe. Private Collection (MO-448). Needlepoint cluster.

Tommy Singer. Private Collection (MO-279). Chip inlay.

Introduction

Determining who has made a well-crafted object is of abiding interest to most people, not only those who collect but also those who house, research, buy, or sell such things. There are a variety of ways to satisfy this urge, some requiring the accumulation of years of experience, but the simplest is to urge the craftsman to place an identifying label or symbol upon his or her work—a trade mark. Such a device used in connection with any artifact presumably points clearly to the origin of the object on which it is placed and identifies the artist. As reasonable as this course sounds it is not quite so easily implemented because both cultural and technical problems arise.

Within the Southwest there are tribes which have suppressed individuality for the security or survival of the group. Among such people the anonymity of the individual is stressed and artisans of great merit would have found the signing or marking of their work inconceivable. This is particularly true when the available market consists only of the members of your own village, all of whom are aware of every other person's capabilities. Hence there is obviously no need to identify one's self. To persuade the craftsman from a tradition such as this to make his work personally known is difficult and when it does occur the mark is often one related to the family or clan and is usually a symbol used by that group.

Other peoples believe that to use one's name indiscriminately reduces its potency and transfers its power to another. If this is coupled with an avoidance of the dead and all things associated with them then it could mean that a signed piece might place a personal name on a dead person, in a grave, or in the hands of a live enemy. Consequently names or anything that might be construed as a personal label are slow to be adopted. It is interesting to note that there is a strong predilection among such people to choose initials which are very impersonal and are usually shared by more than one person.

Obviously many cultural traditions militate against the use of trade marks by Native-Americans, including an individual disinterest in the need, but in addition there are obvious technical problems. A very unsatisfactory result can easily be achieved by tapping a trademark stamp onto the back of a completed mosaic, whereas the same effort on a cast piece always produces the desired mark with no ill effects. Stamps require planning ahead so that they may be used at the proper stage in manufacture. In contrast the innovation of electric engravers in the early 1970s allowed the craftsman to place his or her name, and even address and tribal affiliation, on the article after it was completely finished without harming the piece.

There is also a different attitude toward the markings themselves. Trade- or hallmarks, to those belonging to the Western European culture, are assumed to be a sign that designates a particular product or art and inherently its quality. To the Native-American a trade mark is property which may be borrowed by spouse, relative, or friend. Should the person to whom it belongs die, the mark can be inherited. The emphasis has been shifted to the stamp rather than placed on the uniqueness or quality of the art.

Historically a few individuals began signing their works during the early decades of the 20th century. This occurred at a time that coincided with increasing tourism in the Southwest. The numbers of craftsmen using trademarks slowly grew until after World War II, when the processes of social fermentation among the general population of America sparked massive searches for "roots" and "alternative life ways", and eventually led to an awakened interest in Indians. All Native-Americans, but particularly those in the Southwest, suddenly found themselves in the spotlight of national attention. The effects of this interest were felt most heavily from 1970 to 1976, a time span frequently referred to as the "boom period".

The discovery of the beauty of Native-American art produced thousands of collectors hungry to possess some facet of Indian tradition. In answer to this burgeoning demand, hundreds of Native-Americans took up craftwork, primarily jewelry, and the middlemen multiplied like rabbits. Coupled with this surge of collecting came increasing pressure to know who these artists were and this produced a tidal wave of signed pieces. These run the gamut from individuals who spent more of their time designing their trade mark than they expended on their entire output to

Eskiesose. Heard Museum (NA-SW-Na-J-212). Stamped and hammered work.

Preston Monongye. Heard Museum (NA-SW-Ho-J-42). Cast with set.

J. Blackgoat. Private Collection (MO-438). Stamped and hammered work.

Platero. Private Collection. Applique with set.

Unknown maker. Private Collection (MO-376). Stamped work.

D. Reeves Private Collection (MO-560). Platero style.

Leroy Turquoise. Private Collection. Early shadow box.

Helen Long. Heard Museum (NA-SW-Na-J-121). Effigy.

Preston Monongye. Heard Museum (NA-SW-Ho-J-107). Carved mosaic inlay.

outstanding artists who used insignificant marks or signed erratically. And, of course, an enormous number of artists of all calibers never marked their pieces at all. Almost without exception in jewelry these marks are placed on the back side of the piece. Only a few craftsmen incorporate their marks into the actual design of the article and usually these individuals produce the most contemporary or avant-garde articles.

It should be noted, however, that not all marks placed on an article, particularly of jewelry, are the trademarks of an individual.

More often than not craftsmen produced work made on consignment for traders or wholesalers who supplied the material and paid the craftsmen for the completed pieces. The resultant work was often given a single mark, that of the shop which ordered it and wholesaled the finished item. In other instances tribal enterprises were begun wherein craftsmen combined to form a cooperative or guild to market their own works and thereby eliminate the middle man. A covering trademark was selected to be used in conjunction with that of the individual. Notable among such efforts were the Navajo Arts and Crafts Guild, the Hopi Silvercraft Guild, and the Zuni Cooperative Association. In addition small family shops, often composed of a rather extended family, frequently used only the trademark of the originator of the style even though many contributed to the total production.

Yet another type of mark found only on jewelry is the one that refers to the quality of the material from which the artifact is made. These marks stem from the traditions and practices of the trade guilds of the Middle Ages in Europe. The term "hallmark" became established in England where it was applied to the marks left by the official stamp placed on gold and silver articles at the Goldsmith's Hall in London which attested to the degree of purity of the metal. Today some marks in the Southwest are used for the same purpose although not all pieces carry such marks nor was it the custom in the past to offer this information at all.

In addition there is yet another category of markings often mistaken for trademarks but which are codes placed on articles to indicate the dealer's purchase price for a particular item. By using a wholesale or retail percentage the price of the item can be easily figured without the knowledge of the buyer, supplier, or use of records. These markings resemble initials and are usually scratched in or written in ink. They are based on a ten digit code of non-repeating letters or marks. For example a code might be the phrase **BLACK HORSE** wherein each letter represents a number from one to ten. An article purchased for $5.79 would then be written **KOR**. Obviously such codes are carefully guarded secrets.

The need for collecting trade- or hallmarks has manifested itself frequently in the appearance of short lists of marks in publications on jewelry, craftsmen, or tribes.

Furthermore almost every trader has perforce to maintain lists of the marks used by the craftsmen with whom he works. Despite this there was no general effort being made to systematically record trademarks. This publication is addressed to that need. To recognize both the scope and the limitations of it several points should be considered. Because there is no known measure by which the numbers of craftspeople can be determined it is impossible to determine the percentage of those who sign their work. Consequently this compilation is arbitrarily limited in scope both by the unknown numbers of craftspeople and the amount of time required for research and development of the listings. Foremost among the points that must be kept in mind is the fact that this is *not* an exhaustive work but one, it is hoped, to which additional information may be added. Secondly the fact that there are errors in the data is fully recognized. However the impossibility of removing such errata is apparent when it may require a year to check out a single mark. The elimination of these mistakes requires the cooperation of craftsmen and those who work with them. Third, the many inconsistencies such as the weak representation of kachina carvers, rug weavers, and basket makers, etc. compared with those who make jewelry results from a desire to get the information out rather than await fleeting perfection.

Biographical Entries

ABEITA, KATHY *Isleta*
SILVERSMITH: Piecework.
HALLMARK: Stamped initials in 1/16 Gothic print set on a square plate.

KA

ABEITA, RITA *Navajo*
SILVERSMITH: Piecework.
HALLMARK: Stamped initials in 1/16 Gothic print.

RA

ABEYTA, EUNICE *Laguna*
SILVERSMITH: Shop smith at one time for New Mexico Jewelry Company.
HALLMARK: Stamped name in 3/32 Gothic print, first used in 1975.

E. ABEYTA

ABEYTA, H ? *Laguna*
SILVERSMITH: Shop smith at one time for New Mexico Jewelry Company.
HALLMARK: Stamped name in 3/32 Gothic print, first used in 1975.

H. ABEYTA

ABEYTA, JUAN *Navajo*
SILVERSMITH: Shop smith at one time for New Mexico Jewelry Company.
HALLMARK: Stamped surname and initial of given name, or initials only, in 3/32 Gothic print. Stamps first used in 1975.

J. ABEYTA   JA

ACOYA, ART *Zuni*
SILVERSMITH/LAPIDARIST: Produces a wide variety of pieces, settings, and inlays.
HALLMARKS: Uses either stamped name or initials in Gothic print. The initials are often accompanied by small symbols or are offset.

A. ACOYA

ACQUE, EVELYN *Zuni*
SILVERSMITH/LAPIDARIST: Needlepoint and other work. Producing in 1947.
HALLMARK: Stamped name in 1/16 Gothic print. First used in 1974.

E. ACQUE

ACQUE, GLORIA *Zuni*
SILVERSMITH:
HALLMARK: Stamped name in 1/16 Gothic print. First used in 1975.

G. ACQUE

ADAKAI, FRED *Navajo*
SILVERSMITH: Worked for Atkinson Trading Company ca. 1980.
HALLMARK: Stamped initials in 1/16 Gothic print.

F.A.

ADAKAI, GLEN *Navajo*
SILVERSMITH: Began producing in 1940's.
HALLMARK: Stamped initials in 1/16 Gothic print with symbol of an arrow.

G.A.

ADAKAI, JACK *Navajo*
SILVERSMITH: Predominantly cast work but produces a wide variety of work.
HALLMARK: Stamped name and initials in 1/16 Gothic print. Other stamped initials are freehand.
Spouse: Minnie Adakai who works with him. Son-in-law is John Hornbeck. Name is occasionally spelled Atakai.

JACK ADAKAI   J.A.   Ja   J.A.

ADAKAI, LEN-R *Navajo*
SILVERSMITH: Has worked as a smith for Atkinson Trading Company, Hill's Turquoise ca. 1979.
HALLMARK: Stamped initials in 1/16 or 3/32 Gothic print. First used in 1980.

L.A.

ADAKAI, MINNIE *Navajo*
SILVERSMITH: Cast work as well as a variety of other types. Works with her husband.
HALLMARK: Stamped initials in 1/16 Gothic. Unknown whether she uses her husband's hallmarks.
Spouse: Jack Adakai.

M.A.

ADAMS, DEL *Unknown*
SILVERSMITH:
HALLMARK: Stamped name in 1/16 Gothic print. First used in 1977.

DEL ADAMS

ADAMS, SADIE *Tewa*
POTTER: Produced from ca. 1930-1985.
HALLMARK: Painted and fired drawing of a larkspur.

ADEKY, GILBERT *Navajo*
SILVERSMITH: Worked for First American Traders.
HALLMARK: Stamped name in 1/16 Gothic print first used in 1984 and stamped name with initial in 1/16 Gothic print first used in 1975.

G. ADEKY   GIL ADEKY

AGOODIE, JERRY *Navajo*
SILVERSMITH:
HALLMARK: Stamped name and initial in 1/16 Gothic print first used in 1977.
From area of Pinyon, Arizona.

J. AGOODIE

AGUILAR, BENNY *Santo Domingo*
SILVERSMITH: Works with his wife.
HALLMARK: Stamped combination of the initials of Benny and Frances Aguilar in 1/16 Gothic print. Occasionally in combination with symbols.
Spouse is Frances Aguilar.

BFA

AGUILAR, FRANCES *Santo Domingo*
SILVERSMITH: Works with her husband.
HALLMARK: Shared with Benny. Stamped combination of their initials in 1/16 Gothic print. Sometimes with symbols.
Spouse is Benny Aguilar.

BFA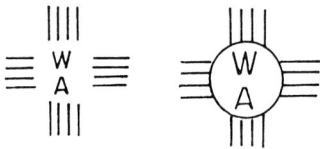

AGUILAR, TONY *Santo Domingo*
HEISHI MAKER: Uses shell and brass.
HALLMARK: Stamped stylized initial.

AGUILAR, WAYNE *Santo Domingo*
SILVERSMITH:
HALLMARK: Stamped initials in 1/16 Gothic print set in sun symbol. Right hand mark first used in 1976.

AHASTEEN, JULIUS *Navajo*
SILVERSMITH:
HALLMARK: Stamped name in 1/16 Gothic print. Same hallmark used by his brother. First used in 1975.
Brother is Tom Ahasteen.
From region of Holbrook, Arizona.

AHASTEEN

AHASTEEN, TOM *Navajo*
SILVERSMITH:
HALLMARK: Uses the same hallmark as his brother, the stamped surname in 1/16 Gothic print. Purchased his hallmark in 1976, a year after his brother.
From region of Holbrook, Arizona.

AHASTEEN

ALBERT, MYRA *Apache*
SILVERSMITH: Peridot settings.
HALLMARK: Stamped initials in 1/16 Gothic print.

MA

ALBERT, RAMON JR. *Hopi*
SILVERSMITH: Overlay work.
HALLMARK: Special stamp of combined initials in 1/16 print, and 1/32 Gothic print of his Hopi name.
From Third Mesa, Arizona.

DALANGYAWMA

ALBERTA, JUAN *Navajo*
SILVERSMITH:
HALLMARK: Stamped initials in 1/16 Gothic print.

JA   M.A.

ALCOTT, MICHAEL *Unknown*
SILVERSMITH:
HALLMARK: Stamped name or initials in 1/32 Gothic print. First stamp used in 1984 and second in 1985.

MIKE ALCOTT

ALESSANDRO, DEBBIE *Navajo*
SILVERSMITH:
HALLMARK: Special stamp of hogan and name in Gothic print 1/8". First used in 1985.
Granddaughter of Kenneth Begay, daughter of Shirley. From region of Window Rock, Arizona.

ALEXIUS, OSCAR *Navajo*
SILVERSMITH: Worked for Chet Jones. Piecework.
HALLMARK: Two lines of 1/16 script on stamp, first used in 1982. Stamped initials 1/16 Gothic print.

Handmade by   O.A.
Oscar Alexius

ALLAPOWA, PATSY *Zuni*
SILVERSMITH/LAPIDARIST: Specializes in very large stones for settings. Began producing in 1967. Works with her husband.
HALLMARK: Her stamped initials and her husband's combined in 1/16 Gothic print. First used in 1967.
Spouse: Thomas Allapowa Jr. Parents are Mary and Lee Weebothee.
[Bell: 1977:43]

TA & PA

ALLOPOWA, THOMAS JR. *Zuni*
SILVERSMITH/LAPIDARIST: Specializes in very large stones for settings. Began producing in 1967. Works with his wife.
HALLMARK: Combined initials of his and his wife's stamped in 1/16 Gothic print. First used in 1967.
Spouse: Patsy Allapowa.
[Bell: 1977:43]

TA & PA

ALLEN, CARL *Navajo*
SILVERSMITH: Also an Indian doctor.
HALLMARK: Special 1/8" stamp of a ceremonial feather. First used in 1985.
From Shiprock, New Mexico region.

ALLISON, D ? *Navajo*
SILVERSMITH: Worked for Hand Made Indian Jewelry Shop as a benchsmith.
HALLMARK: Stamped name and first initial in 1/16 Gothic print used first in 1974. Stamped initials in 3/32" Gothic print first used in 1972.
From Holbrook, Arizona region.

D.ALLISON   D.A.

ALLISON, L ? *Navajo*
SILVERSMITH: Benchsmith.
HALLMARK: Stamped name and initial in 1/16 Gothic print. First used in 1976.
From Window Rock, Arizona region.

L.ALLISON

AMI, MARY *Tewa*
Potter: Began producing ca. 1970.
HALLMARK: Painted and fired bear's head with her name, "Buffalo Maiden", written beside it.
[Stanislawski 1976:65:]

ANDERSON, DOROTHY *Unknown*
SILVERSMITH:
HALLMARK: Special stamp 1/16 Gothic print. First used in 1978.

DMA -∀C

ANDERSON, EDDIE *Navajo*
SILVERSMITH:
HALLMARK: Single letter stamp 1/16 script. First used in 1975.
From Ft. Defiance, Arizona region.

A

ANDERSON, ELIZABETH *Navajo*
SILVERSMITH: Piecework for Atkinson Trading Company.
HALLMARK: Stamped given name in 1/16 Gothic print. First used in 1974.

ELIZABETH A.

ANDERSON, ELLA *Navajo*
SILVERSMITH: Piecework for Atkinson Trading Company before 1976.
HALLMARK: Surname stamped in 1/16 Gothic print.

E.ANDERSON

ANDERSON, EVELYN *Navajo*
SILVERSMITH: Piecework for Atkinson Trading Company.
HALLMARK: Stamped surname and initials both in 1/16 Gothic print. First used in 1974.
Father is Roy Anderson, Sr. and brother is Roy Anderson, Jr.

E.A.

ANDERSON, KATHERINE *Navajo*
SILVERSMITH:
HALLMARK: Special stamp representing bow and arrow(?).

ANDERSON, PAUL *Zuni*
SILVERSMITH/LAPIDARIST:
HALLMARK: Stamped initials in 1/16 Gothic print.

PA

ANDERSON, ROY JR. *Navajo*
SILVERSMITH: Worked for the White Hogan.
HALLMARK: Special stamp of combined initials.
Father was Roy Anderson, Sr. and sister is Evelyn Anderson.

ᚱ   ᴁ

ANDERSON, TOM *Zuni*
SILVERSMITH:
HALLMARK: Stamped initials in 1/16 Gothic print.

TA

ANDERSON, WILBUR *Navajo*
SILVERSMITH: Cement and oil casting. Trained with Kirk at Manuelito, New Mexico. Worked for Woodards ca. 1970.
HALLMARK: Combined initials stamped in 1/16 Gothic print.
[King: 1976:46 referred to as Wilbert Anderson]

WA

ANDERSON, WILLIAM *Navajo*
SILVERSMITH:
HALLMARK: Stamped initials in 1/16 Gothic print.

WA

ANDLER, R ? *Unknown*
SILVERSMITH: Worked for T & R Market in Gallup, N.M.
HALLMARK: Stamped surname in 1/16 Gothic print.

R.ANDLER

ANSELMO, VINCENT *Navajo*
SILVERSMITH: Specializes in applique, large stone settings and filigree.
HALLMARK: Special stamp of a roadrunner.

APACHE, MORGAN *Navajo*
SILVERSMITH: Worked for Albuquerque shops in 1978-9.
HALLMARK: Stamped initials in 1/16 Gothic print.
From Alamo, New Mexico region. Name Apache and Apachito appear to be interchangeable.

MA

APACHE, STEVEN *Navajo*
SILVERSMITH: Worked for Albuquerque shops in 1978-9.
HALLMARK: Stamped initials in 1/16 Gothic print.
From Alamo, New Mexico region. Name Apache and Apachito appear to be interchangeable.

SA

APACHITO, ARCHY *Navajo*
SILVERSMITH: Worked in Albuquerque shops in 1978-9.
HALLMARK: Special stamped A's.
From Alamo, New Mexico region.

AA

APACHITO, BENNY *Navajo*
SILVERSMITH: Worked for Hill's Turquoise.
HALLMARK: Stamped initials in 1/16 Gothic print.
From Alamo, New Mexico region.

BA

APACHITO, CLINTON *Navajo*
SILVERSMITH: Worked for Hill's Turquoise.
HALLMARK: Stamped initials in 1/16 Gothic print. First used in 1977.

C.A.

APACHITO, GENEVIEVE *Navajo*
SILVERSMITH: Worked in Albuquerque shops in 1978-9. Also for Hill's Turquoise.

HALLMARK: Stamped initials in 1/16 Gothic print. GPA first used in 1977.
Spouse is Raymond Apachito, mother is Rita Pino.
From Alamo, New Mexico region.

GPA   G.A.

APACHITO, MORGAN see **Apache, Morgan**

APACHITO, RAYMOND *Navajo*
SILVERSMITH: Worked in Albuquerque shops in 1978-9 and for Hill's Turquoise.
HALLMARK: Stamped initials in 1/16 Gothic print. First used in 1977.
Spouse is Genevieve Apachito.
From Alamo, New Mexico region.

R.J.A.

APACHITO, ROBERT (BOBBY) *Navajo*
SILVERSMITH: Worked for Hill's Turquoise.
HALLMARK: Stamped initials in 1/16 Gothic print. First used in 1977.

RCA

APACHITO, STEVEN see **Apache, Steven**

APACHITO, VELMA *Navajo*
SILVERSMITH: Worked in Albuquerque shops in 1978-9.
HALLMARK: Stamped initials in 1/16 Gothic print.
From Alamo, New Mexico region.

VA

APODACA, LINDA *Unknown*
May not be a silversmith. No information on the individual.
HALLMARK: Variety of stamped names and initials all in 1/32 Gothic print first appearing in 1984-5. May represent a dealer.

DASLIN   ANNIE   PTL

ARAGON, VIDEL *Santo Domingo*
SILVERSMITH: Produced chiseled, filed, and stamped designs on carinated wire. Producing since ca. 1950.
HALLMARK: Special stamps.
[King: 1976:10]

ARGULO, E. *Unknown*
SILVERSMITH/LAPIDARIST: Needlepoint.
HALLMARK: Stamped initials in 1/16 Gothic print.

EA

ARMSTRONG, RAYMOND *Navajo*
SILVERSMITH:
HALLMARK: Stamped initials and symbol.

ARRAGOS, VIRGIL *Santo Domingo*
SILVERSMITH:
HALLMARK: Stamped initials in 1/16 Gothic print.

VA

ARVISO, FLOYD *Navajo*
SILVERSMITH:
HALLMARK: Stamped initials in 1/16 Gothic print.
From Cottonwood, Arizona region.

FA

ARVISO, KIRK *Navajo*
SILVERSMITH:
HALLMARK: Stamped initials in 1/16 Gothic print.
From Chinle, Arizona region.

KA

ARVISO, LEO *Navajo*
SILVERSMITH:
HALLMARK: Stamped symbol and initials in 1/16 Gothic print.

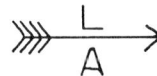

ARVISO, PAUL *Zuni*
SILVERSMITH/LAPIDARIST: Specializes in scenes done in overlay work.
HALLMARK: Stamped hallmark of initials in 1/16 Gothic print, also engraved surname and initials in both script and printing.

PA   ARVISO   Parviso

ARVISO, PONTIAC *Navajo (?)*
SILVERSMITH:
HALLMARK: Stamped name with symbols, letters in 1/8" Gothic print. First used in 1978.
From Lupton, Arizona region.

P🟤NTIXc

ARVISO, SUSIE *Unknown*
SILVERSMITH:
HALLMARK: Stamped surname and initials in 1/16 Gothic print. First used in 1978.

S.A.ARVISO

ARVISO, WILBUR PAUL *Navajo*
SILVERSMITH:
HALLMARK: Stamped offset initials in 1/16 Gothic print. Chiseled surname with symbol.

ASHEET, FRED *Navajo*
SILVERSMITH:
HALLMARK: Stamped initials in 1/16 Gothic print. First used in 1974.
From Church Rock, New Mexico region.

F.A.

ASHLEY, ALICE *Navajo*
SILVERSMITH:
HALLMARK: Stamped surname in 1/16 Gothic print. First used in 1975.
From Mentmore, New Mexico region.

A.ASHLEY

ASHLEY, CECIL *Navajo*
SILVERSMITH: Began producing ca. 1975.
HALLMARK: Stamped initials in 1/16 Gothic print.

CA   C$_A$

ASHLEY, FANNIE *Navajo*
SILVERSMITH:
HALLMARK: Stamped surname in 1/16 Gothic print. First used in 1974.
From St. Michaels, Arizona region.

F.ASHLEY

ASHLEY, J ? *Navajo*
SILVERSMITH:
HALLMARK: Stamped surname in 1/16 Gothic print. First used in 1974.
From St. Michaels, Arizona region.

J.ASHLEY

ASHLEY, MONROE *Navajo*
SILVERSMITH:
HALLMARK: Stamped surname and initial in 1/16 Gothic print. First used name and NAVAJO in 1974.
From Flagstaff, Arizona region.

ASHLEY   A
NAVAJO

ATENCIO, FRANK *Santo Domingo*
SILVERSMITH:
HALLMARK: Chiseled initials and symbol.

ATSITTY, GILBERT *Navajo*
SILVERSMITH:
HALLMARK: Stamped surname in 1/16 Gothic print. First used in 1974.
From Houck, Arizona region.

G.ATSITTY

ATSITTY, THOMAS *Navajo*
SILVERSMITH:
HALLMARK: Stamped surname in 1/16 Gothic print. First used in 1974. Chisel cut initials are earlier.

   T.ATSITTY

ATTAKAI, P ? *Navajo*
SILVERSMITH: Worked for Bernie Dominguez.
HALLMARK: Stamped surname in 1/16 Gothic print. First used in 1975.
From Gallup, New Mexico region.

P.ATTAKAI

AVERY, MARY SMITH *Navajo*
SILVERSMITH: Worked for Atkinson Trading Company.
HALLMARK: Stamped name in 1/16 Gothic print. First used in 1974. Her stamp and current name are different.
From Gallup, New Mexico region.

MARY S. LEW

BACA, HENRY *Unknown*
SILVERSMITH:
HALLMARK: Stamped and joined initials in 1/4" Gothic print. First used in 1976.

HB

BACA, LORENZO *Mescalero/Isleta*
SILVERSMITH/PAINTER/SCULPTOR:
HALLMARK: Two tracks. Appear to be lizard tracks.

BAHE, FIDEL *Navajo*
SILVERSMITH: Benchsmith for Rocking Horse Ranch.
HALLMARK: Stamped symbols and letters.
From Phoenix, Arizona.

T✳LE

BAHE, LOUISE *Navajo*
SILVERSMITH:
HALLMARK: Stamped initial in 1/16 Gothic print in symbol.

[heart with L]

BAHE, S? *Navajo*
SILVERSMITH: Worked for Felix Indian Jewelry.
HALLMARK: Stamped surname in 1/16 Gothic print. First used in 1977.

S.BAHE

BAHE, SAM *Navajo*
SILVERSMITH: Specializes in heavy cast rings. Worked for John Kennedy in the 1960s, Joe Tanner in the 1970s. Stopped producing in the early 1980s due to poor vision.
HALLMARK: Both engraved and stamped script. Resisted signing his work for many years. When he did begin to sign he used an overly large script that almost destroyed the work.
From Houck, Arizona region.

S B

BAHE, S.M. *Navajo*
SILVERSMITH:
HALLMARK: Stamped initials and name in 1/16 Gothic print. Name first used in 1975.
From either Rock Point or Chinle, Arizona.

SB   S.M.BAHE

BAHE, TOM *Navajo*
SILVERSMITH: Specializes in overlay and spin casting. Worked for Atkinson Trading Company.
HALLMARK: Stamped full name and surname with initial in 1/16 Gothic print. Stamp for full name first used in 1978.
From Gallup, New Mexico region.

TOM BAHE   T.BAHE

BAHI, DINI TSAI *Navajo*
SILVERSMITH/GOLDSMITH:
HALLMARK: Stamped initials in 1/16 Gothic print.

D.T.B.

BAHI, JOE *Navajo*
SILVERSMITH:
HALLMARK: Stamped full name in 1/16 Gothic print. Stamp first used in 1979.
From Lupton, Arizona region.

JOE BAHE

BAIN, NELLIE *Navajo*
SILVERSMITH:
HALLMARK: Stamped initial with symbol in 1/16 Gothic print.

N⌒

BALOO, JOHN *Navajo*
SILVERSMITH: Demonstrating silver craft work in 1964.
HALLMARK: Stamped script initials.
From Lower Greasewood, Arizona region.

JB

BANTEAH, ALBERT *Zuni*
SILVERSMITH/LAPIDARIST: Specializes in bird designs. Produces mosaic, channel, and etched inlay. Learned his craft from Jake Haloo and began producing in 1970. Works with his wife.
HALLMARK: Stamped surname and initials in 3/32 Gothic print using a combination of his and his wife's initials. Also engraves the same combination of initials with his surname and his own full name.
Spouse is Dolly Banteah, his brother is Valentino Banteah.
[Bell: 1975:77] [Levy: 1980:19]

A.&D.BANTEAH   A.D. Banteah   Albert Banteah
ADB   A   A&D   A&DB

BANTEAH, DOLLY *Zuni*
SILVERSMITH/LAPIDARIST: Specializes in bird designs. Produces mosaic, channel, and etched inlay. Learned the craft from her father and began producing in 1970. Works with her husband.
HALLMARK: Stamped surname and initials in 3/32 Gothic print are a combination of her and her husband's initials. First used in 1974. Also uses an engraved combination of their initials and surname, a later mark.
Spouse is Albert Banteah, father Jake Haloo, and sisters Nancy Haloo and Lolita Natachu. Half brother is Jacob Livingston.
[Bell: 1975:77] [Levy: 1980:19]

A.&D.BANTEAH
A.DB   A&D   A & DB

BANTEAH, GARY *Zuni*
SILVERSMITH:
HALLMARK: Stamped combined initials of his and his wife's in 1/16 Gothic print. Stamp first used in 1978. Also engraves the same combination of initials with his surname.
Spouse is Serena Banteah.

G.S.B.   G.S. Banteah

BANTEAH, MATILDA *Zuni*
SILVERSMITH/LAPIDARIST: Specializes in geometric designs with heavy channel separations. Entirely self-taught, she began producing in 1973. She does the stone work and her husband the silver.
HALLMARK: Stamped combination of her and her husband's initials.
Spouse is Valentino Banteah.
[Levy: 1980:23]

VMB

BANTEAH, SERENA *Zuni*
SILVERSMITH: Works with her husband.
HALLMARK: Stamped combined initials of her and her husband's in 1/16 Gothic print. Stamp first used in 1978. Also engraves the same combination of initials with his surname.
Spouse is Gary Banteah.

G.S.B.

BANTEAH, VALENTINO *Zuni*
SILVERSMITH/LAPIDARIST: Specializes in geometric designs with heavy channel separations. Entirely self-taught, he began producing in 1973. His wife does the stone work and he does the silver.
HALLMARK: Stamped combination of his and his wife's initials.
Spouse is Matilda Banteah, brother is Albert Banteah.
[Levy: 1980:23]

VMB

BARBER, HENRY *Unknown*
SILVERSMITH: Worked for Ortega.
HALLMARK: Stamped hallmark of his and his wife's full names in 1/16 Gothic print. Stamp first used in 1980.
Spouse is Linda Barber.

HENRY & LINDA BARBER

BARBER, LINDA *Unknown*
SILVERSMITH: Worked for Ortega.
HALLMARK: Stamped hallmark of her and her husband's full name in 1/16 Gothic print. Stamp first used in 1980.
Spouse is Henry Barber.

HENRY & LINDA BARBER

BARTON, BERNARD *Unknown*
SILVERSMITH:
HALLMARK: Stamped initials in 1/16 Gothic print.

BB

BARTON, DAVID *Navajo (?)*
SILVERSMITH:
HALLMARK: Stamped name in 1/16 Gothic print. Stamp first used in 1984.
From Winslow, Arizona region.

DEE BARTON

BASSELENTE, MARIE *Zuni*
SILVERSMITH:
HALLMARK: Stamped surname and initial in 1/16 Gothic print. Stamp first used in 1976.

M.BESSELENTE

BATALA, ART *Hopi*
SILVERSMITH: Specializes in overlay. Began producing in 1975.
HALLMARK: Stamped initial in 1/16 Gothic print. Also uses a combined set of initials.
[Wright: 1982:95]

A   AB

BATTE, B ? *Unknown*
SILVERSMITH:
HALLMARK: Stamped symbol.
From Alamogordo, New Mexico region.

◇◇✦◇◇

BEBO, YVONNE *Navajo*
SILVERSMITH: Worked for Atkinson Trading Company ca. 1980.
HALLMARK: Stamped initials in 1/16 Gothic print.
From Gallup, New Mexico region.

YB

BECENTI, ANNIE *Navajo*
SILVERSMITH: Worked for Atkinson Trading Company.
HALLMARK: Stamped full name in 1/16 Gothic print. Stamp first used in 1974. Surname with initials also in 1/16, Gothic print used first in 1975.
Spouse is Eugene Becenti.
From Gallup, New Mexico region.

ANNIE BECENTI   A1 BECENTI

BECENTI, BENJAMIN *Navajo*
SILVERSMITH/LAPIDARIST: Specializes in inlay work.
HALLMARK: Stamped initials in 1/16 Gothic print. Brother is Robert Becenti.

BB

BECENTI, EUGENE *Navajo*
SILVERSMITH: Worked for Atkinson Trading Company.
HALLMARK: Stamped surname with initials in 1/16 Gothic print. Stamp for E.BECENTI first used in 1974. Stamp for E.T. BECENTI first used in 1975.
Spouse is Annie Becenti.

E.BECENTI   E.T.BECENTI

BECENTI, ROBERT *Navajo*
SILVERSMITH/LAPIDARIST: Specializes in inlay work.
HALLMARK: Stamped initials is 1/16 Gothic print.
Brother is Benjamin Becenti.

RB

BECK, VICTOR *Navajo*
SILVERSMITH/LAPIDARIST: Specializes in contemporary designs and asymmetrical work. Producing in early 1970s. Output is sporadic because of political career.
HALLMARK: Stamped surname or full name in 1/16 Gothic print. Full name stamp first used in 1982.
Brother is Clifford Beck, noted artist.

VICTOR BECK   BECK

BEDALL, TIM *Navajo*
SILVERSMITH/GOLDSMITH:
HALLMARK: Stamped initials in 1/16 Gothic print.

T.B.

BEDONI, JOHN *Navajo*
SILVERSMITH/LAPIDARIST:
HALLMARK: Stamped stylized initial J.
From Keams Canyon region.

J

BEDAH, T. *Navajo*
SILVERSMITH: Worked for J & D Jewelry Sales.
HALLMARK: Stamped surname in 1/16 script. Stamp first used in 1978.
From Gallup, New Mexico region.

T.Bedah

BEEDAH, TIM *Zuni*
SILVERSMITH/GOLDSMITH:
HALLMARK: Engraved name or initials in script.

Tim Beedah   T.B.

BEGAY, A ? *Navajo*
SILVERSMITH: Worked for Bernie Dominguez.
HALLMARK: Stamped surname and initial in 1/16 Gothic print.
From Gallup, New Mexico region.

A.BEGAY

BEGAY, ANNA *Navajo*
SILVERSMITH: Specializing in cement casting with stabilized turquoise settings.
HALLMARK: Stamped initials in 1/16 Gothic print.
From Grants, New Mexico region.

AB

BEGAY, ANTHONY *Zuni*
SILVERSMITH/LAPIDARIST: Specializes in inlaid peyote birds. Works with Roscoe Scott.
HALLMARK: Stamped initials in 1/16 Gothic print. Often initials are set on a small rectangular plate.

A.B.   A.B.

BEGAY, B ? *Navajo*
SILVERSMITH: Worked for Steve Bowser.
HALLMARK: Stamped surname and initial in 1/16 Gothic print. Stamp first used in 1976.

B.BEGAY

BEGAY, BARBARA *Navajo*
SILVERSMITH: Worked for Canyon Silver Company.
HALLMARK: Stamped joined initials.
From Sanders, Arizona region.

BEGAY, BOBBY *Navajo*
SILVERSMITH:
HALLMARK: Stamped initials in 1/16 Gothic print and a special 3/32 stamp with misaligned letters.
From Sheep Springs, New Mexico region.

B.B.   BYE

BEGAY, CARL *Navajo*
SILVERSMITH: Specializes in large stones in floral pieces.
HALLMARK: Stamped given name initial and symbol. Letter is in 1/16 Gothic print.

C ✴

BEGAY, CARL ALLEN or CARLOS *Navajo*
SILVERSMITH:
HALLMARK: Stamped given name initial with symbol. Letter is in 1/16 Gothic print.
From Tuba City, Arizona region. Carl, Carl Allen and Carlos Begay may be the same person.

C⌒   C⌒

BEGAY, CAROLYN *Navajo*
SILVERSMITH:
HALLMARK: Stamped symbol with initials WB in 1/16 Gothic or larger print. Stamp is shared with her husband.
Spouse is Wilson Begay.

WB

BEGAY, CHARLES *Navajo*
SILVERSMITH: Specialized in open and cast work. Began producing in the late 1920s and continued through World War II.
HALLMARK: Stamped initial C with symbol.

BEGAY, CLYDE *Navajo*
SILVERSMITH:
HALLMARK: Stamped initials in 1/16 Gothic print. Stamp first used in 1984. Second stamp in same print combines his initials with those of his wife in two lines.
Spouse is Roseanne Begay.
From Canyoncito, New Mexico region.

CB   RAB
      CB

BEGAY, D.M. *Navajo*
SILVERSMITH:
HALLMARK: Stamped initials in 1/16 Gothic print.

D.M.

BEGAY, E ? *Navajo*
SILVERSMITH: Worked for Steve Bowser.
HALLMARK: Stamped surname and initial in 1/16 Gothic print.

E.BEGAY

BEGAY, EDDIE *Navajo*
SILVERSMITH: Worked for Canyon Silver Company.
HALLMARK: Stamped full name in 1/16 script. Stamp first used in 1975. Initials in 1/16 Gothic print first used in 1975. Two special stamps of 3/4" feathers also date from 1975.
From Sanders, Arizona region.

Eddie Begay   E.B.

BEGAY, EDISON *Navajo*
SILVERSMITH:
HALLMARK: Stamped initials in 1/16 Gothic print.

EB

BEGAY, ELLA MAE *Navajo*
SILVERSMITH:
HALLMARK: Stamped combined initials in 1/16 Gothic print.
Spouse is Johnny Mike Begay.
From St. Michaels, Arizona region.

BEGAY, ELOUISE *Navajo*
SILVERSMITH:
HALLMARK: Stamped initials in 1/16 Gothic print. Stamp first used in 1976.
From Continental Divide, New Mexico region.

E.B.

BEGAY, ELSIE *Navajo*
SILVERSMITH: Worked for Atkinson Trading Company before 1976
HALLMARK: Stamped surname and initial in 1/16 Gothic print.
From Gallup, New Mexico region.

E.BEGAY

BEGAY, F.M. *Navajo*
SILVERSMITH:
HALLMARK: Stamped surname and initials in 1/16 Gothic print. Stamp first used in 1976.
From Lukachukai, Arizona region.

F.M.BEGAY

BEGAY, FRANCES *Navajo*
SILVERSMITH:
HALLMARK: Stamped full name in 1/32 Gothic print. Stamp first used in 1983.
From Santa Fe, New Mexico region.

FRANCES BEGAY

BEGAY, FRANCIS M. *Navajo*
SILVERSMITH:
HALLMARK: Stamped surname and initials in 1/16 Gothic print. Stamp first used in 1975. Second stamp of initials only, in 1/16 Gothic print.
From Tuba City, Arizona region.

F.M.BEGAY   F.M.B.

BEGAY, GEORGE *Navajo*
SILVERSMITH:
HALLMARK: Stamped initials in 1/16 Gothic print.
Nephew is Roland Begay.
From Jones Ranch, New Mexico region.

GB

BEGAY, HARRY H. *Navajo*
SILVERSMITH: Specializes in Navajo scenes done in overlay.
HALLMARK: Stamped initials in both 1/32 and 1/4 Gothic print. Stamp first used in 1977. Second stamp of name and initials.
From Gallup, New Mexico region.

HHB   H.H.BEGAY

BEGAY, HARVEY *Navajo*
SILVERSMITH: Sophisticated contemporary work. Began as a benchsmith in the White Hogan during school, from the 8th grade through high school. In 1979 began career as a craftsman designer in precious stones and metals.
HALLMARK: Stamped initials in 1/16th Gothic print. Some of the initials are combined; each variation may occur plain or on a fringed plate.

Father was Kenneth Begay, noted silversmith. Sister is Sylvia Begay Radcliffe. Harvey received a degree in Aeronautics at Arizona State University-Tempe and served a number of years in the U.S. Navy Air Corp eventually working as a test pilot. In 1973 he opened his own gallery in Steamboat Springs, Colorado.

BEGAY, HELEN *Navajo*
SILVERSMITH: Specialized in flexible bracelets.
HALLMARK: Chisel stamped full name.

HELEN BEGAY

BEGAY, HOWARD *Navajo*
SILVERSMITH:
HALLMARK: Special stamps of Navajo head 3/8. First used in 1977.
From St. Michaels, Arizona region.

BEGAY, IDA *Navajo*
SILVERSMITH: Worked for Montana Mining Company.
HALLMARK: Stamped full name in 1/16 Gothic print. Stamp first used in 1975.

IDA.BEGAY

BEGAY, J.M. *Navajo*
SILVERSMITH:
HALLMARK: Surname and initials stamped in 3/32 Gothic print. Stamp first used in 1976.
From Lukachukai, Arizona region.

J.M.BEGAY

BEGAY, JEROME *Navajo*
SILVERSMITH:
HALLMARK: Stamped offset initials in 1/16 Gothic print.

—J_B—

BEGAY, JIMMY *Navajo (?)*
SILVERSMITH:
HALLMARK: Stamped initials in 1/16 Gothic print.

JB

BEGAY, JOE *Navajo*
SILVERSMITH: Worked for Montana Mining Company in 1974, then for Indian Hammers and Atkinson Trading Company in 1976. Specializes in channel inlay.
HALLMARK: Stamped surname and initial in 1/16 Gothic print. Stamp first used in 1974.
Deceased.

J.BEGAY

BEGAY, JOE G. *Navajo*
SILVERSMITH:
HALLMARK: Stamped initials in 1/16 Gothic print.
From Window Rock, Arizona region.

JGB

BEGAY, JOHN G. *Navajo*
SILVERSMITH: Began work for John Yellowhorse in 1973. Later worked at the White Hogan.
HALLMARK: Stamped initials either separate or joined on square fringed plates.

BEGAY, JOHNNY MIKE *Navajo*
SILVERSMITH: Specialized in flat work and boxes. Worked for Dean Kirk, John Kennedy, and White Hogan.
HALLMARK: Stamped initials JMB joined, either set on a fringed plate or plain. In times of marital disputes his work may have appeared without a mark when his wife had taken his stamp. Spouse is Ella Mae Begay. He is now deceased.
From Houck, Arizona region.

JMB JMB

BEGAY, JOHN WHITE *Navajo*
SILVERSMITH: Worked for Atkinson Trading Company.
HALLMARK: Stamped surname and initials in 1/16 Gothic print. Stamp first used in 1977.
From Gallup, New Mexico region.

J.W.BEGAY

BEGAY, KENNETH *Navajo*
SILVERSMITH: Began as a blacksmith at Ft. Wingate, New Mexico. Learned silversmithing working with Ambrose Roanhorse. Specialized in flat ware. Benchsmith for White Hogan during the 1950s. Instructor in silversmithing at Navajo Community College in Tsaile, Arizona during the 1960s and 70s.
HALLMARK: Consistently used a stamped KB in 1/16 Gothic print set on a fringed plate. Occasionally used a plain square plate. Spouse was Eleanor Begay, son Harvey Begay, daughter Sylvia Begay Radcliffe. Clan brother of George, Alvin, and Allen Kee. Deceased.

 KB

BEGAY, KEYONNIE *Navajo*
SILVERSMITH: Worked for Atkinson Trading Company.

HALLMARK: Stamped initials with the first two joined in 1/16 Gothic print. Stamp first used in 1973.
From Gallup, New Mexico region.

JKB

BEGAY, L ? *Navajo*
SILVERSMITH: Smith for Richardson Trading Company.
HALLMARK: Stamped surname and initial in 1/16th Gothic print. Stamp first used in 1975.

L.BEGAY

BEGAY, LARRY *Anglo*
SILVERSMITH:
HALLMARK: Stamped initials with unknown symbol.
See Loren Begay.

BEGAY, LEONARD *Navajo*
SILVERSMITH: Brothers Leonard and Robert work together.
HALLMARK: Stamped hallmark of given name initials in 1/16 Gothic print. Brothers use the same stamp.
Brother is Robert Begay.

RLB

BEGAY, LEROY *Navajo*
SILVERSMITH:
HALLMARK: Stamped initials and symbol in 1/16 Gothic print. Stamp first used in 1975.
From Holbrook, Arizona region.

BEGAY, LOREN *Anglo*
SILVERSMITH/DEALER:
HALLMARK: Stamped offset initials in 1/16 Gothic print. Used the name Larry Begay and Running Horse as well.
Use of the name Begay implied that this individual was Navajo which he was not.

LB

BEGAY, MANUEL *Navajo*
SILVERSMITH:
HALLMARK: Stamped initials.

MEB

BEGAY, MARIE *Navajo*
SILVERSMITH:
HALLMARK: Stamped initials in 1/16 Gothic print. Stamp first used in 1978. Also uses a joined M and B stamp.

From Thoreau, New Mexico region.

M.F.

BEGAY, MORRIS *Navajo*
SILVERSMITH:
HALLMARK: Stamped script M. Stamp first used in 1976.

M

BEGAY, NORMA JEAN *Navajo*
SILVERSMITH:
HALLMARK: Stamped initials joined in a cluster.

NB

BEGAY, PAULINE *Navajo*
SILVERSMITH: Smith for Atkinson Trading Company.
HALLMARK: Stamped full name in 1/16 Gothic print. Stamp first used in 1974.
From Gallup, New Mexico region.

PAULINE BEGAY

BEGAY, R.A. *Navajo*
SILVERSMITH:
HALLMARK: Stamped surname and initials in 1/16 Gothic print. Stamp first used in 1983.

R.A.BEGAY

BEGAY, R.H. *Navajo*
SILVERSMITH: Specializes in overlay scenes, particularly horses and wagons.
HALLMARK: Stamped surname and initials in 1/16 Gothic print.

R.H.BEGAY

BEGAY, RICHARD C. *Navajo*
SILVERSMITH:
HALLMARK: Stamped surname and initials in 1/16 Gothic print. Stamp first used in 1984.
From Pinyon, Arizona region.

R.C.BEGAY

BEGAY, RICHARD T. *Navajo*
SILVERSMITH: Smith in Flagstaff shops.
HALLMARK: Stamped surname and initials in 1/16 Gothic print. Stamp first used in 1976.
From Holbrook, Arizona region.

R.T.BEGAY

BEGAY, ROBERT *Navajo*
SILVERSMITH: Specializes in Zuni style inlay. Primarily making Apache dancers during the 1970s. Smith for Bernie Dominguez.
HALLMARK: Stamped initials in 1/16 Gothic print using his brother Leonard's initials and his own. Stamp first used in 1975. Also uses a stamp of his surname and initial in 1/16 Gothic print, used first in 1975.
Brother is Leonard Begay.
From Gallup, New Mexico region.

R.BEGAY

BEGAY, ROLAND *Navajo*
SILVERSMITH: Specializes in story teller scenes in his pieces.
HALLMARK: Stamped joined initials in 1/16 Gothic print. Stamp first used in 1975.
Uncle is George Begay.
From the Vanderwagon or Jones Ranch region.

BEGAY, ROSEANNE *Navajo*
SILVERSMITH:
HALLMARK: Stamped initials of 1/16 Gothic print. One stamp combines her initials with those of her husband.
Spouse is Clyde Begay. Her uncle is Raymond Apachito.
From Canyoncito region.

RA   RAB
      CB

BEGAY, SAM *Navajo*
SILVERSMITH: Specialized in hand casting, oil and cement. Produced from mid-1930s into the 80s. Trained by the Kirks. Worked as smith for Kirks, Woodards, and Turpen. Currently having eye trouble.
From the Manuelito, New Mexico region.

SB

BEGAY, T ? *Navajo*
SILVERSMITH: Smith for Steve Bowser.
HALLMARK: Stamped surname and initial in 1/16 Gothic print. Stamp first used in 1976.

T.BEGAY

BEGAY, T. ? *Navajo*
SILVERSMITH:
HALLMARK: Stamped joined initials and symbol in 1/14" square. Stamp first used in 1981.
From Winslow, Arizona region.

BEGAY, TOM H. *Navajo*
SILVERSMITH: Specializes in gold rings backed with silver.
HALLMARK: Full name in 1/16 Gothic print. Stamp first used in 1976. Also uses a stamp with the first three letters enlarged.
From Jones Ranch, New Mexico region.

TOM BEGAY   THBEGAY

BEGAY, VICTOR MOSES *Navajo*
SILVERSMITH: Specializes in large bracelets with cast animals.
HALLMARK: Stamped initials in 1/16 Gothic print.

VMB

BEGAY, W ? *Navajo*
SILVERSMITH:
HALLMARK: Surname and location in two lines of 1/32 Gothic print. Stamp first used in 1985.
From Lukachukai, Arizona region.

W.BEGAY
LUK.AZ

BEGAY, WILSON *Navajo*
SILVERSMITH: Specializes in sand cast, chiselwork and heavy stone settings. His wife shares in the work.
HALLMARK: Stamped initials in 1/16 Gothic print set inside or under a hat symbol. These are often set on round or pentagonal plates. His wife uses his stamps.
Spouse is Carolyn Begay.
From the Manuelito, New Mexico region.

B

BEGAY, ZEARL *Navajo*
SILVERSMITH:
HALLMARK: Stamped initials in 1/16 Gothic print. Stamp first used in 1974.
From Blue Gap Mission region in Arizona.

ZB

BEGAYE, SAM C. *Navajo*
SILVERSMITH:
HALLMARK: Stamped surname and initials in 1/16 Gothic print. Stamp first used in 1978.
From Ft. Defiance, Arizona region.

S.C.BEGAYE

BELLSON, SHIRLEY *Zuni*
SILVERSMITH:
HALLMARK: Surname and initials in 1/16 Gothic print. Stamp first used in 1973. May contain the initials of her husband.

J.S.BELLSON

BENALLY, ALICE *Navajo*
SILVERSMITH: Smith for Atkinson Trading Company.

HALLMARK: Stamped surname in 1/16 Gothic print. Stamp first used in 1975.
Spouse is Edward Benally, Sr.

A. BENALLY

BENALLY, BETTY *Navajo*
SILVERSMITH:
HALLMARK: Stamped initials in 1/16 Gothic print.

B&B

BENALLY, DAVID *Navajo*
SILVERSMITH:
HALLMARK: Stamped.
From Farmington, New Mexico region.

XX

BENALLY, EDWARD SR. *Navajo*
SILVERSMITH:
HALLMARK: Stamped surname.
Spouse is Alice Benally, son is Edward Benally, Jr.
From the Canyoncito, New Mexico region.

E.BENALLY

BENALLY, EMIL *Navajo*
SILVERSMITH:
HALLMARK: Stamped initials and symbol in 1/16 Gothic print.

BENALLY, ERNEST *Navajo*
SILVERSMITH/LAPIDARIST: Specializes in inlay. Smith and stoneworker for Sunburst Handcrafts since 1977.
HALLMARK: Stamped number is used for inlay work. Stamped initials and script name and symbol. Special stamp with symbol first used in 1982. Initials are 1/16 Gothic print.

2      EB

BENALLY, JOSEPHINE *Navajo*
SILVERSMITH:
HALLMARK: Stamped initials.

JB

BENALLY, KEE JOE *Navajo*
SILVERSMITH: Specialized in flat ware and wrought work. Worked also as a designer. Benchsmith for Woodards Indian Shop for 15 years.
HALLMARK: Stamped initials in 1/16 Gothic print. Also used engraved initials.

KJB   K.J.B.

BENALLY, L ? *Navajo*
SILVERSMITH:
HALLMARK: Stamped surname with "handmade" in smaller type on second line.

L.BENALLY
HANDMADE

BENALLY, P.K. *Navajo*
SILVERSMITH: Specializes in channel work and inlay. Benchsmith for Rocking Horse Ranch.
HALLMARK: Stamped surname and initials in 1/16 script. Stamp first used in 1984.

P.K.Benally

BENALLY, RITA B. *Navajo*
SILVERSMITH/LAPIDARIST: Specializes in inlay. Benchsmith and stone worker for Sunburst Handcrafts.
HALLMARK: Stamped initials in 1/16 Gothic print. This stamp first used in 1973. Numerical stamp used for Sunburst Handcrafts.

R.B.B.   1

BENEVIDEZ, JOSE *Santa Domingo*
SILVERSMITH:
HALLMARK: Stamped initials in 3/32 letters.

JKB

BENN, SHIRLEY *Hopi/Tewa*
SILVERSMITH: Specializes in kachinas, animal necklaces, natural objects.
HALLMARK: Stamped surname and her initials and her husband's in 1/16 Gothic print. Also a stamp in 1/32 script of both of their full names. This stamp first used in 1981.
Spouse is Virgil Benn.

V.&S.BENN

BENN, VIRGIL *Paiute*
SILVERSMITH: Specializes in kachinas, animal necklaces, natural objects.
HALLMARK: Stamped surname and his initials and his wife's in 1/16 Gothic print. Also a stamp in 1/32 script of both of their full names. This stamp first used in 1981.
Spouse is Shirley Benn.

V.&S. BENN   Shirley & Virgil Benn

BENNETT, B ? *Navajo*
SILVERSMITH: Smith for Atkinson Trading Company.
HALLMARK: Surname and initial in 1/16 Gothic print. Stamp first used in 1983.

B.BENNETT

BENNETT, BETTY *Navajo*
SILVERSMITH: Smith for Atkinson Trading Company before 1980.

HALLMARK: Stamped initials in 1/16 Gothic print.

B.J.B.

BENNETT, ELIZABETH *Navajo*
SILVERSMITH: Specializes in making beads. Production somewhat erratic.
HALLMARK: Stamped initials in 1/16 Gothic print.
Spouse was Jimmie Toddie (first wife). John Burnside is her father, Tom Burnside her uncle, and Frank Burnside her brother. Dormitory matron at the school.
From Pine Springs, Arizona region.

E.B.

BENNETT, LEE *Navajo*
SILVERSMITH: Smith for Atkinson Trading Company.
HALLMARK: Stamped surname and initial in 1/32 Gothic print. Stamp first used in 1983.

L.BENNETT

BENNETT, RAYMOND *Navajo*
SILVERSMITH: Smith for Atkinson Trading Company.
HALLMARK: Stamped surname and initial in 1/16 Gothic print. Stamp first used in 1978.

R.BENNETT

BENTON, HERMAN *Unknown*
SILVERSMITH:
HALLMARK: Initials in 3/32 Gothic print. Stamp first used in 1974.
From Holbrook, Arizona region.

H.D.B.

BESSELENTE, M. *Zuni*
SILVERSMITH:
HALLMARK: Stamped surname and two initials in 1/16 Gothic print. Stamp first used in 1975.

M.D.BESSE ENTE

BETONEY, B ? *Navajo*
SILVERSMITH: Produces eccentric pieces.
HALLMARK: Stamped surname and initial with a second line reading Navajo in mismatched type. Stamp first used in 1985.

B.BETONEY
NAVAJO

BETONI, ETHEL *Apache*
SILVERSMITH: Peridot settings.
HALLMARK: Stamped initials.

E B

BEYUKA, EDWARD *Zuni*
SILVERSMITH/LAPIDARIST: Specializes in mosaic and channel inlay of dance figures. Drum beads. Figures of eagle dancers, roadrunners, etc.
HALLMARK: Stamped initials either underlined or not. Stamped surname and initial as well as a macaw head.
Spouse was formerly Madeline Beyuka.

EAB   EAB   E.BEYUKA

BEYUKA, JONATHAN *Zuni*
SILVERSMITH:
HALLMARK: Stamped initials.

JB

BEYUKA, MADELINE *Zuni*
SILVERSMITH/LAPIDARIST: Specializes in mosaic and channel inlay. Designs are Zuni women derived from her former husband's work. She learned the craft from her brother-in-law and began producing independently in 1954.
HALLMARK: Stamped initials in 1/16 Gothic print, occasionally placed over and under.
Former spouse was Edward Beyuka.
[Levy: 1980:28]

MB   M
**   B**

BIA, SAM *Navajo*
SILVERSMITH:
HALLMARK: Stamped symbol.
From Witch Wells, Arizona region.

✪

BICENTI, RAYMOND *Navajo*
SILVERSMITH:
HALLMARK: Stamped initials.
[IACA Bull. Nov/Dec. 1981]

RHVB

BICKLE, ESTHER *Navajo*
SILVERSMITH: Smith for Atkinson Trading Company.
HALLMARK: Stamped surname and initial in 1/16 Gothic print. Stamp first used in 1975.

E.BICKLE

BICKLE, L ? *Navajo*
SILVERSMITH: Smith for Indian Hammers.
HALLMARK: Stamped surname and initial in 1/16 Gothic print. Stamp first used in 1976.

L.BICKLE

BILAGODY, E ? *Navajo*
SILVERSMITH:
HALLMARK: Stamped surname and initial in 1/16 Gothic print. Stamp first used in 1982.
From Gallup, New Mexico region.

E.BILAGODY

BILL, EMERSON see **BILLY, EMERSON**

BILL, LORENZO *Navajo*
SILVERSMITH: Smith for Chet Jones.
HALLMARK: Two line stamp in 1/8 script. First used in 1980.

Created by Lorenzo Bill

BILLIE, ? *Unknown*
SILVERSMITH: Smith for Cooper's Indian Store.
HALLMARK: Stamped name in 1/16 Gothic print. Stamp first used in 1981.

BILLIE

BILLIE, BETTY ROSE *Navajo*
SILVERSMITH: Specializes in cast work in oil and cement. Trained and worked for the Kirks at Manuelito. Smith for Woodards, Tanners, and Indian Hammers.
HALLMARK: Stamped initials and surname with initials in 1/16 Gothic print. Surname stamp first used in 1976.

BRB   B.R.BILLIE

BILLIE, HENRY *Navajo*
SILVERSMITH: Smith for Woodards and L.J. Jackson.
HALLMARK: Stamped initials in 1/16 Gothic print first used in 1975. Stamped full name in same print first used in 1976.
From Winslow, Arizona region.

H.J.B.   HENRY BILLIE

BILLIE, J ? *Navajo*
SILVERSMITH: Smith for Native Sons Trading Post.
HALLMARK: Stamped surname and initial in 1/16 Gothic print. First used in 1984.

J.BILLIE

BILLIE, JOE G. *Navajo*
SILVERSMITH: Also works in shell, stone, and leather.
HALLMARK: Stamped initials.

JGB

BILLIE, JOHN JIM *Navajo*
SILVERSMITH:
HALLMARK: Stamped initials.

JJB

BILLIE, J.K. *Navajo*
SILVERSMITH: Smith for Indian Hammers.
HALLMARK: Stamped surname and initials in 1/16 Gothic print. Stamp first used in 1976.

J.K.BILLIE

BILLIE, T? *Navajo*
SILVERSMITH: Smith for Blackbird Trading Company.
HALLMARK: Stamped surname in 1/16 Gothic print. Stamp first used in 1985.

T./BILLIE

BILLIE, TOM see **BILLY, TOM**

BILLISON, ? *Navajo*
SILVERSMITH/LAPIDARIST: Specializes in inlaid birds.
HALLMARK: Stamped initials.

ARB

BILLY, EMERSON (BILL, EMERSON or EMERSON) *Navajo*
SILVERSMITH/GOLDSMITH: Specializes in goldwork. Smith for Chet Jones.
HALLMARK: Stamped initials in 1/16 Gothic print. Stamped given name in 1/16 script. First used in 1980. Second version using stamped given name and initial in 1/16 script. Stamped arrowhead with name 1/4 x 3/16 first used in 1974.
From Crownpoint, New Mexico region.

E. B.   *Emerson B*

BILLY, MARY *Navajo*
SILVERSMITH: Smith for Atkinson Trading Company.
HALLMARK: Stamped full name in 1/16 Gothic print. Stamp first used in 1974.

MARY BILLIE

BILLY, TOM (BILLIE, TOM) *Navajo*
SILVERSMITH:
HALLMARK: Stamped surname in 1/16 Gothic print first used in 1983. Initials in same lettering.
From Dilkon, Arizona region.

T.BILLY   TB   TJB

BINI, DENE TSOSIE *Navajo*
SILVERSMITH:
HALLMARK: Stamped initials in 1/16 Gothic print or with an out-sized letter T. May use the Morgan family stamp as well.
From Manuelito, New Mexico region.

DTB   DTB

BINS, COLEEN ANNE *Unknown*
SILVERSMITH:
HALLMARK: Elaborate monogram 3/16 stamp. First used in 1985.
From Santa Fe, New Mexico region.

BITSUI, JIM *Navajo*
SILVERSMITH: Specializes in chip inlay.

HALLMARK: Stamped joined initials.

BITSUI, MARDI *Navajo*
SILVERSMITH: Smith for Don Woodard.
HALLMARK: Stamped surname in 3/32 Gothic print. Stamp first used in 1982.

BLACKGOAT, ALICE *Navajo*
SILVERSMITH: Specializes in squashblossom necklaces.
HALLMARK: Stamped hallmarks of initials in 1/16 Gothic print or a stamp of a goat's head.

AB

BLACKGOAT, ARLENE *Navajo*
SILVERSMITH: Smith for Max Sandoval.
HALLMARK: Stamped 1/16 Gothic print initials over second line NAVAJO. Stamp first used in 1976.

A.B.
NAVAJO

BLACKGOAT, BEN *Navajo*
SILVERSMITH:
HALLMARK: Stamped initials.

BB

BLACKGOAT, CARSON *Navajo*
SILVERSMITH:
HALLMARK: Stamped given name in 1/16 Gothic print. Stamp first used in 1984.
From Gallup, New Mexico region.

CARSON B

BLACKGOAT, H ? *Navajo*
SILVERSMITH:
HALLMARK: Stamped surname in 1/16 Gothic print. Stamp first used in 1975.

H.BLACKGOAT

BLACKGOAT, JENNIE *Navajo*
SILVERSMITH:
HALLMARK: Stamped surname in both 1/16 and 3/32 Gothic print. Stamps first used in 1975.
From Gallup, New Mexico region.

J.BLACKGOAT

BLACKGOAT, L ? *Navajo*
SILVERSMITH:
HALLMARK: Stamped surname in 1/16 Gothic print. Stamp first used in 1981.
From Gallup, New Mexico region.

L.BLACKGOAT

BLANCARTE, JUAN F. *Unknown*
SILVERSMITH:
HALLMARK: Stamped surname in 1/32 Gothic print. Stamp first used in 1981.
From Clifton, Arizona region.

J. BLANCARTE

BLATTS, RICHARD *Navajo*
SILVERSMITH:
HALLMARK: Stamped symbol.

BLY, JACK *Santo Domingo*
SILVERSMITH: Specialized in chip inlay. During the 1970's specialized in goldwork. Designs are claws and water serpents.
HALLMARK: Stamped initials in 1/16 Gothic print.
Note: Name may be Jack Blything.

J.B.

BOBELU, CAROLYN *Zuni*
SILVERSMITH:
HALLMARK: Two line stamp on plate. Name is in 1/16 Gothic print. Stamp first used in 1979. Also uses a symbol and another stamp for initials.
Married name is Starks.

   CAROLYN BOBELU   ⋈   CMB

BOBELU, OWEN *Zuni*
SILVERSMITH/LAPIDARIST: Specializes in curvilinear channel inlay. Learned from his wife's mother and began producing in 1962. Works with his wife.
HALLMARK: Engraved signature of him and his spouse in script. Spouse is Rosalita Bobelu.
[Levy:1980:33]

Owen & Rose
Bobelu - Zuni

BOBELU, ROSALITA *Zuni*
SILVERSMITH/LAPIDARIST: Specializes in curvilinear channel inlay. Learned from her mother and began producing in 1962. Works with her husband.
HALLMARK: Engraved signature of her and her spouse in script. Spouse is Owen Bobelu.
[Levy:1980:33]

Owen & Rose
Bobelu - Zuni

BOHLEN, AURELIA *Apache*

BONNEY, BERNICE *Navajo (?)*
SILVERSMITH:
HALLMARK: Stamped offset initials in 1/16 Gothic print. Stamp first used in 1981.

B
 B

BONNEY, EMMA *Navajo (?)*
SILVERSMITH:
HALLMARK: Stamped initials in 3/32 Gothic print. Stamp first used in 1985.
Sister-in-law of Rinna Leyba.

E.L.B.

BOONE, ? *Santo Domingo*
SILVERSMITH/LAPIDARIST: Specializes in inlay.
HALLMARK: Stamped surname.

BOONE

BOONE, A ? *Santo Domingo (?)*
SILVERSMITH:
HALLMARK: Stamped surname in 1/16 Gothic print. Stamp first used in 1983.

A.BOONE

BOONE, ALEX *Zuni*
SILVERSMITH/LAPIDARIST: Specializes in inlay.
HALLMARK: Stamped surname and initials. Initials combined with another individual.
Note: May be the same person as BOONE.

A&M BOONE

BOONE, LENA *Zuni*
LAPIDARIST: Specializes in fetishes and inlays.
HALLMARK: Stamped hallmark of her and her husband's given names in 1/32 script.
Spouse is Rigney Boone, mother is Edna Leki.
[Bell:1977:21]

Lena & Rigney   *W/*

BOONE, PAULINUS *Zuni*
SILVERSMITH:
HALLMARK: Stamped initials over small print Zuni.

PB

BOONE, PERLETTA *Zuni*
SILVERSMITH/LAPIDARIST: Specializes in thin inlaid bracelets.
HALLMARK: Stamped surname in 1/16 Gothic print. Stamp first used in 1976.

R.P.BOONE

BOONE, RIGNEY *Zuni*
LAPIDARIST: Specializes in fetishes and inlays of birds and bears
HALLMARK: Stamped hallmark of his and his wife's given names in 1/32 script.
Spouse is Lena Boone.
[Bell:1977:21]

Lena & Rigney

BOOQUA, ALLEN *Zuni*
SILVERSMITH: Smith for Atkinson Trading Company.
HALLMARK: Stamped surname for 1/16 Gothic print. Stamp first used in 1973.

A.BOOQUA

BOOQUA, GLENDORA *Zuni*
SILVERSMITH/LAPIDARIST:
HALLMARK: Stamped initials in 1/16 Gothic print. Combined initials of hers and her husband who works with her.
Spouse is Rickell Booqua.

RGB

BOOQUA, MARLENE *Zuni*
SILVERSMITH/LAPIDARIST:
HALLMARK: Stamped surname in 1/16 Gothic print. Stamp first used in 1984.

C.M.BOOQUA

BOOQUA, RICKELL *Zuni*
SILVERSMITH/LAPIDARIST:
HALLMARK: Stamped initials in 1/16 Gothic print. Combined initials of his and his wife's who works with him.
Spouse is Glendora Booqua.

RGB

BOWANNA, BERTHA *Navajo (?)*
SILVERSMITH:
HALLMARK: Stamped initials.

BB

BOWANNIE, ADELINE *Zuni*
SILVERSMITH/LAPIDARIST: Specializes in channel inlay.
HALLMARK: Stamped three lines of full name and location. 1 1/2 x 3/16" mark.

ADELINE
BOWANNIE
ZUNI,NM

BOWANNIE, DELIA *Zuni*
SILVERSMITH/LAPIDARIST: Specializes in channel inlay of butterflies. Learned from her husband and then began independent work in 1974.
HALLMARK: Stamped initials combining hers and his. Both use the same stamp.

Spouse is Fadrian Bowannie.
[Levy:1980:27]

F.D.B.

BOWANNIE, EARLENE *Zuni*
SILVERSMITH/LAPIDARIST:
HALLMARK: Stamped full name in 1/16 script. Stamp first used in 1982.

Earlene Bowannie

BOWANNIE, FADRIAN *Zuni*
SILVERSMITH/LAPIDARIST: Learned his craft from his sister. Began producing in 1974. Specializes in channel inlaid butterflies. He and his wife work independently on similar designs.
HALLMARK: Stamped joint initials. Both he and his wife use the same stamp.
Spouse is Delia Bowannie.
[Bell:1976:13]

F.D.B.

BOWANNIE, FRED *Zuni*
SILVERSMITH/LAPIDARIST: Specializes in cameo inlaid rings, kachinas, and dome rings. Began producing in 1935.
HALLMARK: Stamped initials either over and under or in combination with Zuni.
Spouse is Lula Bowannie.

FB ZUNI   F/B

BOWANNIE, JOHN Q. *Zuni*
SILVERSMITH/LAPIDARIST: Specializes in mosaic and channel inlay.
HALLMARK: Stamped joint initials of him and his wife in 1/16 Gothic print. Stamp first used in 1974. Both use the same stamp.
Spouse is Rosalie Bowannie, parents are Fred and Lula Bowannie.
[Bell:1977:51]

J.R.B.

BOWANNIE, LULA *Zuni*
SILVERSMITH/LAPIDARIST: Specializes in cameo inlay, dome rings, and kachina designs. Began producing in 1935.
HALLMARK: Stamped hallmark of initials or initials with word ZUNI attached. Uses a different mark than her husband.
Spouse is Fred Bowannie, daughter Adeline Yawakia.

L.B.   L.B.ZUNI

BOWANNIE, ROSALIE *Zuni*
SILVERSMITH/LAPIDARIST: Specializes in mosaic and channel inlay.
HALLMARK: Stamped joint initials of her husband and hers in 1/16 Gothic print. Stamp first used in 1951. Both use the same stamp.
Spouse is John Q. Bowannie.
[Bell:1976:51]

J.R.B.

BOWEKATY, AGNES *Zuni*
SILVERSMITH/LAPIDARIST: Specializes in needlepoint. Began producing in 1951.
HALLMARK: Stamped surname and joint initials of her and her husband. Both use the same stamps.
Spouse is Hugh Bowekaty.
[Bell:1977:7]

H.&A.BOWEKATY   H.BOWEKATY   H&A

BOWEKATY, BERNARD *Zuni*
SILVERSMITH/LAPIDARIST: Specializes in "snake eye" sets in squash blossom necklaces.
HALLMARK: Stamped back to back joined initials followed by ZUNI.
[Bell:1977:44]

ƁB ZUNI

BOWEKATY, HUGH *Zuni*
SILVERSMITH/LAPIDARIST: Specialized in needlepoint. Began producing in 1951.
HALLMARK: Stamped surname with one initial, in two sizes, 1/16 and 1/32 Gothic print. Stamp first used in 1974. Second stamp combines his and his wife's initials and given name and was first used in 1983. Stamped joint initials are also used.
Spouse is Agnes Bowekaty.
[Bell:1977:7]

H.&A.BOWEKATY   H.BOWEKATY   H&A

BOWEKATY, LUCILLE *Zuni*
SILVERSMITH/LAPIDARIST: Specializes in needlepoint clusters, and some inlay.
HALLMARK: Stamped initials of hers and her husband's. Often set on a plate.
Spouse is Samson Bowekaty.
[Bell:1977:14]

S & L   ₛBᴸ

BOWEKATY, SAMSON *Zuni*
SILVERSMITH/LAPIDARIST: Specializes in needlepoint clusters, and some inlay.
HALLMARK: Stamped initials of his and his wife's. Often set on a plate.
Spouse is Lucille Bowekaty.
[Bell:1977:14]

S & L   ₛBᴸ

BOWIE, ? *Unknown*
SILVERSMITH:
HALLMARK: Stamped surname in 3/32 Gothic print. Stamped symbol of a C or a crescent moon or a combination with the name. other two.

C. BOWIE   ☾BOWIE

BOWIE, GERALDINE *Navajo*
LAPIDARIST: Works for Sunburst Handcrafts.

HALLMARK: Stamped numerical mark.

7

BOWMAN, RICHARD *Navajo*
SILVERSMITH:
HALLMARK: Stamped surname in 1/16 Gothic print. Stamp first used in 1975.
From Mexican Springs, New Mexico region.

R.BOW

BOYD, DELPHINE *Navajo*
LAPIDARIST: Bench worker for Sunburst Handcrafts.
HALLMARK: Stamped numerical designation.

5

BOYD, GAY *Navajo*
SILVERSMITH: Specializes in hollow ware.
HALLMARK: Personalized stamp of full name.

Jay Boyd

BOYD, H ? *Navajo*
SILVERSMITH:
HALLMARK: Stamped surname in 1/16 Gothic print. Stamp first used in 1979.
From Holbrook, Arizona region.

H.BOYD

BOYD, JAMES *Navajo*
SILVERSMITH:
HALLMARK: Stamped joined initials in personalized script.
From Whitewater region.

JB

BOYD, JULIA *Navajo*
LAPIDARIST: Benchworker for Sunburst Handcrafts.
HALLMARK: Stamped numerical mark.

6

BOYD, RAYMOND *Navajo*
SILVERSMITH: Specializes in inlaid birds in Zuni style. Smith for Ortega.
HALLMARK: Stamped full name in 1/16 Gothic print. Stamp first used in 1980.

H. BOYD

BOYD, VIRGIL *Navajo*
SILVERSMITH:
HALLMARK: Stamped special symbol 1/8" square.
From Ft. Wingate, Arizona region.

BRADFORD, VIRGINIA *Anglo (?)*
SILVERSMITH:
HALLMARK: Stamped special symbol.

BRADLEY (SECIWA), CHARLOTTE (FLOWER) *Zuni*
SILVERSMITH:
HALLMARK: Stamped special symbols of flowers with name 1/4 x 3/8".
Uses the name Seciwa as well.

BRADLEY, GEORGE *Zuni*
SILVERSMITH:
HALLMARK: Stamped specialized initials in script 1/4 x 3/8".

BRADLEY, TOM *Navajo/Zuni*
SILVERSMITH:
HALLMARK: Stamped two-line surname and tribal affiliation in 3/32 Gothic print. Stamp first used in 1975.

T. BRADLEY
NAV-ZUNI

BRADY, WILBER *Navajo*
SILVERSMITH:
HALLMARK: Special stamp of winged initials 3/16 x 3/32". Stamp first used in 1975.

BROWN, BENJAMIN *Unknown*
SILVERSMITH:
HALLMARK: Stamped initials in 3/32 Gothic print. Stamp first used in 1975.
From Grand Canyon region.

B.BR

BROWN, CEA *Navajo*
SILVERSMITH: Specializes in chip inlay.
HALLMARK: Stamped initials partly reversed and occasionally joined.

CB   CB

BROWN, DAISY *Navajo*
SILVERSMITH:
HALLMARK: Stamped initials in 3/32 Gothic print. Stamp first used in 1974.
From Shiprock, New Mexico region.

D.B.

BROWN, DARRELL *Choctaw*
SILVERSMITH:
HALLMARK: Stamped initials.

DB

BROWN, GILBERT *Navajo*
SILVERSMITH:
HALLMARK: Stamped abridged surname in 1/16 and 3/32 Gothic print. Stamps first used in 1975.
From Lupton, Arizona region.

G.BRN

BROWN, MARIE *Navajo*
SILVERSMITH:
HALLMARK: Stamped surname in 1/16 Gothic print. Stamp first used in 1973.
From Gamerco, New Mexico region.

M.BROWN

BUCKLE, E ? *Navajo*
SILVERSMITH: Smith for Totso Trading Post.
HALLMARK: Stamped name and double initials in 1/16 Gothic print. Stamp first used in 1981.
Spouse is J. Buckle.
From Lukachukai, Arizona region.

J.&E. BUCKLE

BUCKLE, J ? *Navajo*
SILVERSMITH: Smith for Totso Trading Post.
HALLMARK: Stamped name and double initials in 1/16 Gothic print. Stamp first used in 1981.
Spouse is E. Buckle.
From Lukachukai, Arizona region.

J&E BUCKLE

BURNHAM, VIRGINIA *Navajo*
SILVERSMITH: Produced for Canyon Silver Company.
HALLMARK: Stamped joined initials in 1/16 Gothic print. Stamp first used in 1976.
Spouse is Bruce Burnham.

VB

BURNSIDE, ANN *Navajo*
SILVERSMITH:
HALLMARK: Stamped initials shared with spouse. One in Gothic print, the other in personalized print.
Spouse is Milton Burnside.

MB   *MB*

BURNSIDE, FRANK *Navajo*
SILVERSMITH:
HALLMARK: Stamped surname in 3/32 Gothic print. Stamp first used in 1976.
Father is John Burnside, sister is Elizabeth Bennett.
From Mentmore, New Mexico region.

F.BURNSIDE

BURNSIDE, JOHN *Navajo*
SILVERSMITH: Specialized in cast work. Demonstrated silver craft work at numerous events during the 1960s. Having eye trouble nowadays.
HALLMARK: Stamped initials in 1/16 Gothic print.
Brother is Tom Burnside, sister Mabel Burnside Meyer, daughter Elizabeth Bennett, nephews Chester and Franklin Kahn.

JHB   JB

BURNSIDE, L ? *Navajo*
SILVERSMITH:
HALLMARK: Stamped initials in Gothic print.

LB

BURNSIDE, MILTON *Navajo*
SILVERSMITH:
HALLMARK: Stamped initials shared with spouse. One in Gothic print the other in personalized print.
Spouse is Ann Burnside.

MB   *MB*

BURNSIDE, TOM *Navajo*
SILVERSMITH: Specializes in castwork using big bold stones and leaves. Presumably learned his craft from Charlie Houck.
HALLMARK: Stamped initials in Gothic print.
Brother is John Burnside, sister Mabel Burnside Meyer, daughter is Peggy Lynch (noted Pine Springs weaver.)

T.B.

BURRIS, D ? *Unknown*
SILVERSMITH:
HALLMARK: Stamped surname or initials in either 1/16 or 3/32 Gothic print. Stamp for surname first used in 1975.
From Claremore, Oklahoma region.

D.BURRIS   D.B.

BUSH, CURLEY JR. *Apache*
LAPIDARIST: Peridot settings.
HALLMARK: Stamped initials.

JR.

BYJOE, PHILLIP *Navajo*
SILVERSMITH:
HALLMARK: Stamped shared initials in 1/16 Gothic print. Stamp first used in 1979.
From Lukachukai, Arizona region.

P.& V.BYJOE

CACHINI, A ? *Zuni*
SILVERSMITH: Specializes in chip inlay.
HALLMARK: Stamped surname in 1/16 Gothic print. Stamp first used in 1975.

A.CACHINI

CACHINI, FRED *Zuni*
SILVERSMITH:
HALLMARK: Stamped initials in 3/32 Gothic print. Stamp first used in 1974.

F.C.

CACHINI, SYBIL *Zuni*
SILVERSMITH:
HALLMARK: Stamped full name in 1/16 Gothic print. Stamp first used in 1977.

SYBIL CACHINI

CADMAN, DOLORES — *Unknown*
SILVERSMITH: Smith for Ortega.
HALLMARK: Stamped full name in 1/16 Gothic print. Stamp first used in 1980.

DOLORES CADMAN

CADMAN, JULIA — *Navajo*
SILVERSMITH: Specializes in overlay. Smith for the T & R Market.
HALLMARK: Stamped surname in 1/16 Gothic print. Stamp first used in 1976. Stamped initial also.

J.CADMAN   J

CADMAN, L ? — *Unknown*
SILVERSMITH: Smith for the T & R Market.
HALLMARK: Stamped surname in 1/16 Gothic print. Stamp first used in 1976.

L.CADMAN

CADMAN, M ? — *Navajo (?)*
SILVERSMITH: Smith for T & R Market.
HALLMARK: Stamped surname in 1/16 Gothic print. Stamp first used in 1976.

M.CADMAN

CAHUILLA MARGARET — *Morongo*
SILVERSMITH: Specializes in ring watches.
HALLMARK: Stamped initials in personalized 3/32 print. Married name is Gonzales, also goes by the name Red Elk.

C/M (in arch symbol)

CALABAZA, JUANITA ABEITA — *Isleta*
SILVERSMITH:
HALLMARK: Stamped initials in different print sizes.

Jac   J.A.C.

CALABAZA, MITCHELL — *Santo Domingo or Picuris*
SILVERSMITH: Smith for Peshlakai Ltd.
HALLMARK: Stamped initials in 1/8 print surrounded by large initial M. Stamp first used in 1977.

[CLBZ] (within M shape)

CALABAZA, OLIVIA — *Zuni*
SILVERSMITH/LAPIDARIST:
HALLMARK: Stamped initials in 1/16 Gothic print. The C is almost closed and more resembles an 0 than a C.
Spouse was formerly Ronnie Calabaza.

ROC
ZUNI N M

CALABAZA, RONNIE — *Zuni*
SILVERSMITH/LAPIDARIST: Began producing in 1978.
HALLMARK: Stamped initials in 1/16 Gothic print. The C is special in that it resembles an 0 more than a C. This mark was copied by Phillipine craftsmen duplicating his work but they read it as ROO and put this on their fake Indian jewelry. Divorced in 1986 he now uses only the RC. Former spouse was Olivia Calabaza. His mother is Rosalie Pinto.

ROC   RC
ZUNI N M

CALAVAZA, EFFIE — *Zuni*
SILVERSMITH/LAPIDARIST: Specializes in sandcasting and incorporates large stones. Snake designs. She began producing in 1956 after learning the craft from her husband. She uses both her husband's and her own designs.
HALLMARK: Stamped hallmark of her husband's or her given name with Zuni underneath in 1/16 Gothic print. The mark EFFIE C. is used as a family mark by Effie and three daughters. She shared her spouse's mark until his death ca. 1970.
Spouse was Juan Calavaza. Daughters are Georgiana Yatsattie, Gloria Jean Garcia, and Susie Calavaza. Note: Jewelry is indistinguishable.
[Bell:1976:22] [Levy:1980:61]

JUAN C.   EFFIE C.
ZUNI   ZUNI

CALAVAZA, JOAN — *Zuni*
SILVERSMITH:
HALLMARK: Stamped initials.

JC   JC

CALAVAZA, JOSE — *Zuni*
SILVERSMITH:
HALLMARK: Stamped full name with Zuni on second line in 1/16 Gothic print. Stamp first used in 1974. Second stamp of surname with Zuni on second line in 1/32 Gothic print. Stamp first used in 1976. Engraved signature used nowadays.

JOSE CALAVAZA   J.CALAVAZA   J. Calavaza
ZUNI   ZUNI

CALAVAZA, JUAN — *Zuni*
SILVERSMITH/LAPIDARIST: Specialized in sandcasting. One of the few Zuni to do so. Worked also in channel and mosaic inlay. Designs of snakes surrounded by large nugget settings. Began producing in the early 1930s.
HALLMARK: Stamped initials or initials with an arrow. In later years used a stamp of his given name which he shared with his spouse.
Spouse was Effie Calavaza. He was deceased ca. 1970.

J. C.   J.C.→

CALAVAZA, SUSIE — *Zuni*
SILVERSMITH/LAPIDARIST: Specializes in sandcasting of snake designs with heavy nugget settings. Learned her craft from her mother, and work is indistinguishable.
HALLMARK: Stamped initials in 1/16 Gothic print accompanied by either an arrow or in a second line ZUNI. The two line stamp was first used in 1973.
Father was Juan Calavaza and mother Effie. Sisters are Georgiana Yatsattie and Gloria Jean Garcia.

S.C.   ←S.C.
ZUNI

CALAVAZA, VIOLA — *Zuni*
SILVERSMITH/LAPIDARIST:

HALLMARK: Stamped full name in 1/16 Gothic print. Stamp first used in 1974. Also uses stamped initials attached to the word Zuni.

VIOLA CALAVAZA   VCZUNI

CALAVAZA, WAYNE   *Zuni*
SILVERSMITH:
HALLMARK: Engraved given name. Same signature also used as a stamp.

Wayne C.

CALDITO, RAY   *Navajo*
SILVERSMITH:
HALLMARK: Stamped initials in Gothic print.
From San Antonio Springs, New Mexico region.

R.C.

CALLAWAY, MARY L.   *Navajo*
SILVERSMITH:
HALLMARK: Stamped initials in 1/16 Gothic print. Stamp first used in 1977.
From Prewitt, New Mexico region.

M. L.C.

CALVIN, MICHAEL D.   *Navajo*
SILVERSMITH:
HALLMARK: Stamped surname and initials in 1/16 Gothic print. Stamp first used in 1977.
From Chinle, Arizona region.

M.D.CALVIN

CALVIN, SADIE   *Navajo*
SILVERSMITH: Specializes in making molds for original castings as well as standard silver craft. Smith for D.G. Mudd.
HALLMARK: Special stamp of a bird.
Sister is Sarah Dubois.

CAMBRIDGE, NORMAN   *Navajo*
SILVERSMITH: Smith for Moqui Trading Post.
HALLMARK: Stamped initials or surname in 1/32 Gothic print preceded by 1/16 initials.

NFC   N.F.CAMBRIDGE

CANDELARIA, RAMA   *Navajo*
SILVERSMITH:
HALLMARK: Stamped initials.

R.C.

CARILLO, FRANK   *Laguna*
SILVERSMITH:
HALLMARK: Stamped initials in 1/16 Gothic print. Stamp first used in 1985.
From Albuquerque, New Mexico region.

F.C.

CARL, HATTIE   *Hopi*
POTTER: Produced from ca. 1900 to 1951.
HALLMARK: Painted and fired symbol representing a "cloud flower".

CARL, SYBIL   *Tewa*
POTTER: Began producing ca. 1960.
HALLMARK: Painted and fired representation of a tadpole.

CARROL, MICHAEL (MIKE)   *Navajo*
SILVERSMITH: Specialized in ball peen work. Began producing in the 1950s. Smith for the White Hogan.
HALLMARK: Stamped initials often set on a fringed plate. Deceased in 1965.
[King:1976:10]

MC   MC

CARUSETTA, THOMAS   *Unknown*
SILVERSMITH:
HALLMARK: Stamped given name in 1/16 script. Stamp first used in 1982. Stamped initials in 1/32 Gothic print.
From Sedona, Arizona region.

Thomas   TJC

CARVISO, E ?   *Navajo*
SILVERSMITH: Smith for Atkinson Trading Company.
HALLMARK: Stamped surname in 1/16 Gothic print. Stamp first used in 1976.

E.CARVISO

CARVISO, EMMA   *Navajo*
SILVERSMITH:
HALLMARK: Stamped combination of letter and numeral in 1/16 Gothic print. Stamp first used in 1982.
From Fort Wingate, New Mexico region.

W/3   W/3

CARVISO, W (?) JR.   *Navajo*
SILVERSMITH:
HALLMARK: Stamped surname in 1/16 Gothic print. Stamp first used in 1975.

W.CARVISO JR

CASSADORE, WHITMAN JR.   *Apache*
LAPIDARIST: Peridot settings.
HALLMARK: Stamped initials in Gothic print.

WC

CASTILLO, BESSIE   *Navajo*

SILVERSMITH: Simple designs.
HALLMARK: Stamped initials in Gothic print.
From Torres, New Mexico region.

B.C.

CASTILLO, ROSE see **ROSE DRAPER.**

CASUSE, MARY *Unknown*
SILVERSMITH:
HALLMARK: Stamped initials in 1/16 Gothic print.

MRC

CASUSE, RICHARD *Hopi*
SILVERSMITH: Overlay work (?).
HALLMARK: Stamped symbol of water with initials in 1/16 Gothic print. Stamp first used in 1976.

CASUSE, S? *Hopi*
SILVERSMITH:
HALLMARK: Special stamp of sun face with initials. Stamp first used in 1976.

CATING, WESLEY *Navajo*
SILVERSMITH:
HALLMARK: Stamped initials in Gothic print.

WC

CAYATINETO, P ? *Isleta/Sandia*
SILVERSMITH:
HALLMARK: Stamped surname in 1/16 Gothic print and engraved signature also.

P.CAYATINETO   *P.Cayatineto*

CELENCIO, L ? *Zuni*
SILVERSMITH:
HALLMARKS: Stamped symbol of a man and another of an initial.

CELLECION, ANGELA *Zuni*
SILVERSMITH/LAPIDARIST: Specializes in cast crosses and kachina figures in channel and mosaic inlay. Began producing in 1942. Works with her husband.
HALLMARK: Stamped combination of her and her husband's initials in 1/16 Gothic print. The stamps are used jointly.
Spouse is Oliver Cellecion.
[Bell:1975:12]

OJC & AC   OJC
             &
             AC

CELLECION, OLIVER *Zuni*
SILVERSMITH/LAPIDARIST: Specializes in cast crosses and kachina figures in channel and mosaic inlay. Began producing in 1942. Works with his wife.
HALLMARK: Stamped combination of his and his wife's initials in 1/16 Gothic print. Stamps used jointly with his wife.
Spouse is Angela Cellecion.

OJC & AC   OJC
             &
             AC

CELLECION, LELA *Zuni*
SILVERSMITH/LAPIDARIST: Specializes in carved stone. Also produces sun faces and geometric designs in mosaic and channel inlay.
HALLMARK: Stamped initials in 1/16 Gothic print first used in 1973. Also uses an engraved signature.
Spouse is Roger Cellecion.
[Bell:1977:12]

RLC

CELLECION, ROGER *Zuni*
SILVERSMITH/LAPIDARIST: Specializes in carved stone. Also produces sun faces and geometric designs in mosaic and channel inlay.
HALLMARK: Stamped initials in 1/16 Gothic print first used in 1973. Also uses an engraved signature shared with his wife.
Spouse is Lela Cellecion.
[Bell:1977:12]

RLC

CHACO, EDDY *Navajo*
SILVERSMITH: Smith for Ney Trading Post.
HALLMARK: Stamped full name in 1/32 Gothic Print.

EDDY CHACO

CHAMA, FELIX *Unknown*
SILVERSMITH: Contemporary Jewelry
HALLMARK: Stamped initials in Gothic print framed.

F.D.

CHAMBERS, MARY JANE *Unknown*
SILVERSMITH:
HALLMARK: Stamped initials in Gothic print.

MJC

CHAPELLA, GRACE *Tewa*
POTTER:
HALLMARK: Painted and fired representation of a bear paw. Deceased.

CHAPO, BEN *Navajo*
SILVERSMITH:
HALLMARK: Stamped initals half reversed in 3/32 Gothic print. Stamp first used in 1974.
From Prewitt, New Mexico region.

CHARLEY, J? *Navajo*
SILVERSMITH: Smith for Bernie Dominguez.
HALLMARK: Stamped surname in 1/16 Gothic print first used in 1975.

J. CHARLEY

CHARLEY, L? *Navajo*
SILVERSMITH: Smith for Bernie Dominguez.
HALLMARK: Stamped surname in 1/16 Gothic print first used in 1975.

L. CHARLEY

CHARLEY, LENA CHIO *Tewa*
POTTER: Produced from 1933 to 1961.
HALLMARK: Painted and fired symbol of a corn ear. Supposed to represent blue corn.

CHARLEY, RIC *Navajo*
SILVERSMITH/GOLDSMITH: Specializes in contemporary jewelry.
HALLMARK: Stamped letter C first used in 1973. Second stamp in 1974 was an R inside of an elaborate C. This is now often cast as a part of the piece.
From Scottsdale, Arizona region.

CHARLEY, ROSE *Navajo*
SILVERSMITH:
HALLMARK: Stamped initials or initials of Rose and spouse and surname in 1/32 Gothic print. Stamp with surname first used in 1980.
From Dilcon, Arizona region.

Y&R   Y&R CHARLEY

CHARLEY, STANLEY *Navajo*
SILVERSMITH:
HALLMARK: Stamped combined initials with symbol 3/32".
From Tuba City, Arizona region.

CHARLIE, DARLENE *Zuni*
SILVERSMITH/LAPIDARIST: Specializes in small rounded settings. Learned from her parents and began producing in 1974. She does the stone work and her husband the metal.
HALLMARK: Her stamped initials and her husbands in 1/16 Gothic print.
Spouse is Dickie Charlie. Parents are Lee and Mary Webothee.
[Bell:1977:22] [Levy:1980:57]

D/DC

CHARLIE, DICKIE *Zuni*
SILVERSMITH/LAPIDARIST: Specializes in small rounded settings. Learned from his wife's parents. Began producing in 1974. He does the metal work and his wife the stone work.
HALLMARK: His stamped initials and his wife's in 1/16 Gothic print.
Spouse is Darlene Charlie.

D/DC

CHARLIE, FELIX *Zuni*
SILVERSMITH/LAPIDARIST: Specializes in geometric channel inlay. Began producing in 1966. Works with his wife on some pieces.
HALLMARK: Engraved freehand initials used by wife also.
Spouse is Yvonne Charlie.
[Levy:1980:30]

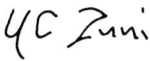

CHARLIE, H? *Navajo*
SILVERSMITH: Smith for Richardson Trading Company.
HALLMARK: Stamped surname in 1/16 Gothic print. Stamp first used in 1975.

H.CHARLIE

CHARLIE, JOHN *Navajo*
SILVERSMITH: Piecework.
HALLMARK: Stamped surname with elaborate initial.

J. CHARLIE

CHARLIE, TOMMIE *Navajo*
SILVERSMITH:
HALLMARK: Stamped initials in Gothic print.

TC

CHARLIE, YVONNE *Zuni*
SILVERSMITH/LAPIDARIST: Specializes in geometric channel inlay. Works with her husband on some pieces. Self-taught.
HALLMARK: Engraved freehand initials used by both her and her husband.
Spouse is Felix Charlie.
[Levy:1980:30]

CHARVEZE, TED *Isleta(?)*
SILVERSMITH/GOLDSMITH: Specializes in contemporary craft pieces.
HALLMARK: Stamped or cast representation of an eagle. Formerly in the foreign car sales business in Kansas.
[Arizona Highways: V.55, #4:1979]

CHATTER, DELBERT *Navajo*
SILVERSMITH:
HALLMARK: Stamped initials in 1/16 Gothic print.
From Winslow, Arizona region.

DC

CHATTER, JACK B. *Navajo*
SILVERSMITH:
HALLMARK: Stamped initials in 3/16 Gothic print. Stamp first used in 1974.
From Tuba City, Arizona region.

J.B.C.

CHAVARRIA, HARRY *Santa Clara*
SILVERSMITH: Specializes in use of wood and other exotic materials in his pieces. Designs are strong geometrics. Works in gold as well.
HALLMARK: Stamped large C with small attached H.
Formerly worked for the United States Forest Service.
[Arizona Highways: V.55, #4:1979]

CHAVEZ, ALFRED *Santo Domingo*
SILVERSMITH:
HALLMARK: Stamped initials in Gothic print.

A.C.

CHAVEZ, BEN *Unknown*
SILVERSMITH:
HALLMARK: Stamped initial surrounded by larger one. Small initial is 1/16 Gothic print. Stamp first used in 1985.

CHAVEZ, C *Unknown*
SILVERSMITH: Smith for T & R Market
HALLMARK: Stamped surname in 1/16 Gothic print. Stamp first used in 1976.

C.CHAVEZ

CHAVEZ, CHRISTOPHER *Unknown*
SILVERSMITH:
HALLMARK: Stamped two line full name in 1/16 Gothic print. Stamp first used in 1984.
From Los Angeles, California region.

CHRIS
CHAVEZ

CHAVEZ, EILEEN *Zuni*
SILVERSMITH/LAPIDARIST: Specializes in channel inlay. Also produces pieces with heavy nugget settings.
HALLMARK: Initials stamped in 1/16 Gothic print with small ZUNI below. Stamp first used in 1974.
Spouse is Sabin M. Chavez.
[Bell:1976:27]

S.M.C.   SMC
ZUNI

CHAVEZ, EVELYN *Navajo*
SILVERSMITH:
HALLMARK: Stamped personalized initials in 3/32 letters.
Spouse is John Chavez.
From Canyoncito, New Mexico region.

EC

CHAVEZ, FELIX *Zuni*
SILVERSMITH/LAPIDARIST:
HALLMARK: Stamp shared with spouse, offset joined initials of both.
Spouse is Mary Ann Chavez.

MFC

CHAVEZ, H.E. *Unknown*
SILVERSMITH:
HALLMARK: Stamped surname in 1/16 Gothic print. Stamp first used in 1974.

H. E. CHAVEZ

CHAVEZ, JIMMIE *Unknown*
SILVERSMITH:
HALLMARK: Stamped surname in 1/16 Gothic print. Stamp first used in 1974.
From Gallup, New Mexico region.

J. CHAVEZ

CHAVEZ, JOHN *Navajo*
SILVERSMITH:
HALLMARK: Stamped initials in different size Gothic print. Larger initial is 3/32".
Spouse is Evelyn Chavez.
From Canyoncito, New Mexico region.

Jc

CHAVEZ, LUCIANO *Santo Domingo*
SILVERSMITH:
HALLMARK: Stamped initials in Gothic print.

LC

CHAVEZ, MARY *San Felipe*
SILVERSMITH: Navajo style work.
HALLMARK: Stamped initials in Gothic print.

MAC   MC

CHAVEZ, MARYANN *Zuni*
SILVERSMITH/LAPIDARIST:
HALLMARK: Stamp of offset joined initials of husband and wife. Stamp used by both.
Spouse is Felix Chavez.

MFC

CHAVEZ, PHILLIP *Unknown*
SILVERSMITH:
HALLMARK: Stamp with large initial letter and 1/16 Gothic print on the remainder.

CHAVEZ

CHAVEZ, PHYLLIS *Unknown*
SILVERSMITH:

HALLMARK: Stamp of 3/16 symbol. Stamp first used in 1983 and set on a plate. Second stamp used in 1984.
From Albuquerque, New Mexico region.

CHAVEZ, RAMOS *Unknown*
SILVERSMITH:
HALLMARK: Stamped offset and joined initials. Stamp of an animal also, possibly a coyote.

CHAVEZ, SABIN M. *Zuni*
SILVERSMITH/LAPIDARIST: Specializes in channel inlay. Also produces pieces with heavy nugget settings.
HALLMARK: Stamped initials in 1/16 Gothic print. Stamp with no periods first used in 1976. Stamp with periods first used in 1974.
Spouse is Eileen Chavez.
[Bell:1976:27]

S.M.C.   SMC

CHAVEZ, TRINNIE *Santo Domingo*
SILVERSMITH:
HALLMARK: Stamped initials and second line of pueblo in upper and lower case 1/16 Gothic print. Stamp first used in 1983.

TRC
s. d. pueblo

CHAVEZ, VIDAL *Zuni*
SILVERSMITH/LAPIDARIST:
HALLMARK: Engraved signature and pueblo.

Vid Chavés Zuni

CHEAMA, ANGELITA *Zuni*
SILVERSMITH/LAPIDARIST: Specializes in cluster work of large irregular stones. Learned from her parents and began producing in 1952.
HALLMARK: Stamped given name in Gothic print first appeared in 1970. Second stamp of surname and initial.
Son is Wayne Cheama.
[Bell:1976:28]   [Levy:1980:60]

ANGIE C.   A. CHEAMA

CHEAMA, C ? *Zuni*
SILVERSMITH:
HALLMARK: Stamped surname in 1/16 Gothic print. Stamp first used in 1973.

C. CHEAMA

CHEAMA, MARVELYNE *Zuni*
SILVERSMITH/LAPIDARIST:
HALLMARK: Engraved personalized printed given name with Zuni beneath it.

Marvelyne C.
ZUNI

CHEAMA, WAYNE *Zuni*
SILVERSMITH: Specializes in nugget work.
HALLMARK: Stamped surname in 1/16 Gothic print that first appeared in 1973. A second stamped given name in 1/16 Gothic print also was first used in 1973.
Mother is Angie Cheama.

W. CHEAMA   WAYNE C.

CHEE, ANITA *Navajo*
SILVERSMITH:
HALLMARK: Stamped symbol with Gothic print initials inside it. Shared with spouse.
Spouse is Wilfred Chee.

CHEE, BETTY JEAN *Navajo*
SILVERSMITH:
HALLMARK: Stamped joined initials 3/8 x 5/16" in a monogram. First used in 1974.
From Lupton, Arizona region.

JBC

CHEE, BILLY *Navajo*
SILVERSMITH:
HALLMARK: Stamped special mark 1/16 x 3/16". First used in 1975.
From Mentmore, New Mexico region.

CHEE, D ? *Navajo*
SILVERSMITH:
HALLMARK: Stamped surname in 1/16 Gothic print. Stamp first used in 1974.

D. CHEE

CHEE, DONALD *Navajo*
SILVERSMITH: Smith for Hill's Turquoise.
HALLMARK: Stamped full name in two lines in 3/32 Gothic print with personalized first letters. Stamp first used in 1977. Second stamp a single line of full name in 1/16 Gothic print.
From Torreon, New Mexico region.

     DONALD CHEE

CHEE, HOWARD *Navajo*
SILVERSMITH:
HALLMARK: Stamped initials in 1/16 Gothic print first used in 1975.
From Pinyon, Arizona region.

H.D.C.

CHEE, IRENE R. *Navajo*
SILVERSMITH: Smith for Montana Mining Company.
HALLMARK: Stamp of full name in 3/32 Gothic print first used in 1975. Second stamp of surname in 1/16 Gothic print first used in

1979.
From Mentmore, New Mexico region.

IRENE CHEE   I.R.CHEE

CHEE, JOE *Navajo*
SILVERSMITH: Specialized in channel work. Smith for Kirk's from 1958-1970, and for Joe Tanner from 1970-74.
HALLMARK: Stamped initials and a second stamp of full name in two lines with enlarged capitals.
Mark Chee's younger brother.

JC   JOE CHEE

CHEE, KEE *Navajo*
SILVERSMITH:
HALLMARK: Stamp of surname in 1/16 Gothic print first used in 1974.
From Vanderwagon, New Mexico region.

K.Y.CHEE

CHEE, LEE *Navajo*
SILVERSMITH: Specialized in concho belts. Began producing in 1974.
HALLMARK: Stamped initials in 1/16 Gothic print first used in 1974.
From Gallup, New Mexico region.

LC

CHEE, LEONARD T. *Navajo*
SILVERSMITH:
HALLMARK: Stamped surname in 1/16 Gothic print first used in 1975.
From Gallup, New Mexico region.

L.T.CHEE

CHEE, MARK *Navajo*
SILVERSMITH: Specialized in heavy silver in old style designs. Began polishing silver in a store in Santa Fe for $5.00 a week. Bought a few tools and used them all his life. Benchsmith for the Wooden Indian at Embudo, New Mexico.
HALLMARK: Stamp of a bird with name in the body in Gothic print. Several versions of this mark but rather than being a separate stamp they may be due to the angle of strike.
Elder brother of Joe Chee. Born at Lukachukai, Arizona in early 1900s. Went to Ft. Defiance Boarding School from the age of 10 until the 11th grade.

CHEE, NELVIN *Navajo*
SILVERSMITH:
HALLMARK: Stamped initials. (This mark does not fit the name of the person who uses it.)

C.W.

CHEE, P ? *Navajo*
SILVERSMITH: Smith for State Line Indian Jewelry.
HALLMARK: Stamp of surname in 3/32 Gothic print first used in 1975. Stamp of surname with enlarged capitals also used.

From Window Rock, Arizona region.

   P.CHEE

CHEE, ROSE A. *Navajo*
SILVERSMITH:
HALLMARK: Stamped surname in 3/32 Gothic print first used in 1979. Earlier stamp of surname in 1/16 Gothic print with an arrow set on a plate was used in 1977.
From Gallup or Vanderwagon, New Mexico regions.

   R. CHEE

CHEE, S.R. *Navajo*
SILVERSMITH: Smith for Felix Indian Jewelry.
HALLMARK: Stamped surname in 1/16 Gothic print first used in 1976.

S.R.CHEE

CHEE, V *Navajo*
SILVERSMITH: Smith for Felix Indian Jewelry.
HALLMARK: Stamped surname in 1/16 Gothic print first used in 1977.

V.CHEE

CHEE, WILFORD *Navajo*
SILVERSMITH: Smith for Atkinson Trading Company before 1980.
HALLMARK: Stamped initials in Gothic print.

WC

CHEE, WILFRED *Navajo*
SILVERSMITH:
HALLMARK: Stamped symbol with initials in Gothic print inside it. Shared with spouse.
Spouse is Anita Chee.

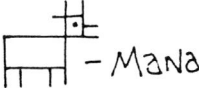

CHEEDA, ZELLA *Hopi*
POTTER:
HALLMARK: Painted and fired rendering of a deer.

-Mana

CHEROMIAH, ETHEL *Unknown*
SILVERSMITH:
HALLMARK: Stamped full name in 1/16 Gothic print. Stamp first used in 1973.
From Blue Water, New Mexico region.

ETHEL CHEROMIAH

CHIPITO, HILDA *Zuni*
SILVERSMITH/LAPIDARIST: Specializes in inlaid work.
HALLMARK: Stamped extended initials.

CHIQUITO, IRENE *Navajo*
SILVERSMITH: Piecework.
HALLMARK: Stamped initials in Gothic print.
Daughters are Katherine and Kathleen Chiquito.

IC

CHIQUITO, KATHERINE *Navajo*
SILVERSMITH: Piecework.
HALLMARK: Stamped initials in Gothic print set one above the other.
Mother is Irene Chiquito and sister is Kathleen Chiquito.

K
C

CHIQUITO, KATHLEEN *Navajo*
SILVERSMITH: Piecework.
HALLMARK: Stamped initials in Gothic print set one above the other on an angle, the only difference in the two sisters' marks.
Mother is Irene Chiquito and sister is Katherine Chiquito.

CHIZOMANA also **ISHII** or **CHIYO F.** *unknown*
EMBROIDERY, BASKETRY:
HALLMARK: A painted or sewn symbol of a plumed bird or the name Chizomana, a corruption of the Hopi term for small bird girl. Stranded in Holbrook, Arizona, she was taken in by Chief Joe Secakuku who operated a small shop there. She took the name of Chirro Mana and claimed adoption into the Hopi tribe. Chief Joe Secakuku disputed this saying it had never happened.

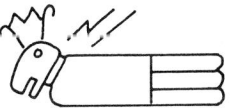   CHIZOMANA

CHRISTENSEN, JOHN *Sauk Fox*
HEISHI MAKER: Specializes in spider web heishi.
HALLMARK: Indian name in 1/32 Gothic print stamped on the findings. Stamp first used in 1980.

KEOKUK

CHRISTIE, TOM *Unknown*
SILVERSMITH: Either an individual smith or a shop.
HALLMARK: Stamped surname in 1/16 Gothic print first used in 1985. Second stamp a monogram in script. This stamp ends in an S whereas the first does not.

CHRISTIE   *christies*

CHUKACHI, MARIA *Hopi*
SILVERSMITH: Produces Navajo style jewelry.
HALLMARK: Stamped surname in 1/16 Gothic print first used in 1982.

M.CHUKACHI

CHURCH, ROGER EARL *Navajo*
SILVERSMITH: Specializes in wrought work with nugget settings.
HALLMARK: Engraved signature in 1965-1975.
From Tuba City, Arizona.

R Earl Church

CLAH, JESSIE *Navajo*
SILVERSMITH: Specialized in letter openers.
HALLMARK: Stamped initials in Gothic print with a symbol of an arrow.

J.C.⟩⟶

CLARK, CARL *Navajo*
SILVERSMITH:
HALLMARK: Stamped design with initials incorporated in it.
Spouse is Irene Clark.
From Phoenix area.

CLARK, DELBERT *Navajo*
SILVERSMITH:
HALLMARK: Stamp with two initials and one surname. Possibly shared with spouse. Gothic print.

D.&J.CLARK

CLARK, DENET *Navajo*
SILVERSMITH: Benchsmith for White Hogan.
HALLMARK: Stamped Gothic print initials.
Deceased.

DC

CLARK, DONNY *Navajo*
SILVERSMITH: Specializes in floral designs with nugget settings. Uses claws also. Wife works with him.
HALLMARK: Stamped double D, his first initials and his wife's. Gothic print.
Spouse is Dorothy Clark.

DD

CLARK, DOROTHY *Navajo*
SILVERSMITH: Specializes in floral designs with nugget settings. Uses claws also. Works with her husband.
HALLMARK: Stamped double D, the first initial of her husband and herself. Gothic print.
Spouse is Donny Clark.

DD

CLARK, HENRY *Navajo*
SILVERSMITH: Specializes in boxes. Benchsmith for the Navajo Arts and Crafts Guild in 1962.
HALLMARK: Stamped H with an enlarged C joined to it.

HC

CLARK, IRENE *Navajo*
SILVERSMITH:
HALLMARK: Stamped design with initials incorporated in it. Second stamp is a design set on a plate. She shares the first hallmark with her husband.
Spouse is Carl Clark.
From Phoenix area

CLARK, JAMES *Navajo*
SILVERSMITH:
HALLMARK: Stamped star.

CLARK, JOHN D. *Zuni*
SILVERSMITH/LAPIDARIST: Inlay work.
HALLMARK: Stamped initials in Gothic print.

DC

CLARK, LOUISE *Navajo*
SILVERSMITH:
HALLMARK: Stamped initials in Gothic print.

LC

CLAW, EUNICE *Navajo*
SILVERSMITH:
HALLMARK: Stamped surname in 1/16 Gothic print. Stamp first used in 1974.

E.CLAW

CLAW, JESSIE *Navajo*
SILVERSMITH: Worked for Atkinson Trading Company.
HALLMARK: First used stamped initials in Gothic print. Second stamp of surname in Gothic print first used in 1974. Other stamps include an abbreviated set of initials and the symbol of a man.

JFC   J.      JC

CLAW, MARY *Navajo*
SILVERSMITH: Smith for Atkinson Trading Company.
HALLMARK: Stamped full name in 1/16 Gothic print first used in 1974.

MARY CLAW

CLAW, PAUL JR. *Navajo*
SILVERSMITH:
HALLMARK: Stamped initials in joined monogram 3/16". Second stamp is the same but set on a plate and first used in 1977.
From Chinle, Arizona region.

CLAWSON, WAYNE *Navajo (?)*
SILVERSMITH:
HALLMARK: Stamped and engraved hallmark 1/32 x 3/32". First used in 1983.
From Ramah, New Mexico region.

Poco

CLEVELAND, FRANK *Navajo*
SILVERSMITH:
HALLMARK: Joined initials. Same as Fred Cleveland's mark. Brother is Fred Cleveland (?). Some confusion exists as to whether Frank and Fred Cleveland are separate individuals.

CLEVELAND, FRED *Navajo*
SILVERSMITH/PAINTER: Worked during the 1960s in silver. In 1972 entered a painting contest and since that time has worked in the new medium.
HALLMARK: Joined initials. Same as Frank Cleveland.
Spouse is Ruby Cleveland. Undetermined whether Fred and Frank are separate individuals or brothers.
From Alamo, New Mexico region.

CLEVELAND, RUBY *Navajo*
SILVERSMITH:
HALLMARK: Joined initials.
Spouse is Fred Cleveland.

   RC

CLY, JOHN *Zuni (?)*
SILVERSMITH/LAPIDARIST: Produces inlaid hearts and some goldwork.
HALLMARK: Stamped initials in Gothic print, stamp of surname in 1/16 Gothic print, and double initials with surname in 1/32 Gothic print. Surname stamp first used in 1977 and the double initial mark in 1985.
Spouse is Raphina Cly.

J.C.   CLY   J&R CLY

CLY, RAPHINA *Zuni*
SILVERSMITH/LAPIDARIST: Working with her husband she produces inlaid hearts and some goldwork.
HALLMARK: Stamped surname with her and her husband's initials. Stamp first used in 1985.
Spouse is John Cly.

J&R CLY

CLY, SARAH *Navajo*
SILVERSMITH:
HALLMARK: Stamped surname in 1/16 Gothic print, first used in 1974.
From Gallup, New Mexico region.

S.CLY

COAN, FRANCES (FANNY) *Navajo*
SILVERSMITH: Specializes in hand cast silver from carved stone molds. Works with her husband.
HALLMARK: Stamped initials in Gothic print, shared with spouse.
Spouse is Jim Coan.

JFC

COAN, JIM *Navajo*
SILVERSMITH: Specializes in hand cast silver from carved stone molds. Works with his wife.
HALLMARK: Stamped initials in Gothic print shared with spouse.
Spouse is Frances Coan. He is related to Louise Coan and Phillip Cone.
[King:1976:46]

JFC

CODY, ART see **HAUNGOAH**

CODY, SADIE *Navajo*
SILVERSMITH:
HALLMARK: Stamped symbol with attached C.

COIN, EDGAR *Hopi*
SILVERSMITH: Produces overlay.
HALLMARK: Stamped symbol.
[Wright:1982:87]

COIN, WILLIE *Hopi*
SILVERSMITH: Produces overlay work.
HALLMARK: Stamped symbol.
[Wright:1982:83]

COLLATETTA, SARAH *Hopi*
POTTER:
HALLMARK: Painted and fired.

Sec

COLTON, AL *Hopi*
POTTER: Contemporary interpretations of Sikyatki pottery.
HALLMARK: Incised Hopi name.
Great nephew of Elizabeth White.

Qoyawayma

COMER, MARY JONES *Zuni*
SILVERSMITH:
HALLMARK: Stamped initials in Gothic print.

M.J.C.

COMOSONA, CHIMO *Unknown*
SILVERSMITH:
HALLMARK: Stamped surname in 1/32 Gothic print. Stamp first used in 1985.
From Ft. Defiance, Arizona region.

C.COMOSONA

CONCHA, PABLITA *Unknown*
SILVERSMITH:
HALLMARK: Stamped symbol of feather or leaf.

CONE, YONAH *Cherokee*
SILVERSMITH: Produces small jewelry and stone carvings. Learned silversmithing on the reservation and began production ca. 1972.
HALLMARK: Stamped letters that appear to be part of the Cherokee alphabet.

COOCHWIKVIA, MARCUS *Hopi*
SILVERSMITH: Produces overlay work.
HALLMARKS: Chisel cut initials or stamped bear paw. First used in 1975.
[Wright:1982:94]

COOCHWYTEWA, RICKY *Hopi*
SILVERSMITH: Produces overlay work.
HALLMARK: Stamped symbol of a bear paw.
Father is Victor Coochwytewa.
[Wright:1892:95]

COOCHWYTEWA, VICTOR *Hopi*
SILVERSMITH/GOLDSMITH: Produces overlay work. Smith for Kopavi International. Began producing in the 1940s. Traditional designs.
HALLMARK: Stamped symbol of clouds.
Son is Ricky Coochwytewa.
[Wright:1982:83]

COOCHYUMPTEWA, JOE *Hopi*
SILVERSMITH: Produces overlay work.
HALLMARK: Stamped symbol of a Hopi pipe.
Uncle is John Coochyumptewa.
[Wright:1982:92]1

COOCHYUMPTEWA, JOHN *Hopi*
SILVERSMITH: Produces overlay work.
HALLMARK: Stamped symbol of a tobacco leaf or initials in Gothic print.
Nephew is Joe Coochyumptewa.
[Wright:1982:95]

 JLC

COONSIS, E ? *Zuni*
SILVERSMITH:
HALLMARK: Stamped surname in 1/16 Gothic print. Stamp first used in 1975.

E.P.COONSIS

COONSIS, HARLAN *Zuni*
SILVERSMITH/LAPIDARIST: Specializes in mosaic inlay of birds, often without borders. Learned his craft in school and by watching his parents. Began producing ca. 1975.
HALLMARK: Stamped surname with his and his wife's initials in 1/16 Gothic print first used in 1985. Also uses stamped initials of the two of them alone in the same print and a stamp of surname with a symbol. Stamps are shared with spouse.
Spouse is Rolanda Coonsis.
[Levy:1980:20]

H.R.COONSIS ZUNI   H.R.C.
                    ZUNI

 H. R. COONSIS

COONSIS, ROLANDA *Zuni*
SILVERSMITH/LAPIDARIST: Specializes in carved mosaic inlay. Learned her craft from watching her parents and began production in 1975. She does the stone work and her husband the metal.
HALLMARK: Stamped surname in 1/16 Gothic print first used in 1985. Stamp of shared initials in same print and with a symbol also. Stamps are shared with spouse.
Spouse is Harlan Coonsis.
[Levy:1980:20]

H. R. COONSIS ZUNI   H.R.C.
                      ZUNI

H. R. COONSIS

COOYATE, RANSOM *Zuni*
SILVERSMITH/LAPIDARIST: Produces silver-backed coral pieces. Began producing ca. 1950. Mainly repair work. Worked for Dean Kirk, Katie Noe, and 14 years for M.L. Woodard.
HALLMARK: Stamped letter inside larger initial.

CORD *(?)* *Unknown*
SILVERSMITH: ? Blackstar Studios.
HALLMARK: Stamped name in 1/32 Gothic print first appearing in 1983.

CORD

COREY, MARY JANE *Zuni*
SILVERSMITH:
HALLMARK: Stamped initials in Gothic print.

MJC

CORIZ, JUANITA *Santo Domingo*
HEISHI MAKER:
HALLMARK: Stamped surname in Gothic print on findings.

J.CORIZ

CORIZ, LEO *Santo Domingo*
SILVERSMITH:
HALLMARK: Stamped full name in 1/16 Gothic print. Stamp in 5/32 script not of his initials.

Umy   LEO CORIZ

CORIZ, RAYMOND *Santo Domingo*
SILVERSMITH: Navajo style of overlay work. Began producing in 1972.
HALLMARK: Stamped initials with diagonals.

\R CORIZ   \R C

CORN, JOHN see **JIM COAN**

COUYANCE, CLARK *Zuni*
SILVERSMITH/LAPIDARIST:
HALLMARK: Engraved personalized printing.

C. Couyancy

COWBOY, ANNIE *Navajo*
SILVERSMITH: Benchsmith/pieceworker for Sunburst Handcrafts since 1976.
HALLMARK: A single initial in Gothic print.
Brother is Jerry Cowboy and sister Ella Cowboy.

A

COWBOY, D ? *Navajo*
SILVERSMITH: Smith for Montana Mining Company.
HALLMARK: Stamped surname in 1/16 Gothic print. Stamp first used in 1974.

D. COWBOY

COWBOY, ELLA *Navajo*
SILVERSMITH: Benchsmith with Sunburst Handcrafts since 1976.
HALLMARK: Single stamped initial in Gothic print or double initials over and under and separated by small STERLING.
Jerry Cowboy is her brother and Annie Cowboy her sister.

E   E
       STERLING
       E

COWBOY, JERRY *Navajo*
SILVERSMITH: Benchsmith for Atkinson Trading Company. Smith for Sunburst Handcrafts off and on since 1977.
HALLMARK: Stamped surname in 1/16 Gothic print first used in 1975 or a single stamped initial in same print.
Sisters are Ella and Annie Cowboy.

J. COWBOY   C

CRAIG, CARSON *Navajo*
SILVERSMITH:
HALLMARK: Stamped personalized initial.

NAVAHO

CRAIG, HYSON *Navajo*
SILVERSMITH: Smith for Montana Mining Company and for Atkinson Trading Company.
HALLMARK: Stamped surname in 1/16 Gothic print first appeared in 1975. In 1976 a circular stamp with joined initials, name, and IHMSS on a plate appeared. He has also used stamps of joined initials and of his surname with symbol and IHMSS below. Used first and fourth stamps at Woodards.
Brother is Wesley Craig.

H. CRAIG   H.CRAIG IHMSS

CRAIG, MARIE *Navajo*
SILVERSMITH:
HALLMARK: Stamped surname in 1/16 Gothic print first appearing in 1974.

M.CRAIG

CRAIG, WESLEY *Navajo*
SILVERSMITH:
HALLMARK: Stamped full name in 1/16 Gothic print. First used in 1974. Stamp of 1/16 Gothic print initials. Also full name in same print accompanied by IHM S/S.
Brother is Hyson Craig.

WES CRAIG   WC   WES CRAIG IHM S/S

CRAWFORD, EUGENE (GENE) *Navajo*
SILVERSMITH/LEATHERWORKER:
HALLMARK: Stamped initials with or without symbol.
Spouse is Marion Crawford.

GC    G.C.

CRAWFORD, YVONNE *Unknown*
SILVERSMITH:
HALLMARK: Stamped surname in 1/16 Gothic print. First appeared in 1985.
From Gallup, New Mexico region.

Y. CRAWFORD

CRESTO, R? *Navajo (?)*
SILVERSMITH:
HALLMARK: Stamped surname in 1/16 Gothic print. Stamp first appeared in 1973.
From Gallup, New Mexico region.

R. CRESTO

CROSS, EARL *Unknown*
SILVERSMITH:
HALLMARK: Stamped initial C around a 3/32" cross.
From Alpine, Arizona region.

⊕

CUNEJO, JOAQUIN *Unknown*
SILVERSMITH:
HALLMARK: Stamped surname in 1/16 Gothic print. Stamp first appeared in 1976. Second stamp is the same but with a sun symbol.

J. CUNEJO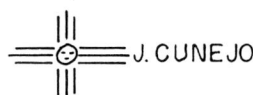

CURLEY, M (?) *Navajo (?)*
SILVERSMITH:
HALLMARK: Stamped surname in 1/32 Gothic print. Stamp first appeared in 1984.
From Albuquerque, New Mexico region.

M. CURLEY

CURLEY, NELSON *Navajo*
SILVERSMITH:
HALLMARK: Stamped surname in 1/32 Gothic print. Stamp first appeared in 1984.
From Albuquerque, New Mexico region.

N. CURLEY

CURLEY, PRESTON *Navajo*
SILVERSMITH: Bead maker.
HALLMARK: Stamped initials on metal tag.
From Grants, New Mexico region.

PC

CURLEY, ROBERT *Navajo*
SILVERSMITH: Demonstrated silver craft at Hubbell's Trading Post in 1981-83.
HALLMARK: Stamped initials with C enlarged.

RC

CURLEY, STANLEY *Navajo*
SILVERSMITH: Specializes in chip inlay.
HALLMARK: Stamped letter and symbol.
Brother-in-law of Tommy Singer.

⌒N

CURTIS, MAX *Unknown*
SILVERSMITH:
HALLMARK: Stamped cursive initials 3/16" square. First used in 1981.

m̃

CURTIS, THOMAS *Navajo*
SILVERSMITH: Benchsmith for Rockinghorse Ranch in 1985.
HALLMARK: Stamped initials, stamped surname, and stamped surname and initial in 1/16 Gothic print.

T.C.   CURTIS   T. CURTIS

CURTIS, TONI *Navajo*
SILVERSMITH:
HALLMARK: Stamped offset initials in Gothic print.

T
 C

CUSTER, B ? *Navajo*
SILVERSMITH: Smith for Atkinson Trading Company.
HALLMARK: Stamped surname in 1/16 Gothic print. Stamp first used in 1976.

B. CUSTER

CUSTER, N ? *Navajo*
SILVERSMITH: Smith for Atkinson Trading Company.
HALLMARK: Stamped surname in 1/16 Gothic print. Stamp first used in 1976.

N. CUSTER

CUSTER, NANCY *Navajo*
SILVERSMITH:
HALLMARK: Stamped initials in Gothic print. May be the same person as CUSTER, N.

NC

DALE, KAREN *Unknown*
SILVERSMITH: Smith for Mark Lindsay and First American Traders.
HALLMARK: Stamped full name and stamped surname in 1/16 Gothic print. Full name stamp first used in 1978. The surname stamp first used in 1981.

KAREN DALE   K. DALE

DALTON, ROBERT *Unknown*
SILVERSMITH:
HALLMARK: Stamped initials and symbol.

DALTON, SYLVIA *Hopi*
POTTER: Began producing ca. 1970.
HALLMARK: Painted and fired symbol of a plant.

DAMON, GILBERT *Navajo*
SILVERSMITH: Specializing in chip inlay.
HALLMARK: Stamped personalized initial or both initials in Gothic print.
From Sawmill, Arizona region.

    G/D

DAN, FRANKIE *Navajo*
SILVERSMITH:
HALLMARK: Stamped surname in 1/16 Gothic print. Stamp first used in 1975.
From Many Farms, Arizona region.

F. DAN

DAVID, DONALD *Navajo*
SILVERSMITH: Specializes in flatware, serving pieces, and belts. First began producing in 1972.
HALLMARK: Stamped initials in Gothic print.

DD

DAVID, E.J. *Navajo*
SILVERSMITH:
HALLMARK: Stamped initials joined and offset in personalized letters 1/8" square. Stamp first used in 1974.
From Sedona, Arizona region.

DAVID, FRANK *Navajo*
SILVERSMITH:
HALLMARK: Stamped initials in 3/32 Gothic print. Stamp first used in 1975.
From St. Michaels, Arizona region.

FD

DAVID, TOM *Navajo*
SILVERSMITH:
HALLMARK: Stamped initials in 1/16 Gothic print. Stamp first used in 1975.
From Gallup, New Mexico region.

T.D.

DAVIS, CAROLINE *Navajo*
SILVERSMITH: Smith for Atkinson Trading Company.
HALLMARK: Stamped surname in 1/16 Gothic print first used in 1971. Second stamp in 1/32 Gothic print first used in 1981.

C. DAVIS

DAVIS, CLYDE *Navajo*
SILVERSMITH: Smith for Atkinson Trading Company.
HALLMARK: Stamped full name in 1/16 Gothic print first used in 1975. Second stamp of surname in 3/32 Gothic print first used in 1978.

CLYDE DAVIS   C. DAVIS

DAVIS, MIKE *Navajo*
SILVERSMITH: Smith for Atkinson Trading Company.
HALLMARK: Stamped surname in 1/16 Gothic print. Stamp first used in 1974.

M. DAVIS

DAVIS, P ? *Navajo*
SILVERSMITH: Smith for Atkinson Trading Company.
HALLMARK: Stamped surname in 1/16 Gothic print. Stamp first used in 1974.

P. DAVIS

DAVIS, R ? *Navajo*
SILVERSMITH:
HALLMARK: Stamped surname in 1/32 Gothic print. Stamp first used in 1981.

R. DAVIS

DAW, LOLA *Navajo (?)*
SILVERSMITH:
HALLMARK: Stamped full name in 1/16 Gothic print. Stamp first used in 1978.
From Gamerco, New Mexico region.

LOLA DAW

DAWAHOYA, BERNARD (MASAQUEVA) *Hopi*
SILVERSMITH: Specializes in overlay work. Began producing ca.

1956. Owns and manages Dawa's Craft Shop, Second Mesa, Arizona.
HALLMARK: Stamped symbol of a snow cloud.
[Wright:1982:88]

DAWAHOYA, BUEFORD *Hopi*
SILVERSMITH: Specializes in overlay work. Began producing in 1975.
HALLMARK: Stamped symbol of a snow cloud.
Brother is Bernard Dawahoya.
[Wright:1982:95]

 BD

DAY, CHALMERS *Hopi*
SILVERSMITH: Specializes in elaborate overlay scenes in silver. Worked as demonstrator at Indian Gallery.
HALLMARK: Stamped symbols of a bird beak, a badger (?) foot, the initial C, and surname.

  C. C. DAY

DAYEA, LEROY *Navajo*
SILVERSMITH: Smith for Atkinson Trading Company.
HALLMARK: Stamped full name in 1/16 Gothic print. Stamp first used in 1974.

LEROY DAYEA

DAYEA, MARY *Navajo*
SILVERSMITH:
HALLMARK: Stamped joined initials or underscored initials.
Spouse is Tom Burnside.
From Chinle, Arizona region.

DEDMAN, D ? *Navajo*
SILVERSMITH: Smith for T & R Market.
HALLMARK: Stamped surname in 1/16 Gothic print. Stamp first used in 1976.

D. DEDMAN

DELENA, LITA *Zuni*
LAPIDARIST: Fetish maker since 1941.
HALLMARK: Stamped on findings in 1/16 Gothic print. First used in 1976.
Spouse is Sam Delena. Father is George Haloo Cheechee.

L. DELENA
ZUNI , N.M.

DELGARITO, B ? *Navajo*
SILVERSMITH: Smith for Atkinson Trading Company.
HALLMARK: Stamped surname in 1/16 Gothic print. Stamp first used in 1974.

B. DELGARITO

DELGARITO, ROY NEZ *Navajo*
SILVERSMITH:
HALLMARK: Stamped in personalized 1/16 script initials. Stamp first used in 1976.
From Prewitt, New Mexico region.

R. N. D.

DELVIN, JOHN *Navajo*
SILVERSMITH: Smith for Sunburst Hand Crafts since 1984.
HALLMARK: Stamped single initial in 1/16 Gothic print.

D

DENET, MARYAN *Hopi/Tewa*
POTTER:
HALLMARK: Painted and fired full name in personalized print.
Spouse is Joseph H. Denet, kachina carver.

DENETCLAW, CLARENCE JR. *Navajo*
SILVERSMITH:
HALLMARK: Stamped initials shared with spouse in 1/16 Gothic print. Stamp first used in 1975.
From Tohatchi, New Mexico region.

H & C. D. C. JR.

DENETDEAL (DEAL), DONALD *Navajo*
SILVERSMITH:
HALLMARK: Stamped initials and symbol set on a square plate.
Uncle is Ambrose Roanhorse.

DENETSO, TOM *Navajo*
SILVERSMITH: Specializes in bead necklaces. Began producing ca. 1972.
HALLMARK: Single stamped initial in 1/16 Gothic print.

D

DENNIS, ALEC *Hopi*
SILVERSMITH: Specializes in overlay work. Began producing around 1952.
HALLMARK: Stamped initials.
From Mishongnovi, Arizona.

AD

DENNIS, PHILBERT *Hopi*
SILVERSMITH: Specializes in silver overlay work. Began producing in 1974.
HALLMARK: Stamped initials in personalized print. Usually in offset positions. First stamp used is the one with separate initials.
[Wright:1982:95]

DENNISON, LESTER *Unknown*
SILVERSMITH:

HALLMARK: Stamped full name in 1/32 Gothic print, first used in 1978. Second stamp in 3/32 abridged name with symbol of a bear paw.

LES DENNISON

DESOTO, JOE *Unknown*
SILVERSMITH:
HALLMARK: Stamped (?) symbol 1/8".

DEWA, ANDREW *Zuni*
SILVERSMITH/LAPIDARIST: Specializes in mosaic and bas-relief inlay. Designs are usually kachina dancers.
HALLMARK: Stamped surname with or without the word Zuni and initials in 1/16 Gothic print. Stamp with surname over word Zuni first used in 1973. Second stamp with surname first used in 1974.
Brother is Don Dewa.
[Bell:1976:46]

A.C.DEWA   AD   A. DEWA
                    ZUNI

DEWA, DON C. *Zuni*
SILVERSMITH/LAPIDARIST: Specializes in inlay and cluster work.
HALLMARK: Stamp of shared initials and surname in 1/16 Gothic print first used in 1974. Second stamp of full name in 1/16 Gothic print first used in 1982.
Spouse is Velma E. Dewa. Andrew Dewa is his brother.
[Bell:1976:24]

D&V DEWA   D&V   DON C.   D.&V. DEWA
ZUNI   ZUNI   DEWA

DEWA, VELMA E. *Zuni*
SILVERSMITH/LAPIDARIST:Specializes in inlay and cluster work.
HALLMARK: Shares stamped surname with her own and her husband's initials in Gothic 1/16 print. This stamp was first used in 1982 and differs from the first shared one.
Spouse is Don C. Dewa. Parents are Seff and Loretto Eriacho.
[Bell:1976:24]

D.&V. DEWA

DEWESEE, JEANETTE *Zuni*
SILVERSMITH/LAPIDARIST:
HALLMARK: Stamped full name in 1/16 Gothic print first used in 1978. Second stamp shared by her husband and herself uses his surname in 1/16 Gothic print and was first used in 1978.
Spouse is Ed Watasilo.

JEANETTE   ED & JEANETTE
DEWESEE   WATASILO

DICK, JOHNNY *Navajo*
SILVERSMITH:
HALLMARK: Stamped initials in Gothic print.

JD

DICKENS, L ? *Navajo*
SILVERSMITH: Smith for Atkinson Trading Company.
HALLMARK: Stamped surname in 1/16 Gothic print. Stamp first used in 1975.

L.DICKENS

DICKENS, SARAH *Navajo*
SILVERSMITH:
HALLMARK: Stamped surname in 1/16 Gothic print and stamped full name in 1/16 Gothic print, first used in 1974.

S. DICKENS   SARAH DICKENS

DICKSON, BENNIE *Navajo*
SILVERSMITH:
HALLMARK: Stamped initials in Gothic print.
This may be the same individual as Bennie Dickinson.

BD   B.D.

DICKSON, LARRY *Zuni*
SILVERSMITH/LAPIDARIST: Specializes in channel inlay in designs of sun faces.
HALLMARK: Stamp of surname with double initial being that of his own and his wife's.
Spouse is Lorinda Dickson.
[Bell:1975:58]

L/L DICKSON

DICKSON, LORINDA *Zuni*
SILVERSMITH/LAPIDARIST: Specializes in channel inlay in designs of sun faces.
HALLMARK: Shared with spouse, the stamp uses both of their initials with her husband's surname in 1/16th Gothic print.
Spouse is Harry Dickson, mother is Marietta Soseah.
[Bell:1975:58; Bell:1976:60]

L/L DICKSON

DISHTA, CHARLENE *Zuni*
SILVERSMITH:
HALLMARK: Stamped initials over word Zuni in Gothic print.

CD
ZUNI

DISHTA, DUANE A. *Zuni*
SILVERSMITH/PAINTER: Produced silver work in 1974. Began as a kachina carver in the early 1960s. Switched to painting in the late 1960s.
HALLMARK: Stamped surname in 1/16 Gothic print first used in 1975.

D.A.DISHTA

DISHTA, LENA *Zuni*
SILVERSMITH/LAPIDARIST: Specializes in small round channel inlay pieces. Creates her own "flower" designs. Learned from her mother and began producing at age 7 in 1958.
HALLMARK: Stamped surname in 1/16 Gothic print. Stamp first used in 1975. Her earlier pieces are not signed.

L.DISHTA

DISHTA, ROBERT *Zuni*
SILVERSMITH/LAPIDARIST: Specializes in channel inlay.
HALLMARK: Stamped surname in 1/16 Gothic print. Stamp first used in 1974.

R.DISHTA

DISHTA, V ? SR. *Zuni*
SILVERSMITH:
HALLMARK: Stamped surname in 3/32 Gothic lettering first used in 1974. Second stamp uses combined initials of his own and his wife's initials with his surname in 1/16 Gothic print and was first used in 1974.
Spouse's name is not known for certain but may be Lena Dishta.

V.DISHTA SR.   V & L DISHTA

DIXON, DON *Unknown*
SILVERSMITH:
HALLMARK: Initial stamped in 1/8" and 1/16" Gothic print. Stamps first used in 1977.

DIXON, JEAN *Navajo*
SILVERSMITH: Smith for Sunburst Handcrafts since 1978.
HALLMARK: Stamped single initial in Gothic print.

J

DIXON, S ? *Navajo*
SILVERSMITH: Specializes in chip inlay bolo ties.
HALLMARK: Stamped initials with caret inserted above or below.

DODGE, LAWRENCE (LARRY) *Navajo*
SILVERSMITH: Specializes in chip inlay.
HALLMARK: Uses several symbols but most often a sun symbol with the letter L inside it.
Tommy Singer is his brother-in-law. He also uses the name of Leonard Dodge.

DODGE, LEONARD see **DODGE, LAWRENCE**

DODGE, STANLEY CARROL *Navajo*
SILVERSMITH: Specializes in stamp work.
HALLMARK: Uses a stamped symbol.

DODSON, W ? *Unknown*
SILVERSMITH: Smith for Indian Hammers.
HALLMARK: Stamped surname in 1/16 Gothic print. Stamp first used in 1976.

W. DODSON

DOUGLAS, WILLIAM *Unknown*
SILVERSMITH:
HALLMARK: Stamped surname in 1/16 Gothic print. Stamp first used in 1974.

W. DOUGLAS

DRAPER, LOWELL *Navajo*
SILVERSMITH: Benchsmith for the White Hogan. Began producing in 1973.
HALLMARK: Stamped initials in 1/16 Gothic print set in different patterns. The preferred mark is an L with the D slightly offset and joined to it.
From Canyon del Muerto, Arizona region.

DRAPER, ROSE CASTILLO *Navajo*
SILVERSMITH: Produces simple pieces. Benchsmith/pieceworker in Albuquerque shops in 1978-79.
HALLMARK: Stamped initials in Gothic print are of her name before she married.
Spouse is Lee Draper. Her mother is Bessie Castillo.
From either Alamo, New Mexico or Cuba, New Mexico region.

RD   RC

DUBE, J.P. *Anglo (?)*
SILVERSMITH:
HALLMARK: Stamped surname in personalized script.

DUBOIS, ALICE *Navajo*
SILVERSMITH:
HALLMARK: Stamped initial A in personalized script. When she assists her husband in making jewelry she uses his hallmark.
Spouse is Jake Dubois.

DUBOIS, JAKE *Navajo*
SILVERSMITH:
HALLMARK: A personalized initial stamp is used most of the time. When his wife helps a combined stamp of their initials in personalized script is used.
Spouse is Alice Dubois.

DUBOISE, BEN *Navajo*
SILVERSMITH:
HALLMARK: Stamped initial and symbol. The initial is in 1/16 Gothic print and was first used in 1977.

B↓

DUBOISE, SARAH *Navajo*
SILVERSMITH: Specializes in making beads. Learned the craft from her sister.
HALLMARK: Stamped initials in 1/16 Gothic print either ordinary or separated by a diagonal. The mark is often set on a circular or lozenge shaped plate. The stamp with ordinary initials was first used in 1975. Sister is Sadie Calvin.
From Gallup, New Mexico region.

S.D.   S/D

DURAN, BERNARD *Hopi*
SILVERSMITH:
HALLMARK: Stamped initials and symbol in a 1/4" form. First used in 1973. Ordinary initials on a lozenge-shaped plate are 3/16 x 5/16" in size, also used first in 1973.
From Old Laguna, New Mexico region.

DURAN, TOM *Picuris*
SILVERSMITH: Smith for Peshlakai, Ltd.
HALLMARK: Stamp of surname with elongated T is used in 3/16, 1/8, and 1/16 Gothic print. All were first used in 1976.
Spouse is a woman from Santa Clara.
From Santa Clara, New Mexico.

ᵗURAN

DURKEE, MICHAEL *Anglo*
SILVERSMITH: Specializes in silver and ironwood.
HALLMARK: Stamped full name in 1/16 Gothic print.

MICHAEL DURKEE

EAGLESTAR, DENNIS *Unknown*
SILVERSMITH:
HALLMARK: Stamped abridged name in 1/16 Gothic print. Stamp first used in 1984.
From Deming, New Mexico region.

EAGLE

EARL, VIVIAN *Hopi*
POTTER:
HALLMARK: Painted and fired mark of a badger paw.
Later called Vivian Mumzewa. Husband was Earl Mumzewa, noted drum maker.

EDAAKIE, DENNIS *Zuni*
SILVERSMITH/LAPIDARIST: Specialist in mosaic inlay. Common motif is hummingbird. Specialized in two-sided turning pendants done in mosaic inlay. A pioneer in this type of inlay, producing as early as 1965.
HALLMARK: Stamped given name in 1/16 Gothic print first used in 1970. Also uses his name and that of his wife with his surname. From 1965-70 he used a stamped symbol of a parrot's beak.
Spouse is Nancy Edaakie.
[Bell:1976:22]

DENNIS E.   DENNIS EDAAKIE
             NANCY

EDAAKIE, EVANGELITA *Zuni*
SILVERSMITH/LAPIDARIST:
HALLMARK: Stamped surname in 1/16 Gothic print first used in 1975.

E. EDAAKIE

EDAAKIE, JENNIE *Zuni*
SILVERSMITH/LAPIDARIST:
HALLMARK: Stamped surname with a combination of her and her husband's initials in 1/16 Gothic print.
Spouse is Myron Edaakie.

M.&J. EDAAKIE

EDAAKIE, MARY ANN *Zuni*
SILVERSMITH/LAPIDARIST:
HALLMARK: Stamped combination of her and her husband's first initials in 1/16 Gothic print. Uses Zuni in small print below.
Spouse is Zeno Edaakie.

ZME
ZUNI

EDAAKIE, MYRON *Zuni*
SILVERSMITH/LAPIDARIST:
HALLMARK: Stamped surname with combined initials of his and his wife's in 1/16 Gothic print.
Spouse is Jennie Edaakie.

M.&J.EDAAKIE

EDAAKIE, NANCY *Zuni*
SILVERSMITH/LAPIDARIST: Specializes in the mosaic inlay of birds and animals, particularly hummingbirds. Also produces two-sided turning pendants. Uses husband's designs but both execute them. Began producing in 1965 at the same time as her husband.
HALLMARK: Uses her husband's hallmarks. Stamp of a macaw or parrot beak from 1965 to 1970. A stamp of his given name from 1970-73. A third stamp combining their given names with his surname in 1984. The lettering is in 1/16 Gothic print.
Spouse is Dennis Edaakie.
[Bell:1975:22]

DENNIS E.   DENNIS EDAAKIE
             NANCY

EDAAKIE, THEODORE (TED) *Zuni*
SILVERSMITH/LAPIDARIST: Specializes in channel inlay and open work. Produced from the early 1930's through the 1960's.
HALLMARK: Stamped initials on a small square plate.

|TE|

EDAAKIE, ZENO *Zuni*
SILVERSMITH/LAPIDARIST:
HALLMARK: Stamped initials of his wife's and his initials with Zuni in small type below. Letters are in Gothic print.
Spouse is Mary Ann Edaakie.

ZME
ZUNI

EDAKIE, JACK *Zuni*
SILVERSMITH: Specializes in gold applique on silver. Formerly a pieceworker for Don Hoel.
HALLMARK: Stamped full name in 1/16 Gothic print.

JACK EDAKIE

EDDIE, ISABEL *Navajo*
SILVERSMITH:
HALLMARK: Stamped special combination of initials.

EDISON, E ? *Navajo*
SILVERSMITH: Smith for Andy Madrid.
HALLMARK: Stamped surname in 3/32 Gothic print first used in 1976.

EDISON

EDMUNDSON, BUDDY LIGHTFOOT *Osage*
SILVERSMITH: Began producing around 1970, primarily seen in the Albuquerque area.
HALLMARK: Special stamp with a small B on the back of a large E. Stamp surname in 3/32 Gothic print, first seen in 1983.
From White Bluff, Oklahoma region.

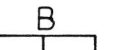   B. LIGHTFOOT

EDSITTY, A ? *Navajo*
SILVERSMITH: Smith for Atkinson Trading Company.
HALLMARK: Stamped surname in 1/16 Gothic print. Stamp first used in 1976.

A. EDSITTY

EDWARDS, VERGIE *Apache*
LAPIDARIST: Peridot settings.
HALLMARK: Stamped initials in Gothic print.

VE

ELDRED, STEVE *Unknown*
SILVERSMITH:
HALLMARK: Two-line stamp of full name in 3/16 Gothic print. Stamp first used in 1979.
From Truckee region.

STEVE
ELDRED

ELLIOT, CHAVIS *Zuni*
SILVERSMITH:
HALLMARK: Stamped initials in Gothic print.

CE

ELLOT, R ? *Navajo*
SILVERSMITH: Piece worker.
HALLMARK: Stamped surname in 1/16 Gothic print. Stamp first used in 1973.

R. ELLOT

ELTHE, L ? *Unknown*
SILVERSMITH: Smith for Steve Bowser.
HALLMARK: Stamped surname in 1/16 Gothic print. First used in 1976.

L. ELTHE

EMANUEL, JAMES N. *Unknown*
SILVERSMITH:
HALLMARK: Stamped initials in 1/32 Gothic print. Stamp first used in 1980.
From Fayetteville, North Carolina.

JNE

EMERSON see **EMERSON, BILL**

EMERSON, NELSON *Navajo*
SILVERSMITH:
HALLMARK: Two line stamp of full name in 1/16 Gothic print. First used in 1975.
From Ft. Wingate, New Mexico region.

NELSON
EMERSON

ENDITO, ETTA *Navajo*
SILVERSMITH: Smith or pieceworker for Atkinson Trading Company before 1980.
HALLMARK: Stamped initials in 1/16 Gothic print.

EE

ENDITO, RANDY *Navajo*
SILVERSMITH: Smith for Atkinson Trading Company.
HALLMARK: Stamp of full name in 1/32 script first used in 1983. Stamp of initials in 1/16 Gothic print first used in 1983.

Randy Endito   R.E.

ENRICO, F ? *Unknown*
SILVERSMITH: Smith for Bernie Dominguez.
HALLMARK: Stamped surname in 1/16 Gothic print. Stamp first used in 1975.

F. ENRICO

EPALOOS, JENNIE *Zuni*
SILVERSMITH:
HALLMARK: Stamped initials in 1/16 Gothic print. Stamp first used in 1974. May use the Peynetsa stamp as well.
See Jane Peynetsa.

J.E.

ERIACHO, CHRISTINE *Zuni*
SILVERSMITH/LAPIDARIST: Specializes in petit point.
HALLMARK: Combined initials of Christine and husband stamped in 1/32 Gothic print. Stamp of combined initials with surname in 1/16 Gothic print first used in 1974.
Spouse is Daniel Eriacho.
[Bell:1976:32]

DCE   D&C ERIACHO

ERIACHO, DANIEL *Zuni*
SILVERSMITH/LAPIDARIST: Specializes in petit point.
HALLMARK: Stamp of combined initials of Donald and wife in 1/32 Gothic print. Stamp of combined initials with surname in 1/16 Gothic print first used in 1974.
Spouse is Christine Eriacho.
[Bell:1976:32]

DCE   D&C ERIACHO

ERIACHO, DONALD *Zuni*
SILVERSMITH/LAPIDARIST: Specializes in geometric mosaic inlay but does a wide variety of styles including cluster work.
HALLMARK: Stamp of combined initials of Donald and wife in 1/16 Gothic print. Stamp of full names of him and his wife in 1/16 Gothic print. Stamp of surname with combined initials in 1/32

Gothic print. Stamp of a bear paw. Stamp of personalized combined signature. In addition much of their work is signed with an engraver and the signatures often vary.
Spouse is Viola Eriacho. Parents are Sefferino and Loretta Eriacho. [Bell:1976:43]

DVE   DON & VIOLA ERIACHO
D.&V. ERIACHO   D.&V. Eriacho
Don & Vie Eriacho   Zuni

ERIACHO, GLENDA *Zuni*
SILVERSMITH/LAPIDARIST:
HALLMARK: Stamped surname in 1/16 script first used in 1975. Stamped surname in 1/16 Gothic print first used in 1985.

G. Eriacho   G. ERIACHO

ERIACHO, KIRK *Zuni*
SILVERSMITH/LAPIDARIST:
HALLMARK: Stamped surname in 1/16 Gothic print first used in 1974. Stamp of combined names of Kirk and wife in 3/32 script first used in 1974. Stamp of surname in 3/32 script first used in 1975. Stamp of first name in 3/32 script first used in 1976.
Spouse is Mary Eriacho.

K.ERIACHO   Kirk & Mary   Eriacho
Kirk

ERIACHO, MARY *Zuni*
SILVERSMITH/LAPIDARIST:
HALLMARK: Shares her husband's stamp of combined names of Mary and husband in 3/32 script, first used in 1975. Also uses a stamp in 1/16 Gothic print of her given name set on a plate. Stamp of given name in 3/32 script first used in 1976.
Spouse is Kirk Eriacho.

Kirk & Mary   [MARY]   Mary

ERIACHO, SEFFERINO *Zuni*
SILVERSMITH/LAPIDARIST: Specializes in tear drop cluster work. Began producing ca. 1935.
HALLMARK: Stamped surname in 1/16 Gothic print first used in 1975. Initials are those of Sefferino and his wife. Earlier work was not marked.
Spouse is Loretta Eriacho, son is Donald Eriacho.

S.L.ERIACHO

ERIACHO, VIOLA *Zuni*
SILVERSMITH/LAPIDARIST: Specializes in geometric mosaic inlay and petit point as well as a wide variety of other styles.
HALLMARK: Shares her husband's stamps. Stamp of combined initials of Viola and husband's in 1/16 Gothic print. Stamp of full names of Viola and husband in 1/16 Gothic print. Stamp of surname with combined initials in 1/32 Gothic print. Stamp of a bear paw. Stamp of personalized combined signature. In addition much of their work is signed with an engraver and the signatures vary.
Spouse is Donald Eriacho.

DVE   DON & VIOLA ERIACHO
D.&V. ERIACHO   D.&V. Eriacho
Don & Vie Eriacho   Zuni

ESALIO, HOWARD *Zuni*
SILVERSMITH:
HALLMARK: Stamped initials in 1/16 Gothic print. Stamp first used in 1974.

H.E.

ESCALIO, LAWRENCE *Zuni*
SILVERSMITH:
HALLMARK: Stamped surname in 1/16 Gothic print first used in 1974. The variation in the hallmark and the name came from an error in ordering the stamp.

L.ESALALIO

ETSATE, BETTY *Navajo*
SILVERSMITH: Specializes in needlepoint, making primarily squashblossom necklaces and conchos.
HALLMARK: Stamp of initials, abridged initials, and given name all in 1/16 Gothic print. She also signs her work in personalized print with an engraver.

B.A.E.   BE   BETTY   BETSATE

ETSITTY, ANN *Zuni*
SILVERSMITH:
HALLMARK: Stamped initials in Gothic print.

A.E.

ETSITTY, E ? *Navajo*
SILVERSMITH: Smith for Atkinson Trading Company.
HALLMARK: Stamped surname in 1/16 Gothic print. Stamp first used in 1976.

E. ETSITTY

ETSITTY, FRED *Navajo*
SILVERSMITH: Smith for Canyon Silver Company.
HALLMARK: Stamped initials in Gothic print.

F.E.

ETSITTY, MARIE *Navajo*
SILVERSMITH: Pieceworker for Canyon Silver Company.
HALLMARK: Stamped initials in Gothic print. Stamped surname in 1/16 Gothic print first used in 1976.
From Sanders, Arizona region.

M.E.   M.ETSITTY

ETSITTY, N ? *Navajo*
SILVERSMITH: Smith for Atkinson Trading Company.
HALLMARK: Stamped surname in 1/32 Gothic print. Stamp first used in 1981.

N.ETSITTY

ETSITTY, NANCY *Navajo*
SILVERSMITH:
HALLMARK: Stamped surname in 1/16 Gothic print. Stamp first used in 1975.
From Chinle, Arizona region. There is a possibility that this is the same person as the preceding.

N.ETSITTY

ETSITTY, RAYMOND *Navajo*
SILVERSMITH:
HALLMARK: Stamped initials in 1/16 Gothic print. Stamp first used in 1973.
From Mentmore, New Mexico region.

C.T.E.

ETSITTY, RICHARD *Navajo*
SILVERSMITH:
HALLMARK: Stamped initials in 1/16 Gothic print. Stamp first used in 1977.
From Many Farms, Arizona region.

R.E.

ETSITTY, TOM *Navajo*
SILVERSMITH: Pieceworker for Canyon Silver Company.
HALLMARK: Stamped initials in Gothic print.
From Sanders, Arizona region.

T.E.

ETSITTY, V ? *Navajo*
SILVERSMITH: Specializes in solid silver bracelets. Pieceworker for Montana Mining Company.
HALLMARK: Stamped surname in 1/16 Gothic print. Stamp first used in 1975.

V.ETSITTY

ETSITTY, YAZZIE *Navajo*
SILVERSMITH:
HALLMARK: Stamped initials in 1/16 Gothic print. Stamp first used in 1973.
From Many Farms, Arizona region.

Y.K.E.   Y K E

EUSTACE, BEATRICE *Zuni*
SILVERSMITH:
HALLMARK: Stamped symbol with initials in Gothic print below. Combined initials of her husband and herself in Gothic print.
Spouse is Ken Eustace.

K.& B.E.

EUSTACE, BEN *Zuni*
SILVERSMITH: Specializes in foliate work.
HALLMARK: Stamped symbol of an eagle used around 1950 was destroyed by his children and never replaced. Also uses stamped initials in Gothic print.
Spouse is Felicita or Felice Eustace.

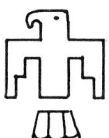   B.E.

EUSTACE, CHARLOTTE *Zuni*
SILVERSMITH/LAPIDARIST: Specializes in carved stones with foliate settings. Began producing in 1973. She and her husband divide the work. She does the silver and he carves the stones.
HALLMARK: Stamped initials of her husband in 1/16 Gothic print are used by both.
Spouse is Nelson Eustace.

NE

EUSTACE, CHRISTINE *Zuni/Cochiti*
SILVERSMITH: Specializes in contemporary silver resembling Danish silver work.
HALLMARK: Stamped combined initials of her husband and her own. Stamped initials in 1/16 Gothic print. First used in 1984.
Spouse is Al Newman (Anglo). Sister is Linda Eustace. Brothers are Joe and Nelson Eustace. Mother is Felicita Eustace and father Ben Eustace.

CAE   CE

EUSTACE, FELICITA *Cochiti*
SILVERSMITH: Specializes in foliate silver first produced ca. 1956.
HALLMARK: Stamped initials in Gothic print.
Spouse is Ben Eustace. Children are Linda, Joe, Christine, and Nelson Eustace.

F.E.

EUSTACE, JOE *Cochiti/Zuni*
SILVERSMITH:
HALLMARK: Stamped initials in Gothic print.
Spouse is Ada Chavez. Sisters are Linda and Christine Eustace. Brother is Nelson Eustace. Parents are Ben and Felicita Eustace.

JE

EUSTACE, JOLENE A. *Unknown*
SILVERSMITH:
HALLMARK: Stamped initials in 1/16 Gothic print. First used in 1985.

JAE

EUSTACE, KEN *Zuni*
SILVERSMITH:
HALLMARK: Combined initials of his wife and himself in Gothic print.
Spouse is Beatrice Eustace.

K.&B.E.

EUSTACE, LINDA *Cochiti/Zuni*
SILVERSMITH:
HALLMARK: Stamped initials in Gothic print.
Parents are Ben and Felicita Eustace. Brothers and sisters are Christine, Joe, and Nelson Eustace.

LE

EUSTACE, LOUVINA *Zuni*
SILVERSMITH:
HALLMARK: Stamped joined and offset initials in 3/16 personalized print. Stamp first used in 1977.

EUSTACE, NELSON *Cochiti/Zuni*
SILVERSMITH: Specializes in carved stone and foliate silver. Designs used are those made and patented by his father. Began

producing in 1973. Shares the work with his wife. She does the silver and he carves and sets the stones.
HALLMARK: Stamped initials in Gothic print. Also used by his wife.
Spouse is Charlotte Eustace. Parents are Ben and Felicita Eustace. Brothers and sisters are Joe, Linda, and Christine Eustace.

NE

EUSTACE, ROLAND — *Zuni*
SILVERSMITH/LAPIDARIST: Specializes in mosaic animal inlays.
HALLMARK: Stamped given name and ZUNI in 1/16 Gothic print.
Stamp first used in 1975.
Spouse is Ann Eustace (?).

ROLAND E.
ZUNI

EUSTACE, SENSA — *Zuni*
SILVERSMITH:
HALLMARK: Stamped initials in 1/16 Gothic print. Stamp first used in 1974.

S.E.

EUSTIS, FRANCIS — *Zuni*
SILVERSMITH:
HALLMARK: Stamped initials in Gothic print.

FE

FELICIANO, ? — *Unknown*
SILVERSMITH:
HALLMARK: Stamped name in 3/32 Gothic print. Stamp first used in 1974. The name may represent either a surname or a given name.

FELICIANO

FELIX, DUFFY — *Unknown*
SILVERSMITH:
HALLMARK: Stamped given name in 1/16 Gothic print. Stamp first used in 1979.
From Holbrook, Arizona region.

DUFFY

FENDENHEIM, JAMES — *Papago*
SILVERSMITH: Began producing in 1982.
HALLMARK: Stamped initial with symbols.

—F—

FERNANDO, LILLIAN — *Navajo*
SILVERSMITH:
HALLMARK: Stamped initials in ordinary form or with an enlarged L.

LF |F

FERREIA, JEANNE — *Apache*
LAPIDARIST: Peridot settings.
HALLMARK: Stamped personalized printing of initials.

JF

FERSEN, NINA — *Anglo (?)*
SILVERSMITH:
HALLMARK: Stamped symbol.

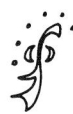

FOUTZ, JOHN ALLEN — *Anglo*
SILVERSMITH:
HALLMARK: Chisel cut initials. Hallmark placed on the fourth bead in necklaces.

FRAGUA, VERA — *Apache*
LAPIDARIST: Peridot settings.
HALLMARK: Stamped initials in Gothic print.

VF

FRANCIS, ERMA — *Navajo*
SILVERSMITH: Smith for Atkinson Trading Company.
HALLMARK: Stamped surname in 1/16 Gothic print. Stamped full name in 1/16 Gothic print first used in 1974.

E. FRANCIS   ERMA FRANCIS

FRANCIS, JAMES — *Zuni*
SILVERSMITH: Specializes in cast silver from hand-carved stone molds.
HALLMARK: Stamped initials joined in personalized print.

JF

FRANCISCO, HELEN — *Navajo*
SILVERSMITH:
HALLMARK: Stamped and joined initials in specialized print with elaboration.

HF

FRANCISCO, LILLIAN — *Laguna*
SILVERSMITH:
HALLMARK: Stamped initials in 1/16 Gothic print. Stamp first used in 1975.

LF

FRANCISCO, NELSON M. — *Santa Domingo*
SILVERSMITH:
HALLMARK: Stamped symbols of star and moon in 1/16 and 1/8" sizes.
From Bayard, New Mexico region.

FRANCISCO, ROGER — *Navajo*
SILVERSMITH:
HALLMARK: Stamped initials in Gothic print.

RVF

FRANK, J ? *Navajo*
SILVERSMITH:
HALLMARK: Stamped surname in 1/16 Gothic print. Stamp first used in 1974.

J.FRANK

FRANK, JERRY J. *Zuni*
SILVERSMITH:
HALLMARK: Stamped single initial in Gothic print.

J.

FRANK, JIMMY *Navajo*
SILVERSMITH: Specializes in chip inlay.
HALLMARK: Stamped initials in Gothic print.

JF

FRANK, JOHNNIE *Navajo (?)*
SILVERSMITH:
HALLMARK: Stamped initials in 3/32 Gothic print. Stamp first used in 1974.
From Winslow, Arizona region.

J.F.

FRANK, PAUL *Navajo*
SILVERSMITH:
HALLMARK: Stamped initials in Gothic print.

PF

FRANKLIN, JEROME *Navajo (?)*
SILVERSMITH:
HALLMARK: Two line stamp using surname and "Handmade" in 1/16 Gothic print. Stamp first used in 1977.
From region around Leupp Boarding School, Leupp, Arizona.

J. FRANKLIN
HANDMADE

FRANKLIN, NELSON *Navajo*
SILVERSMITH:
HALLMARK: Stamp of surname in 1/16 Gothic print. Stamp first used in 1976.
From Leupp, Arizona region.

N.FRANKLIN

FRED, NATHAN JR. *Hopi*
SILVERSMITH: Specializes in overlay work. Began producing ca. 1969.
HALLMARK: First stamp is of personalized print joined and offset. First used in 1973. Second stamp is of joined initials with the symbol of an arrow first used in 1975.
Father is Nathan Fred, Sr.

FREDENBERG, DENNIS *Unknown*
SILVERSMITH:
HALLMARK: Stamped initial in 3/32 script. The initial can be either an H or a Y. The stamp was first used in 1978.
From Window Rock, Arizona region.

GACHUPIN, LAURA *Jemez*
POTTER:
HALLMARK: Painted and fired symbol of a corn plant. The hallmark is that of her sister.
Sister is Maxine Toya.

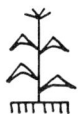

GAHATE, BART *Zuni*
SILVERSMITH: Works in gold as well.
HALLMARK: Stamped initials in Gothic print.

B.G.

GAHATE, DEWEY *Zuni*
SILVERSMITH/LAPIDARIST: Works with his wife.
HALLMARK: Combined initials of his and his wife's with his surname in 1/16 Gothic print. Stamp first used in 1975.
Spouse is Janette Gahate.

D.J.GAHATE

GAHATE, JANETTE *Zuni*
SILVERSMITH/LAPIDARIST: Works with her husband.
HALLMARK: Her initials combined with her husband's and his surname in 1/16 Gothic print. Stamp first used in 1975.
Spouse is Dewey Gahate.

D.J.GAHATE

GAMBINO, NICOLAS *Mexican*
SILVERSMITH: Began producing in 1971. Benchsmith for White Hogan.
HALLMARK: Stamped initials in 1/16 Gothic print.
From Durango, Mexico.

NG

GARCIA, CATHY *Unknown*
SILVERSMITH:
HALLMARK: Stamped given name in 1/16 Gothic print. Stamp first used in 1974.
From Gallup, New Mexico region.

CATHY G.

GARCIA, DAVID F. *Santo Domingo*
SILVERSMITH:
HALLMARK: Stamped full name in 1/16 Gothic print, first used in 1972. Second stamp of surname in 1/16 Gothic print. Stamp first used in 1985.

DAVID F. GARCIA   D.F.GARCIA

GARCIA, GLORIA JEAN *Zuni*
SILVERSMITH/LAPIDARIST: Specializes in sand casting, channel inlay, and nugget work. Uses snake designs. Her work is indistinguishable from her sister's and her mother's.
HALLMARK: Stamped surname of 1/16 Gothic print first used in 1985.

Her mother's name is Effie Calavaza. Her sisters are Susie Calavaza and Georgiana Yatsattie.

G.J.GARCIA

GARCIA, JOHN C. *Navajo*
SILVERSMITH:
HALLMARK: Stamped surname in 1/16 Gothic print. Stamp first used in 1975.
From Prewitt, New Mexico region.

J.C.GARCIA

GARCIA, JUAN PEDRO *Santo Domingo*
SILVERSMITH: Specializes in foliate work with nugget settings.
HALLMARK: Stamped personalized print of joined initials.

GARCIA, LEAH NAMPEYO *Tewa*
POTTER: Began producing ca.1960.
HALLMARK: Painted and fired symbol of a corn ear.
Deceased.

GARCIA, NELSON *Santo Domingo*
SILVERSMITH/GOLDSMITH:
HALLMARK: Stamped initials in Gothic print, also initials with symbol.
From Phoenix, Arizona region.

NDG

GARCIA, ROSE CHINO *Acoma*
POTTER:
HALLMARK: Painted and fired symbol.

GARCIA, TONY *Unknown*
SILVERSMITH:
HALLMARK: Stamped initials in 1/16 Gothic print.

T.G.

GARNETT, JAMES *Unknown*
SILVERSMITH:
HALLMARK: Stamped symbol of a loggerhead turtle. Stamp first used in 1976.

GARRETT, DONALD F. *Unknown*
SILVERSMITH:
HALLMARK: Stamped initial with symbols in 1/16 Gothic print. Stamp first used in 1985.

~G~

GARRISON, JERRY *Unknown*
SILVERSMITH:
HALLMARK: Stamped initials in Gothic print.

JG

GASHWAZRA, ALFONSO *Hopi*
SILVERSMITH: Specializes in overlay work. Began producing in 1975.
HALLMARK: Chiseled initials joined and offset.
Brother is Bradley Gashwazri.
[Wright:1982:95]

GASHWAZRI, BRADLEY *Hopi*
SILVERSMITH: Specializes in overlay work. Began producing in 1963.
HALLMARK: Stamped initials in 1/16 Gothic print.
Brother is Alfonso Gashwazra.
[Wright:1982:90]

BG

GASPER, ANNIE QUAM *Zuni*
SILVERSMITH/LAPIDARIST: Specializes in channel and mosaic inlay. Designs are of hummingbirds and spiderwebs. Began producing in 1955. Learned the craft from Horace Iule.
HALLMARK: Stamped initials over word Zuni in 1/16 Gothic print. Stamp without periods first used in 1973.
[Bell:1977:52] [Levy:1980:25]

A.Q.G.   AQG
ZUNI   ZUNI

GASPER, ARLAN *Zuni*
SILVERSMITH:
HALLMARK: Stamped initials of Arlan's and his wife's given names with Arlan's surname in 1/16 Gothic print. Stamp shared with wife.
Spouse is Rose Gasper.

A&RG

GASPER, ASHBARRY A. *Zuni*
SILVERSMITH:
HALLMARK: Stamped surname in 1/16 Gothic print. First used in 1974. Second stamp of initials in 3/32 Gothic print first used in 1975.

A.GASPER   A.A.G.

GASPER, CLARA *Zuni*
SILVERSMITH/LAPIDARIST: Specializes in inlay work.
HALLMARK: Stamped husband's surname with both their initials in 1/16 Gothic print. Stamp first used in 1973. Second stamp of husband's surname with both of their initials in 1/8 script first used in 1976. Stamp of her name in 1/8 script.
Spouse is Filbert Gasper.

F.C.GASPER   *F.C.Gasper*   *C.Gasper*

GASPER, ELKUS *Zuni*
SILVERSMITH/LAPIDARIST: Specializes in needlepoint.
HALLMARK: Stamped hallmark in 1/16 Gothic print of surname with small EL offset above was first used in 1974. Second stamp of

surname and abridged given name in 3/32 Gothic print was also used first in 1974.

GASPER, FILBERT *Zuni*
SILVERSMITH/LAPIDARIST: Specializes in inlay work.
HALLMARK: Stamped surname with his and his wife's initials in 1/16 Gothic print, first used in 1973. Second stamp of surname with his and his wife's initials in 1/8 script, first used in 1976.
Spouse is Clara Gasper.

F.C.GASPER *F. C. Gasper*

GASPER, JOSEPH H. *Zuni*
SILVERSMITH/LAPIDARIST:
HALLMARK: Stamped surname in 3/32 Gothic print. Stamp first used in 1975.

J.J.GASPER

GASPER, L.V. *Zuni*
SILVERSMITH/LAPIDARIST:
HALLMARK: Two line stamp of surname and village in 1/16 Gothic print. Stamp first used in 1974.

L.V.GASPER
ZUNI

GASPER, RAYMOND *Zuni*
SILVERSMITH/LAPIDARIST:
HALLMARK: Stamped initials over a symbol in 1/8 Gothic print, first used in 1972. Second stamp of the same device but reversed and set in 1/4 Gothic print, used first in 1973. Third stamp in 1/8 Gothic print, first used in 1974.

GASPER, ROSE *Zuni*
SILVERSMITH/LAPIDARIST:
HALLMARK: Stamped initials of husband and wife with Arlan's surname in 1/16 Gothic print. Shared stamp.
Spouse is Arlan Gasper.

A&RG

GAUSSOIN, CONNIE TSOSIE *Navajo*
SILVERSMITH:
HALLMARK: Stamped symbol of a deer head with NAV below.

GCHACHU, RUBY *Zuni*
SILVERSMITH/LAPIDARIST: Specializes in needlepoint. Began producing in 1960.
HALLMARK: Signs her given name and initial with an engraver.
[Bell:1976:23]

Ruby Gchachu

GCHACHU, SMOKEY *Zuni*
SILVERSMITH/LAPIDARIST: Specializes in needlepoint in contemporary forms. Began producing in 1974. Learned from his mother. He does the silver work and stone carving. His wife sets the stones.
HALLMARK: Signs his first name with an engraver. Mark is shared by his wife.
Spouse is Terry Gchachu.

Smokey

GCHACHU, TERRY *Zuni*
SILVERSMITH/LAPIDARIST: Specialty is needlepoint in contemporary forms. Began producing in 1974. Her husband does the silver work and stone carving. She sets the stones.
HALLMARK: Shares her husband's mark.
Spouse is Smokey Gchachu.

Smokey

GEORGE, JOHN *Navajo*
SILVERSMITH:
HALLMARK: Stamped personalized initials.

JG

GIA, ELLA *Zuni*
SILVERSMITH/LAPIDARIST: Specializes in channel inlay using bird designs, a few squashblossom necklaces.
HALLMARK: Signature of her given name and her husband's full name signed with an engraver.
Spouse is Wesley Gia.

Wesley & Ella Gia

GIA, WESLEY *Zuni*
SILVERSMITH/LAPIDARIST: Specializes in channel inlay using bird designs, a few squashblossom necklaces.
HALLMARK: Signature of his full name with the given name of his wife signed with an engraver.
Spouse is Ella Gia.

Wesley & Ella Gia

GILBERT, WILMA *Apache*
LAPIDARIST: Peridot settings.
HALLMARK: Stamped initials in Gothic print.

WG

GISNIE, ROGER *Navajo (?)*
SILVERSMITH:
HALLMARK: Stamped initials in 1/16 Gothic print. Stamp first used in 1977.
From Holbrook, Arizona region.

RTG

GOLSH, JOSEPH *Kumeyaay or Pala*
SILVERSMITH:
HALLMARK: Stamped personalized and joined initials.
Deceased.

GOLSH, LARRY *Pala*

SILVERSMITH/GOLDSMITH: Specializes in bold geometric castings with single stones.
HALLMARK: May be stamped, chiseled or cast. Occasionally they are incorporated into the design. His hallmark is registered. His first stamp was used from 1970-'74. The second stamp is registered and has been used since 1974. The third stamp is the one incorporated as a design element. Mark is usually 1/8" long. Formerly an architectural student with Ben Goo at Arizona State University and with Paolo Soleri. He is also a painter and sculptor.

GOODLUCK, TEDDY *Navajo*
SILVERSMITH:
HALLMARK: Initials inside symbol are in Gothic print. He seldom uses his mark.

GORDON, DELBERT *Unknown*
SILVERSMITH: Smith for T & R Market.
HALLMARK: Stamped surname in 1/16 Gothic print. Stamp first used in 1976.

D.GORDON

GORULD, JOANNE R. *Navajo (?)*
SILVERSMITH:
HALLMARK: Stamped initials in 1/16 Gothic print. Stamp first used in 1976.
From Crownpoint, New Mexico region.

J.R.G.

GOULD, J.B. *Navajo*
SILVERSMITH:
HALLMARK: Stamped surname in 1/16 Gothic print. Stamp first used in 1974.
From Tohatchi, New Mexico region.

J.B.GOULD

GRAHAM, MIDGE *Unknown*
Possibly this is a shop rather than an individual silversmith:
HALLMARK: Several marks all featuring star in some way. Stamps are in 1/16 Gothic print. The RAINSTAR stamp was first used in 1984.

RAINSTAR   MORNING STAR   LA ☆
MS ☆

GRAY, JOE LEE *Navajo*
SILVERSMITH: Specializes in stamp work and clusters. Began producing in 1970 at the age of 32. Smith for New Mexico jewelry.
HALLMARK: Stamped full name in 1/16 Gothic print.
Spouse is Angelita Gray.
From Church Rock, New Mexico region.

JOE L.GRAY

GRIJALVA, DAVID *Unknown*
SILVERSMITH:
HALLMARK: Stamped full name in 1/16 Gothic print. Stamp first used in 1975. Nickname used in stamp.

DOBBY GRIJALVA

GUARDIAN, ESTHER *Zuni*
SILVERSMITH/LAPIDARIST: Specializes in mosaic inlaid birds with stellate margins on the pieces. Began producing ca. 1966. Did piecework for Albuquerque shops in 1978-79.
HALLMARK: Stamped given names of her husband and herself in 1/16 Gothic print. Used an engraved signature with both their initials until 1973. Stamped surname and both initials in 1/16 Gothic print used from 1976 on.
Spouse is Sammy Guardian.
[Bell:1976:20]

SAMMY (N) ESTHER   S & E Guardian Zuni
E. & S. GUARDIAN

GUARDIAN, SAMMY *Zuni*
SILVERSMITH/LAPIDARIST: Specializes in mosaic inlaid birds with stellate margins on the pieces. Began producing ca. 1966. Did piecework for Albuquerque shops in 1978-79. Works with wife.
HALLMARK: Stamped given names of his wife and himself in 1/16 Gothic print. Used an engraved signature with both their initials until 1973. Stamped surname and both initials in 1/16 Gothic print used from 1976 on.
Spouse is Esther Guardian.
[Bell:1976:20]

SAMMY (N) ESTHER   S & E Guardian Zuni
E. & S. GUARDIAN

GUERNO, FRANK *Navajo*
SILVERSMITH:
HALLMARK: Stamped initials in 1/16 Gothic print.

FG

GUERRO, AMY *Unknown*
SILVERSMITH:
HALLMARK: Stamped full name in Gothic print.

AMY GUERRO

GUERRO, FRANK *Navajo (?)*
SILVERSMITH:
HALLMARK: Stamped initials in Gothic print.
From Alamo, New Mexico region.

F.G.

GUERRO, FRED *Navajo*
SILVERSMITH:
HALLMARK: Stamped initials or stamped given name in Gothic print.
From Puertocito, New Mexico region.

FG   FRED G.

GUERRO, J ? *Unknown*
SILVERSMITH: Smith for New Mexico Jewelry.

HALLMARK: Stamped surname in 3/32 Gothic print. Stamp first used in 1975.
From Los Lunas, New Mexico region.

J.GUERRO

GUERRO, PHILLIP *Unknown*
SILVERSMITH:
HALLMARK: Stamped initials in 3/32 Gothic print, first used in 1975.
From Canyoncito, New Mexico region.

PTG

GUERRO, TONY *Navajo*
SILVERSMITH: Smith for New Mexico Jewelry, Steve Skinner, and Jeff Sutton.
HALLMARK: Stamped full name in 1/16 Gothic print first used in 1975. Stamped surname in 3/32 Gothic print. Stamped two line full name and tribe in 1/32 Gothic print first used in 1983.
From Los Lunas, New Mexico region.

TONY GUERRO   T. GUERRO   TONY GUERRO NAVAJO

GURULE, PRESILIANO *Unknown*
SILVERSMITH:
HALLMARK: Stamped full name in 1/16 Gothic print. Stamp first used in 1978.
From Thoreau, New Mexico region.

PRESSIE GURULE

HALEY, ? *Navajo*
SILVERSMITH: Smith for Atkinson Trading Company.
HALLMARK: Stamped surname in 1/16 Gothic print. Stamp first used in 1982.

HALEY

HALEY, BENJAMIN *Navajo*
SILVERSMITH: Smith for Atkinson Trading Company.
HALLMARK: Stamped surname in 1/16 Gothic print, first used in 1974. Stamped initials in same print.

B.HALEY   B.H.

HALEY, CHRISTINE *Navajo*
SILVERSMITH: Smith for Atkinson Trading Company.
HALLMARK: Stamped surname in 1/16 Gothic print. first used in 1984.

C.HALEY

HALEY, J ? *Navajo*
SILVERSMITH: Smith for Atkinson Trading Company in the 1970s.
HALLMARK: Stamped surname in 1/16 Gothic print, first used in 1974.

J.HALEY

HALEY, JAMES M. *Navajo*
SILVERSMITH: Smith for Atkinson Trading Company during the 1970s.
HALLMARK: Stamped surname in 1/16 Gothic print, first used in 1974.

J.M.HALEY

HALEY, JULIAN *Navajo*
SILVERSMITH: Smith for Atkinson Trading Company before 1976.
HALLMARK: Stamped surname in Gothic print.

J.HALEY

HALEY, PAUL *Navajo*
SILVERSMITH: Smith for Atkinson Trading Company.
HALLMARK: Stamped surname in 1/16 Gothic print, first used in 1974.

P.HALEY

HALEY, PRESLEY *Navajo*
SILVERSMITH: Smith for Atkinson Trading Company.
HALLMARK: Stamped full name in 1/16 Gothic print, first used in 1975. Also stamped given name in 1/16 Gothic print.

PRESLEY HALEY   PRESLEY H.

HALEY, ROBERT *Navajo*
SILVERSMITH: Smith for Atkinson Trading Company.
HALLMARK: Stamped surname in 1/16 Gothic print, first used in 1974.

R.H.

HALEY, WILLIE *Navajo*
SILVERSMITH: Smith for Atkinson Trading Company.
HALLMARK: Stamped surname in 1/16 Gothic print, first used in 1974.

W.HALEY

HALFMOON, CARLOS *Apache*
SILVERSMITH:
HALLMARK: Stamped symbols of crescent moons.

HALOO, NANCY *Zuni*
SILVERSMITH/LAPIDARIST: Specializes in carved mosaic inlay of bird designs. Began producing in 1973. Learned from her father.
HALLMARK: Stamped initials in 1/16 Gothic print.
Father is Jake Haloo, sisters are Dolly Banteah and Lolita Natachu. Half brother is Jacob Livingston.

N.H.

HALOO, PETER III *Zuni*
SILVERSMITH/LAPIDARIST: Specializes in "snake eye" settings. Uses his grandparents' designs. Learned his craft by watching other craftsmen. He began producing in 1965. He does the metalwork and sets the stones and his wife does the polishing.
HALLMARK: Engraved signatures of his and his wife's given names and his surname.
Spouse is Vivian Haloo.
[Bell:1977:38] [Levy:1980:38]

Peter & Vivian Haloo

HALOO, VIVIAN *Zuni*
SILVERSMITH/LAPIDARIST: Specializes in "snake eye" sets. Learned from her husband and other craftsmen. Began producing in 1965. Her husband does the metalwork and sets the stones; she does the polishing.
HALLMARK: Engraved signatures of her given name and her husband's with his surname.
Spouse is Peter Haloo, III.
[Bell:1977:38] [Levy:1980:38]

HAMILTON, ALICE *Navajo*
SILVERSMITH:
HALLMARK: Stamp of joined personalized initials in 1/6" print.

AH

HAMILTON, TONITA (NAMPEYO) *Tewa*
POTTER:
HALLMARK: Painted and fired symbol of an ear of corn.

HANNAWEEKE, ALICE *Zuni*
SILVERSMITH/LAPIDARIST:
HALLMARK: Stamped initials of given names of her and her husband and his surname in Gothic print.
Spouse is Thomas Hannaweka.

T-A. H

HANNAWEEKE, CHARLIE *Zuni*
SILVERSMITH/LAPIDARIST: Specializes in stamp work of his own designs. Learned the craft from his parents and began producing in 1953. He does the metalwork and his wife does the stonework.
HALLMARK: Stamped initials of his and his wife's given names and his surname in Gothic print.
Spouse is Pauline Hannaweeke.
[Levy:1980:37]

CPH

HANNAWEEKE, PAULINE *Zuni*
SILVERSMITH/LAPIDARIST: Specializes in stamp work of her husband's designs. She learned the craft from her husband's parents and began producing in 1953. She does the stone work and her husband the metalwork.
HALLMARK: Stamped initials of her given name and those of her husband in Gothic print.
Spouse is Charlie Hannaweeke.
[Levy:1980:37]

CPH

HANNAWEEKE, THOMAS *Zuni*
SILVERSMITH/LAPIDARIST:
HALLMARK: Stamped initials of his wife's given name and his own and surname in Gothic print, first used in 1975.
Spouse is Alice Hannaweeke.

T-A. H

HANSEN, BO *Unknown*
No information.

HANSEN, FREDA (WOODMAN) *Navajo*
SILVERSMITH:
HALLMARK: Stamped Navajo phrase or name in 1/16 Gothic print, first used in 1975. The same name or phrase in personalized print and a third stamp of a symbol.

BITNI DZEEZ BA'A'   Bɨłnɨ dzeez báá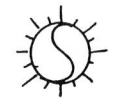

HARMSEN, WILLIAM *Anglo*
SILVERSMITH: Produces erratically.
HALLMARK: Stamped initials.

WDH

HARRIS, EVERETT *Hopi*
SILVERSMITH: Specialized in overlay work. Produced for a short while in the 1940's.
HALLMARK: Stamped symbol of a tobacco leaf 3/16" size.
[Wright:1982:84]

HARRISON, DOUGLAS *Navajo*
SILVERSMITH:
HALLMARK: Stamped initials in Gothic print.

DH

HARRISON, JAMES *Navajo*
SILVERSMITH:
HALLMARK: Stamped initials in Gothic print.
From Gallup, New Mexico region.

JH

HARRISON, JIM *Navajo*
SILVERSMITH:
HALLMARK: Stamped full name in 1/16 script, first used in 1979. Stamped initials in 1/16 Gothic print set on a round plate. Stamped initials in Gothic print set in a symbol.
From Shiprock, New Mexico region.

Jim Harrison

HARUGY, HERBERT *Unknown*
GOLDSMITH:
HALLMARK: Stamped initials in Gothic print.

H.H.

HARVEY, HERBERT C. SR. *Navajo*
SILVERSMITH:
HALLMARK: Stamped full name in 1/16 Gothic print, first used in 1979. Second stamp in Gothic print without the SR.
From Round Rock, Arizona region.

H.C.HARVEY, SR   H.C.HARVEY

HARVEY, HENRY *Navajo*
SILVERSMITH: Smith for Atkinson Trading Company.
HALLMARK: Stamped surname in 1/16 Gothic print, first used in 1983.

HARVEY, L ? *Unknown*
SILVERSMITH: Smith for K.D. Trading Company.
HALLMARK: Stamped surname in 1/16 Gothic print, first used in 1975.

L.HARVEY

HASKIE, FLORENDA *Zuni*
SILVERSMITH/LAPIDARIST: Specializes in a very open needlepoint. Learned from her parents. Began producing in 1972. Works with her husband.
HALLMARK: Stamped surname of her husband in 1/16 Gothic print, first used in 1977. Second stamp of her husband's surname with joined initials of their combined given names in 1/32 Gothic print, first used in 1979.
Spouse is Norbert Haskie. Parents are Hugh and Agnes Boweekaty.
[Bell:1977:55]

N.HASKIE   NF.HASKIE

HASKIE, NORBERT *Zuni*
SILVERSMITH/LAPIDARIST: Specializes in a very open needlepoint. Began producing in 1972. Works with his wife.
HALLMARK: Stamped surname in 1/16 Gothic print first used in 1977. Stamp of surname and combined and joined initials of his and his wife's given names in 1/32 Gothic print, first used in 1979.
Spouse is Florenda Haskie.
[Bell:1977:55]

N.HASKIE   NF.HASKIE

HASTINGS, CALVIN *Hopi*
SILVERSMITH: Specialized in overlay. Produced for a short period after 1948.
HALLMARK: Stamped symbol of a tobacco flower.
[Wright:1982:85]

HATCH, PAUL *Unknown*
SILVERSMITH:
HALLMARK: Stamped symbol with joined initials inside. From Holbrook, Arizona region.

HATTIE, ? *Unknown*
SILVERSMITH: Specializing in needlepoint.
HALLMARK: Stamped surname (?) in 1/16 Gothic print.

HATTIE

HATTIE, ANITA *Zuni*
SILVERSMITH/LAPIDARIST: Specializes in petit point.
HALLMARK: Engraved personalized initials shared with her spouse.
Spouse is Buddy Hattie. Son is Derrick Hattie.
[Bell:1977:18]

A.H.

HATTIE, BITA *Zuni*
SILVERSMITH/LAPIDARIST:
HALLMARK: Stamped full name in Gothic print.

BITA HATTIE

HATTIE, BUDDY *Zuni*
SILVERSMITH/LAPIDARIST: Specializes in petit point.
HALLMARK: Engraved personalized initials of his wife.
Spouse is Anita Hattie.
[Bell:1977:18]

A.H.

HATTIE, BUTCH *Zuni*
SILVERSMITH:
HALLMARK: Stamped given name and initial of surname in 1/16 Gothic print, first used in 1979.

BUTCH-H

HATTIE, DERRICK *Zuni*
SILVERSMITH/LAPIDARIST: Specializes in mosaic and channel inlay but does nugget work also. Learned from his parents. Began producing in 1974.
HALLMARK: Stamped two lines of surname and tribe in 3/32 Gothic print, first used in 1975. Shared with his wife.
Spouse is Vivian Hattie. Parents are Buddy and Anita Hattie.
[Bell:1977:49]

D.V.HATTIE
ZUNI

HATTIE, HARLAN *Zuni*
SILVERSMITH/LAPIDARIST: Specializes in needlepoint. Began producing in 1969.
HALLMARK: Stamped surname in Gothic print with initials of given name. Second stamp of surname in Gothic print with combined initials of given names of his and his wife's in Gothic print and shared with her.
Spouse was Naneen Hattie (deceased).

H.HATTIE   H.N.HATTIE

HATTIE, IVAN *Zuni*
SILVERSMITH:
HALLMARK: Stamped surname with initials of his wife's and his own given names in 1/16 Gothic print, first used in 1974.

I&J.HATTIE

HATTIE, NANEEN *Zuni*
SILVERSMITH/LAPIDARIST: Specialized in needlepoint. Began producing in 1969. Deceased in 1975.
HALLMARK: Stamped combined initials of her spouse's and her own given names with his surname in Gothic print.
Spouse is Harlan Hattie.

H.N.HATTIE

HATTIE, VIVIAN *Zuni*
SILVERSMITH/LAPIDARIST: Specializes in channel and mosaic inlay as well as nugget work. Learned from Anita and Buddy Hattie. Began producing in 1974.
HALLMARK: Stamped surname with combined initials of her spouse's and her own given names in 3/32 Gothic print. Stamp shared with her husband. First used in 1975.

Spouse is Derrick Hattie.
[Bell:1977:49]

D.V.HATTIE
   ZUNI

HAUNGOAH (ART CODY) *Kiowa*
POTTER:
HALLMARK: Painted and fired Indian name in personalized print.

   HAUNGOAH

HAWEE, BILLY RAE *Hopi*
SILVERSMITH: Specialized in overlay work. Began producing in 1959.
HALLMARK: Stamped symbol of a crescent moon and star. Used a stamp of initials in Gothic print also.
[Wright:1982:88]

   BRH

HAWLEY, JOHNNIE B. *Zuni*
SILVERSMITH/LAPIDARIST: Specializes in inlaid work and overlay technique as well.
HALLMARK: Stamped initials in Gothic print.

JBH

HAYDEN, JULIAN *Anglo*
SILVERSMITH: Little production.
HALLMARK: Stamped symbol of a turtle with joined initials inside. Stamp first made in 1936 and registered as a trade mark in 1942.

HEALING, ANNIE NAMPEYO *Tewa*
POTTER: Assisted her mother in decorating her pottery as well as making her own.
HALLMARK: Painted and fired her surname and initial and that of her mother.
Mother was Nampeyo, sister is Fannie Nampeyo Polacca.

A. Nampeyo   Nampeyo

HENRY, ARLENE *Navajo*
LAPIDARIST: Specializes in inlay work. Craftsman for Sunburst Handcrafts.
HALLMARK: Numerical stamp in 1/16 print.

8

HENRY, BERNARD JR. *Navajo*
GOLDSMITH:
HALLMARK: Stamped initials in Gothic print.

B.H.

HENRY, GEORGE *Navajo*
SILVERSMITH/goldsmith:
HALLMARK: Stamped initials in Gothic print. Stamped initial of his wife's and his initials in Gothic 1/16 print. Stamped names of him and his wife and his surname in personalized script. Stamp first used in 1978.
Spouse is Nusie Henry.
From Crownpoint, New Mexico region.

GH   GNH   Geo & Nusie Henry

HENRY, J.R. *Unknown*
SILVERSMITH:
HALLMARK: Stamped symbol 9/16".
From Window Rock, Arizona region.

HENRY, L ? *Navajo*
SILVERSMITH: Smith for Indian Hammers.
HALLMARK: Stamped surname in 1/16 Gothic print, first used in 1976.

L.HENRY

HENRY, NUSIE *Navajo*
SILVERSMITH/GOLDSMITH:
HALLMARK: Stamp of initials of her husband and her own in 1/16 Gothic print. Stamped names of her husband's and her own in personalized script, first used in 1978.
Spouse is George Henry.

GNH   Geo & Nusie Henry

HENRY, WILFORD J. *Navajo*
SILVERSMITH:
HALLMARK: Stamped offset personalized print of initials.

ωJH

HERALD, JIMMY *Navajo*
SILVERSMITH: Specializes in contemporary work.
HALLMARK: Stamp of joined personalized print initials.
Son is Jimmy Herald, Jr.
[King:1976:31]

JH   JH   CH

HERALD, JIMMY JR. *Navajo*
SILVERSMITH: Specializes in contemporary silver work. Uses Frank Patania designs.
HALLMARK: Stamped joined initials of personalized print made with very fine lines.
Father is Jimmie Herald.

JH

HERRERA, ARNOLD *Cochiti*
SILVERSMITH: Specializes in handmade beads.

HALLMARK: Stamped symbol with initials in Gothic print.

HERRERA, KATIE *Navajo*
SILVERSMITH: Piecework.
HALLMARK: Stamped initials in Gothic print.

KAH

HESUSE, HENRY P. *Navajo*
SILVERSMITH:
HALLMARK: Stamped personalized print initials, joined and expanded. Stamp 3/32" in size first used in 1985.
From Nageezi, New Mexico region.

HPH

HILDRETH, BOBBY *Navajo*
SILVERSMITH: Benchsmith for Sunburst Handcrafts from 1982-1986.
HALLMARK: Stamped initials in Gothic print.
Related (?) to Marguerita Hildreth.

B.H.

HILDRETH, MARGUERITA *Navajo*
SILVERSMITH: Benchsmith with Sunburst Handcrafts since 1980.
HALLMARK: Stamped initials in Gothic print.
Related (?) to Bobby Hildreth.

MH

HILL, C. V. *Navajo*
SILVERSMITH: Smith for Bernie Dominguez.
HALLMARK: Stamped surname in 1/16 Gothic print, first used in 1975.

C.V.HILL

HILL, WENDAL J. *Mohawk*
SILVERSMITH:
HALLMARK: Stamped initial with symbol in Gothic print.

H⌒

HINTON, CORNELIA *Apache*
LAPIDARIST: Peridot settings.
HALLMARK: Stamped initials in Gothic print.

CH

HOLDEN, LES *Navajo*
SILVERSMITH:
HALLMARK: Stamped joined initials in personalized print.

H

HOLMES, DOUGLAS *Hopi*
SILVERSMITH: Specializes in silver overlay work. Produced from 1948 to 1961.
HALLMARK: Stamped symbol of a butterfly.
[Wright:1982:85]

HOLMES, EMERY *Hopi*
SILVERSMITH: Specializes in silver overlay. Began producing in 1975.
HALLMARK: Stamped offset initials in Gothic print.
[Wright:1982:95]

EH

HOLTSOI, ERNEST SR. *Navajo*
SILVERSMITH:
HALLMARK: Stamped surname in 1/16 Gothic print. Stamp first appeared in 1982.
From Farmington, New Mexico region.

E.HOLTSOI

HONANIE, PHILLIP *Hopi*
SILVERSMITH: Specializes in silver overlay. Began producing in 1967.
HALLMARK: Stamped initials in Gothic print or symbol of so-called "friendship" mark.
[Wright:1982:89]

   PH

HONANIE, WATSON *Hopi*
SILVERSMITH: Specializes in silver overlay. Began producing in 1973.
HALLMARK: Stamped joined and personalized initials or a symbol of a bear paw with so-called "friendship" mark on its palm.
[Wright:1982:94]

WH

HONIE, AGNES *Tewa*
POTTER:
HALLMARK: Painted and fired symbol of an animal.

HONIE, NORMAN JR. *Hopi*
SILVERSMITH: Specializes in silver overlay. Learned from his father and began producing in 1974.
HALLMARK: Stamped initials in Gothic print or the symbol of a tadpole.
[Wright:1982:95]

NHJR

HONIE, NORMAN SR. *Tewa*
SILVERSMITH: Specializes in silver overlay. Began producing in 1966.
HALLMARK: Stamped symbol of a spider.
Son is Norman Honie, Jr.
[Wright:1982:89]

HONWISIOMA, RANDALL *Hopi*
SILVERSMITH: Specialized in hammered work. Benchsmith for Grave's Indian Store, Skiles, and Vaughn's Indian Store. Produced from 1937—1962.
HALLMARK: Stamped symbol of a macaw.
[Wright:1982:44]

HONWYTEWA, JERRY *Hopi*
SILVERSMITH: Specializes in silver overlay. Began producing in 1972.
HALLMARK: Stamped personalized initials or in Gothic print. Stamp of a symbolized strap.
[Wright:1982:93]

      JH

HONYAKTEWA, JAMES *Hopi*
SILVERSMITH: Specializes in silver overlay.
HALLMARK: Stamp of personalized joined initials.

HONYAKTEWA, NEILSON *Hopi*
SILVERSMITH: Specialized in silver overlay. Produced from 1948 to 1951.
HALLMARK: Stamped symbol of a lizard.
[Wright:1982:85]

HOOIE, DAISY (NAMPEYO) *Tewa*
POTTER:
HALLMARK: Painted and fired symbols of a corn ear and a leaf (?).

HOOIE, NORMAN JR. *Zuni*
SILVERSMITH/LAPIDARIST: Specializes in needlepoint. Began producing in 1962.
HALLMARK: Stamped initials of his wife's and his own initials. Both share the same stamp.
Spouse is Virginia Hooie.
[Bell:1977:47]

NVH

HOOIE, SIDNEY *Zuni*
SILVERSMITH/LAPIDARIST: Specializes in needlepoint. Began producing in 1935.
HALLMARK: Stamped initials in personalized print or in Gothic print.

   SH

HOOIE, VIRGINIA *Zuni*
SILVERSMITH/LAPIDARIST: Specializes in needlepoint. Began producing in 1962.
HALLMARK: Stamped initials or her husband's and her own initials in Gothic print. Shares the mark with her husband.
Spouse is Norman Hooie, Jr.
[Bell:1977:47]

NVH

HORACE, EMERSON *Unknown*
SILVERSMITH:
HALLMARK: Stamped name in 1/16 Gothic print. The stamp first appeared in 1982.
From Oraibi, Arizona region.

QUANNIES

HORNBECK, JOHN *Anglo*
SILVERSMITH: Produces a variety of work. Learned his craft from Preston Monongye. Married into the silvermaking Adakai family.
HALLMARK: Stamped symbol of deer track usually used in a set of two.

HORSE, K ? *Unknown*
SILVERSMITH:
HALLMARK: Stamped surname (?) in 1/16 Gothic print. Stamp first appeared in 1985.

K.HORSE

HOSKIE, BILLY JOHN *Navajo*
SILVERSMITH: Specializes in cast silver using hand-carved stone molds.
HALLMARK: Stamped initials with one enlarged.
[King:1976:46]

BJH

HOSKIE, ERVIN *Navajo*
SILVERSMITH: Produces both contemporary and traditional styles. Works in gold also.
HALLMARK: Stamped personalized initials. Two-line stamp in 1/16 script of full name. This stamp first appeared in 1978.

EH   *Made by Ervin Hoskie*

HOSKIE, ESTHER COAN *Navajo*
SILVERSMITH: Specializes in cast silver from hand-carved stone molds. Began producing in 1964.
HALLMARK: Stamped initials in Gothic print.
From Window Rock, Arizona region.
[King:1976:46]

ECH

HOSKIE, JOHN *Navajo*
SILVERSMITH: Crafts pieces using bear claws. Began producing in the 1970s.
HALLMARK: Stamped full name in 1/16 Gothic print. Stamp first appeared in 1984.
From Orem, Utah region.

JOHN HOSKIE

HOSLER, BOB *Unknown*
SILVERSMITH:
HALLMARK: Stamped surname in 1/16 Gothic print. Stamp first appeared in 1979.

HOSLER

HOTHAN, LANI *Navajo (?)*
SILVERSMITH:
HALLMARK: Stamped given name in 1/16 Gothic print. Stamp first appeared in 1979.
From Chinle, Arizona region.

LANI

HOVALO, EDGAR MILLER *Hopi*
SILVERSMITH: Specialized in overlay silver. Produced from 1948 until his death in the 1950s.
HALLMARK: Punched symbol of a Hopi man's hair knot.
[Wright:1982:86]

HOWARTER, TERRI *Anglo (?)*
SILVERSMITH:
HALLMARK: Stamped symbol of either an animal or joined initials. Mark is 3/32" in size and first appeared in 1985.

HOYUNGOWA, MANUEL *Hopi*
SILVERSMITH: Specializes in silver overlay. Learned from Preston Monongye and the AIIA in Santa Fe. Began producing in 1975. Works with his wife.
HALLMARK: Stamped symbol of strong rain clouds. He has used at least five versions of this as a hallmark. The first version appeared in 1977.
Spouse is Karen Hoyungowa.
[Wright:1982:96]

HUBBARD, GEORGE *Unknown*
SILVERSMITH: Production little if any.
HALLMARK: Stamped initials in 1/16 Gothic print. Stamp first appeared in 1977.
From Provo, Utah region.

G.C.H.

HUGHTE, GEORGEANN *Zuni*
SILVERSMITH/LAPIDARIST: Specializes in channel inlay in simple curvilinear designs. Learned from her parents and began producing ca. 1970. Her husband occasionally helps her.
HALLMARK: Stamped initials of her and her husband's initials. Shared stamp.
Spouse is Rodney Hughte.
[Levy:1980:29]

R.H.G.   RHG

HUGHTE, RODNEY *Zuni*
SILVERSMITH: Specializes in channel inlay in simple curvilinear designs. Began producing ca. 1970. Sporadic producer, he mainly assists his wife.
HALLMARK: Stamped initials of his and his wife's. Shared stamp.
Spouse is Georgeann Hughte.
[Levy:1980:29]

R.H.G.   RHG

HUMEYESTEWA, BYRON *Hopi*
SILVERSMITH: Specializes in silver overlay. Began producing in 1975.
HALLMARK: Stamped joined, or joined and offset initials.
[Wright:1982:96]

HUMEYESTEWA, JAY *Hopi*
SILVERSMITH: Specializes in silver overlay. Began producing in 1976.
HALLMARK: Stamped joined initials, or single initial both with bear claw marks above them.
[Wright:1982:96]

HUMEYESTEWA, MANUEL *Hopi*
SILVERSMITH: Specializes in silver overlay.
HALLMARK: Stamped symbol of an animal (bear?) head or initials in Gothic print.

MH

HUMEYESTEWA, TOM *Hopi*
SILVERSMITH: Specialized in silver overlay. Began producing in 1948 but continued only for a short while.
HALLMARK: Stamped symbols of a bird's head or the entire bird. The bird is supposed to be an eagle.
[Wright:1982:84]

HUMEYESTEWA, WINFIELD *Hopi*
SILVERSMITH: Specializes in silver overlay. Began producing in 1974.
HALLMARK: Stamped symbol of a bear paw with the palm divided and a spot in one part.
[Wright:1982:96]

HUNTER, HAROLD *Hopi*
SILVERSMITH: Specializes in silver overlay.
HALLMARK: Stamped joined personalized initials.

H

HURLEY, RONNIE *Navajo*
SILVERSMITH:
HALLMARK: Stamped initials in Gothic print.

From Canyoncito, New Mexico region.

RH

HUSTITO, ALONZO *Zuni*
SILVERSMITH/LAPIDARIST:
HALLMARK: Stamped symbol of a bear or a bear with 1/16 script initials under it. The total size is 1/4 x 3/32". This latter stamp first appeared in 1974.

HUSTITO, CHARLES *Zuni*
SILVERSMITH/LAPIDARIST:
HALLMARK: Stamped symbols of clouds above rain with initials inside. 1/4" in size.

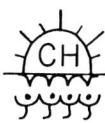 

HUSTITO, SHARON *Zuni*
SILVERSMITH/LAPIDARIST: Specializes in petit point using her sister's designs. Learned from watching her parents. Began producing in 1974. She does all of the work on each piece.
HALLMARK:. Stamped initials in Gothic print.
[Levy:1980:37]

SH

IGNACIO, IRMA *Navajo*
SILVERSMITH: Smith in the Albuquerque shops in 1978-9.
HALLMARK: Stamped initials in Gothic print.
From Torreon, New Mexico region.

I I

ITAIKE, LEE *Unknown*
SILVERSMITH:
HALLMARK: Stamped initials in Gothic print.

L I

IULE, GARY *Zuni*
SILVERSMITH:
HALLMARK: Stamped surname in Gothic print.

G.IULE

IULE, HORACE *Zuni*
SILVERSMITH/LAPIDARIST: Specialized in channel inlay and cast work. Best known for his cast and set crosses. Began producing in 1925 and continued till his death in the 1970s. Helped in his craft by his wife.
HALLMARK: Stamped surname in Gothic print.
Spouse is Lupe Iule.
[Bell:1975:10, 14, 15]

H.IULE

IULE, LUPE *San Felipe*
SILVERSMITH/LAPIDARIST: Specialized in cast and channel work particularly cast crosses. Learned the craft from her husband and began producing in 1937. Formerly helped her husband; she is now assisted by her daughter who does the metalwork.
HALLMARK: Stamped full name in 1/16 Gothic print. First appeared in 1979. Second stamp of surname in 3/32 Gothic print first appeared in 1981. Presumably shared her husband's mark when he was alive.
Spouse was Horace Iule. Children are Celia and Phillip Iule. There are others.
[Levy:1980:63]

LUPE IULE   L.IULE

IULE, PHILLIP *Zuni/San Felipe*
SILVERSMITH/LAPIDARIST: Specializes in cast silver pieces with simple inlay. Learned from his parents.
HALLMARK: Stamped surname in Gothic print.
[Bell:1957:16]

P.IULE

IULE, W ? *Zuni*
SILVERSMITH:
HALLMARK: Stamped surname in 1/16 Gothic print. Stamp first appeared in 1982.

W.IULE

IVERSON, ELMER *Anglo*
SILVERSMITH: Individual smith and shopowner also(?).
HALLMARK: Stamped surname in 1/16 script that first appeared in 1977. Second stamped surname in 1/32 script appeared in 1982.

Iverson   *Iverson's*

JACK, RENA P. *Navajo*
SILVERSMITH:
HALLMARK: Stamped initials in 1/16 Gothic print. Stamp first appeared in 1973.
From Prewitt, New Mexico region.

R.P.J.

JACK, ROSA *Navajo*
SILVERSMITH:
HALLMARK: Stamped initials in Gothic print.

RPJ

JACKSON, DAN *Navajo*
SILVERSMITH:
HALLMARK: Stamped surname set in a symbol of a hogan. Second stamp of surname alone in 1/16 Gothic print, first appeared in 1976.
From Window Rock, Arizona region

   JACKSON

JACKSON, D. A. *Navajo*
SILVERSMITH: Possibly a member of the Jackson family from Manuelito, New Mexico that learned casting under Dean Kirk.
HALLMARK: Stamped surname in 1/16 Gothic print, first appeared in 1975.
From Keams Canyon, Arizona region.

D.A.JACKSON

JACKSON, E ? *Navajo*
SILVERSMITH:
HALLMARK: Stamped initials or stamp of surname in 1/16 Gothic print. Surname stamp first appeared in 1976.
From Window Rock, Arizona region.

EJ   E.JACKSON

JACKSON, GENE *Navajo*
SILVERSMITH:
HALLMARK: Stamped surname in 1/16 Gothic print. Stamp first appeared in 1983.
From Chinle, Arizona region.

JACKSON

JACKSON, JAMES *Navajo*
SILVERSMITH:
HALLMARK: Stamped initial, initials with symbol, or symbol of an animal track.
Possibly related to Virginia and Willie Jackson.

J

JACKSON, LARRY *Navajo*
SILVERSMITH:
HALLMARK: Stamp of joined letters in personalized print. Larry Joe uses the same hallmark but it is not known whether it is the same individual with two names or separate persons.

JACKSON, MARTHA *Navajo*
SILVERSMITH:
HALLMARK: Stamp of surname in Gothic print. Stamped symbol of a hogan.

JACKSON

JACKSON, MARY E. *Navajo*
SILVERSMITH:
HALLMARK: Stamp of a single initial in 1/16 Gothic print which appeared first in 1978. Also uses a stamp of three initials in Gothic print.
From Winslow, Arizona region.

E   MEJ

JACKSON, MURRAY *Walapai*
SILVERSMITH: Specializes in silver overlay. Began producing in 1977.
HALLMARK: Stamped joined and offset initials in personalized print.
[Wright:1982:96]

MJ

JACKSON, R ? *Navajo*
SILVERSMITH: Smith for Bowser and Begay.
HALLMARK: Stamped surname in 1/16 Gothic print. Stamp first appeared in 1976.

R.JACKSON

JACKSON, RAYMOND *Navajo*
SILVERSMITH:
HALLMARK: Stamped hallmark of symbol of a rainbow 3/8" in size with 1/16 Gothic print initials inside it.
From Winslow, Arizona region.

JACKSON, T ? *Navajo*
SILVERSMITH:
HALLMARK: Stamped initials either personalized or in Gothic print. Stamped surname in Gothic print.

TJ   TJ   T.JACKSON

JACKSON, VIRGINIA *Navajo*
SILVERSMITH:
HALLMARK: Stamped animal track or initial with symbol.
Possibly related to Willie or James Jackson.

J

JACKSON, WILLIE *Navajo*
SILVERSMITH:
HALLMARK: Stamped animal track or initial with symbol.
Possibly related to Virginia or James Jackson.

J

JAKE, HARRY *Navajo*
SILVERSMITH:
HALLMARK: Stamped initials in 3/32 Gothic print. Stamp first appeared in 1974.
From Prewitt, New Mexico region.

H.J.

JAMES, ? *Navajo*
SILVERSMITH:
HALLMARK: Stamped single initial in Gothic print.

J

JAMES, ALICE *Navajo*
SILVERSMITH:
HALLMARK: Stamped surname in 1/16 Gothic print. Stamp first appeared in 1975.
From Chinle, Arizona region.

A.JAMES

JAMES, BAHE *Navajo*
SILVERSMITH:
HALLMARK: Stamped surname in 1/16 Gothic print. Stamp first used in 1975.
From Ganado, Arizona region.

B.JAMES

JAMES, DELLA *Navajo*
SILVERSMITH: Specializes in squashblossoms. Producing by 1970.
HALLMARK: Stamped joined initials of her spouse. Shared

stamp.
Spouse is Francis James.

JAMES, DENNIS *Navajo*
SILVERSMITH:
HALLMARK: Stamped initials in Gothic print.

DJ

JAMES, ELDON *Hopi*
SILVERSMITH: Specializes in silver overlay. Began producing in 1962 and continued until his death in 1979.
HALLMARK: Stamped symbol of a rabbit head. Chiseled initials or a stamped combination of rabbit head and personalized initials. [Wright:1982:88]

JAMES, FRANCIS *Navajo*
SILVERSMITH: Specializes in squashblossoms. Began producing in 1970. Smith for the Tanners. Wife works with him.
HALLMARK: Stamped joined initials. Stamp used by wife.
Spouse is Della James.

JAMES, JEFFERSON *Navajo (?)*
SILVERSMITH:
HALLMARK: Stamped full name in 1/16 Gothic print. Stamp acquired in 1975.
From Los Lunas, New Mexico region.

JEFFERSON JAMES

JAMES, L ? *Navajo*
SILVERSMITH: Smith for Atkinson Trading Company.
HALLMARK: Stamped surname in 1/16 Gothic print. Stamp first appeared in 1976.

L. JAMES

JAMES, LEONARD *Navajo*
SILVERSMITH: Smith for State Line Indian Jewelry.
HALLMARK: Stamped surname in 3/32 Gothic print. Stamp first appeared in 1975. Second stamp of surname with enlarged first letters and personalized print. State Line Indian Jewelry shop stamp may appear with his.

L. JAMES   L. JAMES

JAMES, LEWELLEN *Navajo*
SILVERSMITH:
HALLMARK: Stamp of given name in 1/16 Gothic print. Stamp first appeared in 1975.
From Sanders, Arizona region.

LEWELLEN

JAMES, MARCELLA *Navajo*
SILVERSMITH:
HALLMARK: Registered stamp of initials in Gothic print with sterling below it and a third line for registry mark.

MJ
STERLING
®

JAMES, R. W. *Navajo*
SILVERSMITH: Smith for Indian Hammers in 1976 and for J. Taylor in 1977.
HALLMARK: Stamped surname in 1/16 Gothic print first used in 1976. Second stamp of name in script over a rainbow under which appears a small flute player. Third stamp of an elaborate script R.

R.W. JAMES

JAMES, RAY JR. *Navajo*
SILVERSMITH: Smith for Indian Hammers in 1976. Smith for Canyon Silver Company also.
HALLMARK: Stamped surname in 1/16 Gothic print first appeared in 1976. Stamps of personalized initials with smaller JR. appearing in different positions.

R. JAMES JR   RJ JR

JAMES, RITA *Navajo*
SILVERSMITH:
HALLMARK: Stamped initials in personalized italicized print.

R.J.

JAMES, ROSE MARY *Zuni*
SILVERSMITH:
HALLMARK: Stamped surname in 1/16 Gothic print. Stamp first appeared in 1976.

R.M. JAMES

JAMES, VIRGINIA *Navajo*
SILVERSMITH:
HALLMARK: Stamped initials in 1/16 Gothic print. Stamp acquired in 1975.

V.J.

JAMESON, DON *Navajo (?)*
SILVERSMITH:
HALLMARK: Stamped full name in 1/16 Gothic print. Stamp first used in 1976.
From Gallup, New Mexico region.

DON JAMESON

JAMEZ, P ? *Navajo*
SILVERSMITH: Smith for State Line Indian Jewelry.
HALLMARK: Stamped surname in 3/32 Gothic print. Stamp first used in 1975. Second stamp of surname with personalized initial letters and symbol. Shop stamp for State Line Indian Jewelry may appear with hallmarks.

P. JAMEZ   P☆JAMEZ

JAMEZ, S ? *Navajo*
SILVERSMITH: Specializes in wrought work. Smith for State Line Indian Jewelry.
HALLMARK: Stamped surname in 3/32 Gothic print. Stamp first

used in 1975. Second stamp of surname with personalized initial letters. Shop stamp for State Line Indian Jewelry may appear with these hallmarks.

S.JAMEZ   S.JAMEZ

JAMEZ, SARAH *Navajo*
SILVERSMITH:
HALLMARK: Stamped surname in personalized script with symbol. Stamp first used in 1982. This may be the same individual as the one immediately preceding.
From Gallup, New Mexico region.

S⚹⚹Jamez

JAMON, CLIFF *Zuni*
SILVERSMITH:
HALLMARK: Stamped full name in 1/32 Gothic print. Stamp first appeared in 1982.
From Albuquerque, New Mexico region.

CLIFF JAMON

JAMON, CORNELIA *Zuni*
SILVERSMITH:
HALLMARK: Stamped initials in 1/16 print. Stamp first appeared in 1977.

C.E.J.

JANSEN, D ? *Unknown*
SILVERSMITH:
HALLMARK: Stamped surname in 1/16 Gothic print. Stamp first used in 1980.
From Albuquerque, New Mexico region.

D.JANSEN

JARAMILLO, EDDIE *Zuni*
SILVERSMITH/LAPIDARIST:
HALLMARK: Engraved surname and initials of his wife and his own in personalized script. Shared with his wife.
Spouse is Odelle Jaramillo.

E⚹OJaramillo

JARAMILLO, ODELLE *Zuni*
SILVERSMITH/LAPIDARIST:
HALLMARK: Engraved surname of husband with initials of both hers and her husband's in personalized script.
Spouse is Eddie Jaramillo.

E⚹OJaramillo   O.J.

JENKINS, GRANT *Hopi*
SILVERSMITH: Specialized in hammered work. Began producing before 1924. Benchsmith for stores in Phoenix and Flagstaff.
HALLMARK: Stamped head of coyote and initial H for Hopi. One of the earliest Hopi hallmarks.
[Wright:1982:81]

H

JENKINS, MARSHALL *Hopi*
SILVERSMITH: Specialized in silver overlay work. Began producing in the 1960s. Learned his craft in 1939.
HALLMARK: Stamped symbol of a bear claw. Stamp first used in 1967. Used stamp of Gothic print initials also.
[Wright:1982:81]

    MJ

JENSEN, D ? *Unknown*
SILVERSMITH:
HALLMARK: Stamped surname in 1/16 Gothic print. Stamp first used in 1980.

D.JENSEN

JIM, A ? *Navajo*
SILVERSMITH:
HALLMARK: Stamped surname in Gothic print.

A.JIM

JIM, D.A. *Navajo*
SILVERSMITH: Smith for Atkinson Trading Company.
HALLMARK: Stamped surname in 1/16 Gothic print. Stamp first used in 1976. May be accompanied by the shop stamp for Atkinson Trading Company.

D.A.JIM

JIM, HARRISON *Navajo*
SILVERSMITH: Smith for Richardson Trading Company.
HALLMARK: Stamped surname in 1/16 Gothic print. Stamp first appeared in 1976.

H.JIM

JIM, I ? *Navajo*
SILVERSMITH: Smith for Atkinson Trading Company.
HALLMARK: Stamped surname in 1/16 Gothic print. Stamp first appeared in 1976. Stamp may be accompanied by shop stamp for Atkinson Trading Company.

I.JIM

JIM, IRENE *Navajo*
SILVERSMITH: Smith for Atkinson Trading Company.
HALLMARK: Stamped full name in 1/16 Gothic print. Stamp first used in 1975. Stamp may be accompanied by shop stamp of Atkinson Trading Company. Irene Jim and the person immediately preceding this, I. Jim, may be one and the same.

IRENE JIM

JIM, MARIE LE *Navajo*
SILVERSMITH:
HALLMARK: Stamped surname in 1/16 Gothic print, first used in 1974. Second stamp of hogan with surname in 1/16 Gothic print below first appeared in 1976.
From Vanderwagon, New Mexico region.

M.L.JIM

M.L.JIM

JIM, N ? *Navajo*
SILVERSMITH:
HALLMARK: Stamped surname in 1/16 Gothic print, first used in 1976. May be accompanied by Atkinson Trading Company's shop stamp.

N. JIM

JIM, THOMAS *Navajo*
SILVERSMITH: Specializes in repoussé work. Learned from his grandfather. Began work for John Yellowhorse in Flagstaff and for Al Zuni. Began producing in 1982. Benchsmith for Rocking Horse Ranch.
HALLMARK: Stamped surname in 1/16 script, first appeared in 1982. Uses stamped initials in 1/16 Gothic print also. His mark is accompanied by the shop mark of Rocking Horse Ranch.
Brother is Wilson Jim.

T. Jim   TJ

JIM, WILSON *Navajo*
SILVERSMITH/GOLDSMITH: Makes a variety of pieces in traditional designs. Learned his craft from a cousin.
HALLMARK: Stamped surname in 1/16 Gothic print. Stamped initials in Gothic print. Stamp of personalized initial and name with enlarged capital. Stamp of name with sterling used on a rectangular plate. Took a new mark when he began to work for Rocking Horse Ranch.
Brother is Thomas Jim, grandfather was Bedoni. From a large family, many of whom are silversmiths.

W. JIM   W.J.   STERLING / W. Jim

JIRON, EVELYN *Isleta*
SILVERSMITH:
HALLMARK: Stamped initials in Gothic print either offset or ordinary.

E_JJ   E.J.

JOE, ALFRED *Navajo*
SILVERSMITH:
HALLMARK: Stamped full name in 1/16 Gothic print first used in 1975. Stamp of surname in Gothic print used on an oval plate. Stamp of joined offset initials. Stamp of joined offset initials set on a circular plate or inside a horseshoe.
From Winslow, Arizona region.

-AL JOE-   JOE

JOE, ANDERSON P. *Navajo*
SILVERSMITH/LAPIDARIST: Specializes in lapidary work and shadow box pieces. Began producing ca. 26 years of age.
HALLMARK: Joined personalized initials with an enlarged J. Stamp first used in 1972.
From Gamerco, New Mexico region.

A_J

JOE, ANSON *Navajo*
SILVERSMITH: Smith for Atkinson Trading Company.
HALLMARK: Stamped full name in 1/16 Gothic print, first used in 1974. May be accompanied by the Atkinson Trading Company shop mark.

ANSON JOE

JOE, CHARLIE *Navajo*
SILVERSMITH:
HALLMARK: Stamped given name in Gothic print.

CHARLIE

JOE, CORBET *Navajo*
SILVERSMITH: Specializes in chip inlay.
HALLMARK: Stamped initials in Gothic print.
From St. Michaels, Arizona region.

CJ

JOE, ELLA MAE *Navajo*
SILVERSMITH:
HALLMARK: Stamped initials in 1/16 Gothic print first used in 1974.
From Church Rock, New Mexico region.

E.M.J.

JOE, H ? *Navajo*
SILVERSMITH: Smith for Canyon Silver Company.
HALLMARK: Stamped surname in 1/16 Gothic print. Stamp first used in 1975.

H.JOE

JOE, KEE *Navajo*
SILVERSMITH:
HALLMARK: Stamped initials in Gothic print.

KJ

JOE, LARRY *Navajo*
SILVERSMITH:
HALLMARK: Stamped personalized joined initials 3/32" size. Stamp first appeared in 1974.
It is possible that Larry Jackson and Larry Joe are the same person.

Æ

JOE, MARY *Navajo*
SILVERSMITH: Smith for Atkinson Trading Company.
HALLMARK: Stamped full name in 1/16 Gothic print first seen in 1974.

MARY JOE

JOE, TED *Navajo*
SILVERSMITH: Smith for Atkinson Trading Company.
HALLMARK: Stamped full name in 3/32 Gothic print first appearing in 1980.

TED JOE

JOE, TOM K. *Navajo*
SILVERSMITH:
HALLMARK: Stamped initials in 1/16 Gothic print first used in 1974.
From Ft. Defiance, Arizona region.

T.J.

JOE, TONY *Navajo*
SILVERSMITH:
HALLMARK: Stamped initials in 1/16 Gothic print first used in 1974.
From Winslow, Arizona region.

J/B

JOGAR, ? *Unknown*
SILVERSMITH:
HALLMARK: Stamped 1/4" symbol of a lizard set on an oval plate. Stamp first appeared in 1973.
It is not known whether this name is a surname or a given name.

JOHN, DENNISON *Navajo*
SILVERSMITH:
HALLMARK: Stamped personalized print initials.
Mother is Isabel John, pictorial weaver from Many Farms, Arizona.

DJ

JOHN, KEE *Navajo*
SILVERSMITH:
HALLMARK: Stamped and joined personalized print initials.
Sister is Helen Long.

JOHN, KENNY *Navajo*
SILVERSMITH:
HALLMARK: Stamped initials in Gothic print.

KJ

JOHNSON, C ? *Navajo (?)*
SILVERSMITH:
HALLMARK: Stamped surname in 1/16 Gothic print. Stamp first used in 1974.

C.JOHNSON

JOHNSON, CECIL JR. *Zuni*
SILVERSMITH:
HALLMARK: Stamped initials of his and his wife's in 1/16 Gothic print. Stamp first appeared in 1974.
Wife's name is unknown.

C&C.J.JR.

JOHNSON, DON *Navajo*
SILVERSMITH: Smith for Rocking Horse Ranch.
HALLMARK: Stamped initials and full name in 1/16 Gothic print. These stamps first appeared in 1983. Prior to this he used a two-line stamp in 1/32 script of an earlier name, **DON JUAN**, and New Mexico beneath it. This stamp was first used in 1977.

DON JOHNSON   DJ   *Don Juan New Mexico*

JOHNSON, ETTA *Navajo*
SILVERSMITH: Smith for Steve Skinner.
HALLMARK: Stamped full name in 1/16 Gothic print. Stamp first used in 1976.

ETTA JOHNSON

JOHNSON, FLORENCE *Navajo*
SILVERSMITH: Specializes in Navajo Yei.
HALLMARK: Stamped initials in Gothic print.

FJ

JOHNSON, FREDDIE *Navajo*
SILVERSMITH:
HALLMARK: Stamped offset initials in Gothic print.

F J

JOHNSON, JAMES *Navajo (?)*
SILVERSMITH:
HALLMARK: Stamped initials in elaborate 3/32 script.
From Shiprock, New Mexico region.

J.J.J.

JOHNSON, JANICE *Navajo*
SILVERSMITH:
HALLMARK: Stamped surname in 1/16 Gothic print. Stamp first used in 1975.
From Gallup, New Mexico region.

J.JOHNSON

JOHNSON, JERRY *Navajo*
SILVERSMITH:
HALLMARK: Stamped initials in Gothic print shared with wife.
Spouse is JoAnn Johnson.
From Church Rock, New Mexico region.

J.J.

JOHNSON, JOANN *Navajo*
SILVERSMITH:
HALLMARK: Stamped initials in Gothic print shared with husband.
Spouse is Jerry Johnson.
From Church Rock, New Mexico region.

J.J.

JOHNSON, LEONARD *Navajo*
SILVERSMITH: Pieceworker.
HALLMARK: Stamped initials in Gothic print.

LCJ

JOHNSON, M ? *Navajo*
SILVERSMITH: Smith for Steve Skinner.
HALLMARK: Stamped surname in 3/32 Gothic print. Stamp first used in 1974.

M.JOHNSON

JOHNSON, M.J. *Navajo (?)*
SILVERSMITH: Smith for New Mexico Jewelry.

HALLMARK: Stamped surname in 1/32 Gothic print. Stamp first used in 1974.

M.J.JOHNSON

JOHNSON, MARY ANN *Navajo*
SILVERSMITH:
HALLMARK: Stamped initials in 3/32 print that are probably those of her husband, first used in 1974. Second stamp in 1/16 Gothic print of her initials first used in 1974.
From Gallup, New Mexico region.

JTJ   M.A.J.

JOHNSON, MARY *Navajo (?)*
SILVERSMITH: Smith for Steve Skinner.
HALLMARK: Stamped full name in 1/16 Gothic print. Stamp first used in 1975.

MARY JOHNSON

JOHNSON, MORTY *Navajo (?)*
SILVERSMITH:
HALLMARK: Stamped full name in Gothic print.

MORTY JOHNSON

JOHNSON, PATTERSON *Navajo*
SILVERSMITH: Produces a variety of styles.
HALLMARK: Stamped personalized print initials. Stamp of initials in Gothic with an unknown shop mark.

PJ.   PJ(A)™

JOHNSON, PAUL *Navajo*
SILVERSMITH: Specializes in foliate work. Began producing ca. 1972.
HALLMARK: Stamped given name in upper and lower case Gothic print. Also uses an engraved signature.
From Mentmore, New Mexico region.

Paul J.

JOHNSON, SOCORRO (CORA) *Zuni*
SILVERSMITH/LAPIDARIST: Specializes in petit point and large pieces. Began producing ca. 1961.
HALLMARK: Stamped surname with shared initials of her husband and herself in 1/16 Gothic print. Stamp first used in 1973.
Spouse is Vincent Johnson.
[Bell:1975:40]

V.S.JOHNSON

JOHNSON, TOMMY *Navajo*
SILVERSMITH:
HALLMARK: Stamped surname in 1/16 Gothic print. Stamp first appeared in 1982.
From Gallup, New Mexico region.

TK JOHNSON

JOHNSON, V.G.JOHNSON *Navajo*
SILVERSMITH:
HALLMARK: Stamped full name in 1/32 script.

V.g.JohnsonJohnson

JOHNSON, VINCENT *Zuni*
SILVERSMITH/LAPIDARIST: Specialized in lamps, goblets, and petit point. Began producing ca. 1961.
HALLMARK: Stamped full name with shared initials of his and his wife's in 1/16 Gothic print. Stamp first used in 1973. Shares stamp with his wife.
Spouse is Socorro Johnson.
[Bell:1975:40]

V.S.JOHNSON

JOHNSON, WILLIAM G. *Navajo*
SILVERSMITH:
HALLMARK: Stamped initials in Gothic print. Engraved signature.

W.G.J.   *W.g.Johnson*

JOHNSON, YAZZIE *Navajo*
SILVERSMITH: Specializes in contemporary work in both silver and brass. Self-taught.
HALLMARK: Stamped symbol or letter Y.

Y

JOHNSTON, MRS. H.R. *Navajo*
SILVERSMITH:
HALLMARK: Stamped personalized script initials joined in monogram style, 1/2 x 1/4". Stamp first used in 1975.
From Thoreau, New Mexico region.

JON, S ? *Unknown*
SILVERSMITH: Smith for Felix Indian Jewelry.
HALLMARK: Stamped surname in 1/16 Gothic print. Stamp first appeared in 1977.

S.JON

JONES, FRANCIS *Navajo*
SILVERSMITH: Specializes in cast work, chip inlay, Navajo Yei squashblossoms. Began producing in 1959 at the age of 15.
HALLMARK: Stamped initials with J enlarged.

FJ

JONES, L ? *Navajo*
SILVERSMITH: Smith for Atkinson Trading Company.
HALLMARK: Stamped surname in 1/16 Gothic print. Stamp first used in 1976.

L.JONES

JONES, PAUL *Navajo*
SILVERSMITH:
HALLMARK: Stamped two-line of surname and sterling in 1/16 Gothic print. Stamp first used in 1982.
From Tohatchi, New Mexico region.

P.JONES
STERLING

JONES, RAY JR. *Navajo*
SILVERSMITH:

HALLMARK: Stamped initials in Gothic print.
(Roy James Jr. appears to be the same person.)

RJ JR.

JORDAN, BILLY *Navajo*
SILVERSMITH:
HALLMARK: Stamped surname in 1/16 Gothic print first used in 1975.
From Window Rock, Arizona region.

B.JORDAN

JOSEPH, D ? *Navajo*
SILVERSMITH: Smith for Atkinson Trading Company.
HALLMARK: Stamped surname in 3/32 Gothic print. Stamp first used in 1980.

D.JOSEPH

JOSEYESVA, ROSS *Hopi*
SILVERSMITH: Specializes in silver overlay. Began producing ca. 1971. Sporadic production.
HALLMARK: Stamped symbol of an antelope track.

JOSHEVEMA (LOMAHEFTEWA), VALJEAN *Hopi*
SILVERSMITH: Specializes in overlay silver. Began producing in 1948. Sporadic output.
HALLMARK: Stamped symbol of a crescent moon or stamped initials in Gothic print.
Uses the name Lomaheftewa also.
[Wright:1982:83]

   VJSR

JOSHWESEOMA see **ROBERT LOMADAPKI**

JOSYTEWA, JESSE *Hopi*
SILVERSMITH: Specializes in silver overlay.
HALLMARK: Stamped symbol, stamped offset and joined initials, stamped offset initials with symbol.

JUANCHO, JOANN CHRISTINE *Isleta*
SILVERSMITH:
HALLMARK: Stamped upper and lower case Gothic initials.

JcJ

JUAN, DON see **DON JOHNSON**

JURAN, JOHN R. *Anglo (?)*
SILVERSMITH:
HALLMARK: Stamped symbol with Gothic initials inside. Size 3/16 x 1/4".

KABOTIE (LOMAWYWISA), MICHAEL *Hopi*
SILVERSMITH/PAINTER: Specializes in silver applique. Self-taught. Began producing in 1967 for a short period then began again in the 1980s.
HALLMARK: Stamped initial of surname, stamp of initials registered as a hallmark in 1981, stamp of joined initials. Stamp of Hopi name in script first used in 1979, particularly for paintings.
[Wright:1982:96]

K   MK   ⊛ MK   ∫omAwywssa

KAGENVEAMA, BENNETT *Hopi*
SILVERSMITH: Specializes in silver overlay.
HALLMARK: Stamped symbol of a spider.

KAGENVEMA, RICHARD *Hopi*
SILVERSMITH: Specialized in silver overlay. Began producing in 1948 and continued until his death in 1983.
HALLMARK: Stamped hallmark of a snake's head. Second stamp with the addition of fangs used from 1969 on.
[Wright:1982:86]

KAHN, CHESTER *Navajo*
SILVERSMITH/GOLDSMITH: Benchsmith for White Hogan. Continued on as an independent producer.
HALLMARK: Stamped interlocking personalized initials. Stamped surname in Gothic print.
Nephew of Tom, John, and Mabel Burnside (Meyer). Brother of Franklin Kahn.

   ＜KAHN

KAHN, FRANKLIN *Navajo*
SILVERSMITH:
HALLMARK: Stamped special name in Gothic print.
Brother of Chester Kahn, nephew of John, Tom, and Mabel Burnside (Meyer).

KK DINE

KALESTENA, JACK *Zuni*
SILVERSMITH:
HALLMARK: Stamped or chisel cut symbol.

KALISTEO, DENNIS *Navajo*
SILVERSMITH:
HALLMARK: Stamped initials in Gothic print.

DK

KALISTEWA, QUANITA *Zuni*
SILVERSMITH:
HALLMARK: Stamped initials in Gothic print.

QK

KALLESTEWA, BEN *Zuni*
SILVERSMITH/LAPIDARIST: Specializes in mosaic inlay and cluster and nugget work.
HALLMARK: Stamped initials of spouse and self in Gothic print. Stamp shared with his wife.
Spouse is Reyes Kallestewa.
[Bell:1977:45]

BRK

KALLESTEWA, DENNIS *Zuni*
SILVERSMITH:
HALLMARK: Stamped initials combined and joined.

KALLESTEWA, FARREL *Zuni*
SILVERSMITH/GOLDSMITH:
HALLMARK: Stamped initials in Gothic print.

F.K.

KALLESTEWA, HARVEY *Zuni*
SILVERSMITH:
HALLMARK: Stamped initials and word Zuni in 1/32 Gothic print. Stamp first used in 1983.

J-K ZUNI

KALLESTEWA, JANITA *Zuni*
SILVERSMITH/LAPIDARIST:
HALLMARK: Stamped initials of spouse's and her own in Gothic print. Stamp is shared with her husband.
Spouse is Sibert Kallestewa.

SKJ

KALLESTEWA, JOHN *Zuni*
SILVERSMITH:
HALLMARK: Stamped initials in Gothic print.

JK

KALLESTEWA, LILLY *Zuni*
SILVERSMITH/LAPIDARIST: Specializes in sun's face rings and bracelets.
HALLMARK: Stamped initials of her husband's and her own name in Gothic print offset on an angle. Shared stamp.
Spouse is Ralph Kallestewa.

R.
 L.
  K.

KALLESTEWA, LORRIE *Zuni*
SILVERSMITH/LAPIDARIST: Works with her sister.
HALLMARK: Stamped initials of her sister's and her own in Gothic print, offset.
Sister is Marcie Kallestewa.

M^L_K MLK   M$_L$K

KALLESTEWA, MARCIE *Zuni*
SILVERSMITH/LAPIDARIST: Works with her sister.
HALLMARK: Stamped initials of her sister's and her own in Gothic print, offset.
Sister is Lorrie Kallestewa.

M^L_K MLK   M$_L$K

KALLESTEWA, RALPH *Zuni*
SILVERSMITH/LAPIDARIST: Specializes in Sun's Face rings and bracelets.
HALLMARK: Stamped initials of his wife's and his own name in Gothic print offset at an angle. Shared stamp.
Spouse is Lilly Kallestewa.

R.
 L.
  K.

KALLESTEWA, REYES *Zuni*
SILVERSMITH/LAPIDARIST: Specializes in mosaic inlay and cluster and nugget work. Works with her husband.
HALLMARK: Stamped initials of her husband's name and her own.
Spouse is Ben Kallestewa.
[Bell:1977:45]

BRK

KALLESTEWA, SIBERT *Zuni*
SILVERSMITH/LAPIDARIST:
HALLMARK: Stamped initials of his wife's given name and his own.
Spouse is Janita Kallestewa.

SKJ

KALLESTEWA, SUE-ELLEN *Zuni*
SILVERSMITH/LAPIDARIST: Specializes in mosaic and channel inlay in bold geometric designs. Contemporary work. Began producing in 1967.
HALLMARK: Stamped initials in 1/16 Gothic print.
[Bell:1975:52]

N.S.K.

KANTEENA, RAYBERT *Zuni*
SILVERSMITH/LAPIDARIST: Specializes in carved mosaic inlay and "snake eye" settings. Learned from his mother. Began producing ca. 1972. He does the metal work and his wife does the stone work.
HALLMARK: Engraved initials followed by Zuni.
Spouse is Rhoda Kanteena.
[Levy:1980:21]

RK Zuni

KANTEENA, RHODA *Zuni*
SILVERSMITH/LAPIDARIST: Carved mosaic inlays in raised bezels and "snake eye" settings. Began producing ca. 1972. Her husband does the metal work and she does the stone work.
HALLMARK: Engraved initials followed by Zuni.
Spouse is Raybert Kanteena.
[Levy:1980:21]

RK Zuni

KASKALLA, LEBERT *Zuni*
SILVERSMITH/LAPIDARIST: Specializes in small channel inlay rings. Learned from his mother and uses her designs. Began

producing ca. 1970. Wife helps on some pieces.
HALLMARK: Stamped initials of his wife's given name and his own.
Spouse is Louise Kaskalla.
[Levy:1980:34]

LLK

KASKALLA, LOUISE *Zuni*
SILVERSMITH/LAPIDARIST: Assists her husband.
HALLMARK: Stamped initials of her husband's name and her given name.
Spouse is Lebert Kaskalla.
[Levy:1980:34]

LLK

KASKALLA, RODERICK *Zuni*
SILVERSMITH/LAPIDARIST: Specializes in inlay.
HALLMARK: Engraved full name in personalized print.

RODERICK KASKALLA
ZUNI

KATSENIH, CARRIE *Zuni*
SILVERSMITH/LAPIDARIST: Specializes in needlepoint and small square set stones. Has been producing since she was 18.
HALLMARK: Stamped initials in Gothic print.
[Bell:1977:9]

CK

KAVENA, WILMER *Hopi*
SILVERSMITH/KACHINA CARVER: Specialized in silver overlay. Began producing in 1974.
HALLMARK: Stamped symbol of a hopping frog on silver or joined personalized initials.
[Wright:1982:96]

   WK

KEAMS, CHEE *Navajo*
SILVERSMITH:
HALLMARK: Stamped joined and reversed initials.
Son is Sammy Keams.

JK

KEAMS, SAMMY *Navajo*
SILVERSMITH: Specializes in Zuni cluster work, squashblossoms.
HALLMARK: Stamped underlined initials or chisel cut joined initials.
Father is Chee Keams.

SK

KEE (?) *Navajo*
SILVERSMITH: Smith for Cooper's Store.
HALLMARK: Stamped name in 1/16 Gothic print. Stamp first appeared in 1982.

KEE

KEE, ALLEN *Navajo*
SILVERSMITH: Benchsmith for White Hogan from 1946 to 1962. Worked with Sam Roanhorse and Kenneth Begay. Learned from Ambrose Roanhorse.
HALLMARK: Stamped and joined initials in broad letters. Accompanied by White Hogan shop stamp.
From Steamboat Springs, Arizona region.

AK

KEE, CAROL *Navajo*
SILVERSMITH: Smith for Montana Mining Company.
HALLMARK: Stamped full name in 1/16 Gothic print. Stamp first used in 1975.

CAROL KEE

KEE, E ? *Navajo*
SILVERSMITH: Smith for Atkinson Trading Company.
HALLMARK: Stamped surname in 1/32 Gothic print. Stamp first used in 1981.

E KEE

KEE, ED *Navajo*
SILVERSMITH:
HALLMARK: Stamp of full name, full name with symbol of an arrow and the word Navajo.

ED KEE   ED KEE
          NAVAJO →   ED KEE
                     NAVAJO →

KEE, ELMER (Now called **ANTHONY**) *Navajo*
SILVERSMITH: Fashion jewelry.
HALLMARK: Stamped initials in Gothic print. May have changed his hallmark.
Parents (adoptive) are George and Ella Kee. Uncles are Ivan and Allen Kee.

FK

KEE, GEORGE *Navajo*
SILVERSMITH: Benchsmith at White Hogan.
HALLMARK: Stamped initials in 3/32 print with broad letters.
Brothers are Ivan and Allen Kee. Son is Elmer Kee.
From Steamboat Springs, Arizona region.

GK

KEE, HARRISON *Navajo*
SILVERSMITH:
HALLMARK: Stamped initials in Gothic print. The K in this set of initials often looks like an R.

HK

KEE, I ? *Navajo*
SILVERSMITH: Smith for Atkinson Trading Company.
HALLMARK: Stamped surname in 1/16 Gothic print. Stamp first used in 1980.

I.KEE

KEE, INEZ *Navajo*
SILVERSMITH: Specializes in cast and hollow ware.
HALLMARK: Stamped iniitials in Gothic print with broad letters. Mark is shared with husband.
Spouse is Ivan Kee.

IK

KEE, IRVIN *Navajo*
SILVERSMITH: Smith for Bilagaanas.
HALLMARK: Stamped full name in 1/16 Gothic print. Stamp first used in 1984.

IRVIN KEE

KEE, IVAN *Navajo*
SILVERSMITH: Specializes in cast and hollow ware, also hand-carved stone molds. Benchsmith for White Hogan, Reservation Crafts.
HALLMARK: Stamped initials in Gothic print broad letters, hallmark shared with spouse. White Hogan shop stamp also. Spouse is Inez or Isabelle Kee, brothers are George and Allen Kee. From Steamboat Springs, Arizona region.

KEE, J ? *Navajo*
SILVERSMITH:
HALLMARK: Stamped surname in Gothic print, registered.

J.KEE ®

KEE, MABEL *Navajo*
SILVERSMITH:
HALLMARK: Stamped reversed and joined initials in Gothic print.

KEE, MARIE *Navajo*
SILVERSMITH:
HALLMARK: Stamped full name in 1/16 Gothic print. Stamp first used in 1974.

MARIE KEE

KEE, RICHARD *Navajo*
SILVERSMITH/LAPIDARIST: Specializes in heavy traditional style pieces. Began producing in 1968.
HALLMARK: Stamped initials in Gothic print. Chiseled reversed and joined initials.
From Many Farms, Arizona region.

KEE, SAMSON *Navajo*
SILVERSMITH:
HALLMARK: Stamped initials with symbol in Gothic print.

KEE, T ? *Navajo*
SILVERSMITH:
HALLMARK: Stamped misaligned initials in Gothic print.

K

KEE, VEE *Navajo*
SILVERSMITH: Smith for Atkinson Trading Company.
HALLMARK: Stamped full name in 1/16 Gothic print. Stamp first used in 1983.

VEE KEE

KEETO, LARRY *Navajo*
SILVERSMITH: Smith for Don Mortensen.
HALLMARK: Stamped symbol with shared initials and sur-name in Gothic print alongside the head. Stamp first used in 1977. From Window Rock, Arizona region.

KELLY, JERRY G. *Navajo (?)*
SILVERSMITH:
HALLMARK: Stamped surname in personalized print 1/32". Stamp first used in 1985.
From Window Rock, Arizona region.

KELLEY, ROBERT *Unknown*
SILVERSMITH: Smith for Montana Mining Company and for Bernie Dominguez.
HALLMARK: Stamped full name in 1/16 Gothic print. Stamp first used in 1974.

ROBT. KELLEY

KENDY, LORRAINE *Zuni*
SILVERSMITH:
HALLMARK: Stamped surname in 1/16 Gothic print. Stamp first used in 1973.

L.KENDY

KENTON, SANDRA *Apache*
LAPIDARIST: Peridot settings.
HALLMARK: Stamped initials in Gothic print.

SK

KEWANYAMA, LEROY *Hopi*
SILVERSMITH: Specialized in silver overlay. Began producing in 1955.
HALLMARK: Stamped symbol of a Star Priest's hat or combined initials.
[Wright:1982:87]

KING, ANNA *Unknown*
SILVERSMITH:
HALLMARK: Stamped given name in personalized print 1/16" letters.
From Tijeras, New Mexico region.

Anna

KING, E ? *Navajo (?)*
SILVERSMITH: Smith for Don Mortensen in 1978, for Sophie Cooper in 1983.
HALLMARK: Stamped surname with enlarged capitals in combination of 3/32 and 1/16 Gothic print. Stamp first appeared in 1978. Second stamp the same without any initials appeared the

same year. Third stamp of surname in 1/16 Gothic print appeared in 1983.

E. KING   KING   E.KING

KING, HENRY   *Navajo*
SILVERSMITH:
HALLMARK: Stamped initial in Gothic print with symbol.

H

KING, JIM   *Navajo*
SILVERSMITH:
HALLMARK: Stamped joined and personalized initials. Shared mark.
Spouse is Rita King.

JR

KING, JIMENEZ see **KING, JIMMIE JR.**

KING, JIMMY JR.   *Navajo*
SILVERSMITH:
HALLMARK: Stamped script of joined initials in personalized letters, occasionally with symbols. Stamps with full name in 1/16 and 1/32 script used in 1982 and 83. Usually these are accompanied by a line that says Hand Made, Limited Edition, or American Indian. Stamps shared with spouse until divorce.
Spouse was Reyna King.

R   R   HAND MADE BY Jimmie King Jr.
Jimmie King Jr.   AMERICAN INDIAN
Limited Edition   HAND MADE BY Jimmie King, Jr.

KING, JOHNNY   *Navajo*
SILVERSMITH: Benchsmith for White Hogan.
HALLMARK: Stamped initials in Gothic print with broad letters.

JK

KING, REYNA   *Zuni*
SILVERSMITH:
HALLMARK: Shared former husband's stamps until divorce. Now uses stamped initials in 1/16 Gothic print. This stamp is shared by her new husband.
Former spouse Jimmie King, Jr.; present spouse is Richard (?).

    R&R

KING, RITA   *Navajo*
SILVERSMITH:
HALLMARK: Stamped joined initials in personalized print.
Spouse is Jim King.

JR

KIRK, ANDREW   *Navajo*
SILVERSMITH: Began producing around 1970.
HALLMARK: Stamp of two crescent moons has been used since he began. Second stamp of given name in Gothic initials with number used later.
Younger brother is Michael Kirk.

KIRK 1

KIRK, JOHN   *Unknown*
SILVERSMITH:
HALLMARK: Stamped initials in 1/16 Gothic print. Stamp first used in 1974.

JK

KIRK, MICHAEL   *Navajo*
SILVERSMITH: Began producing in 1971-2. Smith for Legacy Gallery.
HALLMARK: Stamped given name in Gothic print with number used since he began work. Second stamp of surname with initial in 1/32 Gothic print first used in 1985.
Older brother is Andrew Kirk.

KIRK 2   M.KIRK

KIYITE, ALVIN   *Zuni*
SILVERSMITH/LAPIDARIST: Specializes in simple tear drop cluster work of his own design. Learned from watching his brother and sister. Began producing in 1970. Works separately from his wife.
HALLMARK: Stamped shared initials in Gothic print. Wife uses the same mark although she works independently.
Spouse is Donna Kiyite.
[Levy:1980:50]

ADK

KIYITE, DONNA   *Zuni*
SILVERSMITH/LAPIDARIST: Specializes in flat stone tear drop clusters with silver bb's. Creates her own designs. Learned from her husband and began producing ca. 1970. Works independently from her husband.
HALLMARK: Stamped shared initials in Gothic print. Husband uses the same mark although they work separately.
Spouse is Alvin Kiyite.
[Levy:1980:50]

ADK

KIYOOMIA, JOE   *Navajo*
SILVERSMITH:
HALLMARK: Stamped initials in Gothic print.

J.K.

KLIMAJ, STEPHEN J.   *Unknown*
SILVERSMITH:
HALLMARK: Stamped signature in personalized 1/16 script. Stamp first used in 1982.

Stefan L. Klimaj

KNOWLES, MEL   *Anglo*
SILVERSMITH:
HALLMARK: Stamped symbol.
From Santa Fe, New Mexico region.

KOINVA, ELLIOT *Hopi*
SILVERSMITH: Specializes in silver overlay. Began producing in 1974.
HALLMARK: Stamped initials in Gothic print. Stamped symbol of an arrow and a sun. Brother of Lauren Koinva.
[Wright:1982:94]

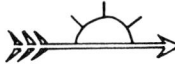   EK

KOINVA, LAUREN *Hopi*
SILVERSMITH: Specialized in silver overlay. Began producing in 1973 and continued till his death in 1981.
HALLMARK: Stamped initials in Gothic print. Stamped symbol of a rattle (3/32 x 1/8").
Brother is Elliot Koinva.
[Wright:1982:94]

   LK

KOMALESTEWA, ALTON *Hopi*
POTTER:
HALLMARK: Painted and fired kilt decoration.

KOMAYOUSE (QUIMAYOUSIE), HERBERT *Hopi*
SILVERSMITH: Specializes in silver overlay. Began producing in 1948.
HALLMARK: Stamped symbol of a spider.
[Wright:1982:85]

KORUH, HAROLD *Hopi*
SILVERSMITH: Specialized in silver overlay. Began producing in 1948. Sporadic production.
HALLMARK: Stamped symbol of a star.
[Wright:1982:84]

KOYAYESVA, LAWRENCE *Hopi*
SILVERSMITH: Specializes in silver overlay. Began producing in 1975.
HALLMARK: Stamped symbol of a ceremonial wand first used in 1975. Second stamp of initials in Gothic print.

LK

KRAUS, ADOLF *Anglo (?)*
SILVERSMITH:
HALLMARK: Stamped initials in 1/16 Gothic print. Stamp first used in 1982.
From Yuma, Arizona region.

AK

KREPPS, DON *Anglo (?)*
SILVERSMITH:
HALLMARK: Stamp of personalized initials in 3/16 print joined and offset. Stamp first appeared in 1985.

KUWANVAYOUMA, KENNETH *Hopi*
SILVERSMITH: Specialized in silver overlay. Began producing in 1970.
HALLMARK: Stamped symbol of a corn plant 3/16" square. Chiseled initials.
[Wright:1982:90]

KYASYOUSIE, RAYMOND *Hopi*
SILVERSMITH: Specializes in silver overlay. Began producing in 1975.
HALLMARK: Stamped joined and offset initials in personalized print.
Brother is Tony Kyasyousie.
[Wright:1982:97]

KYASYOUSIE, TONY *Hopi*
SILVERSMITH: Specializes in silver overlay. Began producing in 1969.
HALLMARK: Stamped symbol of a rabbit stick first used in 1969. Also uses stamp of offset initials in Gothic print and stamps of personalized and joined initials.
Brother of Raymond Kyasyousie.
[Wright:1982:91]

   T_K   TK   TK

L ? JOHNSON *Navajo*
SILVERSMITH: Smith for Montana Mining Company.
HALLMARK: Stamped given name in 1/16 Gothic print. Stamp first used in 1975.

JOHNSON L

LAAHTY, ANDREW *Zuni*
SILVERSMITH/LAPIDARIST: Specializes in channel and mosaic inlay. Sun Chief designs.
HALLMARK: Stamped symbol with initials in Gothic print set on rectangular plate.
Morris Laahte is his father. Name has numerous spellings.

LAAHTE, MORRIS *Zuni*
SILVERSMITH/LAPIDARIST: Specializes in channel and mosaic inlay and general silversmithing.
HALLMARK: Stamped symbols of a sun in more or less detail set on plates about half the time. Wide variety in the mark. Mark is shared by spouse.
Spouse is Sadie Laahte. Son is Andrew Laahty. The name is

interpreted in many ways and may appear as Lahate, Lottie, Latie, Laate, Laahti, Leathy, etc.
[King:1976:10]

LAAHTE, SADIE *Zuni*
SILVERSMITH/LAPIDARIST: Specializes in channel and mosaic inlay as well as wide range of silver pieces.
HALLMARK: Stamped symbols of a sun in more or less detail, set on plates about half of the time. Wide variety in the mark. Mark shared with spouse.
Spouse is Morris Laahte. Son is Andrew Laahty.
[King:1976:10]

LAATE, LARRY *Zuni*
SILVERSMITH/LAPIDARIST: Specializes in carved, channel, and mosaic inlay as well as needlepoint. Designs are both geometric and realistic such as etched and carved ducks.
HALLMARK: Stamped misaligned initials in Gothic print.
[Bell:1977:17]

LAATE, LYGATIE *Zuni*
SILVERSMITH:
HALLMARK: Stamped surname and initials in 1/16 Gothic print. Stamp first used in 1975.

L.EL.LAATE

LABAN, SAMUEL N. *Hopi*
SILVERSMITH: Specialized in silver overlay. Began producing in 1948 and continued until his death in 1955.
HALLMARK: Stamped symbol of a Sun's face.
[Wright:1982:86]

LACKEY, AL *Anglo*
TURQUOISE DEALER:
HALLMARK: Stamped joined initials in personalized print. From Kingman, Arizona region.

7L

LACONSELLO, NANCY HALOO *Zuni*
SILVERSMITH/LAPIDARIST: Specialist in mosaic and channel inlay. Bird motifs. Learned from her father and began producing in 1972. She does the stone work while her husband does the metal work and finishing.
HALLMARK: Stamped combined initials of her spouse's and her own. Engraved signature of both their given names.
Spouse is Ruddell Laconsello. Father is Jake Haloo. Sisters are Dolly Banteah and Lolita Natachu. Half brother is Jake Livingston.
[Levy:1980:18]

RNL   *Ruddell & Nancy*

LACONSELLO, RUDDELL *Zuni*
SILVERSMITH/LAPIDARIST/PAINTER: Specializes in mosaic and channel inlay, also etched mosaic with bird motifs. Learned his craft from his wife. Began producing in 1977. He does the cutwork and finishing while his wife does the stone work.
HALLMARK: Stamped combined initials of his wife's and his own. Engraved signature of both their given names.
Spouse is Nancy Haloo Laconsello.
[Levy:1980:18]

RNL   *Ruddell & Nancy*

LAHI, JULIE O. *Zuni*
SILVERSMITH:
HALLMARK: Stamped full name in 1/16 Gothic print. Stamp first used in 1976.

JULIE O. LAHI

LAKELA, NICK *Zuni*
GOLDSMITH:
HALLMARK: Stamped initials in Gothic print.

N.L.

LALIO, EVELYN *Zuni*
SILVERSMITH:
HALLMARK: Stamped surname in 1/16 Gothic print. Stamp first used in 1980.

E.LALIO

LALIO, LAVONNE *Zuni*
SILVERSMITH/LAPIDARIST:
HALLMARK: Stamped initials in Gothic print.

LL

LALIO, LENA *Zuni*
SILVERSMITH/LAPIDARIST: Specializes in needlepoint combined with round stones in geometric designs. Began producing in 1963.
HALLMARK: Engraved signature of surname and initial.
[Bell:1975:21]

L. LALIO

LALIO, S.M. *Zuni*
SILVERSMITH/LAPIDARIST: Pieceworker for Winfield.
HALLMARK: Stamped surname in 1/16 Gothic print. Stamp first used in 1976.

S.M.LALIO

LAMON, SARA *Zuni*
SILVERSMITH:
HALLMARK: Stamped full name in 1/16 Gothic print. Stamp first used in 1976.

SARA LAMON

LAMSON, SHANNON *Hopi*

SILVERSMITH: Specializes in silver overlay.
HALLMARK: Stamped symbols of a quarter sun. One in 1/16 and the other in 1/8" sizes. Both used first in 1984.

LAMY, JULALITA *Zuni*
SILVERSMITH/LAPIDARIST: Specializes in mosaic inlay kachina figures.
HALLMARK: Engraved initials and name in personalized print.
[Bell:1976:18]

J.L.   *J. Lamy* ZUNI

LANTE, DORIS *Navajo*
SILVERSMITH/LAPIDARIST: Specializes in inlay and cast work.
HALLMARK: Stamped symbol set on a plate.
Sister is Sadie Lante.

LANYATE, HESSER L. *Zuni*
SILVERSMITH/LAPIDARIST: Specializes in mosaic inlay of Knifewing and other stylized birds.
HALLMARK: Engraved name and initials in personalized printing.
Sister is Roberta Banketewa.
[Bell:1977:26]

H.L. LANYATE

LARGO, B ? *Navajo*
SILVERSMITH:
HALLMARK: Stamped surname in 1/16 Gothic print. Stamp first used in 1973.
From Ft. Wingate, New Mexico region.

B. LARGO

LARGO, D.F. *Navajo*
SILVERSMITH: Smith for Bernie Dominguez.
HALLMARK: Stamped surname with double initials in 1/16 Gothic print first used in 1973. Second stamp in 1/16 Gothic print with single initial used first in 1976.
From Thoreau, New Mexico region.

D.F. LARGO   D. LARGO

LARGO, ERN ? *Navajo*
SILVERSMITH: Smith for Bernie Dominguez.
HALLMARK: Stamped surname and part of given name in 1/16 Gothic print. First used in 1975.

ERN LARGO

LARGO, GILBERT *Navajo*
SILVERSMITH/GOLDSMITH:
HALLMARK: Stamped initials in 1/16 Gothic print. Stamp first used in 1977. Shared with spouse.
Spouse is Mary Largo.
From Thoreau, New Mexico region.

M.&G.L.

LARGO, HARRISON *Navajo*
SILVERSMITH: Smith for Bernie Dominguez.
HALLMARK: Stamped full name in 1/16 Gothic print. Stamp first used in 1975.

HARRISON LARGO

LARGO, MARY *Navajo*
SILVERSMITH/GOLDSMITH:
HALLMARK: Stamped initials shared with spouse in two lines. 1/16 Gothic print first used in 1977.
Spouse is Gilbert Largo.
From Thoreau, New Mexico region.

M.&G.L.

LARGO, MAX *Navajo*
SILVERSMITH: Smith for Bernie Dominguez.
HALLMARK: Stamped full name in 1/16 Gothic print. First used in 1975.

MAX LARGO

LARGO, RITA *Navajo*
SILVERSMITH: Smith for Atkinson Trading Company.
HALLMARK: Stamped surname in 1/16 Gothic print first used in 1980.

R. LARGO

LAROCHE, ROSE *Unknown*
SILVERSMITH:
HALLMARK: Stamped signature in 1/16 script. First used in 1980.

Rose La Roche

LARY, JINNY *Navajo*
SILVERSMITH:
HALLMARK: Stamped initials in Gothic print.

JL

LASILOO, MILTON *Zuni*
SILVERSMITH/LAPIDARIST:
HALLMARK: Stamped joined initials in Gothic print.

M

LAWEKA, BILLIE *Zuni*
SILVERSMITH/LAPIDARIST: Specializes in inlay, petit point, and cluster work. Learned from his grandparents. Began producing in 1968. He does the metal work and his wife does the stone work.
HALLMARK: Stamped given names of his wife and himself. Stamps first appeared in 1974. One differs from the other only in the familiarity of his given name.
Spouse is Lucinda Laweka.
[Levy:1980:54]

BILL & LOU   BILLIE & LOU
ZUNI   ZUNI

LAWEKA, LORRAINE *Zuni*
SILVERSMITH/LAPIDARIST: Specializes in inlay, cluster work, needlepoint, and "snake eye" settings. Learned from her mother. Began producing in 1964. Works with her sister. Lorraine does the stone work.

HALLMARK: Engraved signatures of her sister's and her own surnames.
Sister is Shirley Natewa.
[Levy:1980:44]

S. Natewa & L. Laweka

LAWEKA, LUCINDA *Zuni*
SILVERSMITH/LAPIDARIST: Specializes in inlay, petit point, and cluster work. Learned from her husband's grandparents. Began producing in 1968. Husband does the metalwork and she does the stone work.
HALLMARK: Stamped given name of her husband and her own given name. Stamps first appeared in 1974. One differs from the other only in the familiarity of her husband's name.
Spouse is Bill Laweka.
[Levy:1980:54]

BILL & LOU   BILLIE & LOU
ZUNI   ZUNI

LECONELLE, NANCY *Zuni*
SILVERSMITH:
HALLMARK: Stamped initials in Gothic print.

NRL

LEE, ALLISON *Navajo*
SILVERSMITH: Smith for Steve Skinner.
HALLMARK: Stamped surname in 1/16 Gothic print first appeared in 1976. Second stamp of surname in 1/32 Gothic print appeared first in 1977.
From Mexican Springs, New Mexico region.

A. LEE

LEE, ANGELA *Navajo*
SILVERSMITH: Smith for Bill Hall, John S. Skinner, and Steve Skinner at different times.
HALLMARK: Stamped full name in 1/16 Gothic print, first used in 1974. Second stamp of surname in 1/16 Gothic print, first used in 1976.
From Prewitt, New Mexico region.

ANGELA LEE   A. LEE

LEE, ANNIE *Navajo*
SILVERSMITH: Smith for Atkinson Trading Company before 1980.
HALLMARK: Stamped full name of Louise Lee is used by several individuals including Ella Mae and Louise Lee. Name is in 1/16 Gothic print.

LOUISE LEE

LEE, B ? *Navajo*
SILVERSMITH: Smith for Indian Hammers, also for Atkinson Trading Company since 1982.
HALLMARK: Stamped surname in 1/16 Gothic print first appeared in 1976.

B. LEE

LEE, CECIL *Navajo*
SILVERSMITH: Smith for Felix's Indian Jewelry.
HALLMARK: Stamped surname in 1/16 Gothic print, first appeared in 1977.

C. LEE

LEE, CLARENCE *Navajo*
SILVERSMITH: Specializes in applique goblets, etc. Began producing ca. 1978.
HALLMARK: Stamped initials in Gothic print. Stamp of misaligned initials with symbol 1/4" in size first appeared in 1982. Sisters are Sylvia, Cheryl, and Erica Lee.
From Tohatchi-Bitter Water, New Mexico region.

CCL   LE

LEE, DANIEL *Navajo*
SILVERSMITH: Smith for Steve Skinner.
HALLMARK: Stamped full name in 1/16 Gothic print, first used in 1976.

DANIEL LEE

LEE, DORIS *Navajo*
SILVERSMITH: Smith for Steve Skinner.
HALLMARK: Stamped full name in 1/16 Gothic print, first used in 1976.

DORIS LEE

LEE, ELLA MAE *Navajo*
SILVERSMITH: Smith for Atkinson Trading Company before 1980.
HALLMARK: Stamped full name of Louise Lee is used by Annie and Louise Lee also, in 1/16 Gothic print.

LOUISE LEE

LEE, GEORGE *Navajo*
SILVERSMITH: Smith for Atkinson Trading Company.
HALLMARK: Stamped full name in 1/16 Gothic print, first used in 1974. Second stamp of surname in Gothic print.

GEORGE LEE   G. LEE

LEE, IRENE *Navajo*
SILVERSMITH: Specializes in silver beads.
HALLMARK: Stamped initials in Gothic print.
From Window Rock, Arizona region.

IL

LEE, JAMESON *Navajo*
SILVERSMITH: Smith for New Mexico Jewelry in 1974, for Steve Skinner later in the same year and again in 1976.
HALLMARK: Stamped full name in 1/16 Gothic print, first used in 1974. Second stamp of full name in 3/32 Gothic print also used first in 1974.

JAMESON LEE   JAMESON LEE

LEE, LOUISE *Navajo*
SILVERSMITH: Smith for Atkinson Trading Company before 1980.
HALLMARK: Stamped full name in 1/16 Gothic print. Shared with Annie Lee, and Ella Mae Lee.

LOUISE LEE

LEE, L ? *Navajo*
SILVERSMITH: Smith for Indian Hammers and for Atkinson Trading Company in 1980.
HALLMARK: Stamped surname in 1/16 Gothic print, first used in 1976.

L.LEE

LEE, S ? *Navajo*
SILVERSMITH: Smith for Felix Indian Jewelry.
HALLMARK: Stamped surname in 1/16 Gothic print, first used in 1977.

S.LEE

LEE, SAMUEL *Navajo*
SILVERSMITH: Smith for Steve Skinner.
HALLMARK: Stamped full name in 1/16 Gothic print, first appeared in 1976.

SAMUEL LEE

LEE, SHIRLEY *Navajo*
SILVERSMITH: Smith for Steve Skinner.
HALLMARK: Stamped full name in 1/16 Gothic print.

SHIRLEY LEE

LEE, STAN *Navajo*
SILVERSMITH:
HALLMARK: Stamped surname in 1/16 Gothic print, first appeared in 1975.
From Chambers. Arizona region.

S.LEE

LEE, TIMOTHY *Navajo*
SILVERSMITH:
HALLMARK: Stamped full name in two lines of 1/16 Gothic print. First appeared in 1979.
From Mentmore, New Mexico region.

TIMOTHY
LEE

LEE, TOM *Navajo*
SILVERSMITH:
HALLMARK: Stamped initials in 1/16 Gothic print, first appeared in 1974.
From Gallup, New Mexico region.

T.L.

LEE, VIRGINIA *Navajo*
SILVERSMITH: Smith for Atkinson Trading Company.
HALLMARK: Stamped surname in 1/16 Gothic print, first used in 1985.

V.LEE

LEEKELA, ANSON *Zuni*
SILVERSMITH/LAPIDARIST: Specializes in plain geometric inlay. Learned from Stephen Siutza. Began producing in 1976. Shares the work with his wife.
HALLMARK: Stamped initials of his wife's name and his own.
Spouse is Deborah Leekela
[Levy:1980:31]

ADL

LEEKELA, DEBORAH *Zuni*
SILVERSMITH/LAPIDARIST: Specializes in plain geometric channel inlay using designs by Stephen Siutza. Learned from her husband. Began producing in 1976. Shares the work with her husband.
HALLMARK: Stamped initials of her husband's and her own name.
Spouse is Anson Leekela.
[Levy:1980:31]

ADL

LEEKETY, D ? *Zuni*
SILVERSMITH: Smith for Atkinson Trading Company.
HALLMARK: Stamped surname in 1/16 Gothic print, first used in 1974.

D.LEEKITY

LEEKITY, CORINNE *Zuni*
SILVERSMITH/LAPIDARIST:
HALLMARK: Many variations of the initials C and L which are stamped separately resulting in different placements. Shared with spouse.
Spouse is Curtis Leekity.

LEEKITY, CURTIS *Zuni*
SILVERSMITH/LAPIDARIST:
HALLMARK: Many variations of the initials C and L which are stamped separately resulting in different placements. Shared with spouse.
Spouse is Corinne Leekity.

LEEKITY, EDWARD *Zuni*
SILVERSMITH:
HALLMARK: Stamped initials in Gothic print.

E.L.

LEEKITY, EVA *Zuni*
SILVERSMITH/LAPIDARIST:
HALLMARK: Engraved signature and tribe.

Eva Leekity
Zuni

LEEKITY, GEORGE *Zuni*
SILVERSMITH/GOLDSMITH/LAPIDARIST: Specializes in cast work with settings. Uses adaptations of his wife's father's designs. Learned from his wife's father. Began producing in 1972. Works independently from his wife.
HALLMARK: Stamped surname with shared initials of his wife's and his own. The stamp was first used in 1977.
Spouse is Lupeta Leekity, father-in-law is Horace Iule.
[Levy:1980:62]

G.&L.

LEEKITY, LUPETA *Zuni*
SILVERSMITH/LAPIDARIST/GOLDSMITH: Specializes in cast work with settings, usually crosses. Uses adaptations of her father's designs. Learned from her mother and father and began producing in 1972. Works independently from her husband.
HALLMARK: Stamped surname with shared initials of her husband's and her own. The stamp was first used in 1977.
Spouse is George Leekity, her parents are Horace and Lupe Iule, her brother Phillip Iule.
[Levy:1980:62-3]

G.&L.

LEEKITY, MARY *Zuni*
SILVERSMITH/LAPIDARIST: Specializes in small round settings in delicate jewelry. Uses her own designs. Learned from her husband's mother and began producing in 1970. Husband does the metal work and she does the stone work.
HALLMARK: Stamped initials in 1/16 Gothic print. Shared initials.
Spouse is Olson Leekity.
[Levy:1980:35]

O.M.L.

LEEKITY, NANCY *Zuni*
SILVERSMITH/LAPIDARIST:
HALLMARK: Stamped initials of husband's and wife's initials with enlarged surname initial. Stamped symbol also.
Spouse is Paul Leekity.

LEEKITY, NORA *Zuni*
SILVERSMITH/LAPIDARIST/GOLDSMITH: Specializes in mosaic inlay and channel inlay. Designs are usually horses.
HALLMARK: Engraved signature and tribe.
[Bell:1975:39]

NORA LEEKITY-ZUNI

LEEKITY, OLSON *Zuni*
SILVERSMITH/LAPIDARIST: Specializes in small rounded sets ("snake eyes") in delicate jewelry. Uses his own designs. Learned from his mother and began producing in 1970. He does the metal work and his wife the stone work.
HALLMARK: Stamped initials in 1/16 Gothic print. Shared initials.
Spouse is Mary Leekity.
[Levy:1980:35]

O.M.L.

LEEKITY, PAUL *Zuni*
SILVERSMITH/LAPIDARIST:
HALLMARK: Stamped initials of wife's and his own with enlarged surname initial. Stamped symbol also.
Spouse is Nancy Leekity.

LEEKYA, BERNICE *Zuni*
SILVERSMITH/LAPIDARIST: Specializes in channel inlay.
HALLMARK: Stamped initals of her husband's and her own name. One stamp with enlarged surname initial is set vertically, the other is the same but in italics.
Spouse is Robert Leekya.

R|B

LEEKYA, ROBERT *Zuni*
SILVERSMITH/LAPIDARIST: Specializes in channel inlay. Began producing in 1965.
HALLMARK: Stamped initials of his wife's and his own name. One stamp with enlarged surname initial is set vertically, the other is in italics. Also uses stamps of a single initial emphasized by symbol or other means.
Spouse is Bernice Leekya.

R R

LEEKYA, VIRGIL *Zuni*
Fetish maker:
HALLMARK: Stamped or cut mark is a combination of V and L and does not seem to be a crane track.

LEMENTINE (or LEMENTO), ROLAND J. *Zuni*
SILVERSMITH/LAPIDARIST:
HALLMARK: Stamped initials of his wife's and his own in 1/16 Gothic print. Stamp first used in 1982.
Spouse is Julie Lemento.

RJL

LEMENTINO, ELMER *Zuni*
SILVERSMITH/LAPIDARIST: Specializes in small teardrop or "snake eyes" set in flower clusters. Uses his own designs. Learned from his mother and began producing in 1970. Both he and his wife do the metal work and divide the stone work.
HALLMARK: Stamped initials in Gothic print.
Spouse is Mary Lementino, mother is Susan Lemento.
[Levy:1980:58]

EL

LEMENTINO, EVANS *Zuni*
SILVERSMITH:
HALLMARK: Stamped initials in 1/16 Gothic print, first used in 1984.

ECL

LEMENTINO, MARY *Zuni*
SILVERSMITH/LAPIDARIST: Specializes in small tear drop or "snake eye" flower clusters. Uses her own designs. Learned from her husband's mother and began producing in 1970. Both she and her husband do the metal work and divide the stone work.
HALLMARK: Stamped initials in Gothic print.
Spouse is Elmer Lementino.
[Levy:1980:58]

EL

LEMENTO, JULIE *Zuni*
SILVERSMITH/LAPIDARIST:
HALLMARK: Stamped initials of her husband's and her own in 1/16 Gothic print. Stamp first used in 1982.
Spouse is Roland Lementino or Lemento.

RJL

LEONARD, SANDRA *Unknown*
GOLDSMITH:
HALLMARK: Stamped initials in Gothic print.

S.L.

LEOTA, ? *Unknown*
SILVERSMITH:
HALLMARK: Stamped single initial and symbol.

L

LESANSEE, BLAKE *Zuni*
SILVERSMITH/LAPIDARIST: Specializes in inlaid owls. Began producing in 1957. Works with his wife.
HALLMARK: Signed with an engraver, they are variations of the joined initials of his wife's and his own name.
Spouse is Velma Lesansee, daughter is Corinne Shack.
[Bell:1977:4]

VB

LESANSEE, VELMA *Zuni*
SILVERSMITH/LAPIDARIST: Specializes in mosaic inlay owls. Began producing in 1957. Works with her husband.
HALLMARK: Signed with an engraver, they are variations of the joined initials of her husband's and her own name.
Spouse is Blake Lesansee, daughter is Corinne Shack.
[Bell:1977:4]

VB

LESLIE, RENA *Hopi/Tewa*
POTTER: Began producing in 1937.
HALLMARK: Painted and fired symbol of a yellow cloud.

LEW, MARY S. or **AVERY, MARY SMITH** *Navajo*
SILVERSMITH: Smith for Atkinson Trading Company.
HALLMARK: Stamped full name in 1/16 Gothic print, first used in 1974. Apparently uses either name interchangeably.

MARY S. LEW

LEWIS, AL *Navajo*
SILVERSMITH:
HALLMARK: Stamped full name in 1/16 Gothic print, first used in 1974.
From Ft. Wingate, New Mexico region.

AL LEWIS

LEWIS, ART *Navajo (?)*
SILVERSMITH: Specializes in Yei or kachina-like figures set in bas relief with turquoise.
HALLMARK: Stamped symbol of arrow and ?.

LEWIS, AUSTIN *Navajo*
SILVERSMITH:
HALLMARK: Stamped combined initials in personalized print 1/4" square. Stamp first used in 1973.
From Seba Dalkai, Arizona region.

LEWIS, CHARLES *Navajo*
SILVERSMITH: Smith for Woodard and Atkinson Trading Company. Producing in 1971.
HALLMARK: Stamped surname in 1/16 Gothic print, first used in 1976. Also uses stamped initials in personalized print. This latter stamp is hand made.

C.LEWIS   CL

LEWIS, EFFIE *Zuni*
SILVERSMITH: Specializes in overlay with settings.
HALLMARK: Stamped initials in Gothic print.

EL

LEWIS, ERVIN *Navajo*
SILVERSMITH:
HALLMARK: Stamped initials in 1/16 Gothic print. Stamp first used in 1973.
From Prewitt, New Mexico region.

E. L.

LEWIS, J.E. *Navajo*
SILVERSMITH:
HALLMARK: Stamped surname with joined initials in 1/16 Gothic print, first used in 1977.
From Chinle, Arizona region.

JE LEWIS

LEWIS, J. *Navajo*
SILVERSMITH:
HALLMARK: Stamped surname in 1/16 Gothic print, first used in 1974.
From Ft. Wingate, New Mexico region.

J.J.LEWIS

LEWIS, JAMES *Navajo (?)*
SILVERSMITH: Smith for Biligaana.
HALLMARK: Stamped name of shop in 1/32 script, first used in 1978. Probably the shop mark rather than the craftsman.

Biligaana

LEWIS, JIM *Navajo*
SILVERSMITH: Smith for Montana Mining Company.
HALLMARK: Stamped full name with second line of Indian Hand Made Sterling Silver in 1/16 Gothic print. First used in 1974.

JIM LEWIS
  IHMSS

LEWIS, JIMMIE *Navajo*
SILVERSMITH:

HALLMARK: Stamped surname in 1/16 Gothic print. Stamp first appeared in 1976.
From Winslow, Arizona region.

J.LEWIS

LEWIS, MANUEL *Navajo*
SILVERSMITH: Benchsmith at the White Hogan.
HALLMARK: Stamped joined initials in Gothic print.

ML

LEWIS, ROGER A. ("BOYD") *Navajo*
SILVERSMITH: Smith for Montana Mining Company.
HALLMARK: Stamped surname and second line of Indian Hand Made Sterling Silver in 1/16 Gothic print. Stamp. first used in 1973.

R.A.LEWIS
IHMSS

LEWIS, T.A. *Navajo*
SILVERSMITH: Smith for Montana Mining Company.
HALLMARK: Stamped surname and second line of Indian Hand Made Sterling Silver in 1/16 Gothic print.Stamp first used in 1974.

T.A.LEWIS
IHMSS

LEYBA, RINNIE *Zuni (?)*
SILVERSMITH:
HALLMARK: Stamped initials in 1/16 script, first used in 1984.
From Albuquerque, New Mexico region.

LIDASE, MATTHEW *Zuni*
SILVERSMITH:
HALLMARK: Stamped initial is shared with wife's in Gothic print.
Spouse is Rosemary Lidase.

M&R

LIDASE, ROSEMARY *Zuni*
SILVERSMITH:
HALLMARK: Stamped initial shared with husband's in Gothic print.
Spouse is Matthew Lidase.

M&R

LIGHTFEATHER, MELODY *Unknown*
COPYIST:
HALLMARK: Painted or drawn hallmark of a feather. Claims various tribal affiliations including Pima and Jemez but is probably none of these and possibly is not even Indian. Produces baskets, sculptures, and paintings that are not originals.

LIGHTFOOT, BUDDY see **EDMUNDSON**

LINCOLN, AMBROSE or **ROANHORSE, AMBROSE** *Navajo*
SILVERSMITH: Specialized in the old styles of Navajo jewelry. Taught by Wilfred Jones. Became a well-known teacher and taught in Santa Fe Indian School. Many noted silversmiths were his pupils.
HALLMARK: Stamped symbol of a keystone or broken arrowpoint with an A inside it.
From Ft. Wingate, New Mexico region.

LINCOLN, BENSON *Navajo*
SILVERSMITH:
HALLMARK: Stamped surname in 1/16 Gothic print, first used in 1974.
From Gallup, New Mexico region.

B.LINCOLN

LINCOLN, ELAINE *Navajo*
SILVERSMITH:
HALLMARK: Stamped initials in Gothic print.

E.L.

LINCOLN, FRANCIS THOMAS *Navajo*
SILVERSMITH: Specializes in overlay with turquoise inlaid settings.
HALLMARK: Stamped joined and misaligned initials in personalized print.

F

LINCOLN, HERMAN H. *Navajo*
SILVERSMITH:
HALLMARK: Stamped initials in 3/32 Gothic print, first used in 1975.

H.H.L.

LINCOLN, MARY (see **MARY MARIE LINCOLN** also) *Navajo*
SILVERSMITH:
HALLMARK: Stamped script initial M in personalized print. This mark may belong to Mary Marie Lincoln or be the same individual.

LINCOLN, MARY MARIE *Navajo*
SILVERSMITH/LAPIDARIST:
HALLMARK: Stamped given names in 1/32 Gothic print set on a plate.
[The individual above may be the same.
Brother is Lee Yazzie.

MARY MARIE

LINCOLN, RANDOLPH *Navajo*
SILVERSMITH:
HALLMARK: Stamped initial of given name in personalized script.

R

LINCOLN, ROSE *Navajo*
SILVERSMITH:

HALLMARK: Stamped initials in Gothic print.

RL

LINKIN, TULLY *Unknown*
SILVERSMITH:
HALLMARK: Stamped initials in Gothic print set on a plate.

[TL]

LISTER, D.K. *Navajo*
SILVERSMITH:
HALLMARK: Stamped initials in 1/16 Gothic print, first used in 1981. Stamped surname in 1/16 Gothic print, first appeared in 1981. From Indian Wells, Arizona region.

DKL   D.K. LISTER

LISTER, ERNEST C. *Navajo (?)*
SILVERSMITH:
HALLMARK: Stamped full name in 1/16 Gothic print, first used in 1983. Second special stamp of personalized initials in 1/16 print first appeared in 1984.
From Page, Arizona region.

ERNEST C. LISTER   E

LITTLE, JAMES *Navajo*
SILVERSMITH: Specializes in contemporary jewelry inspired by traditional insights. Worked in Flagstaff shops for a period before beginning production on his own ca. 1979.
HALLMARK: Stamped arrowhead with initials inside. Also uses four bars on some of the pieces.
Deaf as a child he survived by polishing silver in Flagstaff shops until noted by the Birkenhoffs from California. His deafness mitigated, he has taught himself skills in business management, social life, and craftsmanship.

LIVINGSTON, B ? *Navajo*
SILVERSMITH: Smith for Atkinson Trading Company.
HALLMARK: Stamped surname in 1/16 Gothic print, first seen in 1976.

B. LIVINGSTON

LIVINGSTON, JACOB I. (Jake) *Navajo*
SILVERSMITH: Specializes in contemporary pieces using inlay. Began producing Zuni style inlay in 1972.
HALLMARK: Stamped surname in 1/16 Gothic print first used in 1974. Second stamp of given name in 1/16 Gothic print first used in 1974. Stamp of surname in 1/16 script, first used in 1975. Stamp of surname with joined initials in 1/16 Gothic print used first in 1979. Half sisters are Nancy Laconsello, Lolita Natachu, Dolly Banteah. From Houck, Arizona region.

J.I. LIVINGSTON   JAKE L.

J-I LIVINGSTON

LIVINGSTON, LORENZO *Navajo*
SILVERSMITH: Began producing in 1972.

HALLMARK: Stamped offset initials in Gothic print.

L_L

LIVINGSTON, MARY *Navajo*
SILVERSMITH/LAPIDARIST: Specializes in mosaic inlay in Zuni style.
HALLMARK: Stamped initials in Gothic print.

ML

LIZER, DAVID *Navajo*
SILVERSMITH:
HALLMARK: Stamped surname in 1/16 Gothic print, first used in 1986.
From St. Michaels, Arizona region.

D. LIZER

LOLOMA, CHARLES *Hopi*
SILVERSMITH/GOLDSMITH/LAPIDARIST: Specializes in all techniques of fashion jewelry. Executes his own designs. Beginning in ceramics he started producing silver work ca. 1955. The most widely known Hopi craftsman.
HALLMARK: Stamped stylized print of his surname in two forms, the earliest being with the M separate from the A. The name may be either stamped or cast.
[Wright:1982:68]

LOMADAPKI (JOSHWESEOMA), ROBERT *Hopi*
SILVERSMITH: Specializes in contemporary jewelry using overlay in most of his pieces. Began producing in 1964.
HALLMARK: Stamped, cast, or engraved surname with Hopi name.
[Wright:1982:97]

LOMADAPKI
JOSHWESEOMA

LOMAHEFTEWA, MARVIN C. *Hopi*
SILVERSMITH: Specialized in silver overlay. Began producing in 1976, deceased in 1985.
HALLMARK: Stamped initials in Gothic print. Stamped initials with symbol of man's hair knot. Stamp of man's hair knot alone. Stamp of symbols of hair knot, spider, and lightning combined.
[Wright:1982:97]

MCL

LOMAHEFTEWA, VALJEAN see **JOSHEVEMA, VALJEAN**

LOMAHONGVA, EDWARD (PHILLIPS) *Hopi*
SILVERSMITH: Specializes in silver overlay. Began producing in 1979.
HALLMARK: Stamped symbol of a road runner head. Stamped initials in Gothic print.
[Wright:1982:97]

E.L.

LOMAHUKVU, CORTEZ *Hopi*
SILVERSMITH: Produces silver overlay. Began in 1948 and ceased by 1951.
HALLMARK: Stamped symbol of the head of the Elder War God.
[Wright:1982:86]

LOMAKIMA, CHARLES T. *Hopi*
SILVERSMITH: Specializes in silver overlay. Began producing in 1948 and continued sporadically for two or three years.
HALLMARK: Stamped symbol of an Antelope rattle.
[Wright:1982:84]

LOMAKIMA, LORNA *Hopi/Tewa*
POTTER: Began producing ca. 1970.
HALLMARK: Painted and fired larkspur like her mother's mark but with the addition of her initials. Second mark is a single flower with her initials.
Mother is Sadie Adams.

LOMATEMA, LEWIS see **LOMAYESTEWA, LEWIS**

LOMAWAIMA, KIRKLAND *Hopi*
SILVERSMITH: Produced silver overlay. Began in 1948 but did not continue for long.
HALLMARK: Stamped symbol of a squash.
[Wright:1982:87]

LOMAWAIMA, PATRICK *Hopi*
SILVERSMITH: Specialized in silver overlay. Began producing in 1965. Sporadic production in recent years.
HALLMARK: Stamped symbol of a snow flake. Stamped symbol of a snow cloud. Stamped initials in Gothic print.
[Wright:1982:89]

LOMAWAIMA, PHILLIP *Hopi*
SILVERSMITH: Specializes in silver overlay.
HALLMARK: Stamped symbol of a cloud.

LOMAWYWISA see **KABOTIE, MICHAEL**

LOMAYAKTEWA, STARLIE *Hopi*
SILVERSMITH: Produced silver overlay. Began in 1948 then ceased shortly there after.
HALLMARK: Stamped symbol of a bluebird (3/32 x 1/4")
[Wright:1982:86]

LOMAYESTEWA, ARTHUR *Hopi*
SILVERSMITH: Specialized in silver overlay.
HALLMARK: Stamped symbol of a deer 1/8" square or stamped initials in Gothic print.
[Wright:1982:97]

LOMAYESTEWA, CLARENCE *Hopi*
SILVERSMITH: Specialized in silver overlay. Began producing in 1948 and continued until 1964 when he stopped.
HALLMARK: Stamped symbol of a kildeer track (3/32 x 1/8")
Brothers are Mark and McBride Lomayestewa.
[Wright:1982:85]

LOMAYESTEWA, DWAYNE *Hopi*
SILVERSMITH: Specializes in silver overlay.
HALLMARK: Stamped symbol of an antelope head. Stamped initials in Gothic print.

LOMAYESTEWA, JESSICA *Hopi*
SILVERSMITH:
HALLMARK: Stamped initials in 1/16 Gothic print. Stamp first used in 1977.
From New York City, New York.

LOMAYESTEWA, KENDRICK *Hopi*
SILVERSMITH: Specializes in silver overlay.
HALLMARK: Stamped symbol of a shooting star (1/8" sq.) Mark first used in 1985.

LOMAYESTEWA, MARCUS *Hopi*
SILVERSMITH: Specializes in silver overlay. Began producing in 1976.
HALLMARK: Stamped symbol of a flute or initials in Gothic print.
Father is McBride Lomayestewa.
[Wright:1982:97]

LOMAYESTEWA, MARK *Hopi*
SILVERSMITH: Specializes in silver overlay. Began producing in 1955.
HALLMARK: Stamped symbol of a snow cloud or initials in Gothic print.

Brothers are Clarence and McBride Lomayestewa.
[Wright:1982:87]

  ML

LOMAYESTEWA, McBRIDE   *Hopi*
SILVERSMITH: Specializes in silver overlay. Began producing in 1955.
HALLMARK: Stamped symbol of lightning (1/16 x 5/16"). Stamped initials in Gothic print.
Brothers are Clarence and Mark Lomayestewa.
[Wright;1982:87]

 MBL

LOMAYESTEWA, "NAN" or FERNANDA   *Hopi*
SILVERSMITH: Specializes in silver overlay.
HALLMARK: Stamped symbol of a sun's face or initials in Gothic print.

LOMAYESTEWA, STETSON   *Hopi*
SILVERSMITH: Specializes in silver overlay.
HALLMARK: Stamped symbol of a star and a moon or initials in Gothic print.

 SL

LOMAYESVA, LEWIS IRVING or LOMAY,   *Hopi*
SILVERSMITH: Specialized in cast work and silver overlay. Began producing in 1949 or earlier. Worked with Ambrose (Roanhorse) Lincoln and Frank Patania.
HALLMARK: Stamped sun symbols with letter L inside. Stamped symbols of snake with the letters LL in Gothic print. Uses the name Loma or Lomay as well as the above names.
[Wright:1982:82]

   LL

LONASEE, ELLEN   *Zuni*
SILVERSMITH/LAPIDARIST: Specializes in petit point in symmetrical balance with silver. Originates her own designs. Learned from watching relatives and began production in 1950. Her husband helps with the stone work.
HALLMARK: Stamped surname with shared initials in 1/16 Gothic print. Stamp shared with her husband and first used in 1975.
Spouse is Lawrence Lonasee.
[Levy:1980:52]

E.L.LONASEE

LONASEE, LAWRENCE   *Zuni*
SILVERSMITH/LAPIDARIST: Petit point with a balance of stones and silver. Learned from watching relatives and began producing in 1950. Uses wife's designs. Wife does the metal work and stone cutting; he does the remainder.
HALLMARK: Stamped surname with shared initials in 1/16 Gothic print. Stamp shared with wife and was first used in 1975.
Spouse is Ellen Lonasee.
[Levy:1980:52]

E.L.LONASEE

LONASEE, L.J.   *Zuni*
SILVERSMITH/LAPIDARIST:
HALLMARK: Stamped surname in 1/16 Gothic print first used in 1975. Engraved signature more recent.

L.J.LONASEE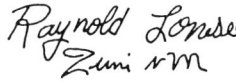

LONCASION, TERRY   *Zuni*
SILVERSMITH/LAPIDARIST:
HALLMARK: Stamped surname in 1/16 Gothic print first used in 1974.

T.LONCASION

LONESEE, RAYNOLD   *Zuni*
SILVERSMITH/LAPIDARIST:
HALLMARK: Engraved signature and tribal affiliation

Raynold Lonsee
Zuni NM

LONEWOLF, JOSEPH   *Santa Clara*
POTTER: Sgrafitto.
HALLMARK: Painted head of a wolf. Accompanied by registration marks indicating piece number and date.

LONG, ALBERT   *Blackfeet/Navajo*
SILVERSMITH:
HALLMARK: Stamped surname in 1/16 Gothic print, first used in 1973.
From either Cottonwood, Arizona or Manuelito, New Mexico regions.

A.LONG

LONG, ALFRED   *Navajo*
SILVERSMITH: Smith for Atkinson Trading Company.
HALLMARK: Stamped surname in 1/16 Gothic print, first used in 1974.

A.LONG

LONG, ALICE   *Navajo*
SILVERSMITH: Smith for Atkinson Trading Company.
HALLMARK: Stamped full name in 1/16 Gothic print, first used in 1974.

ALICE LONG

LONG, CLARENCE   *Navajo*
SILVERSMITH:
HALLMARK: Stamped full name in 1/16 Gothic print, first used in 1979.
From Grants, New Mexico region.

CLARENCE LONG

LONG, EMERSON   *Navajo*
SILVERSMITH:
HALLMARK: Stamped misaligned initials in personalized script

(3/16") inside a circle. This stamp was first used in 1977. From Gallup, New Mexico region.

LONG, HELEN *Navajo*
SILVERSMITH: Specializes in kachina-like figures, Yei figures, and eagle dancers.
HALLMARK: Stamped with initials in Gothic print. Initials in personalized print, or with a single H.
Spouse is Jim Long, brother is Kee John, sons are Phillip and Tom Long.

HL   H L   H

LONG, J. W. *Navajo*
SILVERSMITH: Smith for the Atkinson Trading Company.
HALLMARK: Stamped surname in 1/16 Gothic print. Stamp first appeared in 1975.

J.W.LONG

LONG, JIMMIE *Navajo*
SILVERSMITH:
HALLMARK: Stamped initials in Gothic print or symbol.
Spouse is Helen Long, sons are Phillip and Tom Long. Deceased.

J   JL

LONG, KEE *Navajo*
SILVERSMITH: Smith for Montana Mining Company.
HALLMARK: Stamped full name in 1/16 Gothic print, first appeared in 1975.

KEE LONG

LONG, MARY *Navajo*
SILVERSMITH: Smith for the Atkinson Trading Company.
HALLMARK: Stamped surname in 1/16 Gothic print. first used in 1985.

M.LONG

LONG, PHILLIP *Navajo*
SILVERSMITH: Specializes in kachina-like figures, Yeis, and dancers in the style of his mother.
HALLMARK: Stamped symbol with personalized joined initials.
Parents are Helen and Jimmie Long, brother is Tom Long.

LONG, R ? *Navajo*
SILVERSMITH: Smith for the Montana Mining Company.
HALLMARK: Stamped surname in 1/16 Gothic print, first used in 1974.

R.LONG

LONG, ROLAND *Unknown*
SILVERSMITH/LAPIDARIST: Specializes in inlaid work.
HALLMARK: Engraved signature.

Roland Long

LONG, ROSE HALEY *Navajo*
SILVERSMITH: Benchsmith for Woodard's in 1973 and for Atkinson Trading Company in 1974.
HALLMARK: Stamped full name in 1/16 Gothic print, first used in 1973. Stamped surname in 1/16 Gothic print used in 1974. Stamped full name in 1/16 Gothic print.

ROSE LONG   R.H.LONG   ROSE HALEY LONG

LONG, ROWLAND *Navajo*
SILVERSMITH:
HALLMARK: Stamped two-line initials and ENLAYED above them in 1/16 Gothic print, first used in 1982.
From Gallup, New Mexico region.

ENLAYED
R.L.L.

LONG, SAMMIE *Navajo*
SILVERSMITH:
HALLMARK: Stamped joined personalized script (1/8 x 1/16"). First used in 1972.
From Twin Lakes, New Mexico region.

LONG, TOM *Navajo*
SILVERSMITH:
HALLMARK: Stamped initials in 3/32 Gothic print, first used in 1972. Engraved full name in personalized print.
Parents are Helen and Jimmie Long, brother is Phillip Long.

T.L.   TOM LONG

LONJOSE, ANDREW *Zuni*
SILVERSMITH:
HALLMARK: Two-line stamped initials and tribal affiliation in 1/16 Gothic print. Stamp first used in 1978. Zuni in the stamp is spelled Suni.

AJL
SUNI

LONJOSE, EDITH *Zuni*
SILVERSMITH/LAPIDARIST: Specializes in carved and mosaic inlay, petit point, and cluster work. Learned from her father and began producing around 1950. Works with her husband.
HALLMARK: Stamped cloud symbol with enclosed initials and name in an arc above it. Letters are 1/32 Gothic print. Shares the stamp with her husband.
Spouse is Leonard Lonjose.
[Bell:1975:30,31]

LONJOSE, HELEN *Zuni*
SILVERSMITH:
HALLMARK: Stamped surname in 1/16 Gothic print, stamp first used in 1976.

H.LONJOSE

86 LONJOSE—LOVATO

LONJOSE, JANTA *Zuni*
SILVERSMITH:
HALLMARK: Stamped initials in Gothic print.

JL

LONJOSE, LEONARD *Zuni*
SILVERSMITH/LAPIDARIST: Specializes in carved and mosaic inlay, petit point, and cluster work. Mosaic inlay designs of quail and Apache are his own. Learned from his mother and began producing around 1950. Works with his wife.
HALLMARK: Stamped surname and tribal affiliation in Gothic print. Stamped cloud symbol enclosing initials and surname arched over the clouds in 1/32 Gothic, shared with his wife. Also uses an engraved signature.
Spouse is Edith Lonjose.
[Bell:1975:30,31]

LONJOSE ZUNI

LONJOSE

LONJOSE, MABEL C. *Zuni*
SILVERSMITH:
HALLMARK: Stamped initials and symbols in circle (3/8") first used in 1976. Contains initials other than hers also.

LORETTO, G. *Unknown*
SILVERSMITH: Smith for John S. Skinner.
HALLMARK: Stamped surname in 1/16 Gothic print, first used in 1975.

G.LORETTO

LORETTO, PHILLIP C. *Jemez/Cochiti*
SILVERSMITH: Specializes in contemporary inlay, casting, and hammered work. Uses exotic materials.
HALLMARK: Stamped symbols.
From Navajo, New Mexico or Arizona region.

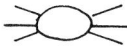

LOVATO, CHARLES *Santo Domingo*
HEISHI MAKER: Works with his wife.
HALLMARK: Personalized initials stamped on findings.
Spouse is Clara Lovato.

CL

LOVATO, CLARA *Santo Domingo*
HEISHI MAKER: Works with her husband.
HALLMARK: Personalized initials stamped on findings.
Spouse is Charles Lovato.

CL

LOVATO, DAN *Santo Domingo*
SILVERSMITH/HEISHI MAKER:
HALLMARK: Stamped single initial in Gothic print. Also uses a single colored strand on the wrapped section of a heishi necklace or a tiny loop with a single stone at the back.

D

LOVATO, HAROLD *Santo Domingo*
SILVERSMITH:
HALLMARK: Stamped initials with symbol, stamped joined initials and initials in Gothic print.
Parents are Mary and Sedillo Lovato.

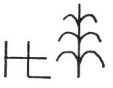 HL

LOVATO, HOMER *Santo Domingo*
SILVERSMITH:
HALLMARK: Stamped initials in Gothic print.

H.L.

LOVATO, JULIAN *Santo Domingo*
SILVERSMITH: Smith for Frank Patania.
HALLMARK: Stamped surname in Gothic print. Stamped symbol with Indian Hand Made placed alongside. This stamp is shared with his wife.
Spouse is Marie Lovato.

J.LOVATO

LOVATO, MANUELITO JUDY *Santo Domingo*
SILVERSMITH/POTTER/BEADWORK/PLASTICS:
HALLMARK: Stamped or painted, joined initials in Gothic print.

ML

LOVATO, MARIE *Santo Domingo*
SILVERSMITH: Smith for Peshlakai, Ltd.
HALLMARK: Stamped surname in 1/16 Gothic print, first used in 1977. Stamped bird symbol with IHM alongside shared with her husband.
Spouse is Julian Lovato.

M.LOVATO

LOVATO. MARY *Santo Domingo*
SHELLWORK: Specializes in inlaid shell, also does castwork decorated by stamping.
HALLMARK: Engraved or stamped initials. Also uses husband's hallmark.
Spouse is Sedalio F. Lovato.

S.D.

LOVATO, MARY C. *Santo Domingo*
SHELLWORK: Specializes in inlaid shells.
HALLMARK: Stamped initials in upper and lower case Gothic print.

McL

LOVATO, SAM *Santo Domingo*
SHELLWORK: Specializes in inlaid shells.
HALLMARK: Engraved, joined and offset initials. Single initial with symbol of an arrow.

LOVATO, SEDALIO F. *Santo Domingo*
SILVERSMITH/SHELLWORKER: Specializes in inlaid shell and cast silver decorated with stamp and chisel. Works with his wife.
HALLMARK: Stamped or engraved initials in Gothic print shared with his wife.
Spouse is Mary Lovato.

S.D.   S.F.L.

LOWE, JOE TOM *Navajo*
SILVERSMITH: Smith for Atkinson Trading Company.
HALLMARK: Stamped full name in 1/16 Gothic print, first used in 1974.

JOE T. LOWE

LOWSAYATEE, MARY HELEN *Zuni*
SILVERSMITH/LAPIDARIST: Specializes in needlepoint earrings. Creates her own designs. Learned from her sister and began producing in 1960. Works alone.
HALLMARK: Stamped initials in Gothic print.
[Levy:1980:49]

MHL

LUCAS, GLENN *Hopi*
SILVERSMITH: Specialized in silver overlay. Began producing around 1966. Smith for Hopicrafts.
HALLMARK: Stamped, joined and offset initials (1/8 x 3/32").
Daughter is Trinidad Lucas.
[Wright:1982:89]

LUCAS, TRINIDAD *Hopi*
SILVERSMITH: Specializes in overlay.
HALLMARK: Stamped initials in Gothic print with enlarged central letter.
Father is Glenn Lucas.

LUCERO, BEVERLY *Cochiti*
SILVERSMITH:
HALLMARK: Stamped numerical mark with symbol.

LUCIO, ERVIN *Zuni*
SILVERSMITH:
HALLMARK: Stamped initials in 1/16 script with tribal affiliation. Stamp first used in 1976.

LUCIO, JOHN *Zuni*
SILVERSMITH/LAPIDARIST: Specializes in needlepoint, inlay, and open work. Designs are frequently eagle dancers. Presumably began producing in 1950. C.G.Wallace attributes pieces to him that were made from 1935 on. It is possible that this was an older generation.
HALLMARK: Stamped initial and surname in Gothic print.
[Bell:1975:50]

J.LUCIO

LUCIO, JOHN B. *Zuni*
SILVERSMITH:
HALLMARK: Stamped full name in 1/16 Gothic print, first used in 1978.

JOHN B. LUCIO

LUCIO, LANDY *Zuni*
SILVERSMITH/LAPIDARIST:
HALLMARK: Engraved signature.

Landy Lucio

LUHELA, NICK *Zuni*
SILVERSMITH/LAPIDARIST: Specializes in channel inlay in floral designs. Works with his wife.
HALLMARK: Engraved signatures of his wife's and his own first name and shared surname.
Spouse is Theresa Luhela.

Nick & Theresa Luhela

LUHELA, THERESA *Zuni*
SILVERSMITH/LAPIDARIST: Channel inlay in floral designs. Works with her husband.
HALLMARK: Engraved signatures of her husband's and her own given names and shared surname.
Spouse is Nick Luhela.

Nick & Theresa Luhela

LUJAN, ARTHUR *Taos*
SILVERSMITH:
HALLMARK: Stamped initials in Gothic print set on an oval plate.
Father is Bobby Lujan.
From Taos Pueblo, New Mexico.

(ARL)

LUJAN, BOBBY *Taos*
SILVERSMITH:
HALLMARK: Stamped initials in Gothic print set on plates of varying shapes.
Son is Arthur Lujan, brother is Jimmie Lujan.
[King:1976:10]

LUJAN, JERRY ORLANDO *Taos*
POTTER:
HALLMARK: Painted and fired signature in personalized print.

J. LUJAN

LUJAN, JIMMIE *Taos*
SILVERSMITH:
HALLMARK: Stamped joined initials on a rounded plate.
Brother of Bobby Lujan. Deceased in 1945.
From Taos Pueblo, New Mexico.

LUJAN, NETTIE *Taos*
SILVERSMITH:
HALLMARK: Stamped cloud symbol.
Spouse is Rick Lujan.
From Taos Pueblo, New Mexico.

LUJAN, RICK *Taos*
SILVERSMITH:
HALLMARK: Stamped cloud symbol.
Spouse is Nettie Lujan.
From Taos Pueblo, New Mexico.

LUKEE, REBECCA *Apache*
LAPIDARIST: Peridot settings.
HALLMARK: Stamped initials in Gothic print.

RL

LUNA, VERA *Zuni*
SILVERSMITH/LAPIDARIST: Specializes in inlay of Gan dancers, cluster work, and squash blossom necklaces. Began producing around 1970.
HALLMARK: Stamped surname in 1/16 Gothic print, first used in 1975. Stamped initials in 3/32 Gothic print, first used in 1975. Stamped symbol of joined initials.

V.LUNA   V.L.   ↓

LUNEO, EUNICE *Zuni*
SILVERSMITH:
HALLMARK: Stamped initials in Gothic print.

E.E.L.

LUPEE, EDDIE *Zuni (?)*
SILVERSMITH:
HALLMARK: Stamped combination of letters.
[King:1976:10]

LYNCH, ELLA *Navajo*
SILVERSMITH: Smith for Atkinson Trading Company.
HALLMARK: Stamped full name in 1/16 Gothic print, first used in 1975. Stamped surname in 1/16 Gothic print first used in 1975.

ELLA LYNCH   E. LYNCH

McCABE, ALBERT *Navajo*
SILVERSMITH:
HALLMARK: Stamped partial initials in 1/16 Gothic print, first used in 1975.
Brother is Allan McCabe.
From Ft. Defiance, Arizona region.

AC

McCABE, ALLAN *Navajo*
SILVERSMITH:
HALLMARK: Stamped initials in 1/16 Gothic print. Stamp first used in 1975.
Brother is Albert McCabe, brother-in-law is Kent Walker.

AMC

McCREA, ERNEST *Navajo*
SILVERSMITH: Smith for Atkinson Trading Company before 1980.
HALLMARK: Stamped initials in 1/16 Gothic print.

E.Mc

McCRORY, JANE *Anglo (?)*
SILVERSMITH:
HALLMARK: Stamped initials in 1/16 Gothic print, first appeared in 1975. Stamped initials in 3/32 Gothic print with underlying bars.

JMc   JMc

McGEE, BOB *Navajo (?)*
SILVERSMITH:
HALLMARK: Stamped full name in 1/16 Gothic print. Stamp first used in 1975.
From Gallup, New Mexico region.

BOBBY McGEE

McHORSE, CHRIS NOFCHISSEY *Navajo*
POTTER:
HALLMARK: Signature painted and fired.

CM C/Horse

McKINSTRY,? *Unknown*
SILVERSMITH:
HALLMARK: Stamped surname in 1/32 Gothic print. Stamp first appeared in 1983.

B.McKINSTRY

McRAE, BILLY *Navajo*
SILVERSMITH/GOLDSMITH:
HALLMARK: Stamped initials in Gothic print.

BM

MADRID, JOSEPH *Unknown*
SILVERSMITH:
HALLMARK: Stamped initials with symbol.

J-M

MAHOOTY, CHESTER B. *Zuni*
SILVERSMITH/LAPIDARIST: Specializes in work with large irregular stone settings. Wife works with him.
HALLMARK: Stamped initials in Gothic print, on larger pieces a

stamped symbol of a badger claw. Shared marks.
Spouse is Dorothy Mahooty.
[Bell:1975:56]

CBM

MAHOOTY, DOROTHY *Zuni*
SILVERSMITH/LAPIDARIST: Specializes in work with large irregular stone settings. Works with her husband.
HALLMARK: Stamped initials in Gothic print. Larger pieces are stamped with the symbol of a badger claw. Shares her husband's marks.
Spouse is Chester B. Mahooty.
[Bell:1975:56]

CBM

MAHOOTY, EUGENE *Zuni*
SILVERSMITH: Specializes in pieces with nugget settings. Works with his wife.
HALLMARK: Stamped initials of his wife's and his own along with tribal affiliation. Shared hallmark.
Spouse is Yvonne Mahooty. His father is Chester Mahooty.
[Bell:1976:50]

EYM
ZUNI

MAHOOTY, G ? *Zuni*
SILVERSMITH:
HALLMARK: Stamped surname in 1/16 Gothic print, first used in 1974.

G.MAHOOTY

MAHOOTY, JAY W. *Zuni*
SILVERSMITH:
HALLMARK: Stamped surname in 1/16 Gothic print, first used in 1985.

J.W.MAHOOTY

MAHOOTY, PAM *Zuni*
SILVERSMITH:
HALLMARK: Stamped full name in 1/16 Gothic print, first used in 1979.

PAM MAHOOTY

MAHOOTY, T ? *Zuni*
SILVERSMITH:
HALLMARK: Stamped surname in 1/16 Gothic print, first used in 1976.

T.MAHOOTY

MAHOOTY, YVONNE *Zuni*
SILVERSMITH: Specializes in pieces with large nugget settings. Learned from her mother. Works with her husband.
HALLMARK: Stamped initials of her husband and her own. Shared hallmark.
Spouse is Eugene Mahooty, mother is Julalita Lamy.
[Bell:1976:50]

EYM
ZUNI

MAKTIMA, DUANE *Hopi*
SILVERSMITH: Specializes in double and triple silver overlay using exotic materials such as ironwood and ivory. Learned in college and began producing in 1974. Originates his own designs.
HALLMARK: Stamped symbol of a parrot head combined with personalized initials. (1/8" sq.)
[Wright:1982:97]

MALAMIC, LOLITA *Zuni*
SILVERSMITH/LAPIDARIST:
HALLMARK: Stamped initials in Gothic print.

LM

MALDONADO, GILBERT *Santo Domingo*
METALWORKER/KACHINA CARVER: Specializes in brass pieces and miniature kachinas.
HALLMARK: Stamped initials in Gothic print.

GM

MALIE, ROSALITA D. (ROSIE) *Zuni*
SILVERSMITH/LAPIDARIST: Specializes in "snake eyes" crosses and other charms. Learned from her mother. Does all the work herself.
HALLMARK: Stamped surname in 1/16 Gothic print. Stamp first used in 1980. Often her pieces are not signed because of size.
[Levy:1980:49]

R.D.MALIE

MANNING, BESS *Unknown*
SILVERSMITH/LAPIDARIST: Specializes in inlay, carved inlay. Worked for J & D Jewelry Sales and for Nugget Gallery.
HALLMARK: Stamped name and type of work in 1/32 script, first used in 1978. Stamp of name in script. Stamp of name and type of work in 1/32 script, two lines, first used in 1983.

Inlay by B. Manning   *Carving by B. Manning*

MANNING, C. ? *Navajo*
SILVERSMITH: Smith for Bowser and Begay in 1976.
HALLMARK: Stamped surname in 1/16 Gothic print, first used in 1976.

C.MANNING

MANNING, GENE *Isleta*
SILVERSMITH:
HALLMARK: Stamped initials in Gothic print.

G.M.

MANSFIELD, A ? *Anglo (?)*
SILVERSMITH: Associated in some manner with the Mansfield Silvercraft Company of Denver.
HALLMARK: Stamp of surname and initial in 3/64 script.

A. Mansfield

MANSFIELD, VERDEN *Hopi*
SILVERSMITH: Specializes in silver overlay.
HALLMARK: Stamped symbol of an antelope.

MANSFIELD, VERNON *Hopi*
SILVERSMITH: Specialized in silver overlay. Began production in 1959
HALLMARK: Stamped symbol of three stars or Orion in 1967. Stamped symbol of two feathers used from 1970 on. Also uses stamp of two initials.
[Wright:1982:88]

 VM

MANUEL, RICK *Papago*
SILVERSMITH: Worked with his wife on her pieces. Taught Roger Ranson, James Fendenheim and Francis Manuel.
HALLMARK: Stamped initials and symbol.

MANUELITO, J ? *Navajo (?)*
SILVERSMITH:
HALLMARK: Stamped surname in 1/16 Gothic print, first used in 1984.

J.MANUELITO

MANYGOATS, B ? *Navajo*
SILVERSMITH: Smith for Moqui Trading Post.
HALLMARK: Stamped surname in 1/16 Gothic print, first used in 1975.

B.MANYGOATS

MANYGOATS, JACKIE *Navajo*
SILVERSMITH: Smith for Max Sandoval.
HALLMARK: Stamped initials with tribal affiliation in two lines of 1/16 Gothic print. Stamp first used in 1976.

J.M.
NAVAJO

MARTIN, ANDREW *Navajo*
SILVERSMITH:
HALLMARK: Stamped surname in 1/16 Gothic print. Stamp first used in 1981.
From Crownpoint, New Mexico region.

MARTIN

MARTIN, BENNY *Navajo*
SILVERSMITH:
HALLMARK: Stamped given name in 1/16 Gothic print, first used in 1978.
From Gallup, New Mexico region.

BENNY M.

MARTIN, G ? *Navajo*
SILVERSMITH: Smith for the Atkinson Trading Company.
HALLMARK: Stamped surname in 1/16 Gothic print, first used in 1975.

G.MARTIN

MARTIN, ROY *Navajo (?)*
SILVERSMITH: Specializes in wrought work.
HALLMARK: Mark is a piece of curled wire soldered to the piece.

MARTIN, VICKI *Navajo*
SILVERSMITH:
HALLMARK: Stamped initials in Gothic print.

VM

MARTINEZ, ARCHIE *Navajo*
SILVERSMITH:
HALLMARK: Stamped abbreviation of name in 1/16 Gothic print. Stamp first used in 1977.
From Ft. Wingate, New Mexico region.

A.MTZ

MARTINEZ, BENNY *Navajo (?)*
SILVERSMITH:
HALLMARK: Stamped initials in Gothic print.

BM

MARTINEZ, BETTY *Zuni*
SILVERSMITH/LAPIDARIST: Specializes in channel inlay in floral designs. Began producing in 1965. She does the stone work for her husband.
HALLMARK: Stamped initials in Gothic print of her own name is used only by Betty. Second stamp combines her husband's initials with her own and is shared.
Spouse is Joseph Martinez.
[Levy:1980:35]

B.M.   JBM

MARTINEZ, DOROTHY *Navajo*
SILVERSMITH:
HALLMARK: Stamped symbol of a star.

MARTINEZ (CHEROMIAH), ETHEL *Navajo*
SILVERSMITH: Benchsmith for Richardson Trading Company.
HALLMARK: Stamped surname in 1/16 Gothic print, first used in 1975. Stamped initials used after she became Ethel Cheromiah.

E.MARTINEZ   EMC

MARTINEZ, EUGENE *Paiute*
SILVERSMITH/GOLDSMITH: Operates a shop in Bishop.
HALLMARK: Stamped combination of symbols and initials in lower case personalized print. (1/2")
From Bishop, California region.

MARTINEZ, GEORGE *Zuni*
SILVERSMITH: Specialized in stamped open work. Producing in 1940.
HALLMARK: Stamped initials with symbols in Gothic print.

>GM<

MARTINEZ, HUBERTA *Zuni*
SILVERSMITH/LAPIDARIST: Specializes in channel inlay, domed and shaped stones in floral designs. Learned from her husband's father and began producing in 1962.
HALLMARK: Stamped shared initials in 1/16 Gothic print. Spouse is Mark Martinez, father-in-law is Joseph Martinez.
[Levy:1980:35]

MHM

MARTINEZ, JOSEPH *Zuni*
SILVERSMITH/LAPIDARIST: Specializes in channel inlay in floral designs. Learned from his father and began producing in 1965. He does the metal work and stone cutting and his wife does the settings.
HALLMARK: Stamped initials shared by his wife and himself. Spouse is Betty Martinez. Father is George Martinez and son is Mark Martinez.
[Levy:1980:35]

JBM

MARTINEZ, JUAN *Zuni*
SILVERSMITH: Specializes in mosaic inlaid clowns. Began producing in 1962. Worked for Atkinson Trading Co.
HALLMARK: Stamped initials in 1/16 Gothic print, first used in 1972. Second stamp of surname in 1/16 Gothic print first used in 1974.

JM   J.MARTINEZ

MARTINEZ, LEO *Navajo (?)*
SILVERSMITH:
HALLMARK: Stamped given name in offset joined personalized print. Stamp first used in 1975. (1/16" print).
From Prewitt, New Mexico region.

LEO

MARTINEZ, MARK *Zuni*
SILVERSMITH/LAPIDARIST: Specializes in channel inlay with domed and shaped stones in floral designs. Learned from his father and began producing in 1974. He and his wife make pieces individually.
HALLMARK: Stamped shared initials in Gothic print. Spouse is Huberta Martinez, father is Joseph Martinez.
[Levy:1980:35]

MHM

MARTZA, LEONARD *Zuni*
SILVERSMITH/LAPIDARIST: Specializes in wrought work and mosaic inlay. Producing in 1948.
HALLMARK: Stamped initials offset or ordinary in Gothic print.

L   LM
M

MASON, EDGAR *Navajo*
SILVERSMITH:
HALLMARK: Stamped surname in 1/16 Gothic print, first used in 1975.
From Crownpoint, New Mexico region.

E.MASON

MASON, JAMES *Navajo*
SILVERSMITH:
HALLMARK: Stamped initials in Gothic print.

JM

MASSIE, DORA *Zuni*
SILVERSMITH/LAPIDARIST:
HALLMARK: Stamped shared initials and husband's surname in 1/16 Gothic print. Stamp first appeared in 1974.
Spouse is Jose Massie.

J.D.MASSIE

MASSIE, JOSE *Zuni*
SILVERSMITH/LAPIDARIST:
HALLMARK: Stamped shared initials and his surname in 1/16 Gothic print. Stamp first appeared in 1974.
Spouse is Dora Massie.

J.D.MASSIE

MASUNGYAMA, TED see **WADSWORTH, TED**

MATEYA, BRUCE *Zuni*
SILVERSMITH/LAPIDARIST: Specializes in square channel inlay. Works with his wife.
HALLMARK: Stamped shared initials with wife in Gothic print. Spouse is Mamie Mateya.
[Bell:1977:50]

MBM

MATEYA, MAMIE *Zuni*
SILVERSMITH/LAPIDARIST: Specializes in square channel inlay. Works with her husband.
HALLMARK: Stamped shared initials with her husband in Gothic print.
Spouse is Bruce Mateya.
[Bell:1977:50]

MBM

MATT, MARY *Navajo*
SILVERSMITH: Smith for Atkinson Trading Company.
HALLMARK: Stamped full name in 1/16 Gothic print first used in 1974.

MARY MATT

MAYES, JOBETH D. *Zuni*
SILVERSMITH/LAPIDARIST: Specializes in free standing settings in shadow box style. Began producing ca. 1971.
HALLMARK: Stamped full name, tribal affiliation and symbol of corn in a triangular form.
[Bell:1976:33]

MEDINA, E. *Zia*
SILVERSMITH:

HALLMARK: Stamped surname in 1/16 Gothic print, first seen in 1977. Stamped symbol of the sun with ZIA enclosed in 1/32 Gothic print first seen in 1977. Total stamp size 3/8".
From San Ysidro, New Mexico region.

E. MEDINA

MEXICANO, MARYANN PLATERO *Navajo*
SILVERSMITH:
HALLMARK: Stamped initials in varying size Gothic style print. Spouse is Larry Mexicano, brothers are Robert and Joey Platero. From Canyoncito, New Mexico region.

MAM

MEYER, RUTH A. *Anglo*
SILVERSMITH:
HALLMARK: Stamped personalized offset initials in script. Stamp first used in 1979, size 1/4".

MIKE, GLORIA *Navajo*
SILVERSMITH/LAPIDARIST: Specializes in inlay. Works for Sunburst Handcrafts.
HALLMARK: Stamped numerical mark.
Sister is Dora Mike.

4

MIKE, DORA *Navajo*
SILVERSMITH: Specialist in inlay. Works for Sunburst Handcrafts.
HALLMARK: Stamped numerical mark.
Sister is Gloria Mike.

3

MIKE, LOIS *Navajo*
SILVERSMITH:
HALLMARK: Stamped surname in 1/32 Gothic print, first used in 1985.
From Gamerco, New Mexico region.

L. MIKE

MILANI, LOLITA *Zuni*
SILVERSMITH/LAPIDARIST: Specializes in solid channel inlay of triangles and curvilinear mosaics. Learned from watching her stepfather. Began producing in 1945.
HALLMARK: Stamped initials in Gothic print.
[Levy:1980:23]

LM

MILLER, EDGAR see HOVALO, EDGAR

MONONGYE, BESSIE *Hopi*
POTTER: Began producing in 1973. Third Mesa potter.
HALLMARK: Painted and fired cloud symbols with name and village.

MONONGYE, JESSIE *Navajo*
SILVERSMITH/LAPIDARIST: Specializes in elaborate and complex designs in mosaic inlay and contemporary silver work. Works with exotic materials. Learned silver smithing from his father.
HALLMARK: Earlier work is marked with the use of an elaborate design that is made from the letter M and a mirror image. Stamped surname with joined initials in Gothic print has been used since 1979.
Parents are Ida Mae Lee and Preston Monongye.

 JMONONGYE

MONONGYE, PRESTON *Mission/Mexican*
SILVERSMITH/LAPIDARIST: Specialist in every silverworking technique particularly in combinations of castwork, overlay, and wrought work. Designs range from traditional to contemporary. Learned silverworking from his uncle and produced from 1939 to 1980. Piecework for most of the traders in the Southwest.
HALLMARK: Earliest hallmark is stamped initials in Gothic print. Continued to use this mark on cast work. Also used a P enclosed in symbols from 1950-1955. Stamps of peyote birds incorporating his initials most commonly used.
Spouse was Ida Mae Lee, son is Jessie Monongye.
[Wright:1982:83]

PM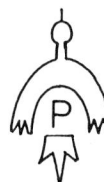

MONTANA, M ? *Unknown*
SILVERSMITH:
HALLMARK: Stamped surname in 1/16 Gothic print, first used in 1975. Stamp may represent the shop, Montana Mining Company.

M. MONTANA

MONTANO, GIBSON *Navajo*
SILVERSMITH: Specializes in castwork.
HALLMARK: Stamped abbreviated given name with symbol in 1/32 Gothic print. Stamp of surname in 1/16 Gothic print first used in 1974.

GIBB 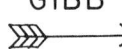 G. MONTANO

MONTOYA, KEE *Navajo*
SILVERSMITH:
HALLMARK: Stamped full name in personalized printing.
From San Antonio Springs, New Mexico.

by Kee Montoya

MOON, CACTUS *Zuni*
SILVERSMITH:
HALLMARK: Stamped symbol.

MOQUINO, JIM — *Santo Domingo*
METAL WORK: Specializes in brass with coral settings.
HALLMARK: Stamped initials in Gothic print.

JM

MORGAN, BEN BILLIE — *Navajo*
SILVERSMITH:
HALLMARK: Stamped full name in 1/16 Gothic print, first used in 1976.
From Crownpoint, New Mexico region.

BEN B. MORGAN

MORGAN, BERTHA — *Navajo*
SILVERSMITH:
HALLMARK: Stamped initial in personalized script. A registered hallmark.

𝓜®

MORGAN, CHARLIE — *Navajo*
SILVERSMITH: Pieceworker.
HALLMARK: Stamped initials in Gothic print.

CM

MORGAN, HERMAN K. — *Navajo*
SILVERSMITH:
HALLMARK: Stamped initials in 1/16 Gothic print, stamp first used in 1977.
From Crownpoint, New Mexico region.

HKM

MORGAN, IDA — *Navajo*
SILVERSMITH: Smith for Atkinson Trading Company before 1980.
HALLMARK: Stamped given name in 1/16 Gothic print.

IDA M.

MORGAN, JACK — *Unknown*
SILVERSMITH:
HALLMARK: Stamped symbol of a bird (1/2").
From Guymon, Oklahoma region.

MORGAN, LOUISE — *Navajo*
SILVERSMITH:
HALLMARK: Stamped surname in 1/16 Gothic print, first used in 1985.
From Lupton, Arizona region.

L. MORGAN

MORGAN, MARY — *Navajo*
SILVERSMITH: Began producing in the 1940'S. Pieceworker for Tobe Turpen's Indian Trading Company.
HALLMARK: Stamped initial M in Roman print. Stamp used most often is double initials in Gothic print.

⋀   MM

MORGAN, TOM — *Navajo*
SILVERSMITH: Pieceworker.
HALLMARK: Stamped offset initials in personalized print.

MORRIS, DEE — *Anglo*
SILVERSMITH:
HALLMARK: Stamped full name in Gothic print.
From Sedona, Arizona.

DEE MORRIS

MORRIS, EARL — *Navajo*
SILVERSMITH:
HALLMARK: Stamped offset initials in 1/16 Gothic print, first used in 1976.
From Tsaile, Arizona region.

M_Y

MORRIS, HENRY — *Navajo*
SILVERSMITH:
HALLMARK: Stamped initials in Gothic print with enlarged T in the center.

HTM

MORRIS, TOM — *Navajo*
SILVERSMITH:
HALLMARK: Stamped initials in Gothic print.
From Winslow, Arizona region.

TM

MORRIS, WILLIE — *Navajo*
SILVERSMITH:
HALLMARK: Stamped and joined initials look more like a double X than his actual initials.

XX

MOTSE, NORA NARANJO — *Unknown*
SILVERSMITH:
HALLMARK: Stamped initials in Gothic print.

NM

MOWA, DAVID — *Hopi*
SILVERSMITH: Specializes in silver overlay. Began producing in 1984.
HALLMARK: Symbol of half a sun face (1/8"), first seen in 1985.

MOWA, TIM — *Hopi*
SILVERSMITH: Specializes in silver overlay.
HALLMARK: Stamped symbol of a flattened triangle.

MUEHLER, DAVID — *Unknown*
SILVERSMITH:

HALLMARK: Stamped initials, possibly shared, in 3/32 Gothic print. Stamp first used in 1973.

H&D

MULL, MARGIE *Apache*
LAPIDARIST: Peridot settings.
HALLMARK: Stamped initials in Gothic print or same initials with an asterisk or star symbol below.

MM   M M
         *

MUNSON, H ? *Navajo (?)*
SILVERSMITH:
HALLMARK: Stamped surname in 1/32 Gothic print, first used in 1983.

H. MUNSON

MUNSON, THOM *Cherokee*
SILVERSMITH:
HALLMARK: Stamped tribal affiliation in 1/32 Gothic print. Stamp first used in 1978.
From Tahlequah, Oklahoma region.

CHEROKEE

MURPHY, BEN *Navajo*
SILVERSMITH: Specializes in castwork.
HALLMARK: Stamped initials in ordinary position or misaligned, in Gothic print and set on plates of differing shapes.

BM

MUSKET, W. J. *Navajo*
SILVERSMITH:
HALLMARK: Stamped surname in Gothic print.

W. J. MUSKET

MYERS, GRACE *Navajo*
SILVERSMITH: Smith for Atkinson Trading Company.
HALLMARK: Stamped surname in 1/16 Gothic print, first used in 1974.

G. MYERS

MYRTLE, ELLEN *Unknown*
SILVERSMITH:
HALLMARK: Stamped surname in 1/32 Gothic print first used in 1980. Second stamp two-line 1/32 Gothic print, first used in 1982.
From Albuquerque, New Mexico region.

MYRTLE   ELLEN
              MYRTLE

NABERS, BILL *Anglo*
SILVERSMITH:
HALLMARK: Stamped two-line mark of surname and "custom made" in 1/16 Gothic print. Stamp first seen in 1981.

CUSTOM MADE
    NABERS

NACITACIO, LOLITA *Zuni*
SILVERSMITH:
HALLMARK: Stamped initials in Gothic print either in an ordinary position or offset.

LN   L_N

NAHA, HELEN *Hopi/Tewa*
POTTER: Began producing in 1950, uses the name Feather Woman. She makes the pottery and now her daughter decorates it.
HALLMARK: Painted and fired representation of a soft feather. Daughter is Sylvia Naha.

NAHA, SYLVIA *Hopi/Tewa*
POTTER: Decorates the pottery made by her mother and does some of her own.
HALLMARK: Painted and fired representation of a soft feather with the initial S below it.

NAJDOWSKI, MIKE *Unknown*
SILVERSMITH:
HALLMARK: Stamped personalized initials (1/16"), first used in 1985.
From Santa Fe, New Mexico region.

CMW

NAKATEWA, ELSIE H. *Zuni*
SILVERSMITH/LAPIDARIST:
HALLMARK: Stamped initials and abbreviated name in 1/16 Gothic print, first used in 1974.

E. H. NAK

NAMINGHA, FLOYD *Hopi*
SILVERSMITH: Specializes in silver overlay. Began producing in 1969.
HALLMARK: Stamped symbol of an antelope rattle.

NAMINGHA, FRANKLIN *Hopi*
SILVERSMITH: Silver overlay. Began producing in 1969.
HALLMARK: Stamped symbol of an ear of corn.

NAMINGA, RACHEL NAMPEYO *Tewa*
POTTER: Produced wares in the tradition of the Nampeyo family.
HALLMARK: Painted and fired full name or initials on small pieces.
Grandmother was Nampeyo, mother Annie Nampeyo Healing.

Rachel Nampeyo   RN

NAMINGHA, RAYMIE *Hopi*
SILVERSMITH: Specializes in silver overlay. Began producing in 1980.

HALLMARK: Stamped symbol of a rattlesnake's rattle. This is the same hallmark used by his deceased uncle. Stamped personalized initials also.
Uncle was Walter Polelonema.
[Wright:1982:97]

NAMINGHA, WARREN　　　　　　　　　　　　　　　*Hopi*
SILVERSMITH: Specializes in silver overlay.
HALLMARK: Stamped symbol of three clouds in a row.

NAMPEYO　　　　　　　　　　　　　　　　　　　*Tewa*
POTTER: By copying and adapting earlier wares, her sense of design and skill in making pottery led to a revival of First Mesa pottery.
HALLMARK: Despite painted and fired names on the bottoms of vessels Nampeyo could not write. As her eyesight faded she progressed from making pottery and decorating it to only moulding the vessels. During these later years she first had her daughter Annie sign her work and later Fannie. Annie's signature contains lower case letters while Fannie's does not.

NAMPEYO   NaMpeyo

NAMPEYO, ANNIE see **HEALING, ANNIE**

NAMPEYO, ELLSWORTH see **POLACCA, ELLSWORTH**

NAMPEYO, FANNIE see **POLACCA, FANNIE**

NAMPEYO, LEAH see **GARCIA, LEAH**

NAMPEYO, RACHEL see **NAMINGHA, RACHEL**

NARANJO, FELINE　　　　　　　　　　　　　　　*Zuni*
SILVERSMITH:
HALLMARK: Stamped initials in Gothic print.

FN

NARANJO, MANUEL　　　　　　　　　　　　　　*Tewa*
SILVERSMITH:
HALLMARK: Stamped surname in Gothic print.

M.NARANJO

NASEYOMA, STEPHEN HYSON　　　　　　　　　*Hopi*
SILVERSMITH: Specializes in silver overlay. Began producing in 1978.
HALLMARK: Stamped joined initials in personalized print 1/8" square.
[Wright:1982:98]

HN

NASH, EDITH　　　　　　　　　　　　　　　　　*Hopi*
POTTER: Traditional designs.
HALLMARK: Painted and fired representation of an ear of corn and husks.
Deceased.

NASTACIO, ALVIN　　　　　　　　　　　　　　*Zuni*
SILVERSMITH/LAPIDARIST:
HALLMARK: Stamped surname and initials in 1/16 Gothic print. Stamp of initials of his wife and his own in the same print. Stamp of his wife's initials and his own with his surname all in 1/16 Gothic and all being used first in 1977.

A&E　　　　A.&E.N.　　　A.&E.NASTACIO
NASTACIO

NASTACIO, AMELIO　　　　　　　　　　　　　*Zuni*
SILVERSMITH/LAPIDARIST: Specializes in pieces featuring Mickey Mouse. Works with his wife.
HALLMARK: Engraved hallmark of his wife's and his own name done in a scroll with the year included.
Spouse is Veronica Nastacio.
[Bell:1975:53]

AMELIO & VERONICA
NASTACIO-ZUNI

NASTACIO, BILLY　　　　　　　　　　　　　　*Zuni*
SILVERSMITH/LAPIDARIST:
HALLMARK: Stamped surname with shared initials of his wife's and his own in 1/16 Gothic print. Stamp first used in 1976.

B&N NASTACIO

NASTACIO, LEROY　　　　　　　　　　　　　*Zuni*
SILVERSMITH:
HALLMARK: Stamped initials in Gothic print.

L.N.

NASTACIO, MYRA　　　　　　　　　　　　　　*Zuni*
SILVERSMITH:
HALLMARK: Stamped initials which differ from one another. Both are in 1/16 Gothic print and were first used in 1973.

M.A.　　M.N.

NASTACIO, RAPHAEL　　　　　　　　　　　　*Zuni*
SILVERSMITH:
HALLMARK: Stamped surname in 1/16 Gothic print, first used in 1975.

R.NASTACIO

NASTACIO, VERONICA　　　　　　　　　　　　*Zuni*
SILVERSMITH/LAPIDARIST: Specializes in pieces featuring Mickey Mouse. Works with her husband.
HALLMARK: Engraved hallmark of her husband's name and her own and tribal affiliation. Stamped unmarried surname and initials with tribal affiliation in 1/16 Gothic print first used in 1977. Stamped given name in 1/16 script first used in 1979. Also uses a stamped plate with given name.
Spouse is Amelio Nastacio.
[Bell:1975:53]

AMELIO & VERONICA　　　*Veronica*
NASTACIO-ZUNI

V.N.POBLANO
ZUNI　　　　　　　　　　　*Veronica*

NATACHU, BERNICE　　　　　　　　　　　　*Zuni*

SILVERSMITH/LAPIDARIST: Specializes in inlaid work.
HALLMARK: Stamped shared initials and surname of husband in 1/16 Gothic print. First appearing in 1974.
Spouse is Gillerimo Natachu.

G.B.NASTACIO

NATACHU, FRED *Zuni*
SILVERSMITH/LAPIDARIST: Specializes in mosaic inlaid Apache Mountain Way dancers, rainbows, and sun faces.
HALLMARK: Stamped initials shared with wife. Stamped surname with his wife's and his own initials in 1/16 Gothic print, first used in 1974.
Spouse is Lolita Natachu.
[Bell:1977:56]

F.L.   F.L.NATACHU

NATACHU, GILLERIMO *Zuni*
SILVERSMITH/LAPIDARIST: Specializes in inlaid work.
HALLMARK: Stamped initials shared with wife. Stamped surname and shared initials in 1/16 Gothic print, first appearing in 1974.
Spouse is Bernice Natachu.

GN   G.B. NATACHU

NATACHU, LOLITA *Zuni*
SILVERSMITH/LAPIDARIST. Specializes in mosaic inlaid Apache Mountain Way dancers, rainbows. and sun Faces.
HALLMARK: Stamped initials shared with her husband. Her initials and her husband's with his surname in 1/16 Gothic print, first used in 1974.
Spouse is Fred Natachu. Sisters are Dolly Banteah and Nancy Haloo. Half brother is Jake Livingston.
[Bell:1977:56]

LN   L_N   F.L.NATACHU

NATEWA, BERNALL *Zuni*
SILVERSMITH/LAPIDARIST:
HALLMARK: Stamped surname in 3/32 Gothic print, first used in 1975. Stamped surname in 1/16 Gothic print, first used in 1982.

B.NATEWA

NATEWA, NEAL *Zuni*
SILVERSMITH/LAPIDARIST: Specializes in needlepoint and inlaid pieces, also carves fetishes.
HALLMARK: Engraved full name of him and his wife as a signature.
Spouse is Shirley Natewa.
[Bell:1975:76]

Neal & Shirley Natewa

NATEWA, ORLINDA *Zuni*
SILVERSMITH/LAPIDARIST: Specializes in channel inlay.
HALLMARK: Stamped full name in 1/16 Gothic print, first used in 1974.

ORLINDA   NATEWA

NATEWA, PITKIN *Zuni*
SILVERSMITH/LAPIDARIST: Specializes in owl designs. Learned from watching his parents. Began producing in 1952. Both he and his wife work on pieces.
HALLMARK: Stamped surname with shared initials in Gothic print.
Spouse is Wanda Natewa.
[Levy:1980:26]

P.W.NATEWA

NATEWA, SHIRLEY *Zuni*
SILVERSMITH/LAPIDARIST: Specializes in needlepoint and "snake eye" settings. Learned from her mother and began producing in 1959. Works with her sister. Each creates her own designs. Shirley does the metalwork and her sister the stone work.
HALLMARK: Engraved names of her and her sister or her and her husband.
Spouse is Neal Natewa, sister is Lorraine Laweka.
[Levy:1980:44]

S. Natewa & Laweka

NATEWA, WANDA *Zuni*
SILVERSMITH/LAPIDARIST: Specializes in channel inlay in geometric forms or in mosaic owl designs. Learned from her parents and began producing in 1952. She works on each piece with her husband.
HALLMARK: Stamped surname with shared initials in Gothic print.
Spouse is Pitkin Natewa.
[Levy:1980:26]

P.W.NATEWA

NATSEWAY, ALLEN *Laguna*
SILVERSMITH:
HALLMARK: Stamped arrow with initial.

NATSEWAY, JAMES *Zuni*
SILVERSMITH:
HALLMARK: Stamped joined and personalized initials in print.

NAVA, DOUGLAS *Taos*
SILVERSMITH:
HALLMARK: Stamped symbol of two mountains or initial.

NAVAJOHN, LEROY *Navajo (?)*
SILVERSMITH:
HALLMARK: Stamped initials joined and misaligned in personalized print.
From Gallup, New Mexico region.

NAVASIE, JOY ANN *Hopi*
POTTER: Traditional and contemporary.
HALLMARK: Painted and fired representation of a frog patterned after her mother's hallmark.
Mother was Pakwa or Frog Woman (a name now adopted by Joy Ann. Her daughter is Maryann Navasie).

NAVASIE, MARYANN *Hopi*
POTTER: Traditional and contemporary.
HALLMARK: Uses her mother's and grandmother's mark with the addition of an M at the bottom. Does not, so far, call herself Frog Woman.
Her mother is Joy Ann Navasie, her grandmother was Pakwa.

NAVENMA, CEDRIC *Hopi*
SILVERSMITH: Specializes in silver overlay. Began producing in 1976.
HALLMARK: Stamped representation of the Little War God's head with a single initial at the bottom. Stamp of initials in 1/16 Gothic print. first used in 1976.
[Wright:1982:98]

 C.N.

NED, ANDREW SR. *Navajo*
SILVERSMITH:
HALLMARK: Stamped surname in 1/16 Gothic print with shared initials. Stamp of surname, shared initials, and tribal affiliation in 1/32 Gothic print. Stamp of surname, shared initials, tribal affiliation, and sterling in 1/32 Gothic print. Third stamp first used in 1984.
From Lukachukai, Arizona region.

A.&V.NED   A.&V.NED   A.&V.NED
               NAVAJO   STERLING
                              NAVAJO

NELSON, CHARLIE *Navajo*
SILVERSMITH:
HALLMARK: Stamped surname in 1/16 Gothic print, first used in 1974.
From Mentmore, New Mexico region.

C.NELSON

NELSON, EDDIE *Navajo*
SILVERSMITH:
HALLMARK: Stamped full name in 3/32 Gothic print, first used in 1973.
From Ft. Wingate, New Mexico region.

ED NELSON

NELSON, J.L. *Navajo*
SILVERSMITH:
HALLMARK: Stamped surname in 1/16 Gothic print, first used in 1974.
From Prewitt, New Mexico region.

J.L.NELSON

NELSON, JERRY *Navajo*
SILVERSMITH:
HALLMARK: Stamped initials joined and offset with symbol in personalized print.

NELSON, JOHN *Navajo*
SILVERSMITH: Specializing in channel inlay. Began producing in 1975.
HALLMARK: Stamped personalized initials in italic Gothic.

NELSON, MATTHEW R. *Navajo*
SILVERSMITH:
HALLMARK: Stamped personalized initials in varying sizes with symbol of a feather. Same stamp set on a roundplate.
From Ganado, Arizona region or Toyei.

NELSON, RUTH *Navajo*
LAPIDARIST: Specializes in the use of amber.
HALLMARK: Stamped initials in Gothic print.

HRN

NELWOOD, M ? *Navajo*
SILVERSMITH: Smith for Indian Hammers, later for the Traditional Traders.
HALLMARK: Stamped surname in 1/16 Gothic print, first used in 1976.

M. NELWOOD

NEQUATEWA, EDDIE *Hopi*
SILVERSMITH: Specialized in silver overlay. Produced from 1948 to 1955.
HALLMARK: Stamped stylized symbol of a turtle.
Deceased.
[Wright:1982:84]

NEVAYAKTEWA, DELBERT *Hopi*
SILVERSMITH: Specialized in silver overlay. Began producing in 1976.
HALLMARK: Stamped symbol of an ear of corn pointed on the tip, first used in 1976. Stamped symbol of an ear of corn more rounded (3/32") used first in 1984.
[Wright:1982:98]

NEWMAN, AL *Anglo*
SILVERSMITH:

HALLMARK: Stamped initials in 3/32 Gothic print.

AL

NEZ, AL *Navajo*
SILVERSMITH: Specializes in cast work, shadow box work as well as a variety of others.
HALLMARK: Stamped full name in 1/16 Gothic print, first used in 1982.
Brother is Gibson Nez.

AL NEZ

NEZ, B ? *Navajo*
SILVERSMITH:
HALLMARK: Stamped surname in 3/32 Gothic print, first used in 1979.
From Prewitt, New Mexico region.

B.NEZ

NEZ, CHESTER *Navajo*
SILVERSMITH:
HALLMARK: Stamped initials in Gothic print with an arrow between them first used in 1983. Stamped surname with shared initials in 1/16 Gothic print first used in 1985.
From Lupton, Arizona region.

   C/J NEZ

NEZ, COOLIDGE *Navajo*
SILVERSMITH:
HALLMARK: Stamped symbol and letters.
From Albuquerque, New Mexico region.

OV

NEZ, GIBSON *Navajo*
SILVERSMITH: Specializes in big bold designs with fine inlay. Does chisel work and traditional designs. Self taught, he began producing in 1976.
HALLMARK: Stamped initials in Gothic print divided by an enlarged Z.
Formerly a stuntman, heavy equipment operator, and present in the Cowboy Hall of Fame as a bronc rider.
Brother is Al Nez.

GZN

NEZ, HENRY *Navajo*
SILVERSMITH:
HALLMARK: Stamped full name in 1/16 Gothic print, first used in 1983.
From St. Michaels, Arizona region.

NEZ, HOSKIE *Navajo*
SILVERSMITH:
HALLMARK: Stamped initials joined with an enlarged N.
From Chinle, Arizona region.

NEZ, JACKSON JARRETT *Navajo*

SILVERSMITH:
HALLMARK: Stamped initials joined by a bar and set on a plate. Print is 3/32 Gothic and was first used in 1974.
From Gallup, New Mexico region.

NEZ, JAMES *Navajo*
SILVERSMITH: Smith for the Atkinson Trading Company.
HALLMARK: Stamped initials with an enlarged J and joined to the N. N is in 1/16 Gothic print.

NEZ, JULIAN *Navajo*
SILVERSMITH:
HALLMARK: Handmade stamp of 3/32 Gothic style print of surname first used in 1985. Second stamp of surname and Jewelry in Gothic print. Third stamp of full name in 1/32 personalized script with Handmade in 1/32 Gothic print below.
From Shiprock, New Mexico region.

J.NEZ   J.NEZ JEWELRY   *Julian Nez* HANDMADE

NEZ, LUCY *Navajo*
SILVERSMITH:
HALLMARK: Stamped full name in 3/32 Gothic print, first used in 1976.
From Thoreau, New Mexico region.

LUCY NEZ

NEZ, ROSEMARY *Navajo*
SILVERSMITH:
HALLMARK: Stamped shared (?) initials in Gothic print.

NEZ, THOMAS *Navajo*
SILVERSMITH:
HALLMARK: Stamped initials in Gothic print. One stamp of initials in line, the other with the letters one above the other.

TN

NEZ, WILFORD *Navajo*
SILVERSMITH: Specializes in cluster and nugget work.
HALLMARK: Stamp of a shield 1/4". Second stamp of the same symbol but accompanied by the stamped surname over the shield.
From Gallup, New Mexico region.

NEZZIE, JIMMIE *Navajo*
SILVERSMITH:
HALLMARK: Stamped surname in 1/16 Gothic print, first used in 1975. Second stamp of surname in 1/32 Gothic print is registered and was first used in 1977.
From Winslow, Arizona region.

J.NEZZIE   ®76
NEZZIE

NEZZIE, WILLIE   *Navajo*
SILVERSMITH:
HALLMARK: Stamped initials in 1/16 Gothic print, first used in 1974. Second stamp of surname in 1/16 Gothic print first used in 1977.
From Winslow, Arizona region.

WN   W.NEZZIE

NIETO, ANNACITA P.   *Zuni*
SILVERSMITH:
HALLMARK: Stamped surname in 1/16 Gothic print, first used in 1975.
Spouse J.J. Nieto (?)

A.P.NIETO

NIETO, DAVIS (DAVE)   *Zuni*
SILVERSMITH/LAPIDARIST: Specializes in needlepoint, "snake eye" settings, and clusters. Taught himself and began producing in 1962. He does the metal work and his wife does the stone work.
HALLMARK: Engraved names of him and his wife who share the same mark.
Spouse is Celia Nieto.
[Levy:1980:51]

Daye & Celia
Nieto zuni

NIETO, CELIA   *Zuni*
SILVERSMITH/LAPIDARIST: Specializes in needlepoint, "snake eyes", and cluster work. Make and use their own designs. Taught herself and began producing in 1962. Her husband does the metal work and she does the stonework.
HALLMARK: Engraved names of herself and her husband and tribal affiliation. Mark is shared with her husband.
Spouse is Davis Nieto.
[Levy:1980:51]

Daye & Celia
Nieto zuni

NIETO, J.J.   *Zuni*
SILVERSMITH:
HALLMARK: Stamped surname in 1/16 Gothic print, first used in 1975.
Spouse is Annacita P. Nieto (?).

J.J.NIETO

NIETO, RAY   *Zuni*
SILVERSMITH/LAPIDARIST: Specializes in very large nugget work and some inlay.
HALLMARK: Stamped initials in 1/16 Gothic print. Stamped initials in 1/16 Gothic print with central initial enlarged, first used in 1974. Stamped surname in 1/16 Gothic print, first used in 1974.
Spouse is Rosemary Nieto.
[Bell:1977:58]

RNR   RNR   R.NIETO

NIETO, ROSEMARY   *Zuni*
SILVERSMITH/LAPIDARIST: Specializes in very large nugget work and some inlay.
HALLMARK: Stamped initials shared with husband in 1/16 Gothic print. Stamped initials in 1/16 Gothic print with enlarged central initial, first used in 1974. Stamped surname in 1/16 Gothic print, first used in 1974.
Spouse is Ray Nieto.
[Bell:1977:58]

RNR   RNR   R.NIETO

NIGHTHORSE, BEN   *Cheyenne*
SILVERSMITH/PAINTER/SCULPTOR: Contemporary and fashion jewelry. Self taught in silver work.
HALLMARK: Stamped full name in 1/16 Gothic print, first used in 1977. Stamped symbol of a pinyon beetle (?) first used in 1977. Stamped name which appears to be an English version of an Indian name in 1/16 Gothic print, first appeared in 1978. Stamped shop (?) mark and address in 1/32 Gothic print first appeared in 1980. Stamped full name and Limited Edition in 1/16 and 1/32 script first used in 1982. Stamp of name and location in 1/32 script first used in 1985.
Judo champion, horseman, politician. Graduate of the University of California, San Jose where he majored in Physical Education and minored in Business and Art. Owner of a quarter horse ranch and General Mgr. for SKY-UTE Downs Race Track and Training Center. Congressman [D], Colorado.

BEN NIGHTHORSE      ARROWTAKER

Painted Mesa
Ben Nighthorse
                               Ben Nighthorse
                               Limited Edition

NIIHA, DARLENE   *Zuni*
SILVERSMITH/LAPIDARIST: Specializes in needlepoint.
HALLMARK: Stamped given name in 1/16 Gothic print, first used in 1980. Stamped shared initials in 1/16 Gothic print, first used in 1980.
Spouse is Jefferson Niiha.
[Bell:1977:35]

DARLENE N.   J&DN

NIIHA, ED. (?)   *Zuni*
SILVERSMITH: Smith for Montana Mining Company.
HALLMARK: Full name (?) stamped in 1/16 Gothic print first used in 1974.

ED.NIIHA

NIIHA, JEANNETTE   *Zuni*
SILVERSMITH:
HALLMARK: Two line stamped surname and tribal affiliation in 1/32 Gothic print, first used in 1976.

J.J.NIIHA
   ZUNI

NIIHA, JEFFERSON   *Zuni*
SILVERSMITH/LAPIDARIST: Specializes in needlepoint.
HALLMARK: Stamped surname in 1/16 Gothic print, first used in 1975. Stamped given name in 1/16 Gothic print first used in 1980. Stamped shared initials with wife in 1/16 Gothic print, first used in 1980.

Spouse is Darlene Niiha.
[Bell:1977:35]

J.NIIHA   JEFF N.   J&DN

NIIHA, VERDEL *Zuni*
SILVERSMITH:.
HALLMARK: Stamped symbol with initials in Gothic print.

NOBLE, E? *Navajo*
SILVERSMITH: Smith for Atkinson Trading Company.
HALLMARK: Stamped surname in 1/16 Gothic print, first used in 1981.

E.NOBLE

NORIEGA, ALTON *Papago*
SILVERSMITH:
HALLMARK: Stamped or chiseled joined initials.
[Bahti:1980:131]

/\N

NOTAH, A? *Navajo*
SILVERSMITH: Smith for Atkinson Trading Company.
HALLMARK: Stamped surname in 1/16 Gothic print, first used in 1981.

A.NOTAH

NUMKINA, DAWSON *Hopi*
SILVERSMITH: Specialized in silver overlay. Began producing in 1948.
HALLMARK: Stamped symbol of lightning.
[Wright:1982:81]

NUMKINA, EARL *Hopi*
SILVERSMITH: Specialized in hammered and cast work. Self-taught, he began producing in 1920 and ended in 1940 when his eyes failed.
HALLMARK: Stamped symbol of a man's head scarf.
[Wright:1982:81]

NUTIMA, JIM *Hopi*
SILVERSMITH: Specializes in silver overlay. Began producing in 1971.
HALLMARK: Stamped initials, kildeer track and water combined in a single stamp.
[Wright:1982:98]

NUTUMYA, SHAROLD *Hopi*
SILVERSMITH: Specializes in silver overlay. Began producing in 1974.
HALLMARK: Stamped initials joined and misaligned.
[Wright:1980:98]

5N

NUVAYAOUMA, ARLO *Hopi*
SILVERSMITH: Produced silver overlay. Began producing in 1969 and ceased by 1982.
HALLMARK: Stamped symbol of an antelope head.
[Wright:1982:90]

NUVAYAOUMA, WILLARD *Hopi*
SILVERSMITH: Specialized in silver overlay. Began producing in 1959 but ceased sometime before his death in 1969.
HALLMARK: Stamped symbol of a feather (3/16" tall).
[Wright:1982:88]

OHMSATTE, BERDIE *Zuni*
SILVERSMITH:
HALLMARK: Stamped shared initials and surname in 1/16 Gothic print, first used in 1976. Second stamp is the same except for symbol over the initials.
Spouse is Silas Ohmsatte.

S   B OHMSATTE   

OHMSATTE, SILAS *Zuni*
SILVERSMITH:
HALLMARK: Stamped shared initials and surname in 1/16 Gothic print, first used in 1976. Second stamp is the same except for symbol over the initials. Stamped 1/16 script of given name, first used in 1977.
Spouse is Berdie Ohmsatte.

S   B OHMSATTE  *Silas O.*

OLGUIN, J? *Unknown*
SILVERSMITH:
HALLMARK: Stamped surname in 1/16 Gothic print, first used in 1976.

J.OLGUIN

ONDELACY, ALBERTA *Zuni*
SILVERSMITH:
HALLMARK: Stamped surname in 1/16 Gothic print, first used in 1978.

A.ONDELACY

ONDELACY, FANNIE *Zuni*
SILVERSMITH/LAPIDARIST: Specializes in large cluster work.
HALLMARK: Stamped surname in 1/16 Gothic print, first used in 1975. Engraved surname in personalized print, probably later than the first mark.
Spouse was Warren Ondelacy.
[Bell:1977:32]

F.W. ONDELACY　　*F.W. Ondalacy*

ONDELACY, SOL　　*Zuni*
SILVERSMITH:
HALLMARK: Stamped given name in 3/32 Gothic print, first used in 1974.

SOL

ONDELACY, WARREN　　*Zuni*
SILVERSMITH/LAPIDARIST: Produced very large Zuni cluster work.
HALLMARK: Used stamped initials for individual work and stamped surname with individual initials for work shared. Spouse was Fannie Ondelacy. Deceased.

F.W. ONDELACY

ONSAE, LARSON　　*Hopi*
SILVERSMITH: Specialized in silver overlay. Began producing in 1957 but ceased sometime after 1962.
HALLMARK: Stamped symbol of a spider.
[Wright:1982:88]

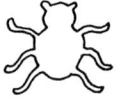

ORTIZ, L?　　*Unknown*
SILVERSMITH: Piecework for Montana Mining Company.
HALLMARK: Stamped surname and initial in 1/16 Gothic print. Individual mark first used in 1974. Mark shared with her husband first used in 1983.
Spouse is Raymond Ortiz.

L.ORTIZ　　　**R&L ORTIZ**

ORTIZ, RAYMOND　　*Unknown*
SILVERSMITH:
HALLMARK: Stamped surname with shared initials in 1/16 Gothic print, first used in 1983.
From Albuquerque, New Mexico region.

R&L ORTIZ

OTHOLE, ADRIAN A.　　*Unknown*
SILVERSMITH:
HALLMARK: Stamped surname in 1/16 Gothic print, first used in 1974.
From Albuquerque, New Mexico region.

AA.OTHOLE

OTHOLE, F?　　*Zuni*
SILVERSMITH: Piecework for Robert Winfield.
HALLMARK: Stamped surname in 1/16 Gothic print, first used in 1977.

F.OTHOLE

PABLITO, ANTHONY　　*Zuni*
SILVERSMITH:
HALLMARK: Stamped surname in 1/16 Gothic print, first used in 1975. Second stamped surname in 1/16 Gothic print, single initial, first used in 1977.

A.L.PABLITO　　**A.PABLITO**

PABLITO, R?　　*Zuni*
SILVERSMITH:
HALLMARK: Stamped surname in 1/16 Gothic print, first used in 1976.

R.PABLITO

PABLO, JOHNNIE　　*Navajo*
SILVERSMITH: Specializes in squashblossoms in shadow box style in very heavy silver. Worked for Zachary and Price in Albuquerque, N.M. Self taught, he was producing in 1977.
HALLMARK: Stamped initials in Gothic print. Stamped full name in Gothic print.

JP　　**JOHNNIE PABLO**

PABLO, SAM　　*Navajo*
SILVERSMITH:
HALLMARK: Stamped initials in Gothic print.

SP

PACQUIN, ISABELLE　　*Zuni*
SILVERSMITH:
HALLMARK: Stamped shared initials with spouse in 1/16 Gothic print, first used in 1974.
Spouse is Sherman Pacquin.

S.&I.P.

PACQUIN, SHERMAN　　*Zuni*
SILVERSMITH:
HALLMARK: Stamped shared initials with spouse in 1/16 Gothic print, first used in 1974.
Spouse is Isabelle Pacquin.

S.&I.P.

PADILLA, BESSIE　　*Navajo*
SILVERSMITH:
HALLMARK: Stamped personalized initials joined in reverse.
From Puertocito, New Mexico region.

BP

PADILLA, J?　　*Unknown*
SILVERSMITH: Smith for New Mexico Jewelry.
HALLMARK: Stamped surname in 3/32 Gothic print, first used in 1975.
From Los Lunas, New Mexico region.

J.PADILLA

PADILLA, PAUL　　*Isleta/Sandia*
SILVERSMITH:
HALLMARK: Stamped initials in Gothic print.

P.D.

PADILLA, WILSON　　*Navajo*
SILVERSMITH: Smith for New Mexico Jewelry.
HALLMARK: Stamped surname in 3/32 Gothic print, first used in 1975. Stamp of initials in Gothic print.
From Los Lunas, New Mexico region.

W.PADILLA   W.P.

PALMER, KEITH *Unknown*
SILVERSMITH:
HALLMARK: Stamped given name in 1/16 print with enlarged capital combined with an arrow. Stamp first used in 1983.

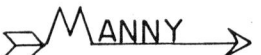

PALOMA, JANICE *Zuni*
SILVERSMITH:
HALLMARK: Stamped surname in 1/16 Gothic print, first used in 1977. Paloma is also used as a family hallmark but size and print type is unknown.

PALOMA

PANTEAH, ALMA *Zuni*
SILVERSMITH/LAPIDARIST: Specializes in cluster work. Began producing in 1945.
HALLMARK: Stamped initials and tribal affiliation in 1/16 Gothic print, first used ca. 1975.
Sisters are Lolita Wyaco and Maxine Wato.
[Bell:1976:38]

A.P.
ZUNI

PANTEAH, AUGUSTINE *Zuni*
SILVERSMITH/LAPIDARIST: Specializes in square stones with twisted wire and large inlays of buffalo and other figures.
HALLMARK: Stamped surname and tribal affiliation in two lines done in 1/16 Gothic print. Occasionally his mark is accompanied by an engraved ZCA the mark of the Zuni Arts and Crafts Cooperative.
Brothers are Florentine, Martin, and Wayne Panteah.
[Bell:1975:32]

A.A.PANTEAH
ZUNI

PANTEAH, ESTHER *Zuni*
SILVERSMITH/LAPIDARIST: Specializes in solid channel work with domed and shaped stones. Uses family designs. Began producing in 1973. Her husband does the stone work and she does the silver work.
HALLMARK: Stamped surname and tribal affiliation in two lines of 1/16 Gothic print, first used in 1979. Stamped surname with given names of her and her husband in two lines of 1/16 Gothic print.
Spouse is Martin Panteah.
[Levy:1980:22]

M.T.PANTEAH   MARVIN & ESTHER
ZUNI   PANTEAH

PANTEAH, FLORENTINE *Zuni*
SILVERSMITH/LAPIDARIST: Specializes in mosaic inlaid figures of buffalo and other animals, also does large stonework settings.
HALLMARK: Stamped surname, tribal affiliation, and location in Gothic print in two lines. Stamped surname and given names of his wife and himself in three lines of 3/32 Gothic print, first used in 1975. Stamp of full name in personalized script.
Spouse is Lela Panteah, brothers are Augustine, Martin, and Wayne Panteah.
[Bell:1975:68]

F.PANTEAH   FLORENTINE
ZUNI, NEW MEXICO   PANTEAH &
                    LELA

Florentine Panteah

PANTEAH, GUS *Zuni*
SILVERSMITH/LAPIDARIST:
HALLMARK: Two-line stamped surname with given names of his wife and himself in 1/16 Gothic print, first used in 1975.
Spouse is Lori Panteah.

GUS & LORI
PANTEAH

PANTEAH, JOSIE *Zuni*
SILVERSMITH/LAPIDARIST: Specializes in channel inlay with wide strips of silver.
HALLMARK: Stamped surname in Gothic print. Stamp of her husband's and her own initials and surname in Gothic print. Stamp shared by her and her husband.
Spouse is Wayne Panteah.
[Bell:1976:37]

PANTEAH   W.J.PANTEAH

PANTEAH, LELA *Zuni*
SILVERSMITH/LAPIDARIST: Specializes in mosaic inlaid figures of buffalo and other animals, also does large stonework settings.
HALLMARK: Three-line stamped surname and given names of her husband and herself in 3/32 Gothic print, first used in 1975.
Spouse is Florentine Panteah.
[Bell:1975:68]

FLORENTINE
PANTEAH &
LELA

PANTEAH, LORI *Zuni*
SILVERSMITH/LAPIDARIST:
HALLMARK: Two-line stamped surname and given names of her husband and her own in 1/16 Gothic print, first used in 1975.
Spouse is Gus Panteah.

GUS & LORI
PANTEAH

PANTEAH, MARTIN *Zuni*
SILVERSMITH/LAPIDARIST: Specializes in channel inlay with raised stones whose edges are shaped. Uses family designs. Learned by watching his mother and began producing in 1973.
HALLMARK: Stamped surname and tribal affiliation in two lines of 1/16 Gothic print, first used in 1979. Stamped surname with given names of him and his wife in two lines of 1/16 Gothic print, first used in 1979.
Spouse is Esther Panteah, brothers are Augustine, Florentine, and Wayne Panteah.
[Levy:1980:22]

M.T.PANTEAH   MARVIN & ESTHER
ZUNI   PANTEAH

PANTEAH, PAULA *Zuni*
SILVERSMITH:
HALLMARK: Stamped surname in 1/16 Gothic print, first used in 1977.

From Mexican Springs, New Mexico region.

P.PANTEAH

PANTEAH, QUINCY *Zuni*
SILVERSMITH/LAPIDARIST: Specializes in petit point. Began producing in 1961. Sporadic production because of political career.
HALLMARK: Stamped surname in Gothic print. Stamped surname with shared initials of his wife's and his own.
Spouse is Rose Panteah. He is a Zuni Tribal Councilman.
[Bell:1975:49]

Q.PANTEAH   R.Q.PANTEAH

PANTEAH, ROSEMARY *Zuni*
SILVERSMITH/LAPIDARIST: Specializes in petit point. Began producing in 1961 with her husband.
HALLMARK: Stamped surname with shared initials of her own and her husband's.
Spouse is Quincy Panteah.
[Bell:1975:49]

R.Q.PANTEAH

PANTEAH, WAYNE *Zuni*
SILVERSMITH/LAPIDARIST: Specializes in channel inlay with wide strips of silver. Began producing in 1973.
HALLMARK: Stamped surname in Gothic print. Stamped surname with shared initials of his own and his wife's in Gothic print.
Spouse is Josie Panteah, brothers are Augustine, Martin, and Florentine Panteah.
[Bell:1976:37]

W.J.PANTEAH   PANTEAH

PAKWA *Hopi*
POTTER: Traditional.
HALLMARK: Painted and fired rendition of a frog. Her name meant frog. Her daughter uses the same mark.
Daughter is Joy Ann Navasie who now calls herself Frog Woman. Granddaughter is Maryann Navasie.

PAQUIN, ALVIN *Zuni*
SILVERSMITH/LAPIDARIST:
HALLMARK: Stamped initials.

AP

PAQUIN, GERALDINE *Unknown*
SILVERSMITH: Smith for Bilagaanas Trading Post.
HALLMARK: Stamped combination of Laguna and Zuni in 1/16 Gothic print. Stamp first used in 1985. Shop mark.
Spouse is Leonard Paquin.
From Canyoncito, New Mexico region.

LAG-ZUN

PAQUIN, LEONARD *Unknown*
SILVERSMITH: Smith for Bilagaanas Trading Post.
HALLMARK: Stamped combination of Laguna and Zuni in 1/16 Gothic print. Stamp first used in 1985. Shop mark.
Spouse is Geraldine Paquin.

From Canyoncito, New Mexico region.

LAG-ZUN

PARKER, D.? *Unknown*
SILVERSMITH:
HALLMARK: Stamped in 1/16 Gothic print, first used in 1973.

INDIAN

PARKER, LENNIE *Zuni*
SILVERSMITH:
HALLMARK: Stamped joined personalized print set on a shield-shaped plate or a triangular plate.

   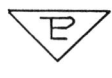

PARKER, TRUDY *Navajo*
SILVERSMITH:
HALLMARK: Stamped surname in 1/16 Gothic print, first used in 1985.
From Ft. Defiance, Arizona region.

T.PARKER

PASELENTE, JANE *Zuni*
SILVERSMITH:
HALLMARK: Stamped surname in 1/16 Gothic print, first used in 1975.

J.PASELENTE

PATANIA, FRANK SR. *Anglo*
SILVERSMITH: Specialized in broad plain silver, nugget settings, shadow box pieces. Strongly influenced native silversmiths.
HALLMARK: Stamped initials offset but joined. Stamped initials in Gothic print. Stamped symbol of a thunderbird enclosing his initials.
From Santa Fe, New Mexico region.

   F.P.

PATANIA, FRANK JR. *Anglo*
SILVERSMITH: Specializes in dishes, hollow ware etc. Not a strong influence in Indian communities.
HALLMARK: Stamped initials offset but joined and with the vertical bar of the P crossed.
From Santa Fe, New Mexico region.

FP

PATTERSON, JIMMIE *Navajo*
SILVERSMITH: Specializes in chip inlay. Began producing in 1975.
HALLMARK: Stamped single initial usually driven very deep.

P

PAUL, BETTY *Navajo*
SILVERSMITH: Smith for Atkinson Trading Company.
HALLMARK: Stamped initials in Gothic print. Stamped full

name in 1/16 Gothic print, first used in 1974.

B.Y.   BETTY PAUL

PAUL, DELORES *Navajo*
SILVERSMITH: Smith for Atkinson Trading Company.
HALLMARK: Stamped surname in 1/16 Gothic print, first used in 1975.

D.PAUL

PAUL, LEO *Navajo*
SILVERSMITH: Smith for Atkinson Trading Company.
HALLMARK: Stamped full name in 1/16 Gothic print, first used in 1976.

LEO PAUL

PAUL, RITA *Navajo*
SILVERSMITH: Smith for Atkinson Trading Company.
HALLMARK: Stamped full name in 1/16 Gothic print, first used in 1974. Stamped surname in 1/16 Gothic print, first used in 1976.

RITA PAUL   R. PAUL

PAVATEA, GARNET *Tewa*
POTTER: Produced from 1950 to 1980.
HALLMARK: Painted and fired representation of a larkspur or her name in personalized print. Flower is the earliest mark.

GARNET PAVATEA

PAWIKI, GRANT *Hopi*
SILVERSMITH: Specializes in silver overlay. Began producing in 1976.
HALLMARK: Stamped initials in Gothic print or stamped symbol of a spider flanked by initials.
[Wright:1982:98]

G⟨⟩P   GP

PAYLASI, IRENE *Zuni*
SILVERSMITH:
HALLMARK: Stamped surname in 1/16 Gothic print, first used in 1976. There is an error in the spelling of the name on the stamp.

I.PAYLUSI

PAYWA, JIM *Zuni*
SILVERSMITH:
HALLMARK: Stamped full name in 3/32 Gothic print, first used in 1982.

JIM PAYWA

PEINA, BERNARD *Zuni*
SILVERSMITH/LAPIDARIST: Specializes in needlepoint. Learned from watching his brother and sister. Began producing in 1974. He does the designs, metal work, and stone work with his wife assisting.
HALLMARK: Engraved surname and given names of him and his wife.
Spouse is Sylvia Peina. Brother is Zigmond Peina.
[Levy:1980:47]

Bernard Sylvia Peina

PEINA, ETHEL *Zuni*
SILVERSMITH/LAPIDARIST: Specializes in needlepoint. Began producing in 1974. Husband does the metal work and she does the stone work.
HALLMARK: Stamped surname in 1/16 Gothic print. Shared mark.
Spouse is Zigmond Peina.
[Levy:1980:46]

Z.PEINA

PEINA, SYLVIA *Zuni*
SILVERSMITH/LAPIDARIST: Specializes in a delicate needlepoint. Learned with her husband from watching his brother. Began producing in 1974. Assists her husband with the metal work.
HALLMARK: Engraved surname and given names of her husband and her own.
Spouse is Bernard Peina.
[Levy:1980:46]

Bernard Sylvia Peina

PEINA, ZIGMOND *Zuni*
SILVERSMITH/LAPIDARIST: Specializes in needlepoint. Learned from watching his sister. Began producing in 1974. He does the metal work and his wife does the stonework.
HALLMARK: Stamped surname in 1/16 Gothic print, shared with his wife.
Spouse is Ethel Peina.
[Levy:1980:46]

Z.PEINA

PEKYTEWA, PAUL *Zuni*
SILVERSMITH:
HALLMARK: Stamped initials of his wife and his own in 1/16 Gothic print, first used in 1973.

C.&.P.P.

PENKETEWA, A? *Zuni*
SILVERSMITH:
HALLMARK: Stamped surname in 1/16 Gothic print, first used in 1974.

A.PENKETEWA

PENKETEWA, CLAUDINE *Zuni*
SILVERSMITH/LAPIDARIST: Specializes in well designed needlepoint chokers.
HALLMARK: Stamped initials in Gothic print.
[Bell:1975:71]

C.P.

PENKETEWA, DOROTHY *Zuni*
GOLDSMITH:
HALLMARK: Stamped initials in Gothic print.

D.P.

PENTEWA, LONNIE A. *Hopi*
SILVERSMITH:
HALLMARK: Stamped initials in Gothic print.

LP

PEONE, LES *Unknown*

L.PEONE

PESHLAKAI, DALTON *Navajo*
SILVERSMITH:
HALLMARK: Stamped symbol of an arrow with a single 3/32 initial in Gothic print, first used in 1974. Stamped symbol of an arrow with two lines of 3/32 Gothic print first used in 1974.
From Ganado, Arizona region.

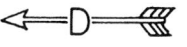   

PESHLAKAI, ETTA *Navajo*
SILVERSMITH:
HALLMARK: Stamped symbol of an arrow with a single initial in 3/32 Gothic print, first used in 1974. Second stamp of two lines of 3/32 Gothic print and the symbol of an arrow, first used in 1974.
From Ganado, Arizona region.

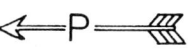   

PESHLAKAI, FRANK *Navajo*
SILVERSMITH:
HALLMARK: Stamped initials in Gothic print.

F.P.

PESHLAKAI, FRED *Navajo*
SILVERSMITH: Traditional silver. Learned from father and uncles. Produced from 1930 to 1960. His tools are now in possession of Dee Morris.
HALLMARK: Stamped initials in Gothic print. Stamped initials in Gothic print with the symbol of an arrow above. Stamped symbol of an arrow with initials in Gothic print in the center of the shaft. One of the first known silversmiths to stamp his work using a plain FP.
Grandson of Atsidi Sani.
Demonstrator in 1934 World's Fair.

F.P.

PESHLAKAI, NORBERT *Navajo*
SILVERSMITH: Contemporary pieces.
HALLMARK: Engraved signature in script. Stamped symbol 3/32" long.
From Crystal, New Mexico region.

Norbert Peshlakai

PESHLAKAI, OTIS *Navajo*
SILVERSMITH:
HALLMARK: Stamped surname in 1/16 Gothic print, first used in 1975.
From Thoreau, New Mexico region.

O.PESHLAKAI

PETE, CURTIS *Navajo*
SILVERSMITH: Smith for Rocking Horse Ranch.
HALLMARK: Stamped surname in 1/16 Gothic print.

C.PETE

PETER, BEN *Navajo*
SILVERSMITH: Smith for Indian Hammers.
HALLMARK: Stamped surname in 1/16 Gothic print, first used in 1977.
From Mentmore, New Mexico region.

B.PETER

PETER, E.? *Navajo*
SILVERSMITH: Smith for Indian Hammers.
HALLMARK: Stamped surname in 1/16 Gothic print, first used in 1976.

E.PETER

PETERMAN, ? *Unknown*
SILVERSMITH:
HALLMARK: Stamped surname in 1/16 Gothic print first used in 1984.

PETERMAN

PEWA, ALBERT *Zuni*
SILVERSMITH/LAPIDARIST:
HALLMARK: Stamped initials in Gothic print. Uses a family stamp also.

AP

PEYKETEWA, CAROL *Zuni*
SILVERSMITH/LAPIDARIST: Specializes in needlepoint in traditional designs. Learned from her mother and began producing in 1973. Her husband does the metal work and the stone cutting while she sets and polishes.
HALLMARK: Engraved surname with her husband's and her own given names in script.
Spouse is Libert Peyketewa.
[Levy:1980:39]

Libert & Carol Peyketewa

PEYKETEWA, LIBERT *Zuni*
SILVERSMITH/LAPIDARIST: Specializes in needlepoint in traditional designs. Taught himself and began producing in 1973. He does the metal work and the stone cutting. His wife polishes and sets the stones.
HALLMARK: Engraved surname with his wife's and his own given names in script.
Spouse is Carol Peyketewa.
[Levy:1980:39]

Libert & Carol Peyketewa

PEYNETSA, AMY *Zuni*
SILVERSMITH/LAPIDARIST: Specializes in small oval stones with silver "beads" around them. Creates her own designs. Learned from her father and began producing in 1955. She does the metalwork and the stone work; her husband helps with the polishing.
HALLMARK: Stamped surname and location in Gothic print. Signs her work with engraved signature also.
Spouse is Joe Peynetsa.

[Levy:1980:42, 43]

A. PEYNETSA, ZUNI N.M.

PEYNETSA, JANE L. *Zuni*
SILVERSMITH:
HALLMARK: Stamped surname in 1/16 Gothic print, first used in 1974. May be shared with Jennie Epaloos.

J.L.

PEYNETSA, MITZI *Zuni*
SILVERSMITH:
HALLMARK: Stamped surname in 1/16 Gothic print, first used in 1974.

M.P. PEYNETSA

PEYNETSA, QUINCY *Zuni*
SILVERSMITH/LAPIDARIST: Produces an inlay resembling Frank Vacit's work.
HALLMARK: Stamped surname and initial.

Q. PEYNETSA

PEYNETSA, SARAH *Zuni*
SILVERSMITH:
HALLMARK: Stamped initials in 1/16 Gothic print, first used in 1974.

S.P.

PEYWA, JEAN *Zuni*
SILVERSMITH:
HALLMARK: Stamped surname in 3/32 Gothic print, first used in 1976. Error in the spelling on the stamp.

J. PEYNA

PHILLIPS, DANIEL *Hopi*
SILVERSMITH: Specializes in silver overlay. Began production in 1970.
HALLMARK: Stamped symbol of a rabbit stick (3/16") first used in 1970. Stylized angular offset initials, first used in 1977.
[Wright:1982:91]

PHILLIPS, LOREN *Hopi*
SILVERSMITH: Specializes in silver overlay. Began producing in 1972.
HALLMARK: Stamped stylized symbol of a rabbit stick first used in 1977. Stamped symbol of a rabbit stick with initials first used in 1973. Chisel stamped combined initials first used in 1972. Last stamp is in two varieties.
[Wright:1982:93]

PHILLIPS, RODERICK *Hopi*
SILVERSMITH: Specializes in silver overlay. Began producing in 1972.
HALLMARK: Stamped sun symbol done with separate stamps.
[Wright:1982:93]

PHILNETTO or NETTO, PHIL *Navajo (?)*
SILVERSMITH:
HALLMARK: Stamped star or floral symbol.
From Canyoncito, New Mexico.

PIASO, CINDY *Navajo*
SILVERSMITH:
HALLMARK: Stamped monogram of combined and joined initials.
From Shiprock, New Mexico region.

C∿P

PIASO, SAM *Zuni*
SILVERSMITH: Smith for the Nakai Trading Company.
HALLMARK: Stamped initials in Gothic print. Stamped given name in Gothic print. Stamped full name in 1/32 Gothic print first used in 1985.

S.P.   SAM PIASO   SAM P

PIASO, VIRGINIA *Navajo*
SILVERSMITH:
HALLMARK: Stamped initials in Gothic print.

VP

PIKE, SNYDER *Apache*
LAPIDARIST: Peridot settings.
HALLMARK: Stamped initials in Gothic print. Appears to be a shared hallmark.

SPE

PINCIO, ROSE *Zuni*
SILVERSMITH:
HALLMARK: Stamped initials in Gothic print.
From Gallup, New Mexico region.

RP

PINO, DAVE *Unknown*
SILVERSMITH:
HALLMARK: Stamped initials in Gothic print.
Spouse is Marie Pino, mother is Rita G. Pino, and sister is Ida Pino.

DP

PINO, GILBERT *Unknown*
SILVERSMITH: Smith for the Albuquerque shops in 1978-9.
HALLMARK: Stamped initials in Gothic print.
Spouse is Offina Pino, mother is Rita G. Pino, and brother is Gilson Pino.
From Alamo, New Mexico region.

G.P.

PINO, HAROG *Unknown*

SILVERSMITH: Smith for the Albuquerque shops in 1978-9.
HALLMARK: Stamped initials in Gothic print.

HP

PINO, HARVEY *Unknown*
SILVERSMITH:
HALLMARK: Stamped offset initials in Gothic print. Uses multiple names so there may be other marks.
From Alamo, New Mexico region.

Hp

PINO, IDA *Unknown*
SILVERSMITH:
HALLMARK: Stamped initials in Gothic print.
Mother is Rita G. Pino, brother is Dave Pino.

IP

PINO, IRA *Unknown*
SILVERSMITH: Smith for the Albuquerque shops in 1978-9.
HALLMARK: Stamped initials in Gothic print.
From Alamo, New Mexico region.

IP

PINO, JACKSON *Unknown*
SILVERSMITH: Smith for the Albuquerque shops in 1978-9.
HALLMARK: Stamped joined initials in Gothic print.
From Alamo, New Mexico region.

JP

PINO, KATHERINE *Unknown*
SILVERSMITH: Smith for the Albuquerque shops in 1978-9.
HALLMARK: Stamped initials in Gothic print.
From Alamo, New Mexico region.

KP

PINO, MARIE *Unknown*
SILVERSMITH:
HALLMARK: Stamped initials in Gothic print.
Spouse is Dave Pino.

MP

PINO, NELLIE *Navajo*
SILVERSMITH: Smith for the Atkinson Trading Company.
HALLMARK: Stamped surname in 1/16 Gothic print, first used in 1976.

N.PINO

PINO, OFFINA *Unknown*
SILVERSMITH: Smith for shops in Albuquerque in 1978-9, also for Hill Turquoise.
HALLMARK: Stamped initials in Gothic print.
Spouse is Gilbert Pino, mother-in-law is Rita G. Pino. From Alamo, New Mexico region.

OP

PINO, RITA G. *Unknown*
SILVERSMITH: Smith for shops in Albuquerque in 1978-9.
HALLMARK: Stamped initials in Gothic print.
Sons are Gilbert and Gilson Pino.
From Torreon, New Mexico region.

R.G.P.

PINTO, ARLINDA ROSE *Zuni*
SILVERSMITH/LAPIDARIST:
HALLMARK: Two-line stamped initials and tribal affiliation in Gothic print.

ARP
ZUNI

PINTO, AUGUSTINE *Zuni*
SILVERSMITH/LAPIDARIST: Specializes in mosaic inlay of kachina figures, also carved inlay.
HALLMARK: Stamped initials in Gothic print in horizontal or vertical line. Shared with spouse.
Spouse is Rosalie Pinto.
[Bell:1976:36]

A.R.P.   A
         R
         P

PINTO, BENNY *Navajo*
SILVERSMITH:
HALLMARK: Stamped initials in Gothic print.

BP

PINTO, ROSALIE *Zuni*
SILVERSMITH/LAPIDARIST: Specializes in carved mosaic inlay of kachina figures.
HALLMARK: Stamped initials in Gothic print in horizontal or vertical line. Shared with spouse.
Spouse is Augustine Pinto.
[Bell:1976:36]

A.R.P.   A   RP
         R
         P

PLATERO, ? *Unknown*
SILVERSMITH: Smith for Cooper's Indian Store.
HALLMARK: Stamped surname in 1/16 Gothic print, first used in 1981.

PLATERO

PLATERO, AGNES *Navajo*
SILVERSMITH:
HALLMARK: Stamped joined initials in personalized print.
From Prewitt, New Mexico region.

AP

PLATERO, ALBERT *Navajo*
SILVERSMITH:
HALLMARK: Stamped initials in Gothic print.

AL /PL

PLATERO, ALICE *Navajo*
SILVERSMITH:
HALLMARK: Stamped initials in Gothic print.

A.P.

PLATERO, ANTOINETTE *Laguna*
SILVERSMITH:
HALLMARK: Stamped initials in 5/32 Gothic print.
From Blue Water, New Mexico region.

AP

PLATERO, BETTY *Navajo*
SILVERSMITH: Pieceworker.
HALLMARK: Stamped initials in 1/16 Gothic print. Stamped surname with shared initials of her husband's and her own in 1/16 Gothic print, first used in 1974.
Spouse is Scotty Platero.
From Thoreau, New Mexico region.

BP   S&B PLATERO

PLATERO, CAROL *Navajo*
SILVERSMITH: Smith in the Albuquerque shops in 1978-9.
HALLMARK: Stamped initials in Gothic print.
From Canyoncito, New Mexico region.

CSP

PLATERO, DON *Navajo*
SILVERSMITH:
HALLMARK: Stamped initials in Gothic print in conjunction with a straight bar placed in different positions.

DP   DP/   DP

PLATERO, F.C. *Navajo*
SILVERSMITH:
HALLMARK: Three-line stamp of tribal affiliation surname and silver content in 1/16 Gothic print. Stamp first used in 1985.

NAVAJO
PLATERO FC
STERLING

PLATERO, FANNIE *Navajo*
SILVERSMITH: Pieceworker.
HALLMARK: Three-line stamp of tribal affiliation, surname and silver content in Gothic print in an oval form. Also uses a single initial in Gothic print.

NAVAJO
FNE PLATERO   F
STERLING

PLATERO, FREDDIE *Navajo*
SILVERSMITH:
HALLMARK: Stamped initials in Gothic print.
From Canyoncito, New Mexico region.

F.P.

PLATERO, HERBERT *Navajo*
SILVERSMITH:
HALLMARK: Stamped initials in Gothic print or stamped and joined initials in the same print style.

HP   HP

PLATERO, INEZ *Navajo*
SILVERSMITH:
HALLMARK: Stamped initials in Gothic print.

I P

PLATERO, JEANETTE *Navajo*
SILVERSMITH:
HALLMARK: Stamped initials in Gothic print.
Spouse is Robert Platero.
From Canyoncito, New Mexico region.

JP

PLATERO, JERRY *Navajo*
SILVERSMITH:
HALLMARK: Stamped initials in Gothic print. Stamped surname in 3/32 Gothic print, first used in 1982.
From Gallup, New Mexico region.

J P   J.PLATERO

PLATERO, JOEY *Navajo*
SILVERSMITH:
HALLMARK: Stamped initials in Gothic print.
Spouse is Maria Platero, brother is Robert Platero and sister Maryann Platero Mexicano.
From Canyoncito, New Mexico region.

JP

PLATERO, JOHN *Navajo*
SILVERSMITH:
HALLMARK: Stamped initials in Gothic print.

J.P.

PLATERO, JOHNSON *Navajo*
SILVERSMITH: Smith for Johnny Pablo.
HALLMARK: Two-line stamped full name in 1/32 Gothic print.
From Albuquerque, New Mexico region.

JOHNSON
PLATERO

PLATERO, JONATHAN *Navajo*
SILVERSMITH:
HALLMARK: Stamped intials in Gothic print.
Deceased.

JP

PLATERO, LEONARD *Navajo*
SILVERSMITH:
HALLMARK: Stamped initials in Gothic print.

LP

PLATERO, LOLITA *Zuni*
SILVERSMITH:
HALLMARK: Stamped surname in 1/16 Gothic print, first used in 1985.
From Canyoncito, New Mexico region.

L.PLATERO

PLATERO, LOUISE or LUCILLE (?) *Navajo*
SILVERSMITH: Specializes in foliate silver work.

HALLMARK: Stamped surname using home-made stamp, first used in 1975.
Spouse is Ramon Platero.
From Little Blue Water, New Mexico region.

L PlAtero

PLATERO, MARIA *Navajo*
SILVERSMITH:
HALLMARK: Stamped initials in Gothic print.
Spouse is Joey Platero.

MP

PLATERO, PREWITT *Navajo*
SILVERSMITH:
HALLMARK: Stamped initials in Gothic print offset in position.

AP
 R
  L

PLATERO, RAMON *Navajo*
SILVERSMITH: Smith in the Albuquerque shops. Specializes in foliate work. Presumably one of the first to use the leaf in silver jewelry.
HALLMARK: Stamped surname in 1/16 Gothic print, first used in 1974. Also hand stamped surname in personalized print.
Spouse is Louise Platero.
[Ariz. Hwy: May, 1979:38]

R. PLATERO   R PlATeRo

PLATERO, ROBERT *Navajo*
SILVERSMITH:
HALLMARK: Stamped initials in Gothic print.
Spouse is Jeanette Platero, brother Joey Platero, sister Maryanne Platero Mexicano.

RP

PLATERO, SAM *Navajo*
SILVERSMITH:
HALLMARK: Stamped given name in Gothic print.

SAM P

PLATERO, SCOTTY *Navajo*
SILVERSMITH: Pieceworker.
HALLMARK: Stamped surname with shared initials in 1/16 Gothic print, first used in 1974.
Spouse is Betty Platero.
From Thoreau, New Mexico region.

S & B PLATERO

PLATERO, THOMPSON *Navajo*
SILVERSMITH: Smith for Roger Hill.
HALLMARK: Stamped initials in 1/16 Gothic print. Uses the stamped representation of a tipi with his initials below it. The tipi mark is that of Roger Hill.
From Albuquerque. New Mexico region.

T.P.

PLATERO, TOM *Navajo*
SILVERSMITH:
HALLMARK: Stamped full name in 1/16 Gothic print, first used in 1975.
From Ft. Defiance, Arizona region.

TOM PLATERO

PLATERO, VERONICA *Navajo*
SILVERSMITH: Smith in the Albuquerque shops in 1978-9.
HALLMARK: Stamped initials in Gothic print.
From Albuquerque, New Mexico region.

V.E.P.

PLATERS, ALICE *Navajo*
SILVERSMITH:
HALLMARK: Stamped joined initials in Gothic print.

MP

PLATERS, JOHN *Navajo*
SILVERSMITH:
HALLMARK: Stamped initials in personalized Gothic style print.

J P

PLUMMER, HARRY *Navajo*
SILVERSMITH: Smith for Atkinson Trading Company in 1974.
HALLMARK: Stamped surname in 1/16 Gothic print, first used in 1974.

H. PLUMMER

POBLANO, MARY L. *Zuni*
SILVERSMITH:
HALLMARK: Stamped surname in 1/16 Gothic print, first used in 1975. Stamped initials in 1/16 Gothic print, first used in 1977.

M.L. POBLANO   M.L.P.

POBLANO, S. *Zuni*
SILVERSMITH/LAPIDARIST: Smith for Robert Winfield.
HALLMARK: Stamped surname in 1/16 Gothic print, first used in 1975.

S. POBLANO

POBLANO, VERONICA see **NASTACIO, VERONICA**

POLACCA, ELLSWORTH see **NAMPEYO, ELLSWORTH**

POLACCA, FANNIE NAMPEYO *Tewa*
POTTER: Began producing ca. 1930. More than any of Nampeyo's other daughters, Fannie's use of the so-called "migration pattern" or "bat wing design" caused this very ancient feature to be identified as Nampeyo's.
HALLMARK: Painted and fired on the vessel. In addition to signing Nampeyo's pottery, Fannie signed her own with her full name and the symbol of an ear of corn. Her printed signature alone was used from ca. 1934 until 1972.
Deceased in 1987.

FANNIE
NAMPEYO

POLACCA, HAROLD — *Tewa*
POTTER:
HALLMARK: Painted and fired mark of a corn plant.

POLACCA, STARLIE — *Hopi-Havasupai*
SILVERSMITH:
HALLMARK: Engraved initials or small figure.

POLACCA, TOM — *Tewa*
POTTER/SILVERSMITH: Ceramics are contemporary carved and heavily decorated wares. Produced a little silver ca. 1970.
HALLMARK: Painted and fired hallmark of a corn plant. Also uses full name in personalized print. Uses the name Tom Nampeyo also.

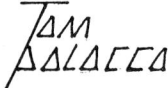 

POLEAHLA, ELAINE — *Hopi*
POTTER: Still producing pottery in 1970.
HALLMARK: Painted and fired corn and cloud symbols with her name printed between.

POLELONEMA, TYLER — *Hopi*
SILVERSMITH: Specialized in silver overlay. Began producing in 1985.
HALLMARK: Stamped symbol of a macaw's beak (1/8"), first used in 1985.

POLELONEMA, WALTER — *Hopi*
SILVERSMITH: Specialized in silver overlay. Produced from 1948 until his death in 1971.
HALLMARK: Stamped symbol of a rattlesnake rattle (1/8"). Stamp is used now by Raymie Namingha.
[Wright:1982:86]

POLEQUAPTEWA, RILEY — *Hopi*
SILVERSMITH: Specializes in silver overlay. Began producing in 1972.
HALLMARK: Stamped symbol of bear claws (1/4 x 5/32") or initials in Gothic print.
[Wright:1982:93]

  RP

POLEVIYOUMA, JACOB JR. — *Hopi*
SILVERSMITH: Specialized in silver overlay. Produced from 1976 until his death in 1987.
HALLMARK: Stamped symbol of a feather (7/32" long) used first in 1976. Stamped initials in Gothic print.
[Wright:1982:98]

 JPJR   JP

POLEYMA, RAMONA — *Hopi*
SILVERSMITH: Smith for Charles Loloma.
HALLMARK: Stamped symbol of an animal with her given name in Gothic print (3/16" in length), first used in 1984. Stamp of a butterfly (3/16" in height), first used in 1984.

POLINGAYSI see **WHITE, ELIZABETH**

POLINGYOUMA, HENRY — *Hopi*
SILVERSMITH: Specialized in silver overlay. Produced silver from 1948 to 1951.
HALLMARK: Stamped symbol of a Sun's Forehead or half sun.
[Wright:1982:85]

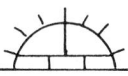

POLINGYOUMA, PHILBERT — *Hopi*
SILVERSMITH: Specialized in silver overlay from 1975 until his death in 1982.
HALLMARK: Stamped symbol of a rabbit's tracks or initials in Gothic print.
[Wright:1982:98]

   PP

POLIVEMA, LARRY — *Hopi*
SILVERSMITH: Specializes in silver overlay.
HALLMARK: Stamped symbol of the Little War God's tracks or a sun symbol. Also uses stamped initials in Gothic print.

    LP

POLIVEMA, LEONARD see **POLIVEMA, LARRY**

PONCHO, BILLY — *Zuni*
SILVERSMITH:
HALLMARK: Stamped surname in 1/16 Gothic print, first used in 1977.

B.PONCHO

PONCHO, CHARLES — *Zuni*
SILVERSMITH/LAPIDARIST: Specializes in channel and mosaic inlay of eagles and other creatures. Began producing in 1953. Works with his wife. Produces a few fetishes.
HALLMARK: Stamped initials of his wife's and his own with their tribal affiliation in Gothic print.
Spouse is Mary Ann Poncho.
[Bell:1975:37]

PONCHO, DAN *Zuni*
SILVERSMITH:
HALLMARK: Two-line stamped full name and "handmade" in 1/16 Gothic print, first used in 1978.

HANDMADE
DAN PONCHO E

PONCHO, DON *Zuni*
SILVERSMITH:
HALLMARK: Stamped surname in 1/16 Gothic print, also tribal affiliation and location in 1/16 Gothic. Name first used in 1977, tribe in 1978.

PONCHO   ZUNI N.MEX

PONCHO, MARY ANN *Zuni*
SILVERSMITH/LAPIDARIST: Specializes in channel and mosaic inlay of eagles and other creatures. A few fetishes also. Began producing in 1953. Works with her husband.
HALLMARK: Stamped initials of her husband's and her own with their tribal affiliation in Gothic print.
[Bell:1975:37]

CMP ZUNI

POOYAMA, ALLEN *Hopi*
SILVERSMITH: Specializes in silver overlay but produces other types as well. Began producing in 1937.
HALLMARK: Stamped ear of corn (1/4 x 1/8") in two different styles. Uses the name Pooyaouma and Nuvahoyouma also.
[Wright:1982:83]

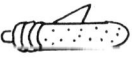

POOYOUMA, LAWRENCE (LARRY) *Hopi*
SILVERSMITH: Specializes in silver overlay. Began producing in 1975.
HALLMARK: Stamped symbol of an ear of young corn. Stamped offset and joined initials in personalized print. Stamped initials in Gothic print.
[Wright:1982:98]

 LAP

POOYOUMA, STEVEN *Hopi*
SILVERSMITH: Specializes in silver overlay. Began producing in 1974.
HALLMARK: Stamped joined and offset initials in personalized print first used in 1974. Stamped representation of a chief's water jug first used in 1977. Stamped representation of a chief's terraced bowl first used in 1982.
[Wright:1982:99]

  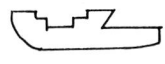

POPOVICH, JANE (YIKAAZBA) *Navajo*
SILVERSMITH:
HALLMARK: Stamped and joined initials with sterling in smaller print.

 STERLING

POSEYESVA, MANUEL *Hopi*
SILVERSMITH: Specializes in silver overlay. Began producing in 1965.
HALLMARK: Stamped symbol of a snow cloud (1/8" sq.).
[Wright:1982:89]

POSEYESVA, PHILBERT *Hopi*
SILVERSMITH: Specializes in silver overlay. Began producing in 1973.
HALLMARK: Stamped offset and joined initials in stylized print (1/8" sq.).
[Wright:1982:99]

POSTON, JAMES *Navajo (?)*
SILVERSMITH:
HALLMARK: Stamped representation of an agave plant (3/32"). From Ramah, New Mexico region.

PRINCE, LEE *Unknown*
SILVERSMITH:
HALLMARK: Stamped surname in 1/16 Gothic print, first used in 1974. Stamped initials joined into monogram in 1/16 print, first used in 1982.
From Claremont, Oklahoma.

L. PRINCE

PUHUYESTEWA, BERT *Hopi*
SILVERSMITH: Produced before World War II. Concha belts.
HALLMARK: Stamped symbol of the head of a Crow Mother kachina.
[Wright:1982:80]

QUALO, EFFIE *Zuni*
SILVERSMITH/LAPIDARIST:
HALLMARK: Stamped full name in 1/16 Gothic print, first used in 1981.

EFFIE QUALO

QUALO, ELLIOT *Zuni*
SILVERSMITH/LAPIDARIST: Specializes in silver boxes, channel, mosaic, and carved inlay. Uses exotic materials such as shell and ironwood with silver. Began producing in the 1960s.
HALLMARK: Single stamp of a deer antler struck twice. Since his death his wife has used his hallmark.

QUALO, JUNE *Zuni*
SILVERSMITH/LAPIDARIST: Specializes in rounded stones surrounded by a high collar to produce a shadow box style. Uses all of her own designs (?). Learned from her mother and began producing in 1965. Design and execution are very similar to her mother's work.
HALLMARK: Engraved signature.
Mother is Myra T. Qualo.
[Levy:1980:58]

June Qualo

QUALO, MYRA T. *Zuni*
SILVERSMITH/LAPIDARIST: Specializes in rounded stones surrounded by a collar to produce almost a shadow box style. Self taught she uses her own designs and does all her own work. Began producing in 1937.
HALLMARK: Engraved signature has probably been used only in recent years.
Daughter is June Qualo.
[Levy:1980:58]

Myra T Qualo

QUAM, ALICE *Zuni*
SILVERSMITH/LAPIDARIST: Specializes in both fetishes and petit point.
HALLMARK: Stamped initials in Gothic print. Stamped shared initials of her own and her husband's.
Spouse is Duane Quam.

A.Q.   A&DQ

QUAM, ANDREW (EMERSON) *Zuni*
FETISHMAKER: Specializes in very large pendants on his fetish necklaces.
HALLMARK: Engraved surname and initial.
[Bell:1975:38]

A.QUAM

QUAM, BONNIE *Zuni*
SILVERSMITH/LAPIDARIST: Specializes in needlepoint and petit point. Began producing in 1953.
HALLMARK: Stamped representation of a frog (1/16" vert.).
Spouse is John Quam.

QUAM, DUANE *Zuni*
SILVERSMITH/LAPIDARIST:
HALLMARK: Stamped shared initials of his wife's and his own in Gothic print.

A&DQ

QUAM, ELSIE *Zuni*
GOLDSMITH:
HALLMARK: Stamped initials in Gothic print.

E.Q.

QUAM, FRANCINE *Zuni*
SILVERSMITH/LAPIDARIST:
HALLMARK: Stamped shared initials of her husband's and her own in Gothic print. Stamped surname with same shared initials in Gothic print. Both stamps first used in 1976.
Spouse is Raymond Quam.

R&F   R&F QUAM

QUAM, GERLINDA *Zuni*
SILVERSMITH:
HALLMARK: Stamped surname in 1/16 Gothic print, first used in 1975.

G.QUAM

QUAM, JOHN *Zuni*
SILVERSMITH:
HALLMARK: Stamped symbol of a frog set on a plate.
Spouse is Bonnie Quam.

QUAM, RAYMOND *Zuni*
SILVERSMITH:
HALLMARK: Stamped surname in 3/32 Gothic print, first used in 1975. Stamped shared initials of his wife's and his own in Gothic print. Stamped surname with shared initials in Gothic print.
Spouse is Francine Quam.

R.QUAM   R&F   R&F QUAM

QUAM, SHIRLEY *Zuni*
SILVERSMITH:
HALLMARK: Stamped surname in 3/32 Gothic print, first used in 1976.

S.QUAM

QUAM, VIRGINIA *Zuni*
SILVERSMITH/LAPIDARIST: Specializes in large nugget work or mosaic inlay in eccentric geometrics. Much of her work is set in gold.
HALLMARK: Stamped surname with shared initials of her husband's and her own in 1/16 Gothic print. Stamp first used in 1975.
Spouse is Wayne Quam.
[Bell:1977:10]

W.&V.QUAM

QUAM, WAYNE *Zuni*
SILVERSMITH/LAPIDARIST: Specializes in large nugget work and mosaic inlay in eccentric geometrics. Much of his work is set in gold.
HALLMARK: Stamped surname in 1/16 Gothic print, first used in 1978. Stamped surname with shared initials of his wife's and his own in 1/16 Gothic print first used in 1975.
Spouse is Virginia Quam.
[Bell:1977:10]

W.QUAM   W.&V.QUAM

QUANDELACY, AMY *Zuni*
SILVERSMITH/LAPIDARIST: Specializes in raised channel inlay with shaped stones and wide silver settings. Distinctive designs

came from her former husband's mother. Learned silversmithing from her husband and began producing in 1976. Usually she and her husband worked individually but if they worked together she did the stone work.
HALLMARK: Stamped initials of her and her husband in in 1/16 Gothic print, first used in 1975. Stamped initials of her husband's and her given names in 3/32 Gothic print, first used in 1975. Two-line stamped shared initials in 1/16 Gothic print first used in 1976. Stamp of given name in 3/32 script, first used in 1984 is an individual stamp. Stamped surname with shared initials in 3/32 Gothic print.
Spouse was formerly Dickie Quandelacy.
[Levy:1980:24]

D&A   D&AQ   D&A
                        Q

D&A QUANDELACY

QUANDELACY, DICKIE   *Zuni*
SILVERSMITH/LAPIDARIST: Specializes in raised channel inlay with shaped stones and wide silver settings. Uses his mother's distinctive designs. Learned from his mother and began producing in 1975. Husband and former wife worked individually most of the time. If working together Dickie did the metalwork.
HALLMARK: Stamped shared initials of his wife's and his own in 1/16 Gothic print, first used in 1975. Stamped shared initials of their given names in 3/32 Gothic print, first used in 1975. Two-line stamped shared initials in 1/16 Gothic print first used in 1976. Stamped surname in 3/32 Gothic print first used in 1975. Stamped surname with shared initials in 3/32 Gothic print. Special stamp with name in 1/32 script not seen.
Former spouse was Amy Quandelacy, mother is Ellen Quandelacy.
[Levy:1980:24]

D&A   D&AQ   D&A   QUANDELACY
                        Q

D&A QUANDELACY

QUANDELACY, ELLEN   *Zuni*
SILVERSMITH/LAPIDARIST: Specializes in channel inlay in curvilinear designs and in fetishes.
HALLMARK: Two-line stamped initials in 1/16 Gothic and tribal affiliation in 1/32 Gothic print. May be either stamped or engraved.
Son is Dickie Quandelacy.
[Bell:1976:44]

E.Q.
ZUNI

QUANIMPTEWA, HARVEY JR.   *Hopi*
SILVERSMITH: Specialized in silver overlay. Began producing in 1976.
HALLMARK: Stamped bluebird track with initials at either side. Stamped initials set at an angle on either side of blue bird track under an arc. Stamped initials in Gothic print (?).
[Wright:1982:99]

HQ

QUIMAYOUISE, HERBERT see **KOMAYOUSE, HERBERT**

QUINTANA, CIPRIANO   *Cochiti*
SILVERSMITH: Contemporary or fashion jewelry.
HALLMARK: Stamped with the name Cippie or Crazyhorse.

CRAZYHORSE   CZH

QUINTANA, JERRY   *Cochiti*
SILVERSMITH:
HALLMARK: Stamped script initials.
Spouse was Terecita Quintana, father is Joseph Quintana.

QUINTANA, JOSEPH H.   *Cochiti*
SILVERSMITH: Specializes in silver overlay.
HALLMARK: Stamped initials with tribal affiliation in very small letters outlined below. Gothic print.
Son is Jerry Quintana.

JHQ
COCHITI

QUINTANA, TERECITA   *Cochiti*
SILVERSMITH:
HALLMARK: Stamp of her initials was made for her by Rogers but she never used it. After her death her husband adapted it to JQ and used it.
Spouse was Jerry Quintana.

QUOTSKUYVA, CAMILLE NAMPEYO   *Tewa*
POTTER: Began producing ca. 1970.
HALLMARK: Painted and fired ear of corn with name.
Mother is Dextra Nampeyo Quotskuyva.

QUOTSKUYVA, DEXTRA NAMPEYO   *Tewa*
POTTER: Contemporary work based on tradition. Began producing ca. 1967.
HALLMARK: Painted and fired representation of an ear of corn with her name.
Mother is Rachel Nampeyo and daughter Camille Quotskuyva.

QUMAWUNU, LOREN see **SAKEVA, LOREN**

QUMYINTEWA, ALDE   *Hopi*
SILVERSMITH: Specializes in silver overlay. Began producing in 1975.
HALLMARK: Stamped symbol of bear paw with mark in center of palm. Stamped initials in Gothic print.
[Wright:1982:99]

    AQ

QURAISHI, MASHALLAH   *Unknown*
SILVERSMITH:

HALLMARK: Stamped full name in 1/16 script with sun symbol alongside, first used in 1980.

RADCLIFFE, SYLVIA BEGAY *Navajo*
SILVERSMITH: Learned from her father.
HALLMARK: Stamped 1/16 script of her given name, first used in 1977.
Father is Kenneth Begay and brother is Harvey Begay.
From Window Rock, Arizona region.

Sylvia

RAFEL, TOM *Navajo*
SILVERSMITH:
HALLMARK: Stamped initials in 1/16 Gothic print with underlying symbol first used in 1975. Stamp of a single personalized initial.
From Prewitt, New Mexico region.

RAINCLOUD, HARRY *Unknown*
SILVERSMITH:
HALLMARK: Stamped representation of a raincloud.

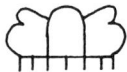

RAINSTAR, ? *Unknown*
SILVERSMITH:
HALLMARK: Stamped name or designation in 1/32 Gothic print first used in 1983.

RAIN-STAR

RAMONE, ANNIE *Unknown*
SILVERSMITH:
HALLMARK: Stamped initials in Gothic print.
Brother-in-law is Frank Ramone, sister is Sally Ramone.

AR

RAMONE, FRANK (FREDDIE?) *Unknown*
SILVERSMITH: Specializes in concho belts.
HALLMARK: Stamped surname in Gothic print.
Spouse is Sally Ramone, sister-in-law is Annie Ramone.

F.RAMONE

RAMONE, GENEVA *Unknown*
SILVERSMITH: Smith for Bernie Dominguez in 1976. Smith for Bilagaanas in 1984.
HALLMARK: Stamped surname in 1/16 Gothic print, first used in 1976.

G.RAMONE

RAMONE, L ? *Unknown*
SILVERSMITH: Smith for Cooper's Indian Store.
HALLMARK: Stamped surname in 1/32 Gothic print, first used in 1984.

L.RAMONE

RAMONE, NELLIE *San Felipe*
GOLDSMITH:
HALLMARK: Stamped initials in Gothic print.

NR

RAMONE, SALLY *Unknown*
SILVERSMITH: Specializes in concho belts. Helps her husband.
HALLMARK: Stamped surname and initial of her husband in Gothic print. Stamped initials of her name in Gothic print.
Spouse is Frank Ramone.

F.RAMONE   S.R.

RANDOLPH, SADIE *Navajo*
SILVERSMITH: Began producing in 1975.
HALLMARK: Stamped script initial in monograph form.

RANSON, ROGER *Papago*
SILVERSMITH: Learned from Rick Manuel and James Fendenheim in 1982.
HALLMARK: Stamped representation of a Papago carrying basket.

RATION, A ? *Navajo (?)*
SILVERSMITH: Smith for Bernie Dominguez.
HALLMARK: Stamped surname in 1/16 Gothic print, first used in 1975.

A.RATION

RATION, CHRISTINE *Navajo (?)*
SILVERSMITH:
HALLMARK: Stamped initials in 1/16 Gothic print, first used in 1974.
From Continental Divide, New Mexico region.

C.R.

RATION, E ? *Navajo (?)*
SILVERSMITH: Smith for Bernie Dominguez.
HALLMARK: Stamped surname in 1/16 Gothic print, first used in 1975.

E.RATION

RATZLAFF, KAREN *Anglo*
SILVERSMITH:
HALLMARK: Stamped representation of a cat's track (3/32"). Stamp first used in 1984.
From Santa Rosa, California.

RAY, SILVER *Unknown*
SILVERSMITH:
HALLMARK: Stamped surname in 3/32 script, first used in 1984.

From Albuquerque, New Mexico region.

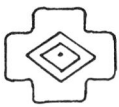

REAGAN, GENE *Navajo*
SILVERSMITH:
HALLMARK: Stamped symbol.
From Tucson, Arizona region.

REANO, JERRY *Santo Domingo*
SILVERSMITH:
HALLMARK: Stamped initials in offset Gothic print.
Spouse is Terry Reano.

J
 B
  R

REANO, JOE *Santo Domingo*
LAPIDARIST: Specializes in turquoise necklaces.
HALLMARK: Stamped initials on metal disk between the beads. Also the addition of a different colored bead at the clasp.

JR

REANO, PERCY *Santo Domingo*
SHELL WORK:
HALLMARK is a representation of an inlaid shell with his initials at the base.

REANO, TERRY *Santa Domingo*
SILVERSMITH:
HALLMARK: Initials stamped on a slant in 1/16 Gothic print.
Spouse is Jerry Reano.

T
 O
  R

REDBIRD, D ? *Unknown*
SILVERSMITH: Smith for Lee Prince.
HALLMARK: Stamped surname in 1/16 Gothic print, first used in 1974.

D.REDBIRD

REDWATER,? *Navajo*
SILVERSMITH:
HALLMARK: Stamped initial and symbol for water.
From Window Rock, Arizona region.

R∿∧

REEVES, H ? *Navajo*
SILVERSMITH: Smith for the T & R Market.
HALLMARK: Stamped surname in 1/16 Gothic print, first used in 1976.

H.REEVES

REEVES, L ? *Navajo*
SILVERSMITH: Smith for Blackbird Trading Company.
HALLMARK: Stamped surname in 1/16 Gothic print, first used in 1985.

L.REEVES

RICKY, MARCIA FRITZ *Hopi*
POTTER: Producing in 1960.
HALLMARK: Painted and fired representation of a flying ant, used before 1965. Same mark with initials used afterwards.

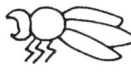

ROAN, JERRY *Navajo*
SILVERSMITH:
HALLMARK: Stamped images of a stick man in two versions. Stamped joined initials in personalized print.

 JR

ROANHORSE, AMBROSE see **LINCOLN, AMBROSE**

ROANHORSE, HENRY *Navajo*
SILVERSMITH: Works with his wife.
HALLMARK: Stamped surname in 1/16 Gothic print, first used in 1978. Shares the stamp with his wife.
Spouse is Louise Roanhorse.
From Gallup, New Mexico region.

ROANHORSE

ROANHORSE, JAMES *Navajo*
SILVERSMITH:
HALLMARK: Stamp of joined initials in personalized print enclosed or accompanied by a horseshoe.

ROANHORSE, LOUISE *Navajo*
SILVERSMITH: Works with her husband..
HALLMARK: Stamped surname of her husband in 1/16 Gothic print, first used in 1978. Shared stamp.

ROANHORSE

ROANHORSE, SAM *Navajo*
SILVERSMITH: Benchsmith for the White Hogan from 1951-52.
HALLMARK: Stamped script initials in personalized print.
Deceased.
1944

SR

ROBERTSON, L ? *Navajo*
SILVERSMITH:
HALLMARK: Two-line stamped surname and tribal affiliation in 1/16 Gothic print, first appeared in 1975.
From Ft. Defiance, Arizona region.

ROBERTSON
  NAVAJO

ROBINSON, HELEN — *Anglo (?)*
SILVERSMITH:
HALLMARK: Stamped word in 1/16 Gothic print, first used in 1980.
From San Rafael, California.

FAITH

ROBINSON, MORRIS (TALAWYTEWA) — *Hopi*
SILVERSMITH: Produced a variety of styles working from 1924 to the 1970s. Smith in the Phoenix and Tucson Shops.
HALLMARK: Stamped representation of a snake with the letter H over its back.
[Wright:1982:81]

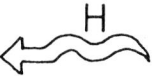

ROCKBRIDGE, RUSS — *Navajo*
SILVERSMITH: Smith for the Rocking Horse Ranch.
HALLMARK: Stamped initials and stamped surname in 1/16 Gothic print, first used in 1985.

RR   R.ROCKBRIDGE

RODGERS, KAY — *Navajo (?)*
SILVERSMITH:
HALLMARK: Stamped given name in script, stamp first used in 1977.
From Window Rock, Arizona region.

Kay

ROGERS, MICHAEL R. — *Paiute/Shoshoni*
SILVERSMITH/SHELL WORKER: Self taught. Began producing in 1978.
HALLMARK: Stamped initials in Gothic print. Stamped surname and tribe in Gothic print. Stamped surname and tribe with a rabbit and the word sterling, also in Gothic print. Stamp of a buffalo.

MR   PAIUTE ROGERS   PAIUTE ROGERS STERLING

ROMANCITO, EMMA — *Zuni*
SILVERSMITH:
HALLMARK: Stamped initials in Gothic print.

ER   ELR

ROMANCITO, JOYCE — *Zuni*
SILVERSMITH: Specializes in cluster work.
HALLMARK: Stamped initials.

JR

ROMERO, ADELAIDO — *Unknown*
SILVERSMITH: Metalwork.
HALLMARK: Stamped initials.

AR

ROMERO, CIPRIANO — *Unknown*
SILVERSMITH:
HALLMARK: Stamped initials in Gothic print.

CR

ROSETTA, DAN — *Santo Domingo*
HEISHI MAKER:
HALLMARK: Placed an eccentric stone on one side near the attachment, turquoise bead among white ones for example.
Deceased ca. 1965-66.

ROSETTA, JOHNNIE (JUAN) — *Santo Domingo*
HEISHI MAKER: Fine beads in the style of his father.
HALLMARK: Stamped initials in special script, his initials combined with those of his wife, on the findings.
Spouse is Marlene Rosetta, father is Ray and mother Mary Rosetta.

JrR.   JrR

ROSETTA, MARLENE — *Santo Domingo*
HEISHI MAKER: Bead maker.
HALLMARK: Stamped initials of her husband and herself.
Spouse is Johnnie (Juan) Rosetta.

JrR   JrR

ROSETTA, MARY — *Santo Domingo*
HEISHI MAKER: Fine beads originated by her husband.
HALLMARK: Stamped combination of her initials and those of her husband. Stamp first used in 1981.
Spouse is Ray Rosetta, son Johnnie Rosetta.

RrrR

ROSETTA, PAUL — *Santo Domingo*
HEISHI MAKER: Began producing ca. 1975.
HALLMARK: Stamped script of full name.

Mr. & Mrs. Paul Rosetta

ROSETTA, RAY — *Santo Domingo*
HEISHI MAKER: Specializes in fine beads which he originated.
HALLMARK: Stamped combination of his and his wife's initials. Stamp first used in 1981.
Spouse is Mary Rosetta, son is Johnnie (Juan) Rosetta.

RrrR

ROSETTA, ROMIJIO — *Santo Domingo*
HEISHI MAKER: Began producing ca. 1975.
HALLMARK: Stamped combined initials back to back with the symbol of an arrow above.

ROSS, EDISON — *Navajo*
SILVERSMITH:
HALLMARK: Stamped representation of a spider.

ROSS, TOMMY — *Anglo*
LAPIDARIST: Specializes in carved turquoise.
HALLMARK: Engraved single initial.

SAHMIE, RANDOLPH *Tewa*
SILVERSMITH: Specializes in silver overlay. Began producing ca. 1966-68.
HALLMARK: Stamped misaligned initials.
[Wright:1982:92]

SAKEVA, LOREN *Hopi*
SILVERSMITH: Specializes in silver overlay. Began producing in 1973.
HALLMARK: Began using a tadpole as his mark in 1976. Now uses initials. All marks are stamped.
[Wright:1982:94]

LQ   LS

SAKEVA, RAYMOND *Hopi*
SILVERSMITH: Specializes in silver overlay.
HALLMARK: Stamped initials in Gothic print.

RS

SAKEWA, DAVID *Santo Domingo*
HEISHI AND FETISH MAKER:
HALLMARK: Etched name on the belly of one of the fetish birds.

DAVID

SAKYESVA, HARRY *Hopi*
SILVERSMITH: Produced both hammered and silver overlay work. Began around 1937.
HALLMARK: Stamped image of a tadpole 1/16" long.
[Wright:1982:83]

SALISTEO, D? *Unknown*
SILVERSMITH: Worked in the Albuquerque area.
HALLMARK: Stamped initials in 3/32 Gothic print. First used in 1980.

D.S.

SALT *Navajo*
SILVERSMITH:
HALLMARK: Stamped name.

MADE BY: SALT

SALT, LARRY L. *Navajo*
SILVERSMITH: Specializes in shadow box and nugget pieces. Began producing ca. 1971.
HALLMARK: Stamped initials both vertical and italic Gothic print.
From Crownpoint, New Mexico region.

LLs   LLS

SALVADOR, JENNIE *Zuni*
SILVERSMITH:
HALLMARK: Combination of her husband's and her own initials.
Spouse is Lloyd Salvador.

L & J

SALVADOR, LLOYD *Zuni*
SILVERSMITH:
HALLMARK: Stamped initials of his wife's name and his own given name.
Spouse is Jennie Salvador.

L & J

SALVIO, ? *Zuni*
SILVERSMITH:
HALLMARK: Stamped initials.

STM

SAM, ALICE *Navajo*
SILVERSMITH:
HALLMARK: Stamped full name in 1/16 Gothic print, first used in 1975.
From Churchrock, New Mexico region.

ALICE SAM

SAM, BENSON *Navajo*
SILVERSMITH: Smith for the Atkinson Trading Company, Woodards. Specialized in overlay crosses with oxydized backs. Began producing in 1975.
HALLMARK: Stamped full name in 1/16 Gothic print. Stamp first used in 1975. Not many pieces are signed.
Spouse is Sadie Sam.

BENSON SAM

SAM, BETTY *Navajo*
SILVERSMITH: Smith for the Atkinson Trading Company.
HALLMARK: Stamped full name in 1/16 Gothic print. Stamp first used in 1976.

BETTY SAM

SAM, JIM *Navajo*
SILVERSMITH: Smith for the Atkinson Trading Company.
HALLMARK: Stamped full name in 1/16 Gothic print. Stamp first used in 1974.

JIM. SAM

SAM, JUNIOR L. *Navajo*
SILVERSMITH: Smith for the Atkinson Trading Company.
HALLMARK: Stamped full name in 1/16 Gothic print. Stamp first used in 1974.

JUNIOR L. SAM

SAM, MARGARET *Navajo*
SILVERSMITH: Smith for Indian Hammers in 1976 and for Atkinson Trading Company in 1974.
HALLMARK: Stamped full name in 1/16 Gothic print, first used in 1974. Stamped surname and initial in 1/16 Gothic print first used in 1976.

MARGARET SAM   M.SAM

SAM, SADIE *Navajo*
SILVERSMITH: Smith for Atkinson Trading Company.
HALLMARK: Stamped full name in 1/16 Gothic print, first used in 1975.
Spouse is Benson Sam.

SADIE SAM

SAM, TULLY *Navajo*
SILVERSMITH: Smith for the Atkinson Trading Company.
HALLMARK: Stamped full name in 1/16 Gothic print, first used in 1974.

TULLY SAM

SAMPSON, CLYDE *Navajo*
SILVERSMITH: Producing in the 1960s.
HALLMARK: Stamped symbol of a star (?).

SAMPSON. LUCY see **BOWEKATY, LUCILLE**

SANCHEZ, ANGELITA B. (ANGIE) (LASILOO) *Zuni*
SILVERSMITH/LAPIDARIST: Specializes in needlepoint, using her own designs. Learned from watching her mother. Began producing in 1955.
HALLMARK: Uses both stamped and engraved hallmarks. Uses the engraved mark most often.
Mother is Lolita Edaakie.
[Levy:1980:50]

A.B.SANCHES   *Angie*   G.A.LASILOO

G.G.A.L.

SANCHEZ, HORACE *Zuni*
SILVERSMITH/LAPIDARIST: Works in both silver and gold. Specializes in needlepoint, set so it looks woven.
HALLMARK: Uses both stamp and engraver. Stamped initials are usually his alone and are set on a plate. A combination of his wife's and his own initials are usually engraved. Stamp with his initials first used in 1981.
Spouse is Morenda Sanchez.
[Bell:1977:29]

[HZ]   HMS

SANCHEZ, LARRY *Unknown*
SILVERSMITH: Worked in the Albuquerque region.
HALLMARK: Stamped full name in 1/16 Gothic print. The name is in error on the stamp but is used anyway. First used in 1986.

HARRY SANCHEZ

SANCHEZ, MORENDA *Zuni*
SILVERSMITH/LAPIDARISTt: Works in both silver and gold. Specializes in needlepoint set so it looks woven.
HALLMARK: Engraved initials of her husband's and her name.
Spouse is Horace Sanchez.
[Bell:1977:29]

HMS

SANCHEZ, TONY *Anglo*
SILVERSMITH: Specializes in overlay work.
HALLMARK: Stamped symbol.

SANCHEZ, WILLARD *Zuni*
SILVERSMITH:
HALLMARK: Stamped surname with combined initials of his wife's and his own given names in 1/16 Gothic print. Stamp first used in 1975.
Spouse is Vela Sanchez.

W.& V.SANCHEZ

SANDERS, ALICE *Navajo*
SILVERSMITH: Smith for the Atkinson Trading Company.
HALLMARK: She uses her husband's hallmark of his initials in 1/16 Gothic print, first used in 1980.
Spouse is Cecil Sanders.

CS

SANDERS,CECIL *Navajo*
SILVERSMITH: Smith for Atkinson Trading Company.
HALLMARK: Stamped initials shared with his wife. Initials in 1/16 Gothic print and were first used in 1980.
Spouse is Alice Sanders.

CS

SANDOVAL, BEN *Unknown*
SILVERSMITH: Pieceworker.
HALLMARK: Stamped given name and initial of surname.

BEN S.

SANDOVAL, DANNY *Navajo*
SILVERSMITH:
HALLMARK: Stamped initials in Gothic print.

DS

SANDOVAL DAVID see **Thunderbolt**

SANDOVAL, GLENN *Navajo*
SILVERSMITH:
HALLMARK: Stamped initials in 1/16 Gothic print, first used in 1977.
From Thoreau, New Mexico region.

GS   G.S.

SANDOVAL, IRENE *Navajo*
SILVERSMITH: Smith for Atkinson Trading Company.
HALLMARK: Stamped initials may be those of Glen Sandoval(?). The stamps she uses are of initials not her own in 1/16 Gothic print and were first used in 1980.

GS   G.S.

SANDOVAL, LARRY *Navajo*
SILVERSMITH: Pieceworker.
HALLMARK: Stamped initials in Gothic print.
Spouse is Sherry Sandoval.

LS

SANDOVAL, LEROY *Navajo*
SILVERSMITH: Pieceworker.
HALLMARK: Stamped misaligned initials in Gothic print.

L$_S$

SANDOVAL, SHERRY *Navajo*
SILVERSMITH: Pieceworker.
HALLMARK: Stamped initials in various arrangements. Occasionally the initials are divided by a diagonal or set along the shaft of an arrow.
Spouse is Larry Sandoval.

SS   ⇐SS⋘

SAUFKIE, ANDREW *Hopi*
SILVERSMITH: Specializes in silver overlay. Began producing in 1971.
HALLMARK: Chisel cut initials used from 1974 until 1980, 1/16". Stamped representation of a bear paw used since 1980.
[Wright:1982:91]

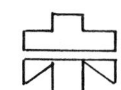 A. S.

SAUFKIE, GRACILDA *Hopi*
SILVERSMITH: Specializes in silver overlay. Began producing in 1965.
HALLMARK: Used a stamped representation of a snow cloud from 1965—1971. Stamp was lost or broken and a new one on the left was used from 1972 on.
Spouse is Lawrence Saufkie.
[Wright:1982:89]

SAUFKIE, LAWRENCE *Hopi*
SILVERSMITH: Specializes in silver overlay. Learned from his father. Began producing in 1947.
HALLMARK: Stamped hallmark is a bear. In later years the name Saufkie in 1/16 Gothic print was added or combined with the bear.
Spouse is Gracilda Saufkie, father is Paul Saufkie.
[Wright:1982:88]

   SAUFKIE

SAUFKIE, PAUL *Hopi*
SILVERSMITH: Produces hammered and wrought silver as well as silver overlay.
HALLMARK: Stamped representation of a snow cloud 1/16" sq.
[Wright:1982:81]

SAUFKIE, WILMER, SR. *Hopi*
SILVERSMITH: Overlay. Produced little.
HALLMARK: The stamped representation of a frog's head.

SA-YESWA *Unknown*
SILVERSMITH:
HALLMARK: Stamped symbol.
From Scottsdale, Arizona region.

SCHENDEL, GENE *Unknown*
SILVERSMITH:
HALLMARK: Stamped initials in personalized print. G is 3/16", the S 3/32" in size.
From Yerington, Nevada region.

GS

SCHLOSSER, MARY LOU *Taos*
SILVERSMITH:
HALLMARK: Stamped name of Kupolo (Cradle Flower) in Gothic print.
Spouse is Carl Schlosser, who does not work in silver.
From Taos, New Mexico region.

KUPOLO

SCHMALLIE, LEONARD *Navajo*
SILVERSMITH: Smith for Robert Gonzales.
HALLMARK: Stamped surname in 1/32 Gothic print with initial in 1/8" script. Initials in 1/16 Gothic print. First stamp used initially in 1984.

ℒSCHMALLIE   ℒSCHMALLIE   LS

SCHMALTZ, MIKE *Unknown*
KNIFEMAKER:
HALLMARK: Stamped surname in 1/16 script on steel. Stamp first used in 1980.

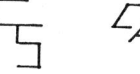

SCOTT, BENNIE KEE *Navajo*
SILVERSMITH:
HALLMARK: Stamped initials in Gothic print.

BKS

SCOTT, COURTNEY AMON *Hopi*
SILVERSMITH: Specializes in silver overlay. Began producing in 1973.
HALLMARK: Stamped initials in misaligned position.
[Wright:1982:99]

SCOTT, DAVE *Navajo*
SILVERSMITH:
HALLMARK: Stamped combined initials.
From Belen, New Mexico region.

SCOTT, EDDIE *Hopi*
SILVERSMITH: Specializing in silver overlay.
HALLMARK: Stamped stylized and misaligned initials.

SCOTT, RAYMOND *Navajo*
SILVERSMITH: Specializes in chip inlay.
HALLMARK: Stamped representations of (?) with initial.

SCOTT, ROSCO *Navajo*
SILVERSMITH: Smith for the Atkinson Trading Company.
HALLMARK: Stamped full name in 1/16 Gothic print first used in 1974. Uses a representation of an arrow also as a stamp.

ROSCO SCOTT

SEAGO, EUNICE *Unknown*
SILVERSMITH:
HALLMARK: Stamped in 1/16 Gothic print. Used first in 1977. From Crescent City, California region.

BLACK STAR

SECAKUKU, MYRON *Hopi*
SILVERSMITH: Specializes in silver overlay. Began producing in 1975.
HALLMARK: Stamped representation of an antelope horn used first around 1977. Also uses initials in Gothic print in normal alignment or one above the other.

M MS M/S

SECAKUKU, SIDNEY JR. *Hopi*
SILVERSMITH: Specializes in silver overlay. Began producing in 1972.
HALLMARK: Stamped representation of an antelope track or an antelope track with an initial.
[Wright:1982:93]

SECAKUKU, SIDNEY SR. *Hopi*
SILVERSMITH: Learned from Paul Saufkie. Began producing before 1940 but has not made any for a long time.
HALLMARK: Stamped representations of a thunderhead.
Sons are Sidney Jr. and Myron Secakuku.
[Wright:1982:82]

SECATERO, RAYNA PLATERO *Navajo*
SILVERSMITH:
HALLMARK: Stamped initials in personalized print.

RPS

SECATERO, TOMMIE *Navajo*
SILVERSMITH:
HALLMARK: Stamped initials in Gothic print, initials in personalized print.
From Canyoncito, New Mexico region.

ST TAS

SECATERO, WILBERT *Navajo*
SILVERSMITH: Smith in the Albuquerque shops.
HALLMARK: Stamped initials in Gothic print.
Spouse was Sarah Pino Secatero, second spouse Josephine Pino Secatero.

W.S.

SECIWA, CHARLOTTE see **BRADLEY, CHARLOTTE**

SECKLETSTEWA, JACKSON *Hopi*
SILVERSMITH: Specializes in silver overlay. Began producing in 1970.
HALLMARK: Stamped representation of a feather. First one used from 1970—1975. Second feather used from 1975 on. Initials are used on small pieces.
[Wright:1982:90]

JS

SEHONGVA, DORAN *Hopi*
SILVERSMITH: Specializes in silver overlay. Began producing in 1975.
HALLMARK: Stamped chisel cut initials in normal position or misaligned.
[Wright:1982:99]

SEHONGVA, ELGENE *Hopi*
SILVERSMITH: Specializes in silver overlay. Began producing in 1973.
HALLMARK: Stamped initials in various combinations or alignments.
[Wright:1982:94]

E/S E/S E/S E/S E/S

SEIBERT, DON *Unknown*
SILVERSMITH: Smith for Jim Rashid at Pow-Wow Traders.
HALLMARK: Stamped full name in 1/16 Gothic print, first used in 1978.

DON SEIBERT

SEKAQUAPTEWA, EMORY JR. *Hopi*
SILVERSMITH: Specialized in overlay. Learned from Harry Sakyesva and began producing ca. 1960. Very sparse production.
HALLMARK: Stamped surname in Gothic print, shared with his brother.
Brother was Wayne Sekaquaptewa.
[Wright:1982:88]

SEKAQUAPTEWA

SEKAQUAPTEWA, PHILLIP *Hopi*
SILVERSMITH: Specializes in silver overlay. Began producing in 1973.
HALLMARK: Stamped initials in Gothic print from April to June of 1973 then used stamp of an eagle track.
[Wright:1982:94]

   PS

SEKAQUAPTEWA, WAYNE *Hopi*
SILVERSMITH: Specialized in silver overlay. Began production in 1960. Founded Hopi Enterprises with his brother Emory. Partnership divided and he changed Hopi Enterprises to Hopicrafts.
HALLMARK: Stamped surname in Gothic print shared with his brother. (For Enterprise and Hopicraft marks see under Shops). Brother is Emory Sekaquaptewa. Wayne is deceased.
[Wright:1982:88]

SEKAQUAPTEWA

SEKAYUMPTEWA, WALLY *Hopi*
SILVERSMITH: Specialized in overlay silver. Produced from 1948 to 1967 when he ceased due to impaired eyesight.
HALLMARK: Stamped representation of crossed arrows.
[Wright:1982:86]

SELINA, WEAVER *Hopi*
SILVERSMITH: Specializes in silver overlay. Began producing ca. 1967.
HALLMARK: Stamped initials in Gothic print but more often the symbol of a rising sun.
[Wright:1982:89]

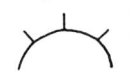   WRS

SEOTEWA, IRMA *Zuni*
SILVERSMITH/LAPIDARIST: Specializes in needlepoint from family designs. She learned from her family and began producing in 1970. She does the stonework and her husband does the metal work.
HALLMARK: Stamped initials of her husband's and her own given names. Engraved given names of her husband's and her own. Spouse was Octavius Seotewa (deceased).
[Levy:1980:40]

O&I   *Octavius & Irma L.*

SEOTEWA, OCTAVIUS *Zuni*
SILVERSMITH/LAPIDARIST: Specialized in needlepoint from family designs. Learned silversmithing from his mother. Began producing in 1970. He did all the silver work and his wife the stone work.
HALLMARK: Stamped initials of his wife's and his given names. Engraved given names of his wife and himself.
Spouse is Irma Seotewa. Mother is Odelle Seotewa.
[Levy:1980:40]

O&I   *Octavius & Irma L.*

SEOTEWA, ODELLE *Zuni*
SILVERSMITH/LAPIDARIST: Specializes in combinations of "snake eye" and rainbow clusters. Creates her own designs in traditional forms. Learned from watching her parents then began producing in 1950. She does both metalwork and stonework.
HALLMARK: Engraved first initials of her husband and herself with his surname.
Spouse is Alex Seotewa, noted painter of kachinas at Zuni.
[Levy:1980:41]

A/O Seowtewa
Zuni, N.M.

SEQUAPTEWA, RAYMOND *Hopi*
SILVERSMITH: Specializes in silver overlay. Began producing in 1970.
HALLMARK: Stamped representation of an ear of corn or initials in Gothic print. Name is occasionally spelled Sekuaptewa.
[Wright:1982:91]

SETALLA, BILL *Hopi*
SILVERSMITH:
HALLMARK: Stamped symbol of corn.
Spouse is a Pima woman.

SETALLA, PAULINE *Hopi*
POTTERY: Began producing ca. 1960.
HALLMARK: Painted and fired representation of a bear's paw.

SEWARD, CHARLES W. *Anglo*
SILVERSMITH:
HALLMARK: Stamped image of an insect 5/32".

SHABIE, LESTER D. *Navajo*
SILVERSMITH:
HALLMARK: Stamped surname in 1/16 Gothic print, first used in 1976.
From Holbrook, Arizona region.

SHABIE   ᒪSHABIE

SHACK, BOBBY *Zuni*
SILVERSMITH/LAPIDARIST: Specializes in channel and mosaic inlay of birds, primarily hummingbirds. Learned from his mother. Both he and his wife work on each piece.
HALLMARK: Engraved surname with the initials of his wife's and his own given names. Initials on small pieces.

Spouse is Corraine Shack. Mother is Thomasine Shack.
[Bell:1976:40,41]

B&C SHACK   B&C

SHACK, CORRAINE *Zuni*
SILVERSMITH/LAPIDARIST: Specializes in channel and mosaic inlay of birds, primarily hummingbirds. She and her husband both work on pieces.
HALLMARK: Engraved surname with the initials of her husband's and her own given names. Initials on small pieces.
Spouse is Bobby Shack.
[Bell:1976:40,41]

B&C SHACK   B&C

SHAKEY, R? *Navajo*
SILVERSMITH: Smith for Atkinson Trading Company.
HALLMARK: Stamped surname in 1/32 Gothic print, first used in 1982.

R.SHAKEY

SHAW, WILLIE *Navajo*
SILVERSMITH:
HALLMARK: Stamped initials in Gothic print.

WS

SHAY, C? *Unknown*
SILVERSMITH: Smith for Ben Touchine.
HALLMARK: Stamped initials and surname in 1/16 Gothic print, first used in 1974. Shared hallmark.

C.&G.SHAY

SHAY, G? *Unknown*
SILVERSMITH: Smith for Ben Touchine.
HALLMARK: Stamped initials and surname in 1/16 Gothic print, first used in 1974. Shared hallmark.

C.&G.SHAY

SHAY, JAMES *Navajo*
SILVERSMITH:
HALLMARK: Stamped misaligned initials in Gothic print.
From Lukachukai, Arizona region.

J_S

SHEECHE, ARDEN *Zuni*
SILVERSMITH:
HALLMARK: Stamped combination of his and his wife's initials in Gothic print.
Spouse is Melinda Sheeche.

MAS

SHEECHE, MELINDA *Zuni*
SILVERSMITH:
HALLMARK: Stamped combination of hers and her husband's initials in Gothic print.
Spouse is Arden Sheeche.

MAS

SHEETS, IRENE *Navajo*
SILVERSMITH:
HALLMARK: Stamped monogram of initials in script.

SHELENDEWA, LINDA *Zuni*
SILVERSMITH:
HALLMARK: Stamped initials and tribal affiliation inside a sun symbol in 1/16 and 3/32 Gothic print.

SHEPHERD, LINCOLN *Navajo*
SILVERSMITH:
HALLMARK: Stamped initials, full name and tribal affiliation in 1/16 script.
From Flagstaff, Arizona region.

SHETIMA, L.L. *Zuni*
SILVERSMITH:
HALLMARK: Stamped surname in 1/16 Gothic print first used in 1975.

L.L.SHETIMA

SHEYKA, ANN *Zuni*
SILVERSMITH/LAPIDARIST: Specializes in channel inlay with engraved details. Learned from watching her mother. Began producing in 1961. She does both stone and metalwork with some assistance from her husband.
HALLMARK: Stamped initial of her husband's given name usually on a plate. Engraved initial and surname of her husband.
Spouse is Porfilio Sheyka.
[Levy:1980:17]

P   P.   P.SHEYKA

SHEYKA, CORINNE *Zuni*
SILVERSMITH/LAPIDARIST:
HALLMARK: Stamped initial of her husband's given name usually on a plate.
Spouse is Porfilio Sheyka.

P   P.

SHEYKA, PORFILIO *Zuni*
SILVERSMITH/LAPIDARIST:
HALLMARK: Stamped initial of a given name, on a plate, stamped symbol of a macaw beak, engraved surname and initial. Shares the initial and surname marks with wife.
Spouses are Ann and Corinne.
Deceased in 1982.

SHIRLEY, ALICE M. *Navajo*
SILVERSMITH:

HALLMARK: Stamped initials in 1/16 Gothic print, first used in 1976.

AMS

SHIRLEY, ANNIE *Navajo*
SILVERSMITH: Smith for Atkinson Trading Company ca. 1974-5.
HALLMARK: Stamped surname is that of Alice Bennally but which ANNIE also uses. In 1/16 Gothic print, the mark was first used in 1975.

A.BENALLY

SHOPTEESE, JOHN *Potawatomi/Sauk-Fox*
SILVERSMITH/GOLDSMITH/SCULPTOR:
HALLMARK: Stamped symbol of a fish, after the Christian symbol, with a pendant initial.
From Albuquerque, New Mexico region.

SHUPLA, HAZEL *Hopi*
POTTER:
HALLMARK: Painted and fired prayer plume or feather.

SHUPLA, IRENE GILBERT *Tewa/Hopi*
POTTER: Began producing in the 1930s.
HALLMARK: Painted and fired representation of a peach flower.

SICE, BERNICE *Zuni*
SILVERSMITH/LAPIDARIST: Produces pieces made with twisted wire and tear drops or rain drops of turquoise. She learned by watching her father and began producing in 1969. She does all of the work on each piece although her husband helps occasionally.
HALLMARK: Stamped initials of her husband's and her own given names with his surname. Shared with her husband.
Spouse is Norman Sice.
[Levy:1980:37]

NBS

SICE, NORMAN *Zuni*
SILVERSMITH: Lends occasional assistance to his wife.
HALLMARK: Stamped initials of his name and the initial of his wife's given name. Shared with his wife.
Spouse is Bernice Sice.
[Levy:1980:37]

NBS

SIEWIYUMPTEWA, ELDON *Hopi*
SILVERSMITH: Specializes in silver overlay.
HALLMARK: Stamped symbol of a cloud. The elongated form is the oldest. The shorter cloud mark 3/16 x 1/8", was first used in 1976. Stamped initials in Gothic print are used in smaller pieces.

  ES

SILVER, MARIE *Navajo*
SILVERSMITH: Smith for the Atkinson Trading Company.
HALLMARK: Stamped surname in 1/16 Gothic print first used in 1974. Second stamp of full name in 1/16 Gothic print first used in 1975.

M.SILVER   MARIE SILVER

SILVER, N? *Navajo*
SILVERSMITH: Smith for Black Hat Trading Post.
HALLMARK: Stamped surname in 1/16 Gothic print, first used in 1974.

N.SILVER

SILVERS, MARY A. *Navajo*
SILVERSMITH:
HALLMARK: Stamped joined initials in 1/16 print.
From Window Rock, Arizona region.

MAS

SILVERS, WAYNE *Navajo*
SILVERSMITH: Smith for Montana Mining Company.
HALLMARK: Stamped surname in 1/16 Gothic print, first used in 1974.

W.SILVERS

SILVERSMITH, JIMMIE *Navajo*
SILVERSMITH: Smith for Atkinson Trading Company.
HALLMARK: Stamped surname in 1/16 Gothic print, first used in 1974.

J.SILVERSMITH

SILVERSMITH, TEDDY *Navajo*
SILVERSMITH: Smith for Atkinson Trading Company.
HALLMARK: Stamped surname and initial in 1/16 Gothic print, first used in 1975.

T.SILVERSMITH

SIMPLICIO, CARMELITA *Zuni*
SILVERSMITH: Specializes in nugget settings and cast work. Foliate designs.
HALLMARK: Stamped surname in Gothic print.
[Bell:1977:42]

SIMPLICIO

SIMPLICIO, DAN *Zuni*
SILVERSMITH/LAPIDARIST: Specializes in mosaic and channel inlay, massive nugget settings, and foliate designs. Learned silversmithing from his uncle and began producing in the 1930s. Well represented in the C. G. Wallace Collection.
HALLMARK: Stamped initials in Gothic print or the stamped representation of a star with a raised boss in the center. It has been said that he used this symbol when he collaborated with another craftsman on a piece.
Uncle was Juan Dideos. His mother was Juan's youngest sister.
[King:1976:10]

   DS

SIMPLICIO, LENA *Zuni*

SILVERSMITH:
HALLMARK: Stamped initials in Gothic print.

LS

SIMPLICIO, MIKE *Zuni*
SILVERSMITH/LAPIDARIST: Produced foliate designs.
HALLMARK: Stamped initial with a tilde above it, given name, and surname with initial in Gothic print. He shared these marks with his wife who continues to use them.
Spouse is Sarah Simplicio. Father is Dan Simplicio.
He is deceased.

  MIKE M.SIMPLICIO M.S.SIMPLICIO

SIMPLICIO, SARAH *Zuni*
SILVERSMITH:
HALLMARK: Stamped surname with double initials in Gothic 1/16" print. Shared hallmark first used in 1975.
Spouse was Mike Simplicio.

M.S.SIMPLICIO

SINGER, CHARLIE *Navajo*
SILVERSMITH: Began producing pieces in "Shiprock style" in the early 1970s.
HALLMARK: Engraved or stamped initials. Stamped symbol of a spade or an arrowhead. Presumably the arrowhead mark is used on Hopi/Navajo pieces.

  CS

SINGER, JACKIE *Navajo*
SILVERSMITH:
HALLMARK: Stamped initials in Gothic print.

J.S.

SINGER, JUAN *Navajo*
SILVERSMITH:
HALLMARK: Stamped joined initials in Gothic print.

JTS

SINGER, TOMMY *Navajo*
SILVERSMITH: Specialized in chip inlay (origin of chip inlay is attributed to the Kirks ca. 1961). Began in the Shiprock region then set up shop in Dilkon, Arizona. Wiped out by Taiwanese imports, he now does traditional silver, heavy ornate pieces. (see Shops T.Singer)
HALLMARK: Uses hallmarks as an individual and as a shop. The most common early mark was some variation on the initial T. This is often accompanied by a quarter moon or a bird form, both derived from Peyote symbolism. Currently he uses a stamped full name mark in 1/16 Gothic print.
Spouse is Rose Singer. Brother-in-law is Lawrence or Leonard Dodge.
[Barnes and Martie:1975:121]

T T꜀ T꜀/S S/T꜀ To

THOMAS SINGER

SINGER, WILLIAM *Navajo*

SILVERSMITH: Specializing in chip inlay. Began producing in 1972.
HALLMARK: Uses a variation of the Singer shop stamp.

SD   S/D

SIOW, LORENE *Zuni*
SILVERSMITH:
HALLMARK: Stamped surname and initial in 1/16 Gothic print. First used in 1978.

L. SIOW

SIOW, THOMAS *Zuni*
SILVERSMITH:
HALLMARK: Stamped surname and initial in 1/16 Gothic print, first used in 1974. Second stamp of initials in 1/16 script, first used in 1975.

T.SIOW   *T.R.S.*

SIUTZA, AVIS *Zuni*
SILVERSMITH/LAPIDARIST: Specializes in channel inlay using flower designs. Learned from Stephen Siutza and began producing in 1973.
HALLMARK: Stamped combined initials of Avis and her husband in Gothic print with tribal affiliation.
Spouse is Herbert Siutza.
[Levy:1980:32]

HAS ZUNI

SIUTZA, HERBERT *Zuni*
SILVERSMITH/LAPIDARIST: Specializes in channel inlay using flower designs. Learned from his father and began producing in 1973.
HALLMARK: Stamped combined initials of Herbert and his wife in Gothic print with tribal affiliation.
Spouse is Avis Siutza, father is Stephen Siutza.

HAS ZUNI

SIUTZA, LOUISE *Zuni*
SILVERSMITH/LAPIDARIST: Specializes in domed inlay using flower designs in turquoise and shell.
HALLMARK: Stamped combination of her husband's initials and her own in Gothic print.
Spouse is Stephen Siutza, son is Herbert Siutza.

N&LS

SIUTZA, STEPHEN *Zuni*
SILVERSMITH/LAPIDARIST: Specializes in domed inlay in flower designs using turquoise and shell. Learned from watching other smiths at work. Began producing in 1955.
HALLMARK: Did not use a stamp before 1973 when he adopted the stamp using his wife's initials and presumably his. The stamp does not reflect his name.
Spouse is Louise Siutza.
[Levy:1980:32]

N&LS

SIWINGYUMPTEWA, DEAN *Hopi*
SILVERSMITH: Specialized in silver overlay. Began producing in 1948 but has not made anything for some time.
HALLMARK: Stamped symbol of a cloud.
[Wright:1982:85]

SIWINGYUMPTEWA, ELDON *Hopi*
SILVERSMITH: Specializes in silver overlay. Began producing in 1968.
HALLMARK: Before 1983 used a stamped symbol of a cloud; after that time he has used the stamped image of a bird.
[Wright:1982:90]

SIWINGYUMPTEWA, LAVERNE *Hopi*
SILVERSMITH: Specialized in silver overlay. Began producing in 1948 but has not made anything for some time.
HALLMARK: Stamped image of a tadpole.
[Wright:1982:85]

SKEET, ROGER *Navajo*
SILVERSMITH: Smith for Tobe Turpen and Tanners. Made concho belts during the 1970s.
HALLMARK: Stamped initials in Gothic print.
Brother is Tony Skeet.

RS

SKEETS, ANDERSON (ANDY) *Navajo*
SILVERSMITH: Specializes in heavy wire open work with leaves. Occasionally works in gold. Smith for Lone Mt. Turquoise Company.
HALLMARK: Stamped elaborated A first used in 1970. Stamped full name in 1/16 Gothic print, first used in 1975.
Father is Roger Skeet.

   ANDERSON SKEETS

SKEETS, IRENE *Navajo*
SILVERSMITH:
HALLMARK: Stamped initials in 1/16 and 3/32 print, first used in 1974.

I.S.

SLEUTH, JERRY *Navajo*
SILVERSMITH:
HALLMARK: Stamped initials of Jerry and his wife (name unknown) in 1/16 Gothic print, first used in 1973. Two separate stamps, one of initials and the other tribal affiliation.
From Gallup, New Mexico region.

J.&I.S. NAVAJO

SLIM, BILLY *Navajo*
SILVERSMITH: Smith for Atkinson Trading Company ca. 1980. Smith also for Canyon Silver Company.
HALLMARK: Stamped initial or surname and initial in 1/16 Gothic print, first used in 1980.
From Sanders, Arizona region.

B   B.SLIM

SLIM, GRACE *Navajo*
SILVERSMITH: Smith for Canyon Silver Company.
HALLMARK: Stamped surname in 1/16 Gothic print, first used in 1975.

G.SLIM

SLIM, HELEN *Navajo*
SILVERSMITH: Smith for the Canyon Silver Company.
HALLMARK: Stamped initials or surname and initial in 1/16 Gothic print, first used in 1975.
From Sanders, Arizona region.

H.S.   H.SLIM

SLIM, MICHAEL L. *Navajo*
SILVERSMITH:
HALLMARK: Stamped full name in 1/16 Gothic print, first used in 1985.
From Albuquerque, New Mexico region.

MICHAEL L. SLIM

SLINKEY, HERMAN *Navajo*
SILVERSMITH:
HALLMARK: Stamped initials in Gothic print.

HS

SLUEIN, JERRY *Navajo*
SILVERSMITH:
HALLMARK: Stamped representation of a Navajo man's head with underlying initials. Initials are 1/32 in height, the head 1/4" square.

SMALL, SERENA *Apache*
LAPIDARIST: Peridot jewelry.
HALLMARK: Stamped initials in regular or misaligned positions.

SS   S
      S

SMALLCANYON, DORIS *Navajo*
SILVERSMITH:
HALLMARK: Stamped abbreviation of the name and initial in script. Mark is registered.

D Smcyn ®

SMILEY, BILLY RAY *Navajo*
SILVERSMITH:
HALLMARK: Stamped initials in Gothic print.

BRS

SMILEY, DAN *Navajo*
SILVERSMITH:
HALLMARK: Stamped initials in Gothic print.

DS

SMILEY, LENA MAE *Navajo*
SILVERSMITH:
HALLMARK: Stamped initials in Gothic print either misaligned or aligned and occasionally accompanied by a star.

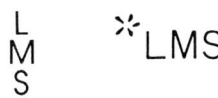

SMILEY, MARTHA *Navajo*
SILVERSMITH:
HALLMARK: Stamped initials in Gothic print.

MS

SMILEY, ROBERT LEE *Navajo*
SILVERSMITH:
HALLMARK: Stamped initials in 1/16 Gothic print, first used in 1978.
From Chinle, Arizona region.

R.L.S.

SMILEY, STELLA *Navajo*
SILVERSMITH:
HALLMARK: Stamped initials both aligned and misaligned in Gothic print.

SS   S
     S

SMITH, BERTHA *Navajo*
SILVERSMITH:
HALLMARK: Stamped italic initial or initial with the symbol of an arrow arched over it.
From Chinle, Arizona region.

SMITH, DENNIS *Navajo*
SILVERSMITH:
HALLMARK: Stamped initials incorporated with either a broken arrow or a curved one with the initials in the middle.

SMITH, EDISON SANDY *Navajo*
SILVERSMITH: Specializes in traditional designs in either gold or silver. Smith for Rockinghorse Ranch.
HALLMARK: Stamped initials in either Gothic print or personalized print.

E.S.S.

SMITH, ED *Navajo*
SILVERSMITH: Began producing in 1975. Works for Phil Woodard.
HALLMARK: Stamped initials in lower case 1/16 script. Stamp first used in 1981.

esm

SMITH, HOWARD *Navajo (?)*
SILVERSMITH:
HALLMARK: Stamped initials in 1/16 Gothic print, first used in 1981.

H.S.

SMITH, LORENZO *Navajo*
SILVERSMITH:
HALLMARK: Stamped symbols of arrows with a single initial beneath. Arrows point either way. Stamp 3/16" and first used in 1983.

SMITH, MARIE *Navajo*
SILVERSMITH: Smith for Atkinson Trading Company.
HALLMARK: Stamped single initial in 1/16 Gothic print, first used in 1980.

S

SMITH, MARY B. *Navajo*
SILVERSMITH: Smith for Atkinson Trading Company.
HALLMARK: Stamped full name in 1/16 Gothic print, first used in 1974. Second stamp of surname and initials in 1/16 Gothic print, first used in 1976.

MARY B.SMITH   M.B.SMITH

SMITH, OLIVER *Navajo*
SILVERSMITH:
HALLMARK: Stamped surname in Gothic print. Engraved signature.
From Guadalupe, Arizona region.

O.SMITH   O. chälh Smith

SMITH, P? *Navajo*
SILVERSMITH: Smith for State Line Indian Jewelry.
HALLMARK: Stamped surname and initial in 3/32 Gothic print, first used in 1975. Second stamp in special print of surname and initial.

P.SMITH   P. Smith

SMITHY, LEONARD *Navajo*
SILVERSMITH:
HALLMARK: Stamped surname in 3/32 Gothic print, first used in 1979.
From Gallup, New Mexico region.

SMITHY

SOCKYMA, MICHAEL *Hopi*
SILVERSMITH: Specializes in silver overlay. Began producing in 1965.
HALLMARK: Stamped symbol of a corn plant used first then switched to combined misaligned initials.
Brother is Mitchell Sockyma.
[Wright:1982:90]

SOCKYMA, MITCHELL *Hopi*
SILVERSMITH: Specializes in silver overlay. Began producing in 1972.
HALLMARK: Stamped image of a turtle first used in 1975. Later switched to misaligned initials very similar to his brother's mark. Brother is Michael Sockyma.
[Wright:1982:93]

SOCKYMA, STEVEN *Hopi*
SILVERSMITH: Specializes in silver overlay. Began producing in 1969.
HALLMARK: Chisel cut mark of misaligned initials in block print. 3/16" square.
[Wright:1982:93]

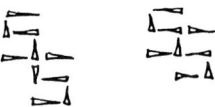

SOLOMON, JUDSON *Zuni*
SILVERSMITH:
HALLMARK: Three line stamp of full name and tribal affiliation in 1/16 Gothic print, first used in 1978.

JUDSON
SOLOMON
ZUNI

SORRELL, ROBERT *Navajo*
SILVERSMITH:
HALLMARK: Stamped surname in Gothic print and stamped initials on smaller pieces in same print.

SORRELL   R.S.

SOSEEAH, GLORIA *Zuni*
SILVERSMITH:
HALLMARK: Stamped surname and initial in 1/16 Gothic print, first used in 1974.

G.SOSEEAH

SOSOLDA, ALVIN *Pima*
SILVERSMITH: Specializes in silver overlay.
HALLMARK: Stamped image of a Pima stylized man, first used in 1983. Mark is 3/16" in height.

SPENCER, ? *Navajo*
SILVERSMITH: Smith for Felix Indian Jewelry.
HALLMARK: Stamped surname in 1/32 Gothic print, first used in 1985.

SPENCER

SPENCER, CHAKA *Anglo/Cherokee (?)*
SILVERSMITH: Produced very little.
HALLMARK: Stamp of a mark referred to by the artisan as a "bear step". A second stamp incorporates the same mark with a stylized bear track and a zigzag arrow. Spencer called himself "Chaka" and said that it meant bear. He also claimed to be part Cherokee. A local Scottsdale character, he died in 1977 or 1978.

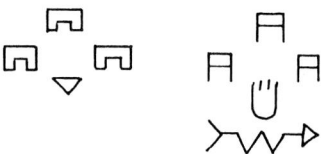

SPENCER, DOROTHY *Navajo*
SILVERSMITH: Smith for the Atkinson Trading Company.
HALLMARK: Stamped surname and initial in 1/32 print, first used in 1985. An earlier stamp used the same surname but a different initial and was first used in 1974. 1/32 Gothic print also.

L.SPENCER   D.SPENCER

SPENCER, E ? *Navajo*
SILVERSMITH: Smith for Felix Indian Jewelry.
HALLMARK: Stamped surname and initial in 1/16 Gothic print, first used in 1976.

E.SPENCER

SPENCER, H? *Navajo*
SILVERSMITH:
HALLMARK: Stamped surname and initial in 1/16 Gothic print, first used in 1974.

H.SPENCER

SPENCER, J. J. *Navajo*
SILVERSMITH: Smith for T&R Market.
HALLMARK: Stamped surname with double initials in 1/16 Gothic print, first used in 1976.

J.J.SPENCER

SPENCER, JOHN *Navajo*
SILVERSMITH: Smith for Atkinson Trading Company.
HALLMARK: Stamped surname and initial in 1/16 Gothic print, first used in 1974.

J.SPENCER

SPENCER, K? *Navajo*
SILVERSMITH: Smith for T&R Market.
HALLMARK: Stamped surname and initial in 1/16 Gothic print, first used in 1976.

K.SPENCER

SPENCER, KEE TSO *Navajo*
SILVERSMITH:
HALLMARK: Stamped initials in 1/16 Gothic print, first used in 1974.
From Gallup, New Mexico region.

K.T.S.

SPENCER, P? *Navajo*
SILVERSMITH: Smith for Montana Mining Company.
HALLMARK: Stamped initial and surname in 1/16 Gothic print, first used in 1974.

P. SPENCER

SPENCER, R? *Navajo*
SILVERSMITH: Smith for Montana Mining Company and later for Atkinson Trading Company.
HALLMARK: Stamped surname and initial in 1/16 Gothic print, first used in 1974.

R. SPENCER

SPENCER, S? *Navajo*
SILVERSMITH: Smith for Vic's Indian Arts and Crafts.
HALLMARK: Stamped surname and initial in 1/16 Gothic print, first used in 1976.

S. SPENCER

SPENCER, W. *Navajo*
SILVERSMITH: Smith for Indian Den Trading Company.
HALLMARK: Stamped surname and initial in 1/32 Gothic print, first used in 1984.

W. SPENCER

SPERICA, BETTY *Navajo*
SILVERSMITH: Produces jewelry in a style similar to Zuni cluster work.
HALLMARK: Stamped initials of her spouse's and her own given names. Shared with her husband.
Spouse is Sam Sperica.

S B

SPERICA, SAM *Navajo*
SILVERSMITH: Produces jewelry in a style similar to Zuni cluster work.
HALLMARK: Stamped initials of his spouse's and his own given names. Shared with his wife.
Spouse is Betty Sperica.

S B

SPURGEON, RICHARD W. *Unknown*
SILVERSMITH:
HALLMARK: Stamped surname in 1/16 Gothic print, first used in 1981.
From Enid, Oklahoma region.

SPURGEON

STAGO, LULA MAE *Navajo*
SILVERSMITH:
HALLMARK: Stamped initials in Gothic print.

LS

STERLING, F.W. *Navajo (?)*
SILVERSMITH:
HALLMARK: Stamped initials and surname in 1/16 Gothic print, first used in 1972.

F.W. STERLING

STEVENS, VERNA *Apache*
LAPIDARIST: Peridot jewelry.
HALLMARK: Stamped initials in Gothic print.

VS

STODDARD, MARY *Tesuque*
SILVERSMITH:
HALLMARK: Stamped initials representing unknown abbreviation in 3/32 Gothic print, first appeared in 1984.
From Tesuque, New Mexico region.

BIFL

STRAIN, CLYDE B. *Unknown*
SILVERSMITH: May represent a shop, Silver Eagle Casting. (see Shops)
HALLMARK: Stamped initial with cross bar in 3/32 print. Stamp first used in 1975.

STRONG, JOHN B. *Unknown*
SILVERSMITH:
HALLMARK: Two line stamp of initials and what appears to be an abbreviation for sergeant in 1/16 Gothic print. A second stamp in similar print, first used in 1978, maybe T-5 rather than T-S.
From Felton, California region.

JBS   T-S
SGT

SULU, MARIETTA *Hopi*
POTTER:
HALLMARK: Painted and fired initials.

MS

SUMATSKUKU, DEWAN *Hopi*
SILVERSMITH: Silver overlay. Produced only during the 1948 classes in silversmithing.
HALLMARK: Stamped image of a coyote head.
[Wright:1982:87]

SUNDT, DANNY D. *Anglo*
CRAFT UNKNOWN.
HALLMARK: Stamped mark in 1/16 print resembles a brand, Rafter D Lazy S.

SUPPLEE, CHARLES *French/Hopi*
SILVERSMITH/LAPIDARIST: Fashion jeweler. Began producing in 1985 after studying with Pierre Touraine.
HALLMARK: Marks are stamped, cast, or set on buttons. The first stamp was stylized initials used in 1984. Second stamp of a stylized sun face was first used in 1985. The hallmark is often worked into the design of the piece being created.
From Flagstaff, Arizona.

 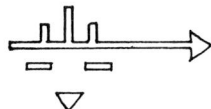

SWINEHART, MARVIN *Anglo (?)*
SILVERSMITH:

HALLMARK: Stamped arrow with a single letter S in the center. 1/4" in length stamp first used in 1984. From Elk City, Oklahoma region.

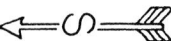

TABAHA, D? *Navajo*
SILVERSMITH: Smith for Hunter's Point Trading Company.
HALLMARK: Stamped surname in 3/32 Gothic print, first used in 1975.

D.TABAHA

TABAHA, S? *Navajo*
SILVERSMITH: Smith for Hunter's Point Trading Company.
HALLMARK: Stamped surname in 3/32 Gothic print, first used in 1975.

S.TABAHA

TADYTIN, L? *Navajo*
SILVERSMITH: Smith for Bernie Dominguez.
HALLMARK: Stamped surname in 1/16 Gothic print, first used in 1975.

L.TADYTIN

TAFOYA, ART *Unknown*
SILVERSMITH:
HALLMARK: Stamped mark is the same as Tommie Singer's and could be a shop mark.

TAFOYA, RAY *Unknown*
POTTER:
HALLMARK: Incised initials in personalized print.

RT

TAFOYA, RICHARD *Santa Clara*
SILVERSMITH: Began producing in the mid 70s.
HALLMARK: Stamp of surname and initial in script. Also uses a stamp called "White Mountain", a stylized representation of a snow-covered peak.

TAHE, VERNA *Navajo*
SILVERSMITH/LAPIDARIST: Specializes in contemporary pieces of heishi and silver.
HALLMARK: Stamped surname in Gothic print. First stamp used is of a stylized mountain with the letter T in 1/32 Gothic print within its outlines. This stamp was first used in 1984. From the Gallup, New Mexico region.

 TAHE

TAKALA, JASON *Hopi*
SILVERSMITH: Specializes in silver overlay and some combinations of gold and silver work. Began production in 1966.
HALLMARK: Stamped representation of a snow cloud 7/32" in length.
[Wright:1982:99]

TALAHEFTEWA, EVANGELINE *Hopi*
BASKETRY: Second Mesa coiled work.
HALLMARK: Stitched coiling on completion end of basket.

TALAHEFTEWA, HERBERT *Hopi*
SILVERSMITH: Specializes in silver overlay.
HALLMARK: Stamped representation of a rainbow.

TALAHEFTEWA, ROY *Hopi*
SILVERSMITH: Specializes in silver overlay. Began producing in 1976.
HALLMARK: Stamped image of a "water deer" or waterstrider. Usually set on a small round plate or button.
[Wright:1982:100]

TALAHEFTEWA, WILLIE ARCHIE *Hopi*
SILVERSMITH: Specializes in silver overlay. Began producing in 1965.
HALLMARK: First stamp of a chief's water jug had a long neck, used from 1965 to 1976. At that date he began using a second stamp with a short broad necked chief's jug, 7/32 x 5/32". First stamp 1/8" square.
[Wright:1982:100]

TALAS, VERNON *Hopi*
SILVERSMITH: Specialized in silver overlay. Began producing in 1948.
HALLMARK: Stamped image of a pipe, 9/32 x 5/32".
Deceased.
[Wright:1982:84]

TALASHIE, ROSALIE *Hopi*
POTTER: Began producing around 1930.
HALLMARK: Painted and fired images of corn ears, corn pollen, or corn tassels. Husband's name means corn tassel/pollen.

TALAYUMPTEWA, CAROLINE *Hopi*

POTTER: Was producing in 1959.
HALLMARK: Painted and fired images of deer tracks, deer tracks with initials, or deer tracks with full name.

TALAYUMPTEWA, ORVILLE   *Hopi*
SILVERSMITH: Made silver overlay. Began producing in 1948 and ceased sometime before 1975.
HALLMARK: Stamped stylized image of a bear paw.
[Wright:1982:85]

TALIMAN, ELIZABETH   *Cochiti*
SILVERSMITH: Specializes in beads. Producing before 1985.
HALLMARK: Stamped joined and misaligned initials.

TAWAHONGVA, BERRA   *Hopi*
SILVERSMITH: Specializes in silver overlay. Began producing in 1983.
HALLMARK: Stamped image of Masau-u's head 1/8" square. Stamp first used in 1985.

TAWAHONGVA, ROY   *Hopi*
SILVERSMITH: Specializes in silver overlay. Began producing in 1972.
HALLMARK: Stamped image of a pipe 7/32 x 3/32" or misaligned initials in Gothic print.
[Wright:1982:100]

TAWANGYAOUMA, RALPH   *Hopi*
SILVERSMITH: Worked in all silver techniques. Began producing before 1939 and continued to mid-1960s. Worked as a shop smith in Phoenix and Tucson.
HALLMARK: Engraved thunderhead with the letter H along side.
[Wright:1982:80]

TAYLOR, BERNICE   *Navajo*
SILVERSMITH:
HALLMARK: Stamped initials in Gothic print with elongated central initial. Engraved initials in freehand printing.

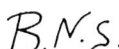

TAYLOR, DALTON   *Hopi*
SILVERSMITH: Specializes in silver overlay. Began producing in 1970.
HALLMARK: Stamped image of a star. In 1973 he used the moon hallmark of Billie Rae Hawee on a few pieces.
[Wright:1982:90]

TAYLOR, HERBERT   *Navajo*
SILVERSMITH:
HALLMARK: Combined and joined initials in Gothic print.

TAYLOR, MILSON   *Hopi*
SILVERSMITH: Specializes in silver overlay. Began producing in 1976.
HALLMARK: Stamped image of a sun or initials in Gothic print.

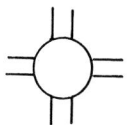   MT

TAYLOR, PATRICK (PAT)   *Navajo*
SILVERSMITH: Smith for the Rockinghorse Ranch in 1985.
HALLMARK: Stamped initial and surname in 1/16 Gothic print. Stamped initials on smaller pieces in the same type. Also uses the image of a cowboy boot in a stamp. Occasionally uses the name Patricio.
From Dilkon, Arizona region.

PT   P.TAYLOR

TEKALA, ANNIE LEE   *Zuni*
SILVERSMITH/LAPIDARIST: Specializes in channel inlay in interlocking oval forms. Learned from her mother and began producing in 1972.
HALLMARK: Engraved freehand printing of her full name and abbreviation of tribal affiliation.
[Levy:1980:28]

Anna Lee Tekala Z.NM.

TEKALA, BERNICE   *Zuni*
SILVERSMITH/LAPIDARIST: Specializes in channel work wristwatch bands. Began producing in the 1940s. Both she and her husband work on the pieces.
HALLMARK: Stamped hallmark of combined and reversed initials of her husband and hers. Stamped abbreviated name with shared initials also used.
Spouse is Rossevelt Tekala.
[Bell:1975:72]

    RBTEKI

TEKALA, LAWRENCE A.   *Zuni*
SILVERSMITH:
HALLMARK: Stamped abbreviation of surname in 1/16 Gothic print. First used in 1975.

TEK

TEKALA, ROOSEVELT *Zuni*
SILVERSMITH/LAPIDARIST: Specializes in channel work watchbands. Began producing in the 1940s. Both he and his wife work on the pieces.
HALLMARK: Stamped combined and reversed initials of his wife's and his given names. Stamped initials and abbreviated surname also used.
Spouse is Bernie Takala.
[Bell:1975:72]

℞ RBTEKI

TELLER, D ? *Navajo*
SILVERSMITH: Smith for Richardson's American Indian Art.
HALLMARK: Stamped initial and surname in 1/16 Gothic print, first used in 1984.

D. TELLER

TENORIO, JAMES *Santo Domingo*
SILVERSMITH: Specializes in pieces with silver overlay on bronze.
HALLMARK: Stamped initials and surname in 1/16 Gothic print, first used in 1985.

J.M. TENORIO

TENORIO, JOE *Santo Domingo*
SILVERSMITH:
HALLMARK: Stamped misaligned initials in Gothic print.

J
T

TENORIO, MARY *Santo Domingo*
SILVERSMITH:
HALLMARK: Stamped misaligned initials with crescent below the initials.

M
T

TERRAZAS, GENEVA *Zuni*
SILVERSMITH:
HALLMARK: Stamped initials of her husband's and her own in Gothic 1/16 print. Stamps first used in 1982.
Spouse is Richard Terrazas.

R.&G.T.   R&GT

TERRAZAS, RICHARD *Mexican*
SILVERSMITH:
HALLMARK: Stamped initials of his wife's and his own in 1/16 Gothic print. Stamps first used in 1982.
Spouse is Geneva Terrazas.

R.&G.T.   R&GT

TEWA, BOBBY *San Juan Tewa/Hopi*
SILVERSMITH: Began producing ca. 1974. Smith for Santa Fe Associates, Inc.
HALLMARK: Stamped initial and surname in 1/16 script, first used in 1980.

BJTewa   BJTewa

TEWAWINA, PAT *Hopi*
SILVERSMITH: Specializes in silver overlay. Began producing in 1976.
HALLMARK: Stamped initials in Gothic print or the image of a snow cloud.
[Wright:1982:100]

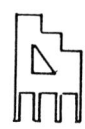   PT

TEWAWINA, STEWART *Hopi*
SILVERSMITH: Specializes in silver overlay. Began producing in 1976.
HALLMARK: Stamped initials in Gothic print or the image of a Kwan Society helmet, the One-Horned Society.
[Wright:1982:100]

   ST

THOMAS, LEROY *Navajo*
(see **THOMPSON, LEROY** and **TURQUOISE, LEROY**)
SILVERSMITH:
HALLMARK: Stamped initials in Gothic print or joined and misaligned initials.

L.T.

THOMAS, LOUISE *Navajo*
SILVERSMITH: Smith for Atkinson Trading Company.
HALLMARK: Stamped initials and surname in 1/16 Gothic print, first used in 1975.

L. THOMAS

THOMAS, M? *Navajo*
SILVERSMITH: Smith for Felix's Indian Jewelry.
HALLMARK: Stamped surname and initial in 1/16 Gothic print. May be a reversed name.

THOMAS M

THOMAS, RICHARD T. *Navajo*
SILVERSMITH:
HALLMARK: Stamped initial in Gothic print.

T

THOMAS, T? *Navajo*
SILVERSMITH: Smith for Traditional Traders.
HALLMARK: Stamped surname and initial in 1/16 Gothic print. First used in 1974.

T. THOMAS

THOMAS, VIRGIL *Hopi*
SILVERSMITH: Specializes in silver overlay. Began producing in 1972
HALLMARK: Stamped or chisel cut combination of initials joined and misaligned. 5/32 x 1/16".

THOMPSON, BEN *Anglo*
SILVERSMITH: Produces Indian style silver work.
HALLMARK: Stamped initials in Gothic print or the image of what appears to be a bailing hook.

BT

THOMPSON, FRANKLIN *Navajo*
SILVERSMITH: Smith for the Atkinson Trading Company.
HALLMARK: Stamped initial and surname in 1/16 print. First used in 1975.

F. THOMPSON

THOMPSON, FRED *Navajo*
SILVERSMITH: Specialized in heavy stamped pieces of silver with many stones. Smith for Tobe Turpen. Producing at the age of 15.
HALLMARK: Stamped full name in 1/16 Gothic print, first used in 1974. Used the Turpen Shop mark with the tilde below the mark.

FRED THOMPSON

THOMPSON, HARDY *Navajo*
SILVERSMITH: Smith for Atkinson Trading Company.
HALLMARK: Stamped initial and surname in 1/16 Gothic print. Stamp first used in 1974.

H. THOMPSON

THOMPSON, JESSIE *Navajo*
SILVERSMITH:
HALLMARK: Stamped joined initials.

JT

THOMPSON, LEROY (see Leroy Thomas) *Navajo*
SILVERSMITH: Smith for Atkinson Trading Company before 1980.
HALLMARK: Stamped initials in 1/16 Gothic print, first used in 1975. Stamped joined initials in block print.

 L.T.

THOMPSON, MARIE *Navajo*
SILVERSMITH: Specializes in sand cast pieces.
HALLMARK: Stamped initials in Gothic print.
From Indian Wells, Arizona region.

M   M.T.

THOMPSON, MELVIN *Navajo*
SILVERSMITH:
HALLMARK: Stamped initials in Gothic print.

MT

THOMPSON, NORMAN *Navajo*
SILVERSMITH:
HALLMARK: Stamped image of Shiprock within a circle; the letter N is just below the mountain outline. Stamp first used in 1976.

THOMPSON, PHILLIP *Navajo*
SILVERSMITH: Smith for the Atkinson Trading Company.
HALLMARK: Stamped initials and surname in 1/16 Gothic print. Stamp first used in 1974.

P. THOMPSON SR.

THOMPSON, S? *Navajo*
SILVERSMITH: Smith for the Atkinson Trading Company.
HALLMARK: Stamped initial and surname in 1/16 Gothic print. Stamp first used in 1974.

S. THOMPSON

THUNDERBOLT, C? *Unknown*
(see **David Sandoval Thunderfoot**)
SILVERSMITH:
HALLMARK: Stamped zigzag of lightning. Also signs himself Thunderbolt and C. Thunderfoot.

THUNDERFOOT, C? *Unknown*
SILVERSMITH:
HALLMARK: Stamped initial and surname in Gothic print. C. Thunderfoot and David Sandoval Thunderfoot may be different individuals.

C. THUNDERFOOT

TOADLENA, J? *Navajo*
SILVERSMITH: Smith for First American Traders.
HALLMARK: Stamped initial and surname in 1/16 Gothic print. Stamp first used in 1975.

J. TOADLENA

TOADLENA, JAMES *Navajo*
SILVERSMITH:
HALLMARK: Stamped initials and surname in 1/16 Gothic print, first used in 1975.
From Vanderwagen, New Mexico region.

J. W. TOADLENA

TODACHEENIE, STELLA *Navajo*
WEAVER:
HALLMARK: Woven signature in a corner of a Ganado rug ca. 1970. May be the first instance of a name being woven into a rug as a hallmark.

Stella Todacheenie

TODACHEENY, JOHNSON *Navajo*
SILVERSMITH: Began producing in 1967. Smith for White Hogan.
HALLMARK: Stamped joined initials in Gothic print.

JT

TODLENA, GORDON *Zuni*
SILVERSMITH:

HALLMARK: Stamped initials in Gothic print.

G.T.

TOLEDO, CURLENE *Navajo*
SILVERSMITH:
HALLMARK: Stamped and joined initials, misaligned and in personalized print.

C/J

TOLEDO, EVA *Unknown*
SILVERSMITH:
HALLMARK: Stamped given name in 1/16 Gothic print, first used in 1984.
From the Santa Fe, New Mexico region.

EVA

TOLEDO, H ? *Unknown*
SILVERSMITH:
HALLMARK: Stamped initial and surname in 1/16 Gothic print, first used in 1984.

H.TOLEDO

TOLEDO, MARY *Navajo*
SILVERSMITH:
HALLMARK: Stamped initials in Gothic print.

M.T.

TOLEDO, RUSSELL *Unknown*
SILVERSMITH:
HALLMARK: Stamped full name in 1/16 Gothic print, first used in 1982.
From Santa Fe, New Mexico region.

RUSSELL TOLEDO

TOLEDO, TONY *Navajo*
SILVERSMITH:
HALLMARK: Stamped misaligned initials and surname in 1/32 Gothic print, first used in 1984. Second stamp of full name in 1/16 Gothic print, first used in 1984.
From Santa Fe, New Mexico region.

TLNAVAJO   TONEY TOLEDO

TOLINO, A.R. *Navajo*
SILVERSMITH:
HALLMARK: Stamped initials and, surname in 1/16 Gothic print, first used in 1973.
From Crown Point, New Mexico region.

A.R.TOLEDO

TOM, CLARENCE B. *Navajo*
SILVERSMITH:
HALLMARK: Stamped initials and surname in 1/16 Gothic print, first used in 1975.
From St. Michaels, Arizona region.

C.B.TOM

TOM, DUANE *Navajo*
SILVERSMITH:
HALLMARK: Stamped joined and misaligned initials in 3/32 Gothic print, first used in 1973.
From Crown Point, New Mexico region.

TOM, ELIZABETH *Navajo*
SILVERSMITH: Smith for the Atkinson Trading Company.
HALLMARK: Stamped initial and surname in 1/16 Gothic print, first used in 1976.

E.TOM

TOM, H.L. *Navajo*
SILVERSMITH:
HALLMARK: Stamped initials and surname in 3/32 Gothic print, first used in 1976.
From Holbrook, Arizona region.

H.L.TOM

TOM, JAMES *Navajo*
SILVERSMITH:
HALLMARK: Stamped initials and surname in 1/16 Gothic print, first used in 1976.
From Holbrook, Arizona region.

J.W.TOM

TOM, JOE *Navajo*
SILVERSMITH:
HALLMARK: Stamped initial with feather, 1/16 print. Stamp first used in 1977.

TOM, LARRY BILL *Navajo*
SILVERSMITH: Smith for Atkinson Trading Company.
HALLMARK: Stamped initials and surname in 1/16 Gothic print.

L.B.TOM

TOOTH, DUANE *Navajo*
SILVERSMITH:
HALLMARK: Stamped images of teeth (?).

TOOTH, JUAN *Navajo*
SILVERSMITH:
HALLMARK: Stamped initials in Gothic print.

JD

TORTALITA, JOE *Santo Domingo*
SILVERSMITH:
HALLMARK: Stamped initials in Gothic print.

JT

TORTALITA, LORENZO *Santo Domingo*
SILVERSMITH:
HALLMARK: Stamped image of a bear paw with initials in block print inside.

TORTALITA, VICKIE — *Santo Domingo*
SILVERSMITH:
HALLMARK: Stamp of bear paw with initials within it in block print. Stamp is 1/4" square and was first used in 1980.

TOUCHINE, BENNY — *Navajo*
SILVERSMITH: Smith for C & B Shay.
HALLMARK: Stamped initial and surname in 1/16 and 1/32 Gothic print. Hallmark is registered.
From Church Rock, New Mexico region.

B.TOUCHINE ®   TOUCHINE

TOUCHINE, EDWARD — *Navajo*
SILVERSMITH:
HALLMARK: Stamped initial and surname in 1/16 Gothic print, first used in 1976.
From Ft. Defiance, Arizona region.

E.TOUCHINE

TOUCHINE, GRACE — *Navajo*
SILVERSMITH/GOLDSMITH:
HALLMARK: Stamped initials in 1/16 Gothic print, first used in 1974.

G.T.

TOYA, MAXINE — *Jemez*
POTTER:
HALLMARK: Painted and fired corn plant. Mark is used by her sister also.
Sister is Laura Gachupin.

TRACEY, LARRY — *Navajo*
SILVERSMITH:
HALLMARK: Special stamp 1/4 x 1/2" of hogan with name above it. Stamp first used in 1977.
From Ganado, Arizona region.

TRACEY, RAY — *Navajo*
SILVERSMITH:
HALLMARK: Stamp of feather with name above in personalized print. One stamp is 1/2 x 1/4", the other is 1/4 x 1/8". Stamps first used in 1976.
From Ganado, Arizona region.

TRACY, STAN — *Unknown*
SILVERSMITH: Smith for Don's Trading Post.
HALLMARK: Stamped full name in 3/32 Gothic print, first used in 1977.

STAN TRACY

TRUEBA, JIM — *Unknown*
SILVERSMITH:
HALLMARK: Stamped joined initials in 3/16 and 5/16" sizes.
From Apache Junction, Arizona region.

JLT   JLT

TRUJILLO, CHARLES — *Unknown*
SILVERSMITH:
HALLMARK: Stamped misaligned initials in 1/16 Gothic print with crescents above and below, first used in 1979.
From Albuquerque, New Mexico region.

TRUJILLO, ERNEST — *Unknown*
SILVERSMITH:
HALLMARK: Stamped initials misaligned in Gothic print.
From Safford, Arizona region.

E
EJT

TRUJILLO, HAROLD — *Navajo*
SILVERSMITH: Smith for Max Sandoval in 1976. Smith for Hill's Turquoise in 1977. Smith for Albuquerque shops in 1978-79.
HALLMARK: Stamped initials and tribal affiliation in two line 1/16 Gothic print, first used in 1976. Second stamp of initials alone in 1/16 Gothic print, first used in 1977.
From Cuba, New Mexico region.

H.T.   H.T.
NAVAJO

TRUJILLO, VELMA — *Navajo*
SILVERSMITH:
HALLMARK: Stamped initials in Gothic print.
From Cuba, New Mexico region.

VT

TRUJILLO, WOODY — *Taos*
SILVERSMITH:
HALLMARK: Stamped surname and tribal affiliation in Gothic print.

WOODY/TAOS

TSABABUTIE, LLOYD — *Zuni*
SILVERSMITH/LAPIDARIST: Specializes in embossed inlay.
HALLMARK: Stamped joined initials in block print.

L

TSABETSAYE, D? — *Zuni*
SILVERSMITH:
HALLMARK: Stamped initial and surname in 1/32 print, first used in 1982.

D. TSABETSAYE

TSABETSAYE, EDITH *Zuni*
SILVERSMITH/LAPIDARIST: Specializes in needlepoint, particularly curved.
HALLMARK: Stamped initials separated by a large Z on a square plate, stamped initials separated by a large Z on a barrel shaped plate 1/4" in size. Stamped initials in 1/32 Gothic print. Barrel shaped plate first used in 1973, initials alone first used in 1982.

 E.T.

TSABETSAYE, EVANGELINE (VANGIE) *Zuni*
SILVERSMITH/LAPIDARIST: Specializes in needlepoint and nugget work. Began producing ca. 1971. Works in both silver and gold.
HALLMARK: Stamped initials, joined and misaligned, of her husband's and her own given name.
Spouse is Griffin Tsabetsaye.
[Bell:1976:42]

 GTV

TSABETSAYE, GRIFFIN *Zuni*
SILVERSMITH/LAPIDARIST: Specializes in needlepoint and nugget work, in both gold and silver. Began producing ca. 1971.
HALLMARK: Stamped initials, joined and misaligned, of his initials and those of his wife.
Spouse is Evangeline Tsabetsaye.
[Bell:1976:42]

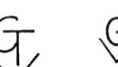  GTV

TSABETSAYE, J? *Zuni*
SILVERSMITH: Smith for Atkinson Trading Company.
HALLMARK: Stamped surname in 1/16 Gothic print, first used in 1976.

J. TSABETSAYE

TSABETSAYE, JOE *Zuni*
SILVERSMITH:
HALLMARK: Stamped initial and numeral in 1/16 Gothic print, first used in 1976.

J-3

TSABETSAYE, ROGER *Zuni*
SILVERSMITH/LAPIDARIST: Specializes in contemporary jewelry using most techniques in silver and inlay. Member of the Southwest Indian Art Project, Institute of American Indian Art. Production and design manager for Indian Arts & Crafts at Zuni. Began production in 1966 or earlier.
HALLMARK: Stamped surname and initial in 1/16 Gothic print, first used in 1976. Stamped surname and initial in 1/32 Gothic print, first used in 1982. Stamped symbol of three feathers. Stamped symbol of Zuni Knife-wing, or Bow Priest's, shield 1/4 x 5/32", first used in 1982.

R. TSABETSAYE

TSABETSAYE, VANGIE (See **Evangeline Tsabetsaye**)

TSADIASE, ? *Zuni*
SILVERSMITH: Smith for Chet Jones.
HALLMARK: Stamped surname in 16 script, first used in 1979.

Tsadiase

TSADIASI, MARY ANN *Zuni*
SILVERSMITH:
HALLMARK: Stamped initials in 1/16 Gothic print, first used in 1977.

M.A.T.

TSADIASI, PERCY J. *Zuni*
SILVERSMITH:
HALLMARK: Stamped initials in 3/32 Gothic print, first used in 1972.

PJT

TSALATE, JOANITA *Zuni*
SILVERSMITH/LAPIDARIST: Specializes in channel inlay.
HALLMARK: Stamped initials in Gothic print, or engraved signature.
[Bell: 1977:64]

JT *Joanita Tsalate*

TSALATE, LINDA *Zuni*
SILVERSMITH:
HALLMARK: Stamped initials in 1/16 Gothic print, first used in 1982.

C.L.T.

TSETHLEKAI, DORIS *Zuni*
SILVERSMITH/LAPIDARIST: Specializes in tiny butterflies with very small settings. Learned from her nephew and began producing in 1974. She does all the work.
HALLMARK: Stamped initials in Gothic print.
[Levy:1980:49]

DT

TSETHLIKAI, IVAN J. *Zuni*
SILVERSMITH/LAPIDARIST: Specializes in butterflies done in channel inlay.
HALLMARK: Stamped symbol of a butterfly in three different sizes and his name engraved on larger pieces.
[Bell:1977:39]

TSETHLIKAI, VIVIAN *Zuni*
SILVERSMITH/LAPIDARIST: Specializes in needlepoint, petit point, and snake eye settings. Began producing in 1951.
HALLMARK: Stamped initials in Gothic print and tribal affiliation.
[Bell:1977:61]

V.T. ZUNI

TSETHLIKIA, LENA *Zuni*
SILVERSMITH/LAPIDARIST: Specializes in mosaic inlay. Both she and her husband work on the same pieces.
HALLMARK: Stamped initials of her husband's and her own given names or full name signed with an engraver.
Spouse is Patrick Tsethlikai.
[Bell:1976:36]

LPT

TSETHLIKIA, PATRICK *Zuni*
SILVERSMITH/LAPIDARIST: Specializes in mosaic inlay. Both he and his wife work on the same pieces. Began in 1960s.
HALLMARK: Stamped initials of his wife's and his own given names or full name signed with an engraver.
Spouse is Lena Tsethlikia.
[Bell:1976:36]

LPT

TSIKEWA, DAVID *Zuni*
LAPIDARIST: Fetish necklaces and heishi.
HALLMARK: Given name stamped on a silver tag in Gothic print or bird track marked on individual pieces.
Spouse is Mary Tsikewa, daughter Lavina Tsikewa. Deceased.
[Ariz Hwys; Aug. 1975]

TSINNIE, DARLENE *Navajo*
SILVERSMITH:
HALLMARK: Stamped combined initials of her husband's and her own initials.
Spouse is Orville Tsinnie.
From Shiprock, New Mexico region.

TSINNIE, ORVILLE *Navajo*
SILVERSMITH: Produces all types of jewelry using many techniques. Began producing ca. 1970.
HALLMARK: Uses a stamped combination of his wife's and his own initials. Several versions of Shiprock with his surname above and Shiprock, New Mexico below in either print or script.
Spouse is Darlene Tsinnie, mother is Ann Yellowhorse.

TSO, BILLIE *Navajo*
SILVERSMITH:
HALLMARK: Stamped surname and initial in Gothic print. May use the name Billie Tsosie as well.

B.TSO

TSO, DAN *Navajo*
SILVERSMITH:
HALLMARK: Stamped full name in 1/16 Gothic print, first used in 1978.
From Cuba, New Mexico region.

DAN TSO

TSO, NELLIE *Navajo*
SILVERSMITH: Specializes in sand cast watchbands. Smith for the Atkinson Trading Company around 1980.
HALLMARK: Stamped full name in Gothic print, surname and initial, variations on the latter.

NELLIE TSO   N.TSO   NTSO   NTso

TSO, PHILLIP *Navajo*
SILVERSMITH:
HALLMARK: Stamped given name or abbreviation of it with initial of surname in 1/16 Gothic print, first used in 1974.

PHIL T.   PHIL T. JR.

TSO, RAYMOND *Navajo*
SILVERSMITH:
HALLMARK: Stamped combined initials first used in 1973. Stamped initials in 3/32 script first used in 1974; two types, one with three initials, the other two. An engraved personalized script ca. 3/32 in size first used in 1976. Stamped combined and misaligned initials 1/8" in height first used in 1982.

TSO, THOMAS (TOMMY) *Navajo*
SILVERSMITH:
HALLMARK: Stamped initials in Gothic print.

T.T.

TSODIA, DELPHINE *Zuni*
SILVERSMITH:
HALLMARK: Engraved signature of full name.

Delphine Tsodia

TSOSIE,? *Navajo*
SILVERSMITH/LAPIDARIST: Specializes in red inlay work.
HALLMARK: Stamped surname in personalized script.

Tsosje

TSOSIE, BILLIE see **TSO, BILLIE**

TSOSIE, BOYD *Navajo*
SILVERSMITH/LAPIDARIST: Specializes in fashion jewelry. Learned the craft from Kenneth Begay at Many Farms Navajo Community College ca. 1970. Works in all techniques but prefers gold to silver. First silversmith in his family.
HALLMARK: First hallmark was a cloud with the letter B below in a single stamp. Since 1985 he has used a stylized stamp of his surname.
Older brother is Richard Tsosie.

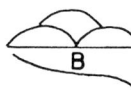

TSOSIE, DOLLY *Navajo*
SILVERSMITH/LAPIDARIST: She and her husband make the inserts for Mary Marie Yazzie.
HALLMARK: Combined initials of her husband's and her given names in Gothic print.
Spouse is Paul Tsosie.

P. D.

TSOSIE, ELKIE *Navajo*
SILVERSMITH:
HALLMARK: Stamped letter X in Gothic print.

X

TSOSIE, HARRISON *Navajo*
SILVERSMITH:
HALLMARK: Stamped symbol embodying letter T.

TSOSIE, IRENE *Navajo*
SILVERSMITH: Smith for Atkinson Trading Company.
HALLMARK: Stamped full name in 1/16 Gothic print, first used in 1974.

IRENE TSOSIE

TSOSIE, JULIA *Navajo*
SILVERSMITH:
HALLMARK: Stamped surname and initial in 1/16 Gothic print, first used in 1978.
From Gallup, New Mexico region.

J. TSOSIE

TSOSIE, KEE *Navajo*
SILVERSMITH:
HALLMARK: Stamped joined and misaligned initials in Gothic print.

K
 T

TSOSIE, LUCIE *Navajo*
SILVERSMITH:
HALLMARK: Stamped surname and initial in 1/16 Gothic print, first used in 1975.
From Chinle, Arizona region.

L. TSOSIE

TSOSIE, MARY E. *Navajo*
SILVERSMITH: Smith for the Atkinson Trading Company.
HALLMARK: Stamped surname and initials in 1/16 Gothic print, first used in 1974.

M.E. TSOSIE

TSOSIE, MELVIN *Navajo*
SILVERSMITH:
HALLMARK: Stamped signature in personalized script.
Related to Boyd and Richard Tsosie.

mel tsosie

TSOSIE, M.J. *Navajo*
SILVERSMITH: Smith for the Atkinson Trading Company.
HALLMARK: Stamped surname and initials in 1/16 Gothic print, first used in 1974.

M.J. TSOSIE

TSOSIE, PAUL *Navajo*
SILVERSMITH: Paul and wife make inserts for Mary Marie Yazzie.
HALLMARK: Stamped intials of his wife's and his given names. Shared with spouse.
Spouse is Dolly Tsosie.

P.D.

TSOSIE, RICHARD *Navajo*
SILVERSMITH: Works in all techniques. Prefers to work in silver. Learned from Kenneth Begay at Navajo Community College in Many Farms, Arizona ca. 1970. Smith for the Tanners for a while.
HALLMARK: First used a three-lobed cloud with initial R below it. In 1985 began using a stylized stamp of his surname.
Brother is Boyd Tsosie.

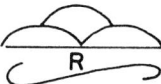

TSOSIE, ROBERTSON T. *Navajo*
SILVERSMITH:
HALLMARK: Stamped initials in 3/32 Gothic print, first used in 1974.
From the Churchrock, New Mexico region.

R.T.T.

TSOSIE, WILSON *Navajo*
SILVERSMITH: Specialized in hammered and wrought work, with nugget sets. Began producing in the late 1940s.
HALLMARK: Stamped surname in 3/32 Gothic print, first used in 1972. Stamped surname with initial in Gothic print. First stamp was joined initials in Gothic print.

WT   TSOSIE   W. TSOSIE

TSOUHLARAKIS, GEORGE E. *Navajo/Greek*
SILVERSMITH/LAPIDARIST: Specializes in fashion jewelry. Began producing in 1972 (age 20). Co-owner of grandfather's Tom A. Lewis Artists, Ltd.
HALLMARK: Stamped symbol which may be incorporated in the design of the piece.

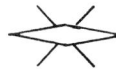

TSUI, LEO S. *Navajo*
SILVERSMITH:
HALLMARK: Stamped initials in 1/16 Gothic print, first used in 1978.
From the Nazlini, Arizona region.

L.S.T.

TUCSON, LEE *Zuni*
SILVERSMITH/LAPIDARIST: Specializes in channel inlay.
HALLMARK: Stamped symbol of a bird or a bird's foot or track.
Wife shares his hallmark.
Spouse is Myra Tucson.

TUCSON, MYRA — *Zuni*
SILVERSMITH/LAPIDARIST: Specializes in channel inlay.
HALLMARK: Stamped symbol of a bird or a bird's foot or track. Husband shares the hallmark.
Spouse is Lee Tucson.

TULLEY, EDISON — *Zuni*
SILVERSMITH:
HALLMARK: Stamped full name in 1/16 Gothic print, first used in 1982.
From the Mentmore, New Mexico region.

EDDY TULLEY

TULLEY, ELSIE — *Zuni*
SILVERSMITH: Smith for the Richardson Trading Company.
HALLMARK: Stamped full name in 1/16 Gothic print, first used in 1975. Stamped surname with initials of her husband's and her given names in 1/16 Gothic print, first used in 1975. Engraved signature of surname and initial also used.

ELSIE TULLEY   B.&E. TULLEY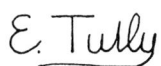

TULLEY, RICHARD — *Navajo*
SILVERSMITH:
HALLMARK: Stamped surname and initial in 3/32 Gothic print, first used in 1975.
From Prewitt, New Mexico region.

R.TULLEY

TUNE, DAVID — *Creek/Navajo/Hopi*
SILVERSMITH:
HALLMARK: Stamped symbols.

TURNER, KEITH — *Anglo*
SILVERSMITH: Produces Indian style jewelry and markets it as such.
HALLMARK: Stamped joined and misaligned initials, sometimes with a symbol.
Uses the name "Kicking Turtle". Has used outlets in Albuquerque, New Mexico and Las Vegas, Nevada.

TURNER, SLIM — *Navajo*
SILVERSMITH:
HALLMARK: Stamped initials in 1/16 Gothic print, first used in 1977.
From Holbrook, Arizona region.

S.T.

TURQUOISE, LEROY see THOMAS, LEROY — *Navajo*
SILVERSMITH: Began producing ca. 1974. Makes his own designs. Smith for White Hogan. Demonstrator at Museum of Northern Arizona in 1976.
HALLMARK: Stamped combination of misaligned initials.
From Bittersprings, Arizona region.

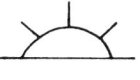 L.T.

TYMA, GILBERT ANDRESS — *Hopi*
SILVERSMITH: Specializes in silver overlay. Began producing in 1975.
HALLMARK: Stamped combination of misaligned initials.
[Wright:1982:100]

TZUNIE, BENJAMIN JR. — *Zuni*
SILVERSMITH/LAPIDARIST: Mosaic inlay and needlepoint are his specialties. Unique in that he numbers his pieces.
HALLMARK: Engraved signature 5/32 x 1" and stamped symbol of a rising sun.
Spouse is Shirley Tzunie.
[Bell:1977:48]

UHASTINE, TOM — *Zuni*
SILVERSMITH:
HALLMARK: Stamped initials in Gothic print.

T.U.

UKASTINE, ALMA — *Zuni*
SILVERSMITH/GOLDSMITH:
HALLMARK: Stamped initials in Gothic print.

A.U.

UKESTINE, CLARISSA — *Zuni*
SILVERSMITH/LAPIDARIST: Specializes in needlepoint.
HALLMARK: Stamped initials of her husband's and her given names with tribal affiliation and location. Mark is shared.
Spouse is Lebeck Ukestine.
[Bell:1977:54]

L&C
ZUNI NM

UKESTINE, DANNY — *Zuni*
SILVERSMITH:
HALLMARK: Stamped given name and initial of surname in 1/16 Gothic print, first used in 1976.

DANNY U.

UKESTINE, JASON — *Zuni*
SILVERSMITH/LAPIDARIST:
HALLMARK: Stamped combination of joined initials in 1/4" and 1/8" Gothic print, first used in 1973. Mark is a combination of his wife's and his given names. Uses the combination with an engraved signature also. Shared with his wife.
Spouse is Pearl Ukestine.

UKESTINE, LEBECK *Zuni*
SILVERSMITH/LAPIDARIST: Specializes in needlepoint.
HALLMARK: Stamped combination of his wife's and his given name initials in Gothic print, with tribal affiliation and location also. Mark shared with his wife.
Spouse is Clarissa Ukestine.
[Bell:1977:54]

L&C
ZUNI NM

UKESTINE, PEARL *Zuni*
SILVERSMITH/LAPIDARIST:
HALLMARK: Stamped combined initials of her husband's and her given names in 1/4 and 1/8" sizes. Uses an engraved signature also with the beginning initials combined.
Spouse is Jason Ukestine.

ULLSTROM, ? *Anglo*
SILVERSMITH:
HALLMARK: Stamped symbol of a horse shoe or an elaborate U.

UNKESTINE, IRMA *Zuni*
SILVERSMITH:
HALLMARK: Stamped surname and initial in 1/16 Gothic print, first used in 1985.

I. UNKESTINE

UPSHAW, JAMES *Navajo(?)*
SILVERSMITH:
HALLMARK: Stamped initials in 1/16 Gothic print, first used in 1973.
From St. Michaels, Arizona region.

J.F.U.

VACIT, FRANK *Zuni*
SILVERSMITH/LAPIDARIST: Specialized in channel and mosaic inlay. Used many techniques. Began producing in the mid 1930s.
HALLMARK: Stamped symbol vaguely resembling a fleur-de-lis. Symbol also used with surname and initial and tribal affiliation.

 F.VACIT ZUNI ⚜

VANCE, HOMER *Hopi*
SILVERSMITH: Smith at Grand Canyon Village.
HALLMARK: Stamped initials in Gothic print.
Deceased.
[Wright:1982:81]

HV

VANDERVER, ANITA *Navajo*
SILVERSMITH: Smith for Atkinson Trading Company.
HALLMARK: Stamped surname in 1/16 Gothic print, first used in 1975.

A VANDERVER

VANDERVER, ANTHONY *Navajo*
SILVERSMITH: Smith for Atkinson Trading Company.
HALLMARK: Stamped surname and initial in 1/16 Gothic print. Two stamps one with name spelled Vandever first used in 1974 and the second with it spelled Vanderver and first used in 1977. Both were purchased by Vanderver.

A.VANDEVER   A.VANDERVER

VANDEVER, LUCY M. *Navajo*
SILVERSMITH:
HALLMARK: Stamped initials in 1/16 Gothic print, first used in 1974.
From Prewitt, New Mexico region.

L.M.V.

VANDEVER, ROY *Navajo*
SILVERSMITH:
HALLMARK: Stamped joined initials in Gothic print. Also uses his signature cut with an engraver.
Spouse is Donna Vandever.
From Prewitt, New Mexico region.

VANDEVER, WILLIAM *Navajo*
SILVERSMITH:
HALLMARK: Stamped combinations of VW joined into a single symbol.

VW   VW   VVV

VAUGHN, TED *Navajo (?)*
SILVERSMITH:
HALLMARK: Stamped surname in 1/16 Gothic print, first used in 1976. Stamped initials combined with a symbol of wings first used in 1977.
From Keams Canyon, Arizona region.

VAUGHN

VELASQUEZ, MARY *San Felipe or Isleta/Sandia*
SILVERSMITH: Favors gold wash work and nugget coral.
HALLMARK: Stamped upper and lower case initials in personalized print. Stamped full name in personalized print.

VERONICA see **NASTACIO, VERONICA**

VICTOR, DARRELL *Apache*
LAPIDARIST: Peridot jewelry.
HALLMARK: Stamped initials in Gothic print.

DV

VINCENT, R? *Navajo (?)*
SILVERSMITH:
HALLMARK: Stamped surname and initial in 1/16 Gothic print, first used in 1974.
From Gallup, New Mexico region.

R.VINCENT

WEAHKEE, TOM *Zuni*
SILVERSMITH/LAPIDARIST: Specializes in story telling inlaid

140 WAATSA—WALLACE

WAATSA, BRYANT JR. *Zuni*
SILVERSMITH/LAPIDARIST: Specializes in needlepoint. Began producing in the 1930s.
HALLMARK: Stamped initials in 3/32 Gothic print, first used in 1974. Stamped surname and initial in 1/16 Gothic print, first used in 1976. Also uses stamped initials with Jr. in 1/16 Gothic print and initials with tribal affiliation in same print.
[Bell:1976:58]

B.W.   B.WAATSA   B.W. JR.   B.W. ZUNI

WAATSA, ERMA *Zuni*
SILVERSMITH:
HALLMARK: Stamped initials in 1/16 Gothic print, first used in 1975.

E.E.W.

WAATSA, EVANS *Zuni*
SILVERSMITH/GOLDSMITH:
HALLMARK: Stamped initials in 3/32 Gothic print, first used in 1974.

E.W.   E.B.W.

WAATSA, LORRAINE *Zuni*
SILVERSMITH:
HALLMARK: Stamped initials in Gothic print.

LW

WADSWORTH, EDISON *Hopi*
SILVERSMITH:
HALLMARK: Stamped symbol 1/8" resembling two T's, first used in 1985.

WADSWORTH, RONALD *Hopi*
SILVERSMITH: Specializes in silver overlay.
HALLMARK: Stamped symbol of an ear of corn with husks.

 RW

WADSWORTH, TED (MASUNGYAMA) *Hopi*
SILVERSMITH: Specializes in silver overlay. Began producing in 1954.
HALLMARK: Stamped initials in 1/16 Gothic print or symbol of rabbitstick.
[Wright:1982:87]

 TW

WADSWORTH, TERRY *Hopi*
SILVERSMITH: Specializes in silver overlay. Began producing in 1975.
HALLMARK: Stamped image of a frog.
[Wright:1982:100]

WALELA, EDISON *Zuni*
SILVERSMITH/LAPIDARIST: Specializes in mosaic inlay. Began producing in 1972.
HALLMARK: Stamped initials and tribal affiliation. First initial is reversed. Shared with wife.
Spouse is Shirley Walela.
[Bell:1977:34]

Ǝ.W. ZUNI

WALELA, SHIRLEY *Zuni*
SILVERSMITH/LAPIDARIST: Specializes in mosaic inlay and needlepoint. Began producing in 1972.
HALLMARK: Engraved signature or use of her husband's stamped hallmark which is his initials with a backward E and the tribal affiliation.
Spouse is Edison Walela.
[Bell:1977:34]

Ǝ.W. ZUNI

WALKER, KENT *Navajo*
SILVERSMITH:
HALLMARK: Stamped initials misaligned.

WALL, STEVE *Mescalero Apache*
SILVERSMITH/SCULPTOR:
HALLMARK: Uses homemade stamp of mountain peaks. Uses the name "Tall Mountain".
From Durango, Colorado and Albuquerque, New Mexico areas.

/\/\/\

WALLACE, ANSELM *Zuni*
SILVERSMITH/LAPIDARIST: Specializes in mosaic and channel inlay. Design called Desert Rose. Began producing ca. 1955.
HALLMARK: Stamped initials of his wife's and his own given names in 1/16 Gothic print, first used in 1979. Stamp with his and his wife's initials and his surname in 1/16 Gothic print first used in 1979. Stamp in the same print with his surname, his wife's given name and the initial of his given name.
Spouse is Rosita Wallace.
[Bell:1976:14]

R.A.W.   R.A.WALLACE   A. ROSITA-WALLACE

WALLACE, JUDY *Zuni*
SILVERSMITH/LAPIDARIST: Specializes in tear drop petit point. Learned from her husband and began producing in 1970. Both do stonework and metalwork.
HALLMARK: Engraved surname and husband's given name initial and tribal affiliation. Shared mark.
Spouse is Vernon Wallace.
[Levy:1980:48]

V. WALLACE-ZUNI

WALLACE, REGINA *Zuni*
SILVERSMITH/LAPIDARIST: Specializes in tear drop needlepoint. Learned from her mother. Uses her own designs. Has been producing since 1970. Does all the work although husband may help polish.
HALLMARK: Engraved initials in personalized print.

R.W.

WALLACE, ROSITA *Zuni*
SILVERSMITH/LAPIDARIST: Specializes in mosaic and channel inlay. Uses Desert Rose design. Began producing ca. 1955.
HALLMARK: Stamped hallmarks in 1/16 Gothic print of her name and her husband's initials, or both their initials, or initials and surname. Used first in 1979. Marks are shared with husband. Spouse is Anselm Wallace.
[Bell:1976:14]

R.A.W. R.A. WALLACE A. ROSITA-WALLACE

WALLACE, VERNON *Zuni*
SILVERSMITH/LAPIDARIST: Specializes in tear drop petit point. Learned from his mother and began producing in 1970. Both he and his wife do stonework and metalwork.
HALLMARK: Engraved surname and initial in personalized print. Mark shared with wife. Uses tribal affiliation also.
Spouse is Judy Wallace.
[Levy:1980:48]

V. WALLACE-ZUNI

WALLEY, N ? *Unknown*
SILVERSMITH: Smith for J&D Jewelry Sales.
HALLMARK: Stamped surname and initial in 1/32" personalized print, first used in 1978.

N WALLEY

WANIKA, TOMMY K. *Unknown*
SILVERSMITH:
HALLMARK: Stamped initials in Gothic print.

T.K.W.

WARNER, RAYMOND *Navajo*
SILVERSMITH: Producing in the mid 1960s and still continuing.
HALLMARK: Stamped initials misaligned with a symbol between.
[King:1976:10]

R / W

WASETA, HELEN *Zuni*
SILVERSMITH/LAPIDARIST: Specializes in channel inlay with designed edges. Learned from her husband and began producing in 1956. She and her husband work separately.
HALLMARK: Uses a stamp of her husband's and her given name initials in Gothic print. Shared with husband.
Spouse is Louie Waseta.
[Levy:1980:27]

H L

WASETA, LOUIE *Zuni*
SILVERSMITH/LAPIDARIST: Specializes in channel inlay with designed edges. Learned from Horace Iule. Began producing in 1956. Works separately from his wife.
HALLMARK: Stamped initials of his wife's and his given names in Gothic print. Shared with his wife.
Spouse is Helen Waseta.
[Levy:1980:27]

H L

WATASILO, EDWARD *Zuni*
SILVERSMITH:
HALLMARK: Stamped complete names of his wife and himself, in 1/16 Gothic print in two lines. First used in 1978.
Spouse is Jeanette Watasilo.

ED & JEANETTE WATASILO

WATCHMAN, LARRY *Navajo*
SILVERSMITH:
HALLMARK: Stamped surname and initial in 1/16 Gothic print. First used in 1984.
From the Vanderwagon, New Mexico region.

L. WATCHMAN

WATCHMAN, LOTTIE *Navajo*
SILVERSMITH/LAPIDARIST: Specializes in inlaid birds.
HALLMARK: Stamped initials in Gothic print.

L.W.

WATSON, G ? *Navajo*
SILVERSMITH: Smith for Atkinson Trading Company.
HALLMARK: Stamped surname and initial in 1/16 Gothic print, first used in 1978.

G. WATSON

WATSON, JEFFERSON *Navajo*
SILVERSMITH:
HALLMARK: Stamped surname and initial in 1/16 Gothic print, first used in 1977.
From Gallup, New Mexico region.

J. WATSON

WATSON, MABEL *Zuni*
SILVERSMITH:
HALLMARK: Stamped initials in 1/16 Gothic print, first used in 1974.

MW

WATSON, MAJOR JOE *Navajo*
SILVERSMITH:
HALLMARK: Stamped initials in 1/16 Gothic print, first used in 1974.
From the Gamerco, New Mexico region.

M.J.W.

WATSON, SARAH *Navajo*
SILVERSMITH: Smith for the Atkinson Trading Company.
HALLMARK: Stamped surname and initial in 1/16 Gothic print, first used in 1974.

WATSON

WAUNEKA, WILBUR *Navajo*
SILVERSMITH: Smith for Indian Hammers.
HALLMARK: Stamped initials in 1/16 Gothic print, and stamped surname and initial in same print, both first used in 1976.

WW   W. WAUNEKA

dinner sets. Began producing in the 1960s.
HALLMARK: Stamp of combined misaligned initials that look like a stick man.
[King:1976:10]

WEATHERFORD, DAVID *Unknown*
SILVERSMITH:
HALLMARK: Stamped representation of a bear paw with a name in personalized 1/16 script, first used in 1978.
From Gallup, New Mexico region.

WEBSTER, C? *Navajo (?)*
SILVERSMITH: Smith for Bernie Dominguez.
HALLMARK: Stamped surname and initial in 1/16 Gothic print, first used in 1975.

C.WEBSTER

WEEBOTHEE, BEVERLY *Zuni*
SILVERSMITH:
HALLMARK: Stamped circle with personalized initials within, 1/4" diameter. First used in 1977.

WEEBOTHEE, LEE *Zuni*
SILVERSMITH/LAPIDARIST: Specializes in a wide variety of techniques, nugget work, mosaic inlay, domed stonework, etc. Began producing in 1945. Wife does the stonework and he does the metalwork using their own designs.
HALLMARK: Stamped given name of his wife's and his own in 1/16 Gothic print first used in 1981. His and his wife's given names and tribal affiliation in 1/16 Gothic print, and 1/16 script. Shared initials in 1/16 script.
Spouse is Mary Weebothee.
[Levy:1980:56]

LEE & MARY   LEE/MARY
              ZUNI   *Lee/Mary* ZUNI
ℒ/𝓂𝓌

WEEBOTHEE, LEONARD *Zuni*
SILVERSMITH/LAPIDARIST: Specializes in petit point, nugget work, and shadow box.
HALLMARK: Engraved initials in personalized print, shared with his wife.
Spouse is Lula Weebothee.
[Bell:1977:30]

LW

WEEBOTHEE, LULA *Zuni*
SILVERSMITH/LAPIDARIST: Specializes in petit point, nugget work, and shadow box.
HALLMARK: Engraved initials in personalized print, shared with her husband.
Spouse is Leonard Weebothee.
[Bell:1977:30]

LW

WEEBOTHEE, MARY *Zuni*
SILVERSMITH/LAPIDARIST: Specializes in a wide variety of techniques: nugget work, mosaic inlay, domed stonework, etc. Began producing in 1945. She does the stonework and her husband the metalwork using their own designs.
HALLMARK: Stamped given name of her husband and her own in 1/16 Gothic print, first used in 1981. Hers and her husband's given names and tribal affiliation in 1/16 Gothic print and in 1/16 script. Shared initials also in 1/16 script.
Spouse is Lee Weebothee.
[Levy:1980:56]

LEE & MARY   LEE/MARY
              ZUNI   *Lee/Mary* ZUNI
ℒ/𝓂𝓌

WEEBOTHEE, MIKE *Zuni*
SILVERSMITH:
HALLMARK: Stamped given name and surname initial in 1/16 Gothic print first used in 1975.

MIKE W.

WEEBOTHEE, TAFT *Zuni*
SILVERSMITH:
HALLMARK: Stamped given name and surname initial in 1/16 Gothic print and first used in 1975.

T.R.W.   T.WEEBOTHEE

WEEKA, ELEANOR *Zuni*
SILVERSMITH/LAPIDARIST: Specializes in needlepoint.
HALLMARK: Stamped given name initial, and surname with initial in 1/16 Gothic print. Stamp first used in 1974.
[Bell:1975:64]

E.   E.WEEKA

WEEKA, W.D. *Zuni*
SILVERSMITH/LAPIDARIST: Specializes in needlepoint and petit point.
HALLMARK: Stamped surname and surname with initials in 1/16 Gothic print. First used in 1975.

WEEKA   W.D.WEEKA

WEEKOTY, FRED *Zuni*
SILVERSMITH: Specializes in beads. Began producing before 1970.
HALLMARK: Stamped initials and tribal affiliation in 1/16 Gothic print or in misaligned and joined print.

F.W.
ZUNI

WEEKOTY, JACK *Zuni*
SILVERSMITH/LAPIDARIST: Specializes in channel inlay. Learned from Horace Iule.
HALLMARK: Stamped initials in Gothic print. Often outlined

with other symbols. May spell his name Weekooty.
[Bell:1975:73]

J.W.

WEIGAND, JAMES *Anglo*
SILVERSMITH: Specializes in channel inlay.
HALLMARK: Used by his daughter also. Stamp first used in 1982.

WERO, FREDDIE *Navajo (?)*
SILVERSMITH:
HALLMARK: Stamped surname and initial in 1/16 Gothic print, first used in 1974.

F.WERO

WESLEY, LEE *Navajo*
SILVERSMITH: Chisel work and triple silver overlay. Also works as a saddle or leather worker.
HALLMARK: Stamped full name or initials in 1/16 Gothic print. Stamp first used in 1976.

LEE WESLEY   LW

WESTIKA, NANCY *Zuni*
SILVERSMITH/LAPIDARIST: Specializes in channel inlay in geometric designs.
HALLMARK: A combination of the initials of her husband's and her given names, engraved or stamped in 1/16 Gothic print. Shared mark. Stamp first used in 1981.
Spouse is Sheldon Westika.
[Bell:1977:60]

S.N.W.

WESTIKA, SHELDON *Zuni*
SILVERSMITH/LAPIDARIST: Specializes in channel inlay in geometric designs.
HALLMARK: Engraved or stamped combination of his wife's and his given name initials in 1/16 Gothic print. Shared mark. Stamp first used in 1981.
Spouse is Nancy Westika.
[Bell:1977:60]

S.N.W.

WHIRLING WIND (MORTON, RAY) *Navajo*
SILVERSMITH: Specializes in hollow work.
HALLMARK: Stamped personalized name or the use of an appliqued symbol for wind.

WHITE, ALICE *Navajo*
SILVERSMITH: Smith for the Atkinson Trading Company.
HALLMARK: Stamped surname and initial in 1/16 Gothic print. Stamp first used in 1974.

A.WHITE

WHITE BUFFALO (PEREZ, MIKE) *Comanche/Mexican*
SILVERSMITH: Fashion jewelry in gold, silver, and precious stones. Smith for the Tanners.
HALLMARK: Stamped symbol of an arrow with the initial W in center. Stamp first used in 1979.
From Farmington, New Mexico region.

WHITE CLOUD, WYLIE *Unknown*
SILVERSMITH: Eagle claw necklaces.
HALLMARK: Stamped symbol of a raincloud.

WHITE EAGLE, CARLOS *Mascalero Apache(?)*
SILVERSMITH: Fashion jewelry in gold, silver, precious stones. Imaginary figures.
HALLMARK: Stamped curvilinear initials.

WHITE, ELIZABETH (POLINGAYSI) *Hopi*
POTTER: Specialized in contemporary forms and designs.
HALLMARK: Incised Hopi name in personalized print.

Polingaysi

WHITE, ELLA MAE *Navajo*
SILVERSMITH: Smith for the Atkinson Trading Company.
HALLMARK: Stamped symbol of an arrow with W in the center. Stamped surname with two initials in 1/16 Gothic print, first used in 1974.

E.M.WHITE

WHITE, F ? *Navajo*
SILVERSMITH: Smith for the Atkinson Trading Company.
HALLMARK: Stamped full name in 1/16 Gothic print, first used in 1974. Stamped surname and initial in 1/16 Gothic print.

F.WHITE

WHITE, JOHN *Navajo*
SILVERSMITH: Smith for Atkinson Trading Company.
HALLMARK: Stamped full name in 1/16 gothic print, stamped surname and initial in 1/16 Gothic print, both first used in 1974.

JOHN WHITE   J.WHITE

WHITE, M ? *Navajo*
SILVERSMITH: Smith for the Atkinson Trading Company.
HALLMARK: Stamped surname and initial in 1/16 Gothic print, first used in 1974.

M.WHITE

WHITE MOUNTAIN (see **Ray Tafoya**)

WHITE, PHILLIP *Navajo*
SILVERSMITH: Smith for the Atkinson Trading Company.
HALLMARK: Stamped surname and initial in 1/16 Gothic print,

first used in 1974.

P. WHITE

WHITEGOAT, DENNISON *Navajo*
SILVERSMITH: Smith for the Atkinson Trading Company.
HALLMARK: Stamped surname and initial in 1/16 Gothic print, first used in 1974.

D. WHITEGOAT

WHITEGOAT, JAMES *Navajo*
SILVERSMITH: Smith for the Atkinson Trading Company.
HALLMARK: Stamped surname and initial in 1/16 Gothic print, first used in 1975.

J. WHITEGOAT

WHITEGOAT, W ? *Navajo*
SILVERSMITH: Smith for the Atkinson Trading Company.
HALLMARK: Stamped surname and initial in 1/16 Gothic print, first used in 1981.

W. WHITEGOAT

WHITETHORNE, HANK *Navajo*
SILVERSMITH:
HALLMARK: Engraved signature of full name.

Hankwhitethorne

WHITEWOLF, ? *Unknown*
SILVERSMITH: Smith for the Blackstar Studios.
HALLMARK: Stamped surname in 1/16 Gothic print, first used in 1983.

WHITEWOLF

WHITMAN, ELIZABETH *Navajo*
SILVERSMITH: Smith for the Atkinson Trading Company before 1980.
HALLMARK: Stamped initials in 1/16 Gothic print.

EWW

WHITMAN, TIM KEE *Navajo*
SILVERSMITH: Smith for Atkinson Trading Company before 1980. Also worked for Woodard's Indian Shop.
HALLMARK: Stamped initials in 1/16 Gothic print.

T.K.W.

WILLETO, MARTHA *Navajo*
SILVER AND GOLDSMITH:
HALLMARK: Stamped initials in Gothic print.
Sister is Sally Ramone.
From Canyoncito, New Mexico region.

MW

WILLETO, SARGENT *Navajo*
SILVERSMITH:
HALLMARK: Stamped script W.

W

WILLETTO, JOE *Unknown*
SILVERSMITH: Smith for Bilagaanas Company.
HALLMARK: Stamped full name in 1/32 Gothic print, first used in 1983.

JOE WILLETTO

WILLETTO, TOM *Navajo*
SILVERSMITH:
HALLMARK: Stamped full name in Gothic print.

TOM WILLETTO

WILLIAMS, ARTHUR J. *Navajo*
SILVERSMITH:
HALLMARK: Stamped initials over the symbol of an arrow first used in 1973.
From Mentmore, New Mexico region.

A.J.W.
➤➤➤

WILLIAMS, BILLIE JR. *Navajo*
SILVERSMITH:
HALLMARK: Stamped initials in 1/16 Gothic print, first used in 1973.

B.W.JR

WILLIAMS, GUY K. *Navajo*
SILVERSMITH:
HALLMARK: Stamped initials in 1/16 Gothic print, first used in 1973. Hallmark is registered.
From Church Rock, New Mexico region.

G.K.W.

WILLIAMS, LAURA *Navajo*
SILVERSMITH:
HALLMARK: Stamped initials in 1/16 Gothic print, first used in 1974.
From Winslow, Arizona region.

L.W.

WILLIAMS, REMULDA *Navajo*
SILVERSMITH: Smith for Bowser/Begay Indian Jewelry.
HALLMARK: Stamped initials in 1/16 Gothic print, first used in 1975. Stamped surname and initial in 1/16 Gothic.

R W   R. WILLIAMS

WILLIE, ANNIE *Navajo*
SILVERSMITH: Smith for the Canyon Silver Company.
HALLMARK: Stamped initials in 1/16 Gothic print, first used in 1975.
From Canyoncito, New Mexico or Sanders, Arizona.

A.W.

WILLIE, CHARLES *Navajo*
SILVERSMITH: Smith for Sunburst Handcrafts since 1981.
HALLMARK: Stamped initials in Gothic print.

CW

WILLIE, HARRISON *Navajo*
SILVERSMITH: Smith for the Atkinson Trading Company.
HALLMARK: Stamped surname and initial in 1/32 Gothic print, first used in 1982.

H. WILLIE

WILLIE, LAURA — *Navajo*
SILVERSMITH:
HALLMARK: Stamped initials in Gothic print.
From Canyoncito, New Mexico region.

LAW

WILLIE, LONNIE — *Navajo*
SILVERSMITH:
HALLMARK: Stamped initials in Gothic print.
From Canyoncito, New Mexico region.

LW

WILLIE, ROBERT — *Navajo*
SILVERSMITH:
HALLMARK: Stamped initials in Gothic print.
From Canyoncito, New Mexico region.

RW

WILSON, AUSTIN — *Navajo*
SILVERSMITH: Specialized in cast and openwork. Producing during the 1930s.
HALLMARK: Stamped symbols of bows and arrows. Deceased ca. 1960. Spouse used his mark, far right, after his death. Spouse is Lucy Wilson.

 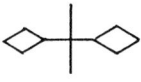 

WILSON, CHEE — *Navajo*
SILVERSMITH:
HALLMARK: Stamped misaligned initials in Gothic print.

C
W

WILSON, EUNISE — *Navaho*
SILVERSMITH:
HALLMARK: Stamped surname with her husband's and her given name initials. Shared mark. First used in 1984.
From Nazlini, Arizona region.

J&E WILSON

WILSON, HENRY — *Navajo*
SILVERSMITH: Began producing in 1964 at age 12.
HALLMARK: Stamped personalized and joined initials.
From Naschitti, New Mexico region.

HW

WILSON, LUCY — *Navajo*
SILVERSMITH:
HALLMARK: Stamped symbols of bows and arrows. After her husband's death ca. 1960 she continued to use his last mark. Spouse was Austin Wilson.

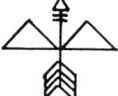

WOLF, CHRISTIN — *Unknown*
SILVERSMITH: Albuquerque shops.
HALLMARK: Stamped initials that are not those of his name. Stamp first used in 1985 is of 1/16 Gothic print. Possibly a shop owner?

J.B.E.

WOLF, JOHN — *Cherokee*
SILVERSMITH/LAPIDARIST: Zuni style fetish birds.
HALLMARK: Personalized print initials joined and misaligned.

WOOD, ALICE K. — *Navajo*
SILVERSMITH:
HALLMARK: Stamped initials in 1/16 Gothic print, first used in 1973.
From Crownpoint, New Mexico region.

A.K.W.

WOOD, ERNEST — *Navajo*
SILVERSMITH:
HALLMARK: Stamped initials in Gothic print.

EW

WOOD, JASPER — *Unknown*
SILVERSMITH:
HALLMARK: Stamped initials in 1/16 Gothic print, first used in 1983.

J.J.W.

WOODS, JOE A. — *Navajo (?)*
SILVERSMITH:
HALLMARK: Stamped full name in 1/16 script. Stamp first used in 1978.
From Gallup, New Mexico region.

Joe G. Woods

WOODY, CLYDE — *Navajo*
SILVERSMITH/LAPIDARIST: Specializes in inlay and stamp work. Despite his hallmark he works alone.
HALLMARK: Stamped double initials in 1/16 Gothic print set usually on a plate. Simple initials with period between was first used in 1980.
From Cortez, Colorado region.

(CW)   (C&W)   CW

WRIGHT, DONALD — *Anglo*
SILVERSMITH: Makes Indian style jewelry.
HALLMARK: Stamped symbol of a rabbit's head with sterling below it.

STERLING

WYACO, BERNIE — *Zuni*
SILVERSMITH:
HALLMARK: Stamped given name initials of her husband and hers. Shared mark.

WYACO, ELANDA *Zuni*
SILVERSMITH/LAPIDARIST: Learned from Roger Tsabetsaye and Fred Bowannie. Creates her own designs and began producing in 1968. Her husband helps with the polishing and she does the remainder.
HALLMARK: Stamped surname and initial in Gothic print.
Spouse is Kerry Wyaco.
[Levy:1980:55]

E.WYACO

WYACO, EVANGELINE L. *Zuni*
SILVERSMITH/LAPIDARIST:
HALLMARK: Stamped full name in 1/16 Gothic print, first used in 1974. Stamped surname with her husband's and her given names in 1/16 Gothic print, first used in 1981. Shared mark.
Spouse is Ray Wyaco.

EVA L.WYACO   RAY & EVA WYACO

WYACO, KERRY *Zuni*
SILVERSMITH/LAPIDARIST: Began producing in 1968. Assists his wife in polishing and doing some of the stone work but also works independently.
HALLMARK: Stamped surname and initial in Gothic print.
Spouse is Elanda Wyaco.
[Levy:1980:55]

K.WYACO

WYACO, RAY *Zuni*
SILVERSMITH/LAPIDARIST:
HALLMARK: Stamped double initials in 1/16 Gothic print. Stamped surname with his wife's and his given names in 1/16 Gothic print, first used in 1981.
Spouse is either Bernie or Evangeline Wyaco.

R & B   RAY & EVA WYACO

WYLIE, ELLA MAE *Navajo*
SILVERSMITH: Smith for the Atkinson Trading Company.
HALLMARK: Stamped surname and initials in 1/16 Gothic print, first used in 1976.

E.M.WYLIE

WYLIE, EULA *Navajo*
SILVERSMITH: Smith for the Atkinson Trading Company.
HALLMARK: Stamped surname and initial in 1/16 Gothic print, first used in 1976.

E.WYLIE

WYLIE, MARY *Navajo*
SILVERSMITH: Smith for the Atkinson Trading Company.
HALLMARK: Stamped surname and initials both with and without periods in 1/16 Gothic print, first used in 1975.

MA WYLIE   M.A.WYLIE

WYLIE, R? *Navajo*
SILVERSMITH: Smith for the Atkinson Trading Company.
HALLMARK: Stamped surname and initial in 1/16 Gothic print, first used in 1976.

R.WYLIE

YAIVA, TRAVIS *Hopi*
SILVERSMITH: Specializes in silver overlay. Began working in 1948. Is not currently producing.
HALLMARK: Symbol of a bear's head.
[Wright:1982:84]

YAMUTEWA, BENNY *Zuni*
SILVERSMITH/LAPIDARIST: Simple channel inlay. Learned from his mother and began producing in 1975. He uses his mother's designs. His wife does the stonework and he does the metalwork.
HALLMARK: Stamped initials of his wife's and his own given names and his surname. Shared mark.
Spouse is Irma Yamutewa.
[Levy:1980:34]

BIY

YAMUTEWA, IRMA *Zuni*
SILVERSMITH/LAPIDARIST: Simple channel inlay. Learned from her mother-in-law and began producing in 1975. Uses her mother-in-law's designs. She does the stonework and her husband does the metalwork.
HALLMARK: Stamped initials of her husband's full name and her own given name. Shaved mark.
Spouse is Benny Yamutewa.
[Levy:1980:34]

BIY

YAMUTEWA, ROGER *Zuni*
SILVERSMITH/LAPIDARIST: Specializes in petit point and snake eyes in flower designs. Learned from his wife's mother and began producing in 1973. He does the stonework and his wife does the metalwork.
HALLMARK: Engraved names of his wife and his own. Shared mark.
Spouse is Victoria Yamutewa.
[Levy:1980:48]

Roger & Victoria Yamutewa
Zuni

YAMUTEWA, VICTORIA *Zuni*
SILVERSMITH/LAPIDARIST: Specializes in petit point and snake eyes in flower designs. Learned from her mother and began producing in 1973. She does the metalwork and her husband the stonework.
HALLMARK: Engraved full names of her husband and her self. Shared mark.
Spouse is Roger Yamutewa.
[Levy:1980:48]

Roger & Victoria Yamutewa
Zuni

YATSATTIE, ANN *Zuni*
SILVERSMITH:
HALLMARK: Stamped surname and initial in 1/16 Gothic print. Stamp first used in 1974.
From Albuquerque, New Mexico region.

A.YATSATTIE

YATSATTIE, POLLY *Zuni*
SILVERSMITH:
HALLMARK: Stamped surname and initial in 1/16 Gothic print, first used in 1973. Stamped full name in 1/16 Gothic print, first used in 1974.

P.YATSATTIE   POLLY-YATSATTIE

YATSAYTE, JOSEPHINE P. *Zuni*
SILVERSMITH:
HALLMARK: Stamped initials and tribal affiliation in 1/16 Gothic print, first used in 1975.

J.P.Y. - ZUNI

YAWAKIA, ADELINE B. *Zuni*
SILVERSMITH/LAPIDARIST: Specializes in mosaic, channel, and raised inlay. Learned from her mother and began producing circa 1950.
HALLMARK: Stamped initials in Gothic print or stamped initials with tribal affiliation.
Mother is Lula Bowannie.
[Bell:1976:10, 11]

A.B.Y.   ZUNI A.B.Y.

YAWAKIA, HENRY *Zuni*
SILVERSMITH:
HALLMARK: Stamped initials in 3/32 script, first used in 1974. Stamped shared initials in 1/16 Gothic print, first used in 1978.

𝓗.𝓑.𝓨.   H & VY

YAWAKIA, LILA *Zuni*
SILVERSMITH:
HALLMARK: Stamped initials in Gothic print.

LY

YAZZIE, A ? *Navajo*
SILVERSMITH: Smith for the T & R Market.
HALLMARK: Stamped surname and initial in 1/16 Gothic print, first used in 1976. (see Antonio Yazzie).

A.YAZZIE

YAZZIE, ALVIN *Navajo*
SILVERSMITH: Smith for the Canyon Silver Company.
HALLMARK: Stamped misaligned and joined initials.
From Sanders, Arizona region.

YAZZIE, ANTONIO *Navajo*
SILVERSMITH:
HALLMARK: Stamped surname and initial in 1/16 Gothic print, first used in 1976. Special misaligned letters 3/16" inside a symbol, first used in 1976.
From Gamerco, New Mexico region.

A.YAZZIE

YAZZIE, BENSON *Navajo*
SILVERSMITH/GOLDSMITH:
HALLMARK: Stamped initials in Gothic print.

B.Y.

YAZZIE, BERTHA *Navajo*
SILVERSMITH:
HALLMARK: Stamped initials in Gothic print.

BLY

YAZZIE, BESSIE *Navajo*
SILVERSMITH: Specializes in shadow box pieces set with turquoise.
HALLMARK: Stamped full name in 1/16 Gothic print, first used in 1974. Stamped initials in 1/16 Gothic print, first used in 1974. Stamped initials with different middle initial in 3/32 Gothic print, first used in 1978.
Spouse is Lee Yazzie.
From Prewitt, New Mexico region.

BESSIE   B.N.Y.   B.A.Y.
YAZZIE

YAZZIE, CHARLENE *Navajo*
SILVERSMITH: Smith for Felix Indian Jewelry and for Atkinson Trading Company before 1980.
HALLMARK: Stamped surname and initial in 1/16 Gothic print, first used in 1977.

C.YAZZIE

YAZZIE, CHARLIE MIKE *Navajo*
SILVERSMITH: Smith for Atkinson Trading Company.
HALLMARK: Stamped initials in 1/16 Gothic print, first used in 1983. Stamped surname with initials in 1/16 Gothic print, first used in 1983.

CMY   C.M.YAZZIE

YAZZIE, DAVID H. *Navajo*
SILVERSMITH:
HALLMARK: Stamped initials in Gothic print.

DHY

YAZZIE, DELORES *Navajo*
SILVERSMITH:
HALLMARK: Stamped initials in Gothic print. (See Don Yazzie's mark)

DRY

YAZZIE, DICK MIKE *Navajo/Hopi*
SILVERSMITH/KACHINA CARVER: Specializes in shadow box pieces and miniature kachinas. Smith for Woodard's Indian Store and Atkinson Trading Company.
HALLMARK: Stamped surname and initials in 1/16 Gothic print, first used in 1974. Stamped initials in 1/16 Gothic print, first used in 1974 also.

D.M.YAZZIE   DMY

YAZZIE, DON *Navajo*
SILVERSMITH:
HALLMARK: Stamped initials in Gothic print. (See Delores Yazzie's mark)

DRY

YAZZIE, DUDLEY *Navajo*
SILVERSMITH:
HALLMARK: Stamped joined and misaligned initials in 1/16 Gothic print, first used in 1976.
From Indian Wells, Arizona region.

YAZZIE, EDDIE *Navajo*
SILVERSMITH: Smith for the Atkinson Trading Company in the 1970's. Smith for shops in Phoenix, Albuquerque, Alaska.
HALLMARK: Stamped surname and initial in 1/16 Gothic print first used in 1975. Initials in 1/16 Gothic print, first used in 1984.

E.YAZZIE   EHY

YAZZIE, ELSIE *Navajo*
SILVERSMITH: Specializes in beads.
HALLMARK: Stamped surname and initial in Gothic print. Stamped initials in normal position or misaligned Gothic print. Sister of Louise Coan and Sarah Duboise.

E.YAZZIE   EY   E
                    Y

YAZZIE, EUGENE JR. *Navajo*
SILVERSMITH:
HALLMARK: Stamped initials in 1/16 Gothic print, first used in 1974.

F.Y.JR.

YAZZIE, EVELYN *Navajo*
SILVERSMITH:
HALLMARK: Stamped full name in 1/16 Gothic print, stamp first used in 1982.
From Mentmore, New Mexico region.

EVELYN YAZZIE

YAZZIE, FRANCIS *Navajo*
SILVERSMITH:
HALLMARK: Stamped script initial of surname and given name.

Y   *F*

YAZZIE, H.D. *Navajo*
SILVERSMITH: Smith for the Atkinson Trading Company.
HALLMARK: Stamped surname and initials in 1/16 Gothic print, first used in 1974.

H.D.YAZZIE

YAZZIE, HARRY *Navajo*
SILVERSMITH:
HALLMARK: Stamped initials in Gothic print.

H.R.Y.

YAZZIE, HELEN *Navajo*
SILVERSMITH:
HALLMARK: Stamped full name and initial in 1/16 Gothic print, first used in 1976. Stamped initials in 1/32 Gothic print, first used in 1977. Stamped surname and initials in 1/16 Gothic print.
Daughter is Mary Yazzie, son is Lee Yazzie, daughter-in-law is Bessie Yazzie.

HELEN C.YAZZIE   HCY   H.C.YAZZIE

YAZZIE, HENRY A. *Navajo*
SILVERSMITH:
HALLMARK: Stamped initials in 1/16 Gothic print, first used in 1978.

H.A.Y.

YAZZIE, IRENE *Navajo*
SILVERSMITH: Smith for Atkinson Trading Company.
HALLMARK: Stamped full name in 1/16 Gothic print, first used in 1974. Stamped surname with initial in 1/16 Gothic print, first used in 1974 also.

IRENE YAZZIE   I.YAZZIE

YAZZIE, J ? *Navajo*
SILVERSMITH: Smith for Bernie Dominguez.
HALLMARK: Stamped surname and initial in 1/16 Gothic print, first used in 1975.

J.YAZZIE

YAZZIE, JASON *Navajo*
SILVERSMITH:
HALLMARK: Handmade stamp of signature in script.

YAZZIE, JIMMY *Navajo*
SILVERSMITH: Specializes in cast work and stamping. Smith for Atkinson Trading Company before 1980.
HALLMARK: Stamped initials (3) in 1/16 Gothic print. Stamped initials (2) in 1/16 Gothic print.

JRY   JY

YAZZIE, JOE *Navajo*
SILVERSMITH: Specializes in wrought work. Began producing in the 1930s.
HALLMARK: Stamped symbol.

YAZZIE, JOE D. *Navajo*
SILVERSMITH: Produced from ca. 1955 to 1975.
HALLMARK: Stamped initials in Gothic print, or stamped representation of a Navajo head inset in a square.
Spouse is Nellie Yazzie. Deceased.

JDY

YAZZIE, LARRY LEE *Navajo*
SILVERSMITH:
HALLMARK: Stamped surname and initials in 1/16 Gothic print, stamp first used in 1976.
From Holbrook, Arizona region.

LL YAZZIE

YAZZIE, LEE *Navajo*
SILVERSMITH/LAPIDARIST: Specializes in inlay of all types. Fashion jewelry in a wide variety of techniques. Smith for Joe Tanner. Collaborated at one time with Preston Monongye.
HALLMARK: Stamped full name in 1/16 Gothic print in either one or two lines.
Spouse is Bessie Yazzie, mother is Helen Yazzie, sister is Mary Marie Yazzie.
[Ariz. Hwys:1979:Apr.:3]

LEE YAZZIE   LEE YAZZIE

YAZZIE, LEO LANDO *Navajo*
SILVERSMITH: Smith for Atkinson Trading Company. Specializes in chip inlay.
HALLMARK: Stamped initials in 1/16 Gothic print, first used before 1980. Stamped initials misaligned or in script

LY   L
      Y

YAZZIE, LEROY F. *Navajo*
SILVERSMITH:
HALLMARK: Stamped initials in 1/16 Gothic print, first used in 1985.

L.F.Y.

YAZZIE, LESLIE *Navajo*
SILVERSMITH:
HALLMARK: Stamped surname in 1/16 Gothic print, first used in 1979.
From Pinyon, Arizona region.

L.YAZZIE

YAZZIE, LUKE BILLY *Navajo*
SILVERSMITH: Specializes in channel work, mother-in-law bells. Producing by the mid 1950s. Smith in Albuquerque shops.
HALLMARK: Stamped initials in Gothic print, sometimes with a symbol.

LBY

YAZZIE, MARIE *Navajo*
SILVERSMITH: Smith for the Atkinson Trading Company before 1976.
HALLMARK: Stamped full name in 1/16 Gothic print, stamped surname and initial in 1/16 Gothic print.

MARIE KEE YAZZIE   M.YAZZIE

YAZZIE, MARY MARIE *Navajo*
SILVERSMITH: Smith for Atkinson Trading Company.
HALLMARK: Stamped full name in 1/16 Gothic print, first used in 1975. Stamped surname and initial in 1/16 Gothic print, first used in 1976.
Mother is Helen Yazzie, brother is Lee Yazzie.

MARY YAZZIE   M.YAZZIE

YAZZIE, MARY CHEE *Navajo*
SILVERSMITH:
HALLMARK: Stamped personalized and misaligned initials often joined.

M^C   MYC

YAZZIE, NELLIE *Navajo*
SILVERSMITH:
HALLMARK: Stamped initials in 1/16 print, first used in 1979. Spouse is Joe D. Yazzie. Related to Herbert Morgan.
From Window Rock, Arizona region.

W.N.Y.

YAZZIE, NELSON *Navajo*
SILVERSMITH: Smith for the Atkinson Trading Company.
HALLMARK: Stamped full name in 1/16 Gothic print, first used in 1976. Stamped surname and initial in 1/16 Gothic print.

NELSON YAZZIE   N.YAZZIE

YAZZIE, PAT *Navajo*
SILVERSMITH: Smith for Woodard's Indian Store.
HALLMARK: Stamped initials in Gothic print.

PY

YAZZIE, RAYMOND C. *Navajo*
SILVERSMITH:
HALLMARK: Stamped signature in 1/16 script first used in 1984.
From Ganado, Arizona region.

Raymond C. Yazzie

YAZZIE, RAYMOND E. *Navajo*
SILVERSMITH: Grand prize winner at Intertribal Ceremonial in Gallup at age 14.
HALLMARK: Stamped surname and initial in Gothic print. Several versions of his initials within the outlines of an arrowpoint. Stamped initials combined into a logo 3/16" first used in 1975.

R.YAZZIE

YAZZIE, RICHARD C. *Navajo*
SILVERSMITH: Producing in mid 1960s. Worked for Bryce Sewell.
HALLMARK: Stamped initials (3) within the outline of an arrowhead with the tip missing.
[King:1976:10]

YAZZIE, RICHARD HENRY *Navajo*
SILVERSMITH: Specializes in traditional pieces, leaves. Began producing in mid 1950s. Smith for John Kennedy, Gallup Indian Trading in 1967-69.
HALLMARK: Stamped initials in 1/16 Gothic print.

RHY

YAZZIE, TIM — *Navajo*
SILVERSMITH:
HALLMARK: Stamped initials in Gothic print occasionally misaligned.

TY

YAZZIE, W? — *Navajo*
SILVERSMITH: Smith for the F&R Market.
HALLMARK: Stamped surname and initial in 1/16 Gothic print, first used in 1976.

W. YAZZIE

YAZZIE, WILBER — *Navajo*
SILVERSMITH:
HALLMARK: Stamped full name in 1/16 Gothic print, first used in 1984. Stamped 3/32 script of initial three letters of given name, first used in 1984 also.
From Ft. Wingate, New Mexico region.

WILBER YAZZIE

YAZZIE, WILLIE A. JR. — *Navajo*
SILVERSMITH: Specializes in overlay work and combinations of silver and copper. Began producing in the late 1950's. Worked for M.L. Woodard.
HALLMARK: Stamped representation of a medicine man's dipper. Father is Willie Yazzie, Sr., who also used dipper as his mark.

YAZZIE, WILSON — *Navajo*
SILVERSMITH:
HALLMARK: Stamped initials in Gothic print accompanied by a five digit number, first used in 1973. Also uses initials alone.

W.Y.   W.Y. 57529

YELLOWHAIR, BILLY — *Navajo*
SILVERSMITH: Specializes in cluster work.
HALLMARK: Stamp of initials of his given name and his wife's. Shared mark.
Spouse is Marie Yellowhair.
From Castle Butte, Arizona region.

B M

YELLOWHAIR, MARIE — *Navajo*
SILVERSMITH: Specializes in cluster work.
HALLMARK: Stamp of initials of her given name and her husband's. Shared mark. Spouse is Billy Yellowhair.
From Castle Butte, Arizona region.

B M

YELLOWHORSE, ANN — *Navajo*
SILVERSMITH:
HALLMARK: Stamped script initials with joined letters.
Son is Orville Tsinnie.
From Shiprock, New Mexico region.

ayh

YELLOWHORSE, DAVID — *Navajo*
SILVERSMITH:
HALLMARK: Stamped full name in 1/32 Gothic print in two lines, first used in 1984. Stamped initials in Gothic print. He also has a stamp that is not of his name in 1/16 Gothic print, first used in 1985.

BY DAVE YELLOWHORSE   LACY RUNNING HORSE

YESSLITH, ? — *Zuni*
SILVERSMITH:
HALLMARK: Stamped surname in 1/16 Gothic print, first used in 1984.
From Phoenix, Arizona region.

YESSLITH

YOUVELLA, RONALD — *Hopi*
SILVERSMITH: Specializes in silver overlay. Began producing in 1974.
HALLMARK: Stamped representation of bear fangs.
[Wright:1982:100]

YOWYTEWA, ARTHUR — *Hopi*
SILVERSMITH: Specializes in silver overlay. Began producing in 1948 and ceased ca. 1970 from impaired eyesight.
HALLMARK: Stamped representation of a Sun face.

YOWYTEWA, HUBERT — *Hopi*
SILVERSMITH: Specializes in silver overlay. Began producing in 1965.
HALLMARK: Uses his father's stamped representation of a Sun's face with his initials stamped along side.
Father is Arthur Yowytewa.
[Wright:1982:91]

YOYOKIE, ELSIE — *Hopi*
SILVERSMITH: Specializes in silver overlay.
HALLMARK: Stamped stylized initials done in the manner of chisel work.
Spouse is Gary Yoyokie.
[Wright:1982:91]

YOYOKIE, GARY — *Hopi*
SILVERSMITH: Specializes in silver overlay. Began producing in 1969.
HALLMARK: Stamped stylized initials done in the manner of chisel work. Stamped representation of a spider. Both marks were used from ca. 1977 on.

[Wright:1982:91]

YUSELEN, GILBERT *Zuni*
SILVERSMITH:
HALLMARK: Stamped surname and initials in 1/16 Gothic print. First used in 1974.

G.T.YUSELEN

YUSELEW, NITA *Zuni*
SILVERSMITH/LAPIDARIST: Specializes in petit point.
HALLMARK: Stamped initials in 1/16 Gothic print, first used in 1974. Engraved initials also.
Father is Old Man Acque.
[Bell:1976:55]

NY

ZUNIE, CHARLENE *Zuni*
SILVERSMITH:
HALLMARK: Stamped surname and two initials in 1/16 Gothic print, first used in 1975.

C-R ZUNIE

ZUNIE, CLYBERT *Zuni*
SILVERSMITH:
HALLMARK: Stamped surname and two initials in 1/16 Gothic print, first used in 1975.

O.C.ZUNIE

ZUNIE, ERNEST *Zuni*
SILVERSMITH:
HALLMARK: Stamped surname and initials in 1/16 Gothic print, first used in 1974.

E.A.ZUNIE

ZUNIE, GENEVA *Zuni*
SILVERSMITH/LAPIDARIST: Specializes in channel and mosaic inlay. Began producing in the 1960s.
HALLMARK: Stamped surname and initials in Gothic print.
Spouse is William Zunie.

W.G.ZUNIE

ZUNIE, HELEN *Zuni*
SILVERSMITH/LAPIDARIST: Specializes in inlay and stamped work using designs of cows, horses, and wagons.
HALLMARK: Stamped surname and initials of spouse and her given names in 1/16 Gothic print, first used in 1974. Spouse is Lincoln Zunie.
[Bell:1977:16]

H-L ZUNIE

ZUNIE, JOE *Zuni*
SILVERSMITH/LAPIDARIST: Specializes in needlepoint. Producing in the 1960s.
HALLMARK: Stamped initials in Gothic print.
[Bell:1975:70]

JZJ

ZUNIE, LINCOLN *Zuni*
SILVERSMITH/LAPIDARIST: Specializes in channel inlay of cows, horses, and wagons, and stamped work.
HALLMARK: Stamped surname and initials of spouse and his given names in 1/16 Gothic, first used in 1974.
Spouse is Helen Zunie, brothers are William and Joe Zunie.
[Bell:1977:16]

H-L ZUNIE

ZUNIE, MICHAEL *Zuni*
SILVERSMITH/LAPIDARIST: Specializes in channel inlay.
HALLMARK: Stamped initials in 3/32 Gothic print of his wife's and his own given names and his surname. Stamp first used in 1977. Spouse is unknown.

M&V ZUNIE

ZUNIE, WILLIAM *Zuni*
SILVERSMITH/LAPIDARIST: Specializes in channel inlay. Began producing in the 1960s.
HALLMARK: Stamped surname and initials in 1/16 Gothic print, first used in 1974.
Spouse is Geneva Zunie.

W.M.ZUNIE

Index I: Initials

INITIALS

A	Ashley, Monroe	AD	Dewa, Andrew
A	Batala, Art	A & D	Banteah, Albert
A	Cowboy, Annie	A & D	Banteah, Dolly
⨝	Aguilar, Tony	A & DB	Banteah, Albert
𝒜	Anderson, Eddie	A & DB	Banteah, Dolly
𝒜	Dubois, Alice	ADB	Banteah, Albert
ʝ	Dubois, Jake	ADB	Banteah, Dolly
Ⓐ™	Johnson, Patterson	ADK	Kiyite, Alvin
»A→	Natseway, Allen	ADK	Kiyite, Donna
(A)	Lincoln (Roanhorse), Ambrose	ADL	Leekela, Anson
𝒜	Skeets, Anderson (Andy)	ADL	Leekela, Deborah
A^A	Acoya, Art	A & DQ	Quam, Alice
AA	Apachito, Archy	A & DQ	Quam, Duane
¥AA	Acoya, Art	A.E.	Etsitty, Ann
*AA	Acoya, Art	A. & E. N.	Nastacio, Alvin
♛AA	Acoya, Art	A. & E. N.	Nastacio, E?
A.A.G.	Gasper, Ashbury A.	AG	Gashwazra, Alonzo
AB	Begay, Anna	AH	Hamilton, Alice
AB	Blackgoat, Alice	a.H.	Hattie, Anita
A B	Bohlen, Aurelia	A⌒H	Herrera, Arnold
A.B.	Begay, Anthony	🐻 a.H.	Hustito, Alonzo
A.B.	Blackgoat, Arlene	AJ	Anderson, Joe P.
ℬ	Batala, Art	A↑J	Joe, Alfred
(A.B.)	Begay, Anthony	AJL SUNI	Lonjose, Andrew
A.B.Y.	Yawakia, Adeline	A.J.W.→	Williams, Art
ZUNI A.B.Y.	Yawakia, Adeline	AK	Kraus, Adolf
AC	McCabe, Albert	A.K.W.	Wood, Alice K.
A.C.	Chavez, Alfred	AL	Lomayestewa, Arthur
AD	Dennis, Alec	AL	Newman, Al

154 INITIALS

ÆL	Jackson, Larry	A.S.	Saufkie, Andrew
ÆL	Joe, Larry	AS	Saufkie, Andrew
7L	Lackey, Al	A.U.	Ukastine, Alma
[AL]	Laahty, A.	A.W.	Willie, Annie
AL./PL	Platero, Albert	ayh	Yellowhorse, Ann
A&M	Boone, Alex	A↑	Yazzie, Alvin
A&M	Boone, M?	(AZ)	Yazzie, Antonio
AMC	McCabe, Allan	B	Begay, Wilson
AMS	Shirley, Alice M.	B	Slim, Billy
A.MTZ	Martinez, Archie	B	Smith, Bertha
amy	Quandelacy, Amy	B/	Chee, Billy
AN	Noriega, Alton	B↓	Dubois, Ben
AP	Paquin, Alvin	B	Smith, Bertha
AP	Pewa, Albert		Tsosie, Boyd
AP	Platero, Antoinette	BA	Apachito, Benny
R	Platero, Agnes	B.A.E.	Etsate, Betty
	Platero, Alice	B.A.Y.	Yazzie, Bessie
A.P ZUNI	Panteah, Alma	BB	Barton, Bernard
		BB	Becenti, Benjamin
AQ	Qumyintewa, Alde	BB	Blackgoat, Ben
A.Q.	Quam, Alice	BB	Bowanna, Bertha
AQG ZUNI	Gasper, Annie Quam	B_B	Bonney, Bernice
A.Q.G. ZUNI	Gasper, Annie Quam	B.B.	Begay, Bobby
AR	Ramone, Annie	B & B	Benally, Betty
AR	Romero, Adelaido	B ZUNI	Bowekaty, Bernard
R	Anderson, Roy	B. BR	Brown, Benjamin
ARB	Billison, ?	BC	Chapo, Ben
A & RG	Gasper, Arlan	B.C.	Castillo, Bessie
		B & C	Shack, Bobby
(ARL)	Lujan, Arthur	B & C	Shack, Corinne
AP R L	Platero, Prewitt	BD	Dawahoya, Bueford
A R P	Pinto, Augustine	BD	Dickson, Bennie
		(BD)	Duran, Bernard
A R P	Pinto, Rosalie	B.D.	Dickson (Dickinson), Bennie
		B D	Duran, Bernard
ARP ZUNI	Pinto, Arlinda Rose	BE	Etsate, Bettie
A.R.P.	Pinto, Augustine	BE	Eustace, Beatrice
A.R.P.	Pinto, Rosalie	B	Begay, Eula Mae

INITIALS 155

⊓B⊓	Edmundson, Buddy Lightfoot	BRK	Kallestewa, Ben
B.E.	Eustace, Ben	BRK	Kallestewa, Reyes
BFA	Aguilar, Benny	BRS	Smiley, Billy Rae
BFA	Aguilar, Frances	BT	Thompson, Ben
BG	Gashwazra, Bradley	(Bw)	Weebothee, Beverly
B.G.	Gahate, Bart	B.W.	Waatsa, Bryant Jr.
⊞	Humiyestewa, Byron	B.W. ZUNI	Waatsa, Bryant Jr.
⊞	Humiyestewa, Byron	B.W. JR.	Waatsa, Bryant Jr.
B.H.	Haley, Benjamin	B.W. JR.	Williams, Billie Jr.
B.H.	Henry, Bernard Jr.	B.Y.	Paul, Betty
B. W. JR.	Hildreth, Bobby	B.Y.	Yazzie, Benson
BIFL	Stoddard, Mary	BYE	Begay, Bobby
BIY	Yamutewa, Billy	C	Cowboy, Jerry
BIY	Yamutewa, Irma	$\mathcal{C}$	Charley, Ric
B.J.B.	Bennett, Betty	C.	Day, Chalmers
BJH	Hoskie, Billy John	C ☼	Begay, Carl
BKS	Scott, Bennie Kee	C ∼	Begay, Carl Allen
[BL]	Lujan, Bobby	C⌒	Begay, Carlos
[L/B]	Lujan, Bobby	C⌒	Begay, Charles
(BL)	Lujan, Bobby	⚘c	Cody Sally
(B/L)	Lujan, Bobby	⊕	Cross, Earl
B/J	Lomadapki, Robert	CA	Ashley, Cecil
BIY	Yazzie, Bertha	C$_A$	Ashley, Cecil
BM	Martinez, Benny	C.A.	Apachito, Clinton
BM	McRae, Billy	⚘	Bins, Coleen Anne
BM	Yellowhair, Billy	CAE	Eustace, Christine
BM	Yellowhair, Marie	CAS	Scott, Courtney Amon
[BM]	Murphy, Ben	CB	Begay, Clyde
(B/M)	Murphy, Ben	Ⓑ	Chavez, Ben
B.M.	Martinez, Betty	⊃B	Brown, Cea
B & N	Nastacio, Billy	⊃B	Brown, Cea
B.N.S.	Taylor, Bernice	C/B	Bradley (Seciwa), Charlotte
BNs	Taylor, Bernice	CBM	Mahooty, Chester B.
B.N.Y.	Yazzie, Bessie N.	CBM	Mahooty, Dorothy
BP	Pinto, Benny	C & C J. JR	Johnson, Cecil Jr.
BP	Platero, Betty	CCL	Lee, Clarence
ℬP	Padilla, Bessie	CD	Dishta, Charlene
BRB	Billie, Betty Rose	CE	Elliot, Chavis
BRH	Hawee, Billy Rae		

156 INITIALS

CE	Eustace, Christine
C.E.J.	Jamon, Cornelia
CH	Hinton, Cornelia
[CH symbol]	Hustito, Charles
[CH RKM symbol]	Hustito, Charles
CJ	Corbet, Joe
[symbol]	Toledo, Curlene
CK	Katsineh, Carrie
[CK symbol]	Kahn, Chester
[K symbol]	Keams, Chee
C/	Celencio, L?
[¢]	Leekity, Corinne
[¢]	Leekity, Curtis
[¢]	Leekity, Corinne
[¢]	Leekity, Curtis
[¢]	Leekity, Corinne
[¢]	Leekity, Curtis
[¢]	Leekity, Corinne
[¢]	Leekity, Curtis
CL	Lewis, Charles
CL	Lovato, Charles
CL	Lovato, Clara
C.L.T.	Tsalate, Linda
CL^W	Wolf, John
CL_W	Wolf, John
CLY	Cly, John
CM	Morgan, Charlie
CM	Cahuilla, Margaret
C	Curtis, Max
[wavy symbol]	Najdowski, Mike
CMB	Bobelu, Carolyn
[symbol]	Lonjose, Mabel C.
CMP ZUNI	Poncho, Charles
CMP ZUNI	Poncho, Mary Anne
CMY	Yazzie, Charlie Mike
C.N.	Navenma, Cedric
[symbol]	Piaso, Cindy
C.P.	Penketewa, Claudine
CPH	Hannaweeke, Charlie
CPH	Hannaweeke, Pauline
C. &. P. P.	Pekytewa, Paul
CR	Romero, Cipriano
ⓡ	Charley, Ric
ⓡ	Cooeyate, Ransom
C.R.	Ration, Christine
C-R ZUNIE	Zunie, Charlene
CS	Sanders, Alice
CS	Sanders, Cecil
[symbol]	Scott, Courtney Amon
CS	Singer, Charlie
[symbol]	Suplee, Charles
CSP	Platero, Carol
[symbol C.T.]	Talayumptewa, Caroline
C.T.E.	Etsitty, Raymond
C W	Willie, Charles
CW	Woody, Clyde
(CW)	Woody, Clyde
C.W.	Chee, Nelvin
(C&W)	Woody, Clyde
(CE)	White Eagle, Carlos
(CWJ)	Trujillo, Charles
D	Delvin, John
D	Denetso, Tom
D	Dixon, Don
D	Lovato, Dan
D	Dixon, Don
←D→	Peshlakai, Dalton
D & A	Quandelacy, Amy
D & A	Quandelacy, Dicky
D.A.	Allison, D?
D & AQ	Quandelacy, Amy
D & AQ	Quandelacy, Dicky
D & A Q	Quandelacy, Amy
D & A Q	Quandelacy, Dicky
DB	Brown, Darrell
D.B.	Brown, Daisy

INITIALS 157

D.B.	Burris, D?	DS	Simplicio, Danny
DC	Chatter, Delbert	DS	Smiley, Dan
DC	Clark, Denet	DS [symbol]	Sehongva, Doran
DC	Clark, John D.	[symbol]	Sehongva, Doran
DCE	Eriacho, Christine	[arrow symbol D/S]	Smith, Dennis
DCE	Eriacho, Daniel	[symbol DuS]	Sundt, Danny S.
DD	Clark, Donny	D.S.	Salisteo, D?
DD	Clark, Dorothy	DT	Tsethlikai, Doris
DD	David, Donald	[symbol]	Tom, Duane
[symbol]	Denetdeal, Donald	DTB	Bini, Dene Tsosie
D/DC	Charlie, Darlene	DTB	Bini, Dene Tsosie
D/DC	Charlie, Dickie	D.T.B.	Bahi, Dini Tsai
DH	Harrison, Douglas	DV	Victor, Darrell
DHY	Yazzie, David H.	DVE	Eriacho, Donald
DJ	James, Dennis	DVE	Eriacho, Viola
DJ	Johnson, Don	E	Cowboy, Ella
DJ [symbol]	John, Dennison	[symbol]	Lincoln, Francis Thomas
DJ	Juan, Don	E.	Weeka, Eleanor
D & V ZUNI	Dewa, Don	EA	Argulo, E?
D & V ZUNI	Dewa, Velma	E.A.	Anderson, Evelyn
DK	Kalisteo, Dennis	EAB	Beyuka, Eddie
[symbol]	Kallestewa, Dennis	EAB	Beyuka, Eddie
DKL	Lister, D.K.	EB	Begay, Edison
DL	Lomayestewa, Dwayne	EB	Benally, Ernest
[symbol]	Maktima, Duane	EB	Betoni, Ethel
D.M.	Begay, D.M.	[symbol E B]	Benally, Emil
DMA -VC	Anderson, Dorothy	E. B.	Begay, Eddie
DMY	Yazzie, Dick Mike	E.B.	Begay, Eloise
DP	Pino, Dave	E.B.	Bennett, Elizabeth
DP	Platero, Don	E. B.	Bill, Emerson
DP/	Platero, Don	[symbol]	Eustace, Louvina
D P/	Platero, Don	E.B.W.	Waatsa, Evans
[symbol]	Phillips, Daniel	EC	Chavez, Evelyn
D.P.	Penketewa, Dorothy	ECH	Hoskie, Esther Coan
DRY	Yazzie, Delores	ECL	Lementino, Evans
DRY	Yazzie, Don	EE	Endito, Etta
DS	Sandoval, Danny	[E STERLING E]	Cowboy, Ella
		E.E.L.	Luneo, Eunice

158 INITIALS

E.E.W.	Waatsa, Irma
EH	Holmes, Emery
ƎH	Hoskie, Erwin
E. H. NAK	Nakatewa, Elsie H.
EHY	Yazzie, Eddie
EJ	Jackson, E.
EJ	James, Eldon
ᙠEJ	James, Eldon
E. J.	Jiron, Evelyn
E J J	Jiron, Evelyn
ℰƊ	David, E.J.
E EJT	Trujillo, Ernest
EK	Kee, Elmer
EK	Koinva, Elliot
∋∈	Kee, Mabel
EL	Lementino, Elmer
EL	Lementino, Mary
EL	Lewis, Effie
EL	Lomahongva, Edward
ⓔℒ	Long, Emerson
E.L.	Leekity, Edward
E.L.	Lewis, Ervin
E.L.	Lincoln, Elaine
E.L. Zuni	Lucio, Ervin
E.L.B.	Bonney, Emma
ELR	Romancito, Emma
ᴿᵃEᵘᵐ	Martinez, Eugene
E. MC	McCrea, Ernest
E.M.C.	Martinez, Ethel
E.M.J.	Joe, Ella Mae
EᴹY	Morris, Earl
E.Q.	Quam, Elsie
E.Q. ZUNI	Quandelacy, Ellen
ER	Romancito, Emma
ᵂR	Yazzie, Raymond
	Siewiyumptewa, Eldon
Eϛ	Sehongva, Elgene
Eϛ	Sehongva, Elgene
Eϛ	Sehongva, Elgene
Eϛ	Sehongva, Elgene
ϛ	Sehongva, Elgene
Ξ	Scott, Eddie
esm	Smith, Ed
E.S.S.	Smith, Edison Sandy
ϵ.S.S.	Smith, Edison Sandy
E. T.	Tsabatsaye, Edith
E.T.	Toledo, Eva
EW	Wood, Ernest
E.W.	Waatsa, Evans
Ǝ.W. ZUNI	Walela, Edison
Ǝ.W. ZUNI	Walela, Shirley
EWW	Whitman, Elizabeth
E Y	Yazzie, Elsie
ᴱY	Yoyokie, Elsie
EYM	Mahooty, Eugene
E Y M	Mahooty, Yvonne
E/Z	Tsabatsaye, Edith
(E/Z)	Tsabatsaye, Edith
F	Platero, Fannie
ʃ	James, Della
ʃ	James, Francis
ʃ	Jones, Francis
⊢	Fendenheim, James
ⅎ	Desoto, Joe
FA	Arviso, Floyd
→fA→	Atencio, Frank
F. A.	Adakai, Fred
F. A.	Asheet, Fred B.
FB ZUNI	Bowannie, Fred
F B	Bowannie, Fred
Fc	Cleveland, Fred
Fc	Cleveland, Fred
Ǝc	Lupee, Ed

INITIALS 159

F.C.	Cachini, Fred		GC	Crawford, Eugene
F.C.	Carillo, Frank		G.C. (with eyelash symbol)	Crawford, Eugene
F. C. LAGUNA	Carillo, Frank		G.C.H.	Hubbard, George
FD	David, Frank		G/D	Damon, Gilbert
(F.D.)	Chama, Felix		GH	Henry, George
F.D.B.	Bowannie, Delia		GIBB (with arrow)	Montano, Gibson
F.D.B.	Bowannie, Fadrian		GK	Kee, George
FE	Eustis, Francis		G.K.W. ®	Williams, Guy K.
F.E.	Etsitty, Fred		ꓧL (symbol)	Lucas, Glenn
F.E.	Eustace, Felicita		GM	Maldonado, Gilbert
FG	Guerno, Frank		GM	Martinez, George
FG	Guerro, Fred		GM	Manning, Gene
F.G.	Guerro, Frank		GN	Natachu, Gillerimo
FJ	Johnson, Florence		GNH	Henry, George
F J (symbol)	Johnson, Fred		GNH	Henry, Nusie
F.K.	Kallestewa, Farrell		GP	Pawiki, Grant
F.L.	Natachu, Frank L.		G⌒⌒P (symbol)	Pawiki, Grant
F.M.B.	Begay, Fancis M.		G.P.	Pino, Gilbert
FN	Naranjo, Feline		GPA	Apachito, Genevieve
FP (symbol)	Patania, Frank		GS	Sandoval, Glenn
FP (symbol)	Patania, Frank Jr.		GS	Sandoval, Irene
(thunderbird FP symbol)	Patania, Frank		GS (script)	Schendel, Gene
◁→FP→◁ (symbol)	Peshlakai, Fred		G.S.	Sandoval, Glenn
F.P.	Patania, Frank		G.S.	Sandoval, Irene
F.P.	Peshlakai, Frank		G.S.B.	Banteah, Gary
F. P.	Platero, Freddie		G.S.B.	Banteah, Serena
→F.P.→ (arrow symbol)	Peshlakai, Fred		ꓧ (symbol)	Tyma, Gilbert Andress
F.W. ZUNI	Weekoty, Fred		G.T.	Todlena, Gordon
ᐯE (symbol)	Weekoty, Fred		G.T.	Touchine, Grace
F. Y. JR.	Yazzie, Eugene Jr.		GTV	Tsabetsaye, Evangeline (Vangie)
ℋ (symbol)	Yazzie, Francis		GTV	Tsabetsaye, Griffin
⇐ (symbol)	Damon, Gilbert		G↓ (symbol)	Tsabetsaye, Evangeline (Vangie)
~G~	Garrett, Donald		G↓ (symbol)	Tsabetsaye, Griffin
G.A.	Apachito, Genevieve		G↓ (symbol)	Tsabetsaye, Evangeline (Vangie)
G.A. (with arrow)	Adakai, Glen		G↓ (symbol)	Tsabetsaye, Griffin
GB	Begay, George		ꓔꓛ (symbol)	Yoyokie, Gary
(symbol)	Bradley, George		ꓔꓛ (symbol)	Yoyokie, Gary
G.BRN	Brown, Gilbert		GꓕN (symbol)	Nez, Gibson
			H	Long, Helen

160 INITIALS

ƕ	Fredenburg, Dennis
H⌒	Hill, Wendall J.
[pig H]	Jenkins, Grant
[H symbol]	King, Henry
[wavy H]	Robinson, Morris
[symbol H]	Tawangyaoma, Ralph
H. & A. ZUNI	Bowekaty, Agnes
H. & A. ZUNI	Bowekaty, Hugh
HAS ZUNI	Siutza, Avis
HAS ZUNI	Siutza, Herbert
H.A.Y.	Yazzie, Henry A.
HB	Begay, Harvey
HB	Baca, Henry
HB	Begay, Harvey
HB	Begay, Harvey
[HB boxed]	Begay, Harvey
[HB ornate]	Begay, Harvey
H.B.Y.	Yawakia, Henry
HC	Chipito, Hilda
HC	Clark, Henry
HC	Craig, Hyson
H & C. D. C. JR	Denetclaw, Clarence Jr.
HCY	Yazzie, Helen C.
H & D	Muehler, David
H.D.B.	Benton, Herman
H.D.C.	Chee, Howard
[HL symbol]	Lovato, Harold
H.E.	Esalio, Howard
HF	Francisco, Helen
HH	Hunter, Harold
H.H.	Harugy, Herbert
HHB	Begay, Harry H.
H.H.L.	Lincoln, Herman H.
H.J.	Jake, Harry
H.J.B.	Billie, Henry
HK	Kee, Harrison
HKM	Morgan, Herman K.
HL	Long, Helen
HL	Lovato, Harold
HL	Waseta, Helen
HL	Waseta, Louie
HL	Long, Helen
HL	Lovato, Harold
H.L.	Lovato, Homer
HMS	Sanchez, Horace
HMS	Sanchez, Morenda
HN	Naseyouma, Stewart Hyson
HN	Nez, Hoskie
HP	Pino, Harog
HP	Platero, Herbert
Hp	Pino, Harvey
HP	Platero, Herbert
HPI	Hesuse, Henry P.
hQ	Cone, Yonah
HQ	Quanimptewa, Harvey Jr.
[symbol HQ]	Quanimptewa, Harvey Jr.
[symbol HQ]	Quanimptewa, Harvey Jr.
H.R.C. ZUNI	Coonsis, Harlan
HRN	Nelson, Ruth
H.R.Y.	Yazzie, Harry
HS	Slinkey, Herman
H.S.	Slim, Helen
H.S.	Smith, Howard
HT	Taylor, Herbert
H.T.	Trujillo, Harold
HTM	Morris, Henry
HV	Vance, Homer
H & VY	Yawakia, Henry
HW	Wilson, Henry
[HY symbol]	Yowytewa, Hubert
(HZ)	Sanchez, Horace
IC	Chiquito, Irene
IE	Eddie, Isabel
IHMS	Indian Hand Made Silver
IHMS/S	Indian Hand Made Sterling Silv
II	Ignacio, Irma
IK	Kee, Inez

INITIALS 161

IK	Kee, Ivan
IL	Lee, Irene
IP	Pino, Ida
IP	Pino, Ira
IP	Platero, Inez
ℐ	Skeets, Irene
I.S.	Skeets, Irene
J	Cadman, Julia
J	Dixon, Jean
J	Jackson, James
J	Long, Jimmy
J	James
J NAVAHO	Craig, Carson
ʲJ	Humiyestewa, Jay
ꓩ	Jackson, James
ꓩ	Jackson, Virginia
ꓩ	Jackson, Willie
(fish symbol)	Shopteese, John
J⋘	Tom, Joe
J.	Frank, Jerry J.
J-3	Tsabetsaye, Joe
JA	Abeita, Juan
JA	Alberta, Juan
Ja	Adakai, Jack
(arrow in circle)	Joe, Alfred
(arrow symbol)	Joe, Alfred
J.A.	Adakai, Jack
J.A.	Adakai, Jack
Jac	Calabaza, Juanita Abeita
JAC	Calabaza, Juanita Abeita
M/B	Eustace, Jolene A.
₣	Foutz, John Allen
JB	Begay, Jimmy
JB	Benally, Josephine
JB	Beyuka, Jonathan
JB	Burnside, John
JB	Baloo, John
JB (chip)	Begay, John G.
–JB–	Begay, Jerome
ℬ	Bitsui, Jim
ℬ	Bitsui, Jim
ℬ	Boyd, James
JB (chip)	Begay, John G.
J.B.	Bly, Jack
J/B	Joe, Tony
JC	Chee, Betty Jean
J.B.C.	Chatter, Jack B.
J.B.E.	Wolf, Christin
JBH	Hawley, John B.
JBM	Martinez, Betty
JBM	Martinez, Joseph
JBR	Reano, Jerry
JBS SGT	Strong, John B.
JC	Calavaza, Joan
JC	Claw, Jessie
JC	Calavaza, Joan
JC	Chee, Joe
Jc	Chavez, John
JC (arrow)	Nez, Chester
J.C.	Calavaza, Effie
J.C.	Calavaza, Juan C.
J.C.	Cly, John
J.C.	Calavaza, Juan
J.C.	Clah, Jessie
JcJ	Juancho, Joanne Christine
ℭ	Claw, Paul Jr.
JD	Dick, Johnny
JD	Tooth, Juan
♭	Dubois, Alice
♫	Dubois, Jake
J & DN	Niiha, Darlene
J & DN	Niiha, Jefferson
JDY	Yazzie, Joe D.
JE	Eustace, Joe
J.E.	Epaloos, Jennie
JF	Frank, Jimmy

162 INITIALS

JF	Ferreia, Jeanne
JF	Francis, James
FJ	Jones, Francis
J.F.	Frank, Johnnie
JFC	Claw, Jessie
JFC	Coan, Frances
JF	Coan, Jim
J F C	Corn, John
J.F.U.	Upshaw, James F.
JG	Garrison, Jerry
JG	George, John
JG	Golsh, Joseph
JGB	Begay, Joe G.
JGB	Billie, Joe G.
JH	Harrison, James
JH	Honwytewa, Jerry
JH	Honwytewa, Jerry
(JH)	Harrison, Jim
(JH)	Harrison, Jim
JH	Herald, Jimmy
JH	Herald, Jimmy
JH	Herald, Jimmy
JH	Honyaktewa, James
JH	Humiyestewa, Jay
JH	Hayden, Julian
JHB	Burnside, John
JH	Herald, Jimmy Jr.
JHJ	Johnson, James
JHQ	Quintana, Joseph H.
J. & I. S. NAVAJO	Sleuth, Jerry
JJ	Josytewa, Jessie
(JJ)	Nez, Jackson
J.J.	Johnson, Jerry
J.J.	Johnson, Joann
J.J.	Billie, John Jim
J.J.W.	Wood, Jasper
JK	Kallestewa, John
JK	King, Johnny
JK	Kirk, John
LK / JK	Kewanyouma, Leroy
J-K ZUNI	Kallestewa, Harvey
J.K.	Kiyoomia, Joe
JK B	Benevidez, Jose
JKB	Begay, Keyonnie
JL	Lary, Jinny
JL	Long, Jimmy
JL	Lonjose, Janta
J	Bedoni, John
⚒	Lewis, Austin
JL	Little, James
J.L.	Lamy, Julalita
J.L.	Lomayestewa, Jessica
JLC	Coochyumptewa, John
JT	Trueba, Jim
JMc	McRory, Jane
JMc	McRory, Jane
JM	Martinez, Juan
JM	Mason, James
JM	Moquino, Jim
JM	Manygoats, Jackie
J-M	Madrid, Joseph
J.M. NAVAJO	Manygoats, Jackie
JMB	Begay, Johnny Mike
MB	Begay, Johnny Mike
JMB	Begay, Johnny Mike
JN	Nelson, John
JN	Nelson, Jerry
JN	Natseway, James
JN	Nez, James
JN	Nutima, Jim
JNE	Emmanuel, James N.
JOE	Joe, Alfred
J P	Pablo, Johnnie
JP	Platero, Jeannette
JP	Platero, Jerry
JP	Platero, Joey

INITIALS 163

JP	Platero, Jonathan		J.S.	Singer, Jackie
JP	Platers, John		[symbol]	Sluein, Jerry
JP	Poleviyouma, Jacob			
♩P	Pino, Jackson		JT	Tortalito, Joe
♩P	Ukestine, Jason		JT	Tsalate, Joanita
♩P STERLING	Popovich, Jane		[symbol]	Tenorio, Joe
J.P.	Platero, John		JT	Thompson, Jessie
[symbol]	Claw, Paul Jr.		JT	Todacheeny, Johnson
[symbol]	Claw, Paul Jr.		JTJ	Johnson, Maryann
[symbol]	Garcia, Juan Pedro		[JTL]	Lujan, Jimmie
JPJR	Poleviyouma, Jacob		JT S	Singer, Juan
J.P.Y. - ZUNI	Yatsayte, Josephine R.		J.W.	Weekoty, Jack
[symbol]	Quintana, Jerry		[JW]	Weekoty, Jack
JR	Reano, Joe		JY	Yazzie, Jimmy
JR	Roan, Jerry Jr.		JZJ	Zunie, Joe
JR	Romancito, Joyce		K	Kabotie, Michael
J.R.	Bush, Curley Jr.		KA	Arviso, Kirk
[symbol]	Johnston, Mrs. H.R.		KA	Abeita, Kathy
[symbol]	King, Jimmie		KAH	Herrera, Katie
[symbol]	King, Reyna		KB	Begay, Kenneth
[symbol]	King, Jimenez		[KB]	Begay, Kenneth
JR	King, Jimmie Jr.		[symbol]	Duran, Bernard
JR	King, Rita		K.& B.E.	Eustace, Beatrice
JR	Roan, Jerry		K.& B.E.	Eustace, Ken
[symbol]	Roanhorse, James		K C	Chiquito, Katherine
UR	Roanhorse, James		K C	Chiquito, Kathleen
JTR	Rosetta, Johnnie		KJ	Joe, Kee
JTR	Rosetta, Marlene		KJ	John, Kenny
JR.	Rosetta, Juan (Johnnie)		[symbol]	John, Kee
JR.	Rosetta, Maria (Marlene)		KJB	Benally, Kee Joe
J.R.B.	Bowannie, John Q.		KJB	Benally, Kee Joe
J.R.B.	Bowannie, Rosalie		KK	Kewanvuyouma, Kenneth
J.R.G.	Goruld, Joanne R.		KP	Pino, Katherine
[JRJ]	Juran, John R.		[symbol]	Kee, Richard
JR M	Rosetta, Johnny		K T	Kee, Tsosie
JR M	Rosetta, Marlene		K T	Tsosie, Kee
[symbol]	Taliman, Elizabeth		K	Turner, Keith
JRY	Yazzie, Jimmy		[symbol]	Turner, Keith
JS	Seckletstewa, Jackson		K.T.S.	Spencer, Kee Tso

164 INITIALS

L	Leota,?
[heart with L]	Bahe, Louise
[sun with L]	Dodge, Lawrence
[cross with L]	Dodge, Lawrence
[sun with L]	Lomayesva, Louis
[sun with L]	Lomayesva, Louis
[arrow L/A]	Arviso, Leo
LA ☆	Graham, Midge
L.A.	Adakai, Len-R
LAG-ZUN	Paquin, Geraldine
LAG-ZUN	Paquin, Leonard
LAP	Pooyama, Lawrence
LAW	Willie, Laura
LB	Burnside, L?
L[animal]B	Begay, Larry
L[animal]B	Begay, Larry
L.B.	Bowannie, Lula
L. B. ZUNI	Bowannie, Lula
LBY	Yazzie, Luke Billy
LBY	Yazzie, Luke Billy
LC	Chavez, Luciano
LC	Chee, Lee
L C	Clark, Louise
L & C ZUNI	Ukestine, Clarissa
L & C ZUNI	Ukestine, Lebeck
LCJ	Johnson, Leonard
LD	Draper, Lowell
LD	Draper, Lowell
LE	Eustace, Linda
LE	Lee, Clarence
LE	Lister, Ernest C.
LEO	Martinez, Leo
[LES hand]	Dennison, Lester
LF	Fernando, Lillian
LF	Francisco, Lillian
LF	Fernando, Lillian
L.F.Y.	Yazzie, Leroy F.
[waves LG]	Golsh, Larry
[waves LG]	Golsh, Larry
H	Holden, Les
LI	Itaike, Lee
L & J	Salvador, Jennie
L & J	Salvador, Lloyd
LJL	Laate, Larry
LK	Koinva, Lauren
LK	Koyayesva, Lawrence
LL	Lalio, Lavonne
LL	Lomayesva, Lewis Irving
L L	
[flower] L.L.	Lomakima, Lorna
[flower] LL	Lomakima, Lorna
LLK	Kaskalla, Leibert
LLK	Kaskalla, Louise
LLS	Salt, Larry L.
LLS	Salt, Larry L.
LM	Malamic, Lolita
L M	Martza, Leonard
L M	Milani, Lolita
L M	Martza, Leonard
LMS	Smiley, Lena Mae
L M S	Smiley, Lena Mae
* LMS	Smiley, Lena Mae
L.M.V.	Vandever, Lucy M.
L/mr	Weebothee, Lee
L/mr	Weebothee, Mary
LN	Nacitacio, Lolita
LN	Natachu, Lolita
LN	Nacitacio, Lolita
LN	Natachu, Lolita
L.N.	Nastacio, Leroy
LP	Pentewa, Lonnie
LP	Platero, Leonard
L P	Polivema, Leonard
LP	Pooyouma, Lawrence (Larry)
[symbol]	Phillips, Loren

INITIALS 165

↯	Phillips, Loren
ᗒ	Prince, Lee
⤫LP⤫	Phillips, Loren
LPT	Tsethlikia, Lena
LPT	Tsethlikia, Patrick
LQ	Qumawunu (Sakeva), Loren
LR/B ☆	Begay, Leroy
2R/S	Tso, Raymond
LS	Sakeva (Qumawunu), Loren
LS	Sandoval, Larry
LS	Schmallie, Leonard
LS	Simplicio, Lena
LS	Stago, Lula Mae
L_S	Sandoval, Leroy
$L	Lovato, Sam
ℒ	Long, Sammie
🏃	Long, Sammie
(L.S. ZUNI)	Shelendewa, Linda
☼	Shelendewa, Linda
L.S.T.	Tsui, Leo S.
LT	Turquoise, Leroy
ᒪT	Thomas, Leroy
L_T	Thompson, Leroy
L_T	Turquoise, Leroy
(hand LT)	Tortalito, Lorenzo
L.T.	Thomas, Leroy
L.T.	Thompson, Leroy
LTD	Draper, Lowell
ℒv	Shepherd, Lincoln
⚓	Luna, Vera
L W	Waatsa, Lorraine
LW	Watchman, Lottie
LW	Weebothee, Leonard
L W	Weebothee, Lula
L W	Wesley, Lee
L W	Willie, Lonnie
L.W.	Williams, Laura
LY	Yawakia, Lila
LY	Yazzie, Leo
L_Y	Yazzie, Leo
ℒy	Yazzie, Leo
M	Thompson, Marie
ℳ	Begay, Morris
ℳ	Lincoln, Mary
ℳ°	Morgan, Bertha
ℳ	Morgan, Mary
∿∿∿	Nadjowski, Mike
(bird m.)	Navasie, Mary Ann
M̃	Simplicio, Mike
⊓⊓	Bitsui, Mardi
MA	Albert, Myra
MA	Apache, Morgan
M.A.	Adakai, Minnie
M.A.	Alcott, Michael
M.A.	Nastacio, Myra
MAC	Chavez, Mary
M.A.J.	Johnson, Mary Ann
MAM	Mexicano, Maryann Platero
(MARY)	Eriacho, Mary
(MARY MARIE)	Lincoln, Mary Marie
MAS	Sheeche, Arden
MAS	Sheeche, Melinda
ΛΑS	Silvers, Mary A.
M.A.T.	Tsadiasi, Mary Ann
MB	Beyuka, Madeline
MB	Burnside, Ann
M B	Burnside, Milton
M/B	Beyuka, Madeline
ℳB	Burnside, Ann
ℳB	Burnside, Milton
⧓	Begay, Marie
MBL	Lomayestewa, McBride
MBM	Mateya, Bruce
MBM	Mateya, Mamie
MC	Carrol, Michael
MC	Chavez, Mary

166 INITIALS

[MC]	Carrol, Michael
M̲	Coochwikvia, Marvin
MCL	Lomaheftewa, Marvin C.
McL	Lovato, Mary C.
[CLBZ]	Calabaza, Mitchell
MY	Yazzie, Mary Chee
MD	Dayea, Mary
MD	Dayea, Mary
M.E.	Etsitty, Marie
MEB	Begay, Manuel
MEJ	Jackson, Mary E.
M.F.	Begay, Marie
M/C	Chavez, Felix
M/C	Chavez, Maryann
M. & G. L.	Largo, Gilbert
M. & G. L.	Largo, Mary
MH	Hildreth, Marguerita
MH	Humeyestewa, Manuel
MHL	Lowsayatee, Mary Helen
MHM	Martinez, Huberta
MHM	Martinez, Mark
m̂l	Weigand, James
MJ STERLING	James, Marcella
MJ	Jenkins, Marshall
MJ	Jackson, Murray
MJC	Chambers, Mary Jane
MJC	Corey, Mary Jane
M.J.C.	Comer, Mary Jones
M.J.W.	Watson, Major Joe
M K	Kabotie, Michael
MK	Kabotie, Michael
ML	Livingston, Mary
ML	Lomayestewa, Marcus
ML	Lomayestewa, Mark
ML	Lasiloo, Milton
ML	Lewis, Manuel
M/L	Lomaheftewa, Marvin
M. L.C.	Callaway, Mary L.
MLK	Kallestewa, Lorrie
MLK	Kallestewa, Marcie
M K L	Kallestewa, Lorrie
M K L	Kallestewa, Marcie
MK L	Kallestewa, Lorrie
MK L	Kallestewa, Marcie
M. L. P.	Poblano, Mary L.
MM	Morgan, Mary
MM	Mull, Margie
M M ✳	Mull, Margie
M.N.	Nastacio, Myra
MP	Pino, Marie
MP	Platero, Marie
MP	Platers, Alice
MR	Rogers, Michael
M & R	Lidase, Matthew
M & R	Lidase, Rosemary
MRC	Casuse, Mary
[glyph]	Nelson, Matthew R.
MS	Secakuku, Myron
MS	Smiley, Martha
MS	Sulu, Marietta
M S	Secakuku, Myron
M S	Secakuku, Myron
M5	Sockyma, Mitchell
M5	Sockyma, Michael
M5	Sockyma, Mitchell
MS ☆	Graham, Midge
MT	Taylor, Milson
MT	Thompson, Melvin
T/M	Morgan, Tom
M/T	Tenorio, Mary
M.T.	Thompson, Marie
M.T.	Toledo, Mary
m v	Velasquez, Mary
MW	Watson, Mabel
MW	Willeto, Martha
MYC	Yazzie, Mary Chee

M?	Yazzie, Mary Chee	NVH	Hooie, Virginia
N⌒	Bain, Nellie	NY	Yuselew, Nita
—N	Curley, Stanley	O.A.	Alexius, Oscar
⌒N	Curley, Stanley	%D	Tsinnie, Darlene
(figure)	Navenma, Cedric	%D	Tsinnie, Orville
NBS	Sice, Bernice	O&I	Seowtewa, Irma
NBS	Sice, Norman	O&I	Seowtewa, Octavius
NC	Custer, Nancy	O.J.	Jaramillo, Odelle
NDG	Garcia, Nelson	OJC & AC	Cellecion, Angela
NE	Eustace, Charlotte	OJC & AC	Cellecion, Oliver
NE	Eustace, Nelson	OJC & AC	Cellecion, Angela
N^F	Fred, Nathan Jr.	OJC & AC	Cellecion, Oliver
⟶NF	Fred, Nathan Jr.	O.M.L.	Leekity, Mary
NFC	Cambridge, Norman F.	O.M.L.	Leekity, Olson
NF/JR	Fred, Nathan Jr.	OP	Pino, Offina
		OV	Nez, Coolidge
NG	Gambino, Nicolas	P	Patterson, Jimmie
N.H.	Haloo, Nancy	P	Sheyka, Ann
NHJR	Honie, Norman Jr.	(P)	Sheyka, Corinne
NJ	Navajohn, Leroy	(P)	Sheyka, Porfilio
NB	Begay, Norma Jean	(P.)	Sheyka, Ann
NL	Lomayestewa, Nan		
N. L.	Lakela, Nick	(P.)	Sheyka, Porfilio
N & LS	Siutza, Louise		
N & LS	Siutza, Stephen		
NM	Motse, Nora Naranjo	⊤P	Tso, Raymond
N/V	Walker, Kent	(figure P)	Monongye, Preston
NR	Ramone, Nellie	(figure P)	Monongye, Preston
JR	Fred, Nathan Jr.	(figure P)	Monongye, Preston
N&R	Nez, Rosemary	←P—≪	Peshlakai, Etta
NRL	Leconelle, Nancy		
N.S.K.	Kallestewa, Sue-Ellen	PA	Anderson, Paul
N̄	Nez, Thomas	P_A	Arviso, Paul
(figure)	Thompson, Norman	P⌒	Arviso, Paul
NTso	Tso, Nellie	⊤Pβ	Boone, Paulinus
NTSO	Tso, Nellie	PC	Curley, Preston
∧N	Noriega, Alton	P.D.	Padilla, Paul
(figure)	Niiha, Verdel	P.D.	Tsosie, Dolly
NVH	Hooie, Norman	P.D.	Tsosie, Paul

168 INITIALS

⊳	Dennis, Philbert
⊳	Dennis, Philbert
⇐—P—⇚	Peshlakai, Etta
PF	Frank, Paul
PH	Honanie, Phillip
(PH)	Hatch, Paul
(A)™	Johnson, Patterson
℞	Johnson, Patterson
PJT	Tsadiasi, Percy J.
PL	Lomawaima, Patrick
P	Prince, Lee
P	Phillips, Loren
P	Phillips, Loren
P	Phillip, Long
P	Phillip, Long
P	Parker, Lennie
P	Parker, Lennie
P|N	Leekity, Nancy
P|N	Leekity, Paul
PM	Monongye, Preston
PP	Polingyouma, Philbert
PP	Poseyesva, Philbert
PP	Tso, Raymond
(P.R.)	Reano, Percy
PS	Sekaquaptewa, Phillip
PT	Taylor, Patrick (Patricio)
PT	Tewawina, Pat
PTG	Guerro, Phillip
PTL	Apodaca, Linda
PY	Yazzie, Pat
QK	Kalistewa, Quanita
ℛ	Garcia, Juan Pedro
ℛ	James, R.W.
ℛ	Lincoln, Randolph
R P	Pincio, Rose
R P	Polequaptewa, Riley
ℛ	Rafel, Tom
ℛ	Leekity, Bernice
ℛ	Leekity, Robert
ℛ	Randolph, Sadie
R	Ross, Tommy
ℛ	Leekya, Robert
ℛ	Manuel, Rick
ℛ	Scott, Raymond
ℛ	Tsosie, Richard
RA	Abeita, Rita
ℛ	Anderson, Roy Jr.
ℛ	Armstrong, Raymond
RAB	Begay, Roseanne
RAB CB	Begay, Clyde
RAB CB	Begay, Roseanne
ℛ	Meyer, Ruth A.
R.A.W.	Wallace, Anselm
R.A.W.	Wallace, Rosita
RB	Becenti, Robert
ℛ	Begay, Roland
ℛ	Tekala, Bernice
ℛ	Tekala, Roosevelt
R & B	Wyaco, Bernie
R & B	Wyaco, Ray
R. B. B.	Benally, Rita B.
RC	Calabaza, Ronnie
RC	Castillo (Draper), Rose
Rc	Cleveland, Ruby
RC	Curley, Robert
Rc	Cleveland, Ruby
Rc	Chavez, Ramos
Rc	Coriz, Raymond
R.C.	Caldito, Ray
R.C.	Candelaria, Rama
R.C.	Casuse, Richard
RCA	Apachito, Robert
(RCJ)	Jackson, Raymond
(RC)	Yazzie, Richard C.
RD	Draper (Castillo), Rose
RD	Dalton, Robert

INITIALS 169

R.E.	Endito, Randy	R[B	Leekity, Robert
R.E.	Etsitty, Richard	RLC	Cellecion, Lela
R & F	Quam, Francine	RLC	Cellecion, Roger
R & F	Quam, Raymond	R.L.K.	Kallestewa, Lilly
R.G.P.	Pino, Rita G.	R.L.K.	Kallestewa, Ralph
R & GT	Terrazas, Geneva	ENLAYED R.L.L.	Long, Rowland
R & GT	Terrazas, Richard		
R. & G. T.	Terrazas, Geneva	R.L.S.	Smiley, Robert Lee
R. & G. T.	Terrazas, Richard	ℛ	Meyer, Ruth
RG	Gasper, Raymond	R∿∿∿	Redwater, ?
RG	Gasper, Raymond	Rm	Rosetta, Mary
RG	Gasper, Raymond	Rm	Rosetta, Ray
RGB	Booqua, Glendora	RN	Namingha, Raymie
RGB	Booqua, Rickell	R.N.D.	Delgarito, Roy Nez
RH	Hurley, Ronnie	RNL	Laconsello, Nancy
R.H.	Haley, Robert	RNL	Laconsello, Ruddell
RHG	Hughte, Georgeann	RNR	Nieto, Rosemary
RHG	Hughte, Rodney	RNR	Nieto, Ray
R.H.G.	Hughte, Georgeann	rNr	Nieto, Rosemary
R.H.G.	Hughte, Rodney	rNr	Nieto, Ray
RHVB	Bicenti, Raymond	ROC ZUNI	Calabaza, Olivia
RHY	Yazzie, Richard Henry	ROC ZUNI	Calabaza, Ronnie
R.J.	James, Rita	RP	Pincio, Rose
RJA	Apachito, Raymond	RP	Platero, Robert
RJ Jr.	Jones. Ray Jr.	RP	Polequaptewa, Riley
RJJR	James, Ray Jr.	RP	Pinto, Rosalie
RJJR.	James, Ray Jr.	RPJ	Jack, Rosa
RJL	Lementino, Julie	R.P.J.	Jack, Rosa
RJL	Lementino, Roland	RPS	Secatero, Rayna Platero
RK	Kee, Richard	RR	Rockbridge, Russ
RK Zuni	Kanteena, Raybert	⊼	Ranson, Roger
RK Zuni	Kanteena, Rhoda	ℛℛ	Romijo, Rosetta
RK	Kyasyousie, Raymond	R & R	King, Reyna
⚔	Kee, Richard	RRL	Leyba, Rinnie
RL	Lincoln, Rose	RS	Sakeva, Raymond
RL	Lukee, Rebecca	RS	Sequaptewa, Raymond
RLB	Begay, Leonard	RS	Skeet, Roger
RLB	Begay, Robert	(RS)	Yazzie, Raymond
R[B	Leekity, Bernice	(RS)	Yazzie, Raymond

170 INITIALS

[symbol with R, S]	Yazzie, Raymond
RS (monogram)	Sahmie, Randolph
R.S.	Sorrell, Robert
RT	Tafoya, Ray
R_T	Tawahongva, Roy
RT (script)	Tso, Raymond
RTG	Gisnie, Roger
R.T.T.	Tsosie, Robertson T.
RV	Vandever, Roy
RV (underlined)	Vandever, Roy
RVF	Francisco, Roger
RW	Wadsworth, Ronald
RW	William, Remulda
R W	Willie, Robert
R.W. (script)	Wallace, Regina
R/W (symbol)	Warner, Raymond
S	Smith, Marie
[symbol]	Skeets, Irene
[sun symbol]	Hanson, Freda
[symbol]	Naha, Sylvia
[symbol]	Secakuku, Sydney Jr.
[symbol]	Secakuku, Sidney Sr.
[symbol]	Secakuku, Sidney Sr.
[symbol]	Lovato, Sam
[symbol]	Smith, Dennis
[symbol]	Smith, Lorenzo
[symbol]	Smith, Lorenzo
[symbol]	Strain, Clyde B.
[arrow symbol]	Swinehart, Marvin
SA	Apache, Steven
[symbol with star]	Charley, Stanley
[star symbol]	Charley, Stanley
SB	Bahe, S.M.
SB	Begay, Sam
S_B	Sperica, Betty
S B	Sperica, Sam
SB (script)	Bahe, Sam
(SBL)	Bowekaty, Lucille
(SBL)	Bowekaty, Samson
S B L	Bowekaty, Lucille
S B L	Bowekaty, Samson
[symbol]	Casuse, S ?
S.C. ZUNI	Calavaza, Susie
[arrow symbol S.C.]	Calavaza, Susie
SD	Singer, William
S/D	Singer, William
S/D	Duboise, Sarah
S/D (script)	Dixon, S ?
S/D	Dixon, S ?
[S/D in oval]	Duboise, Sarah
[S/D in eye]	Duboise, Sarah
S (script)	Scott, Dave
S.D.	Duboise, Sarah
S.D.	Lovato, Mary
S.D.	Lovato, Sedalio
S.E.	Eustace, Sensa
[symbol]	Scott, Eddie
Sec	Collatetta, Sarah
S.F.L.	Lovato, Sedalio F.
SH	Hooie, Sidney
SH	Hustito, Sharon
SH (script)	Hooie, Sidney
[symbol SIE]	Talashie, Rosalie
[symbol SIE]	Talashie, Rosalie
S. & I. P.	Paquin, Isabelle
S. & I. P.	Paquin, Sherman
SK	Kenton, Sandra
SK	Kee, Samson
SKJ	Kallestewa, Janita
SKJ	Kallestewa, Sibert
SL	Lomayestewa, Stetson
[symbol]	Long, Sammie
[symbol]	Lovato, Sam
S.L.	Leonard, Sandra
S & L	Bowekaty, Lucille
S & L	Bowekaty, Samson

INITIALS 171

SMC	Chavez, Eileen	TA	Anderson, Tom
SMC	Chavez, Sabin B.	†A	Atsitty, Thomas
S.M.C. ZUNI	Chavez, Eileen	T-A. H	Hannaweeke, Alice
S.M.C. ZUNI	Chavez, Sabin B.	T-A. H	Hannaweeke, Thomas
S_N	Nutumya, Sharold	T.A & P A	Allapowa, Patsy
S.N.W.	Westika, Nancy	T A & P A	Allapowa, Thomas Jr.
S.N.W.	Westika, Sheldon	TAS	Secatero, Tommie
SOL	Ondelacy, Sol	TB	Billy, Tommy
SP	Pablo, Sam	T.B.	Bedall, Tim
⊥	Pooyouma, Steven	𝒯.ℬ.	Burnside, Tom
S.P.	Peynetsa, Sarah	𝒯.ℬ.	Beedah, Tim
S.P.	Piaso, Sam	TC	Charlie, Tommie
SPE	Pike, Snyder	T C	Curtis, Toni
sP₃	Polacca, Starlie	T.C.	Curtis, Tom
SR	Roanhorse, Sam	T꜀	Singer, Tommy
S.R.	Ramone, Sally	[mono]	Bradley, Charlotte
SS	Sandoval, Sherry	T.D.	David, Tom
SS	Small, Serena	(TE)	Edaakie, Theodore
SS	Smiley, Stella	T.E.	Etsitty, Tom
S S	Sandoval, Sherry	TEK	Tekala, Lawrence A.
S S	Small, Serena	[TG mono]	Goodluck, Teddy
S. S	Smiley, Stella	T.G.	Garcia, Tony
S/S	Sandoval, Sherry	ㄒ	Howarter, Terri
[mono]	Sockyma, Steven B.	T.H.	Hannaweeke, Thomas
[mono]	Sockyma, Steven B.	TJ	Jackson, T ?
←SS—≪	Sandoval, Sherry	TJ	Jim, Thomas
ST	Tewawina, Stewart	T.J.	Joe, Tom K.
Ṣᴛ	Secatero, Tommie	TJB	Billie, Tom
S.T.	Turner, Slim	TJC	Carusetta, Thomas
S_T꜀	Singer, Tommy	TK	Kyasyousie, Tony
S𝕋M	Salvio, ?	T_K	Kyasyousie, Tony
T	Thomas, Richard T.	T̶K̶	Kyasyousie, Tony
T	Singer, Tommy	[mono]	Begay, T ?
兀꜀	Singer, Tommy	T.K.W.	Wanika, Tommy K.
兀	Tafoya, Art	T.K.W.	Whitman, Tim K.
⋀_T	Tahe, Verna	(TL)	Linkin, Tully
⟨P⟩	Tsosie, Harrison	T.L.	Lee, Tom
		T.L.	Long, Tom

172 INITIALS

T̄	Tsababutie, Lloyd
T|d	Lucas, Trinidad
T✻LE	Bahe, Fidel
T̯ᴍ̣	Morgan, Tom
TM	Morris, Tom
(winged V)	Vaughn, Ted
TN	Nez, Tom
Ṇ	Nez, Tom
ᵀᵒ∧	Singer, Tommy
ᵀOᴿ	Reano, Terry
T. P.	Platero, Thompson
⛺ T.P.	Platero, Thompson
T_Q	Quintana, Terecita
TR	Rafel, Tom
TRC	Chavez, Trinnie
s. d. pueblo	
↟	Taliman, Elizabeth
𝒯R𝒮	Siow, Thomas
T.R.W.	Weebothee, Taft
𝒯S.	Tso, Raymond
T-S	Strong, John
Tᶜ S	Singer, Thomas
Tₛₒ	Tso, Raymond
╫	Wadsworth, Eddison
T.T.	Tso, Thomas
T.U.	Uhastine, Tom
⊻	Thomas, Virgil
TW	Wadsworth, Ted
WT	Wilson, Tsosie
⊥̯	Weahkee, Ted
TY	Yazzie, Tim
Ȳ	Yazzie, Tim
U	Ullstrom, ?
Uᵐʸ	Coriz, Leo
VA	Apachito, Velma
VA	Arragos, Virgil
VA	Aragon, Videl
VA (hand)	Aragon, Videl
VB	Burnham, Virginia
VB	Lesansee, Blake
VB	Lesansee, Velma
VBL	Lesansee, Blake
VBL	Lesansee, Velma
VBL	Lesansee, Blake
VBL	Lesansee, Velma
VCZUNI	Calavaza, Viola
VE	Edwards, Vergie
ᶻNᴱ	Niiha, Verdel
V.E.P.	Platero, Veronica
VF	Fragua, Vera
V. J.	James, Virginia
VJSR	Joshveama, Valjean
V.L.	Luna, Vera
VM	Mansfield, Vernon
VM	Martin, Vicki
VMB	Banteah, Matilda
VMB	Banteah, Valentino
VMB	Begay, Victor Moses
VP	Piaso, Virginia
VS	Stevens, Verna
(hand VT)	Trujillo, Velma
(hand VT)	Tortalita, Vickie
V. T. ZUNI	Tsethlkai, Vivian
V W	Vandever, William
VW	Vandever, William
	Vandever, William
𝓤	Willeto, Sargent
𝓦	Boone, Lena
⋀	Noriega, Alton
(winged W)	Brady, Wilber
⬅W⬅	Perez, Mike
⋀	Tafoya, Richard
➤-W-➤	White, Ella Mae
WA	Anderson, William
Wₐ	Arviso, Wilbur Paul
WA	Anderson, Wilbur
≣Wₐ≣	Aguilar, Wayne

INITIALS 173

[symbol]	Aguilar, Wayne	XX	Morris, Willie
[symbol]	Chee, Anita	Y	Johnson, Yazzie
[symbol]	Chee, Wilford	[symbol]	Yazzie, Francis
[symbol]	Begay, Carolyn	[symbol]	Yazzie, Francis
[symbol]	Begay, Wilson	YB	Bebo, Yvonne
[symbol]	Begay, Wilson	YC Zuni	Charlie, Felix
[symbol]	Begay, Wilson	YC Zuni	Charlie, Yvonne
[symbol]	Begay, Wilson	[symbol]	Yazzie, Dudley
W C	Cassadore, Whitman Jr.	Y.K.E.	Etsitty, Yazzie
WC	Cating, Wesley	Y & R	Charley, Rose
WC	Chee, Wilford	ZB	Begay, Zearl
WC	Craig, Wesley	ZB^L	Bowekaty (Sampson), Lucy
WDH	Harmsen, William	ZME	Edaakie, Mary Ann
WG	Gilbert, Wilma	ZME	Edaakie, Zeno
W.G.J.	Johnson, William G.		
WH	Honanie, Watson		
Wil	Yazzie, Wilber		
W.J.	Jim, Wilson		
ωH J	Henry, Wilford Jr.		
yIM	Jim, Wilson		
WK	Krepps, Don		
WK	Kavena, Wilmer		
XX	Morris, Willie		**NUMBERS**
WN	Nezzie, Willie	1	Benally, Rita B.
W.N.Y.	Yazzie, Nellie	2	Benally, Ernest
W.P.	Padilla, Wilson	3	Mike, Dora
WRS	Selina, Weaver	4	Mike, Gloria
WS	Shaw, Willie	5	Boyd, Delphine
W.S.	Secatero, Wilbert	6	Boyd, Julia
[symbol]	Weahkee, Tom	7	Bowie, Geraldine
TW	Tsosie, Wilson	8	Henry, Arlene
WW	Wauneka, Wilbur	81 [symbol]	Lucero, Beverly
W W	Vandever, William	SP$_3$	Polacca, Starlie
W.Y.	Yazzie, Wilson	W/3	Carviso, Emma
W/3	Carviso, Emma	KIRK 1	Kirk, Andrew
W/3	Carviso, Emma	KIRK 2	Kirk, Michael
X	Tsosie, Elkie	W. Y. 57529	Yazzie, Wilson
XX	Benally, David		

Index II: Nicknames and Given Names

Angie	Sanchez, Angelita B.	EFFIE C.	Calavasa, Effie
ANGIE C.	Cheama, Angelita	ELIZABETH A.	Anderson, Elizabeth
Anna	King, Anne	*Emerson*	Billy, Emerson or Bill, Emerson
ANNIE	Apodaca, Linda	*Emerson B*	Billy, Emerson or Bill, Emerson
ARROWTAKER	Nighthorse, Ben	EVA	Toledo, Eva
BENNY M.	Martin, Benny	FAITH	Robinson, Helen
BEN S.	Sandoval, Ben	FRED G.	Guerrero, Fred
BETTY	Etsate, Betty	EL GASPER	Gasper, Elkus
BILL & LOU	Laweeka, Bill and Lucinda	GIBB →	Montano, Gibson
BITNI DZEEZ BA'A'	Hansen (Woodman), Freda	HAUNGOAH	Cody, Al
Bitni dzeez báá	Hansen (Woodman), Freda	IDA M.	Morgan, Ida
BUTCH-H	Hattie, Butch	INDIAN	Parker, E?
CARSON B	Blackgoat, Carson	JAKE L.	Livingston, Jacob
CATHY G.	Garcia, Cathy	JEFF N.	Niiha, Jefferson
CHARLIE	Joe, Charlie	JOE	Joe, Alfred
Charlotte	Bradley (Seciwa), Charlotte	JUAN C.	Calavasa, Juan
CHEROKEE	Munson, Thom	*Kay*	Rodgers, Kay
CHIZOMANA	Chizomana, Ishii	*Kirk*	Eriacho, Kirk
CHRISTIE	Christie, Tom	KIRK 1	Kirk, Andrew
CRAZYHORSE	Quintana, Cipriano	KIRK 2	Kirk, Michael
DALANGYAWMA	Albert, Ramon Jr.	*Kirk & Mary*	Eriacho, Kirk and Mary
DANNY U.	Ukestine, Danny	KK DINE	Kahn, Franklin
DARLENE N.	Niiha, Darlene	KUPOLO	Schlosser, Mary Lou
DAVID	Sakewa, David	LAG-ZUN	Paquin, Leonard and Geraldine
DAVID	Tsikewa, David	LANI	Hothan, Lani
DENNIS E.	Edaakie, Dennis	LEE/MARY	Weebothee, Lee and Mary
L Smcyn	Smallcanyon, Doris	LEE & MARY	Weebothee, Lee and Mary
DUFFY	Felix, Duffy	LEWELLEN	Llewelen, James
		Lena & Rigney	Boone, Rigney and Lena

176 NICKNAMES

Nickname	Name
Hommeyusia	Kabotie, Michael
MANNY	Palmer, Keith
MARTIN	Martin, Andrew
(MARY)	Eriacho, Mary
Mary	Eriacho, Mary
(MARY MARIE)	Lincoln, Mary Marie
Marvelyne C. (ZUNI)	Cheama, Marvelyne
MIKE	Simplicio, Mike
MIKE W.	Weebothee, Mike
MYRTLE	Myrtle, Ellen
Octavius + Irms L	Seowtewa, Octavius and Irene
PALOMA	Paloma, Janice
Paul J	Johnson, Paul
PHIL T.	Tso, Phillip
Poco	Clawson, Wayne
Polingaysi	White, Elizabeth
PONTIXC	Arviso, Pontiac
PRESLEY H.	Haley, Presley
QUANNIES	Horace, Emerson
Qoyawayma	Colton, Al
RAMONA	Poleyma, Ramona
ROANHORSE	Roanhorse, Henry
ROLAND E.	Eustace, Roland
Ruddell & Nancy	Laconsello, Nancy and Ruddell
SAMMY (N) ESTHER	Guardian, Sam and Esther
SAM P	Piaso, Sam
SAM P	Platero, Sam
Silas O.	Ohmsatte, Silas
SMITHY	Smith, Leonard
Smokey	Gchachu, Ruby
Smokey	Gchachu, Smokey
SOL	Ondelacy, Sol
Sylvia	Radcliff, Sylvia Begay
TAHE	Tahe, Verna
Thomas	Carusetta, Thomas
THOMAS M	Thomas, M?
WAYNE C.	Calavasa, Wayne
WAYNE C.	Cheama, Wayne
WES SR	Saufkie, William Sr.
Whirling Wind	Morton, Ray

Index III: Symbols

HUMANS

Celencio, L ?

Claw, Jessie

Haungoah, (Al Cody)

James, R.W.

Luthy, Carl W. (Shop)

Luthy, Carl W. (Shop)

Luthy, Max (Shop)

Polacca, Starlie

Roan, Jerry

Roan, Jerry

Sosolda, Alvin

HUMAN HEADS

Begay, Howard

Begay, Howard

Henry, J.R.

Keeto, Larry

Numkina, Earl

Sluein, Jerry

Yazzie, Joe D.

178 SYMBOLS

HUMAN PARTS

Symbol	Artist
	Aragon, Videl
	Bahe, Louise
	Begay, Carl Allen
	Boyd, Virgil
	Coin, Willie
	Coin, Willie
	Tooth, Duane
	Tooth, Duane

ANIMALS

Symbol	Artist
	Chavez, Ramos
	Cheeda, Zella
	Honie, Agnes
	Howarter, Terri
	Hustito, Alonzo
	Hustito, Alonzo
	Lomayestewa, Arthur
	Mansfield, Verden
	Rocking Horse Ranch
	Rogers, Michael
	Rogers, Michael
	Saufkie, Lawrence
	Saufkie, Lawrence
	Saufkie, Lawrence
	Saufkie, Lawrence

ANIMAL HEADS

Symbol	Artist
	Ami, Mary
	Blackgoat, Alice
	Gaussoin, Connie Tsosie
	Humiyestewa, Manuel
	James, Eldon
	James, Eldon
	Jenkins, Grant
	Knowles, Mel (Shop)
	Lomayestewa, Dwayne

SYMBOLS

Lonewolf, Joseph

Nuvayaoma, Arlo

Sumatzkuku, Dewan

Wright, Don

Yaiva, Travis

ANIMAL TRACKS

Chapella, Grace

Coochwikvia, Marcus

Coochwikvia, Ricky

Day, Chalmers

Dennison, Lester

Earl, Vivian

Eriacho, Donald

Honanie, Watson

Hornbeck, John

Humeyestiwa, Winfield

Jackson, James
Jackson, Virginia
Jackson, Willie

Polingyouma, Philbert

Polivema, Larry

Polivema, Larry

Qumyintewa, Alde

Ratzlaff, Karen

Ross, Josyesva

Saufkie, Andrew

Secakuku, Sidney, Jr.

Secakuku, Sidney, Jr.

Setalla, Pauline

Setalla, Pauline

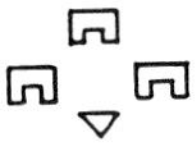

Spencer, "Chaka"

Spencer, "Chaka"

Talayumptewa, Caroline

Talayumptewa, Caroline

180 SYMBOLS

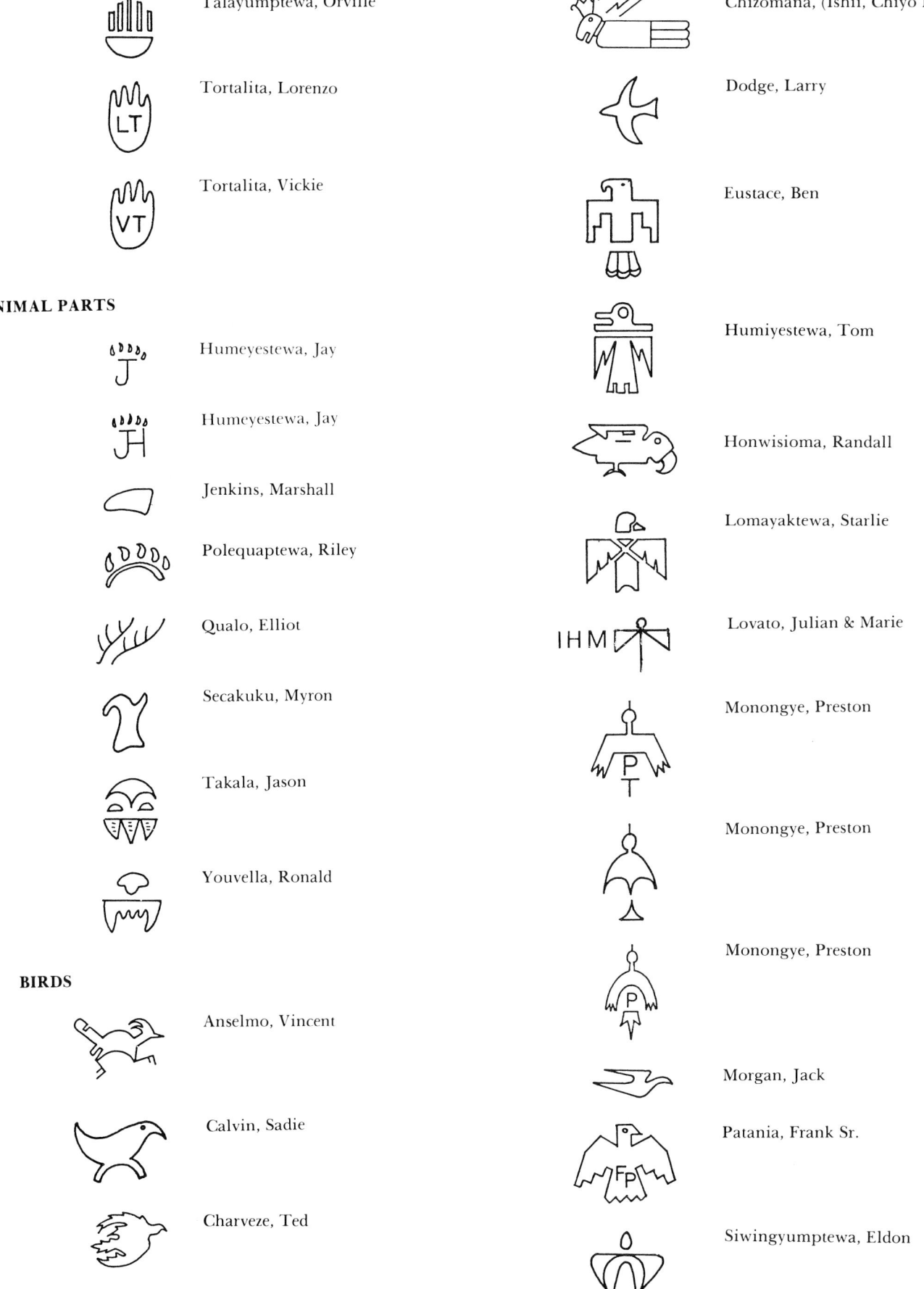

	Talayumptewa, Orville
	Tortalita, Lorenzo
	Tortalita, Vickie

ANIMAL PARTS

	Humeyestewa, Jay
	Humeyestewa, Jay
	Jenkins, Marshall
	Polequaptewa, Riley
	Qualo, Elliot
	Secakuku, Myron
	Takala, Jason
	Youvella, Ronald

BIRDS

	Anselmo, Vincent
	Calvin, Sadie
	Charveze, Ted
	Chizomana, (Ishii, Chiyo F.)
	Dodge, Larry
	Eustace, Ben
	Humiyestewa, Tom
	Honwisioma, Randall
	Lomayaktewa, Starlie
	Lovato, Julian & Marie
	Monongye, Preston
	Monongye, Preston
	Monongye, Preston
	Morgan, Jack
	Patania, Frank Sr.
	Siwingyumptewa, Eldon

SYMBOLS

BIRD HEADS

	Baker, Les (Shop)
	Beyuka, Edward
	Chee, Mark
	Chee, Mark
	Humiyestewa, Tom
	Lomahongva, Edward (Phillips)
	Maktima, Duane

BIRD TRACKS

	Cone, Yonah
	Duboise, Ben
	Leekya
	Lomayestewa, Clarence
	Nutima, Jim
	Quanimptewa, Harvey
	Quanimptewa, Harvey
	Sekaquaptewa, Phillip
	Tsikewa, David
	Tucson, Lee & Myra

BIRD PARTS

	Acoya, Art
	Allen, Carl
	Arviso, Wilbur Paul
	Begay, Eddie
	Begay, Eddie
	Benally, Emil
	Benally, Emil
	Brady, Wilmer
	Concho, Pablita
	Craig, Hyson
	Day, Chalmers
	Edaakie, Dennis & Nancy
	Lightfeather, Melody
	Mansfield, Vernon
	Martinez, Eugene
	Naha, Helen
	Naha, Sylvia

182 SYMBOLS

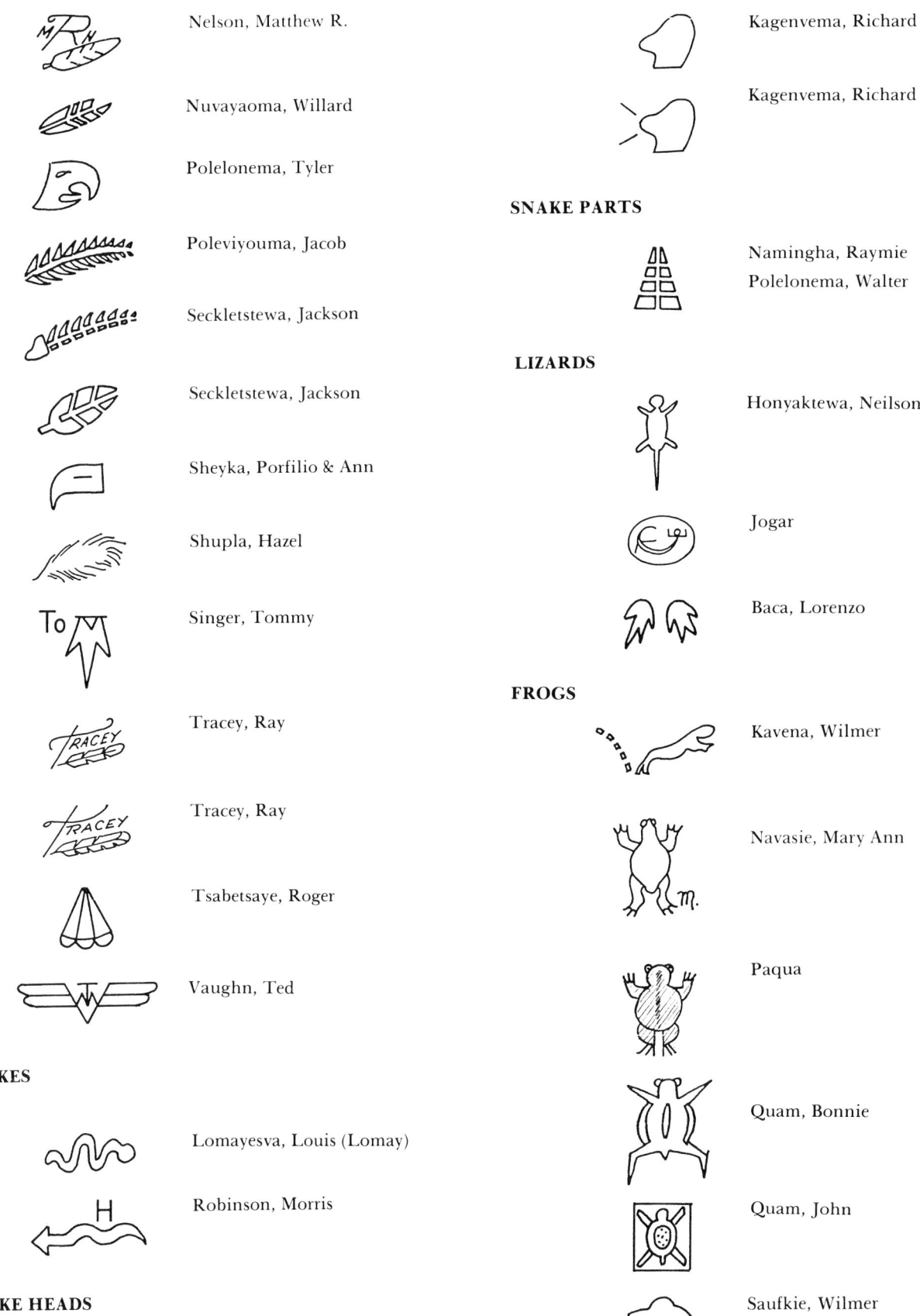

Symbol	Artist
	Nelson, Matthew R.
	Nuvayaoma, Willard
	Polelonema, Tyler
	Poleviyouma, Jacob
	Seckletstewa, Jackson
	Seckletstewa, Jackson
	Sheyka, Porfilio & Ann
	Shupla, Hazel
	Singer, Tommy
	Tracey, Ray
	Tracey, Ray
	Tsabetsaye, Roger
	Vaughn, Ted

SNAKES

| | Lomayesva, Louis (Lomay) |
| | Robinson, Morris |

SNAKE HEADS

	Clark, Carl & Irene
	Kagenvema, Richard
	Kagenvema, Richard

SNAKE PARTS

| | Namingha, Raymie |
| | Polelonema, Walter |

LIZARDS

	Honyaktewa, Neilson
	Jogar
	Baca, Lorenzo

FROGS

	Kavena, Wilmer
	Navasie, Mary Ann
	Paqua
	Quam, Bonnie
	Quam, John
	Saufkie, Wilmer
	Wadsworth, Terry

SYMBOLS

TADPOLES

Carl, Sybil

Honie, Norman Jr.

Sakeva, Loren (Qumawuna)

Sakyesva, Harry

Siwingyumptewa, Laverne

TURTLES

Garnett, James

Hayden, Julian

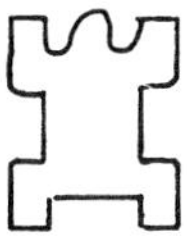

Nequatewa, Eddie

Sockyma, Mitchell

FISH

Shopteese, John

ANTS

Fritz, Marcia

Ricky, Marcia (Fritz)

BUTTERFLIES

Holmes, Douglas

Poleyma, Ramona

Tsethlikai, Ivan J.

Wilson, Austin

DRAGONFLIES

Talaheftewa, Roy

SPIDERS

Honie, Norman

Kagenvema, Bennett

Komayouse, Herbert

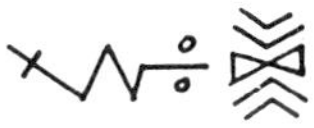

Lomaheftewa, Marvin

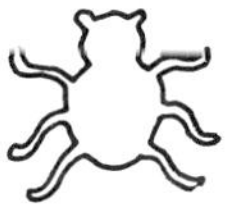

Onsae, Larson

Pawiki, Grant

Ross, Edison

Ross, Edison

Yoyokie, Gary & Elsie

UNKNOWN INSECTS

Leota

184 SYMBOLS

Symbol	Artist
	Loretto, Phillip
	Nighthorse, Ben
	Setalla, Bill
	Seward, Charles W.

CORN PLANTS

Symbol	Artist
	Gachupine, Laura / Toya, Maxine
	Kuwanvayouma, Kenneth
	Lovato, Harold
	Sockyma, Michael
	Sockyma, Michael

CORN EARS

Symbol	Artist
	Charley, Lena Chio
	Charley, Lena Chio
	Garcia, Leah (Nampeyo)
	Garcia, Leah (Nampeyo)
	Hamilton, Tonita (Nampeyo)
	Hooie, Daisy (Nampeyo)
	Namingha, Franklin
	Nash, Edith
	Nevayaktewa, Delbert
	Nevayaktewa, Delbert
	Polacca, Fannie (Nampeyo)
	Pooyama, Allen
	Pooyama, Allen
	Pooyouma, Larry
	Sakeva, Loren
	Sequaptewa, Raymond
	Sequaptewa, Raymond
	Talashie, Rosalie
	Talashie, Rosalie

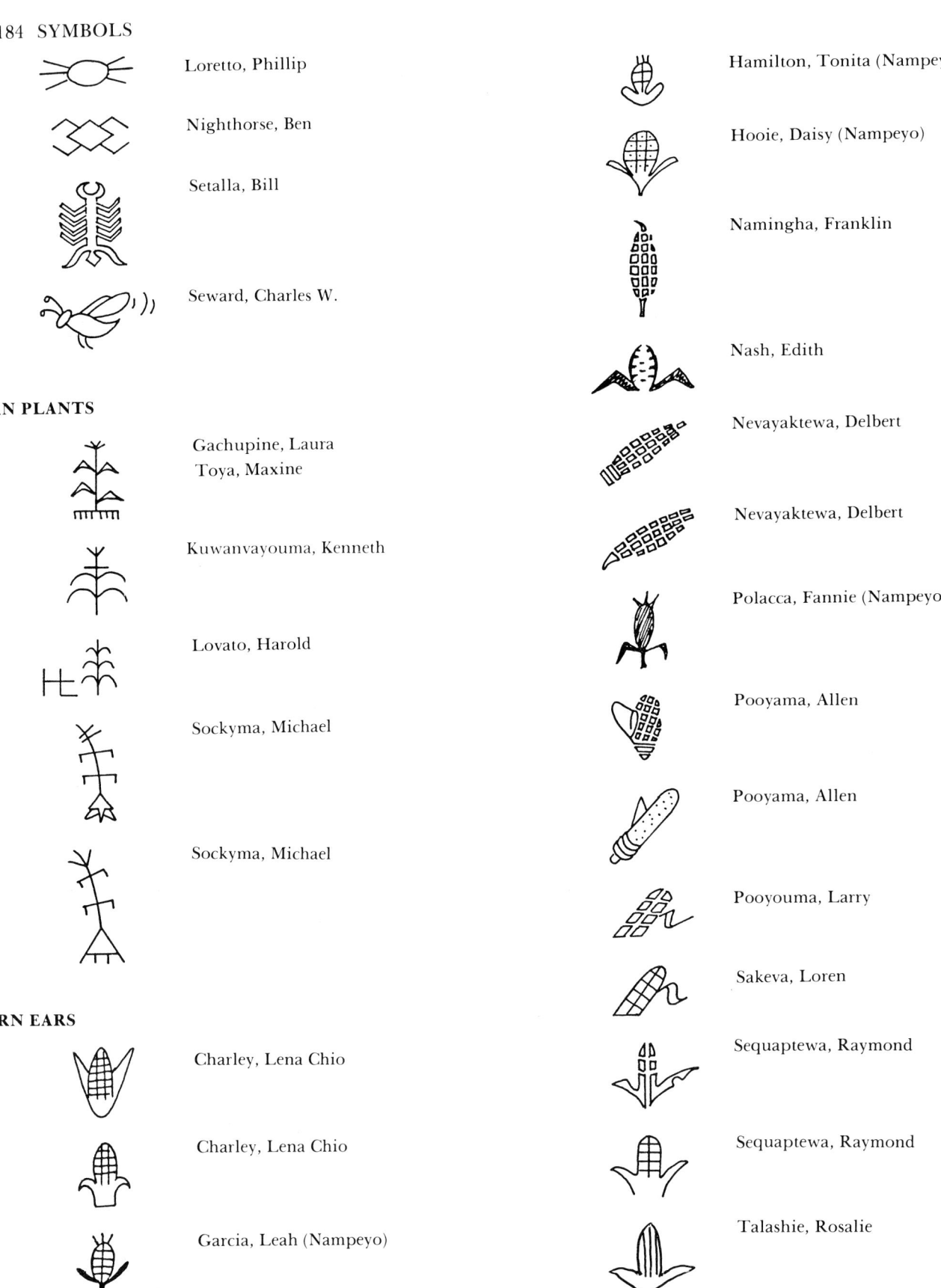

SYMBOLS 185

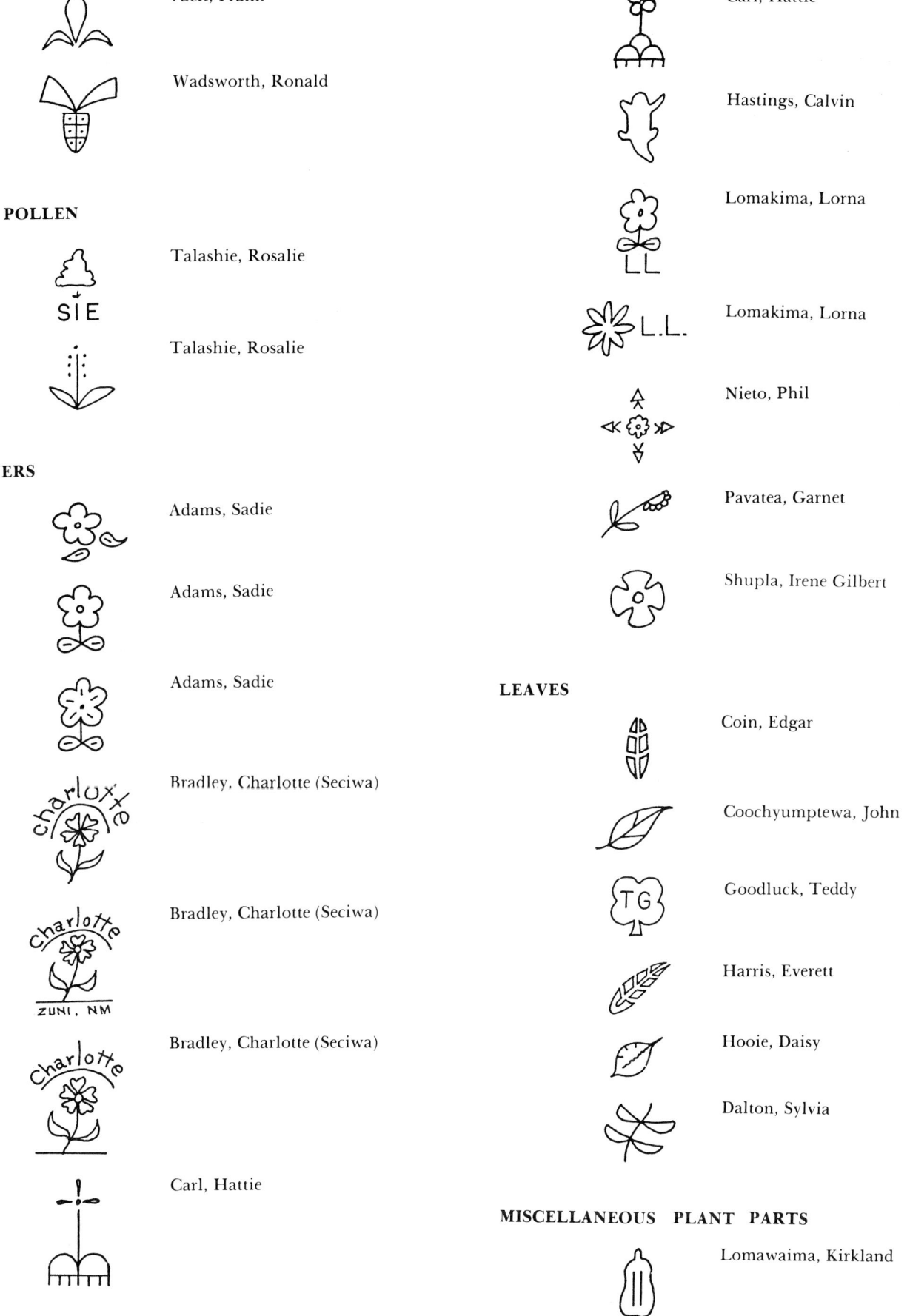

Vacit, Frank

Wadsworth, Ronald

CORN POLLEN

Talashie, Rosalie

Talashie, Rosalie

FLOWERS

Adams, Sadie

Adams, Sadie

Adams, Sadie

Bradley, Charlotte (Seciwa)

Bradley, Charlotte (Seciwa)

Bradley, Charlotte (Seciwa)

Carl, Hattie

Carl, Hattie

Hastings, Calvin

Lomakima, Lorna

Lomakima, Lorna

Nieto, Phil

Pavatea, Garnet

Shupla, Irene Gilbert

LEAVES

Coin, Edgar

Coochyumptewa, John

Goodluck, Teddy

Harris, Everett

Hooie, Daisy

Dalton, Sylvia

MISCELLANEOUS PLANT PARTS

Lomawaima, Kirkland

186 SYMBOLS

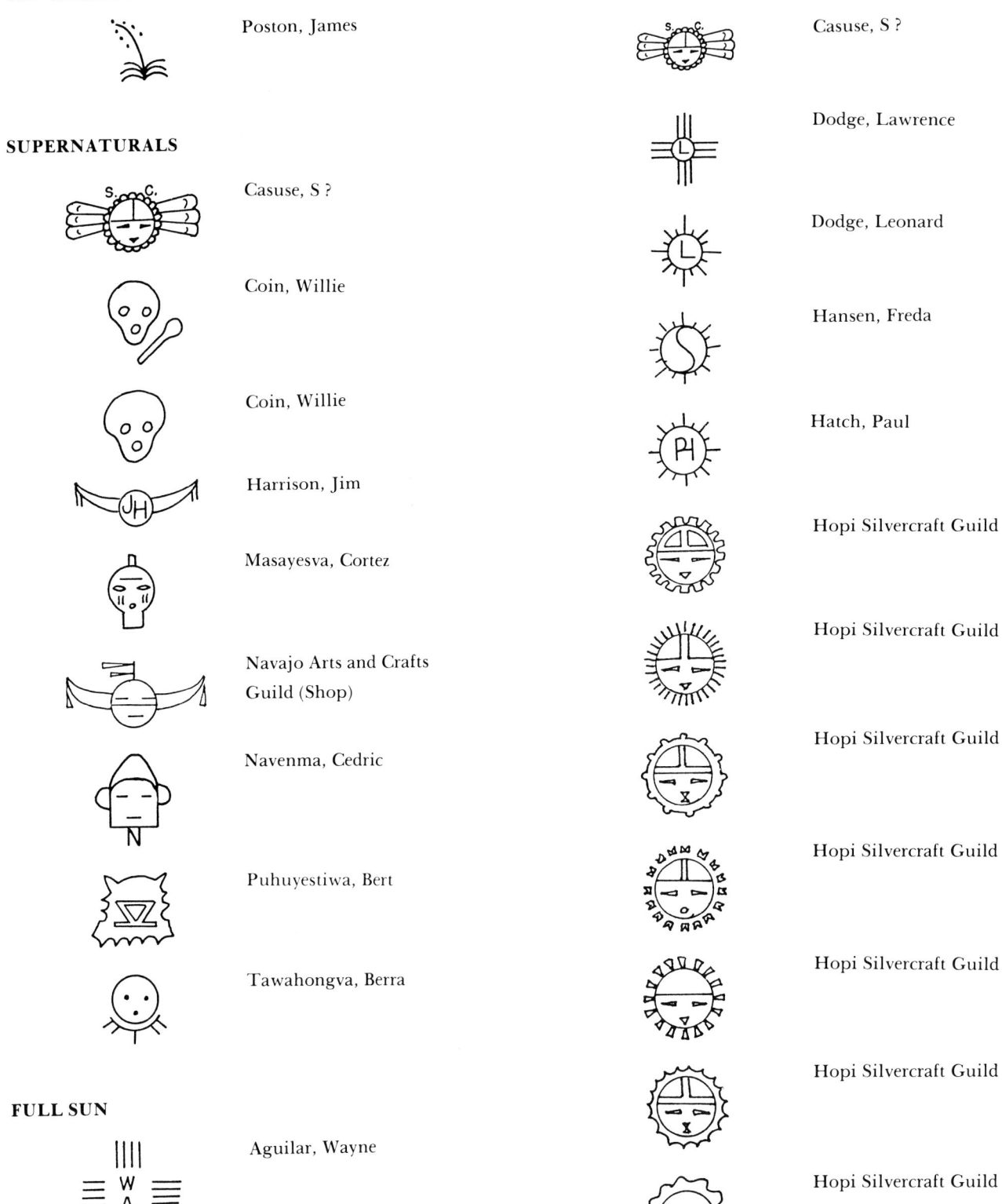

Poston, James

SUPERNATURALS

Casuse, S ?

Coin, Willie

Coin, Willie

Harrison, Jim

Masayesva, Cortez

Navajo Arts and Crafts Guild (Shop)

Navenma, Cedric

Puhuyestiwa, Bert

Tawahongva, Berra

FULL SUN

Aguilar, Wayne

Aguilar, Wayne

Begay, Carl

Casuse, S ?

Dodge, Lawrence

Dodge, Leonard

Hansen, Freda

Hatch, Paul

Hopi Silvercraft Guild

Hopi Silvercraft Guild

Hopi Silvercraft Guild

Hopi Silvercraft Guild

Hopi Silvercraft Guild

Hopi Silvercraft Guild

Hopi Silvercraft Guild

Laahty, Andrew

Laate, Morris & Sadie

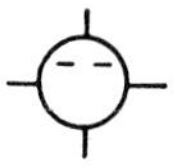

SYMBOLS 187

Laate, Morris & Sadie

Laate, Morris & Sadie

Laate, Morris & Sadie

Laate, Morris & Sadie

Laate, Morris & Sadie

Laban, Samuel N.

Lante, Doris

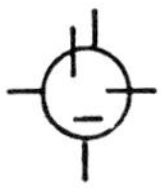

Leekity, Paul & Nancy

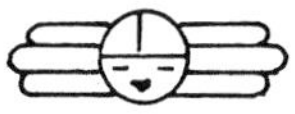

Lomayestewa, Nan

Lomayesva, Louis (Lomay)

Lomayesva, Louis (Lomay)

Medina, E ?

Phillips, Roderick

Polivema, Larry

Shelendewa, Linda

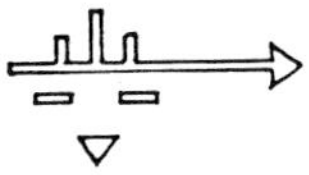

Supplee, Charles

Supplee, Charles

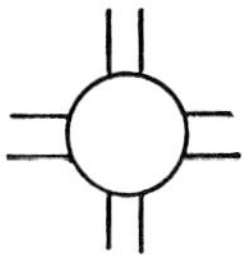

Taylor, Milson

Yowytewa, Arthur

Yowytewa, Hubert

PARTIAL SUN

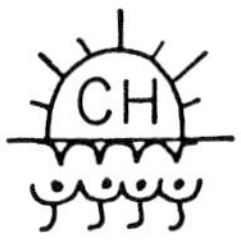

Hustito, Charles

Hustito, Charles

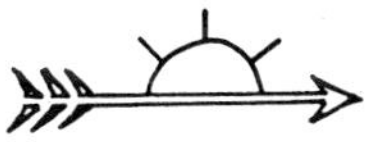

Koinva, Elliot

Lamson, Shannon

Lamson, Shannon

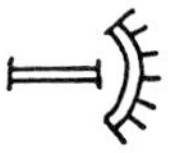

Long, Jimmie

Long, Phillip

Long, Phillip

Mowa, David

Niiha, Verdel

188 SYMBOLS

(rising sun with rays)	Polingyouma, Henry
(half circle)	Selina, Weaver
(half circle with rays)	Tzunie, Benjamin Jr.

MOONS

C (crescent)	Begay, Carl Allen
ℂ	Bowie, C ?
☾BOWIE	Bowie, C ?
☾C	Chavarria, Harvey
☾HAVEZ	Chavez, Phillip
G.C. (with eyelash)	Crawford, Eugene (Gene)
(half moon with rays)	Halfmoon, Carlos
☾	Halfmoon, Carlos
(star in crescent)	Hawee, Billy Rae
H⌒	Hill, Wendall J.
☽	Kirk, Andrew
(crescent with face)	Lomaheftewa, Valjean
(star in crescent)	Lomaheftewa, Stetson
81 (underlined)	Lucero, Beverly
(symbol)	Quanimptewa, Harvey
T☾ / S	Singer, Thomas

T☾	Singer, Thomas
☽	Taylor, Dalton
LBY (in crescent)	Yazzie, Lou Billy

STARS

✧ (4-point with dots)	Batte, B ?
LRB / B ☆	Begay, Loren (Les Baker Shop)
⍟ (pentagram)	Bia, Sam
☆ SA	Charlie, Stanley
☆	Charlie, Stanley / Clark, James / Koruh, Harold
(star with arc)	Fransisco, Nelson M.
MS ☆	Graham, Midge (Shop)
LA ☆	Graham, Midge (Shop)
(star in crescent)	Hawee, Billy Ray
✳	Josytewa, Jessie
✕	Kalestena, Jack
(star figure)	Kewanyama, Leroy
(shooting star)	Lomayestewa, Kendrick
(star in crescent)	Lomayestewa, Stetson

Mansfield, Vernon

Martinez, Dorothy

Mull, Margie

Peshlakai, Norbert

Simplicio, Danny

Smiley, Lena Mae

Talaheftewa, Archie

Taylor, Dalton

Tsosie, Elkie

Tsouhlarakis, George E.

CLOUDS

Carl, Hattie

Carl, Hattie

Coochwytewa, Victor

Dawahoya, Bernard

Dawahoya, Bueford

Hoyungowa, Manuel

Hoyungowa, Manuel

Hoyungowa, Manuel

Hoyungowa, Manuel

Hoyungowa, Manuel & Karen

Leslie, Lena

Lomawaima, Patrick

Lomawaima, Patrick

Lomawaima, Phillip

Lomayestewa, Mark

Lomayestewa, Mark

Lujan, Rick & Nettie

Monongye, Preston

Namingha, Warren

Nava, Douglas

Nelson, Jerry

Poseyesva, Manuel

Raincloud, Nancy

Saufkie, Gracilda

190 SYMBOLS

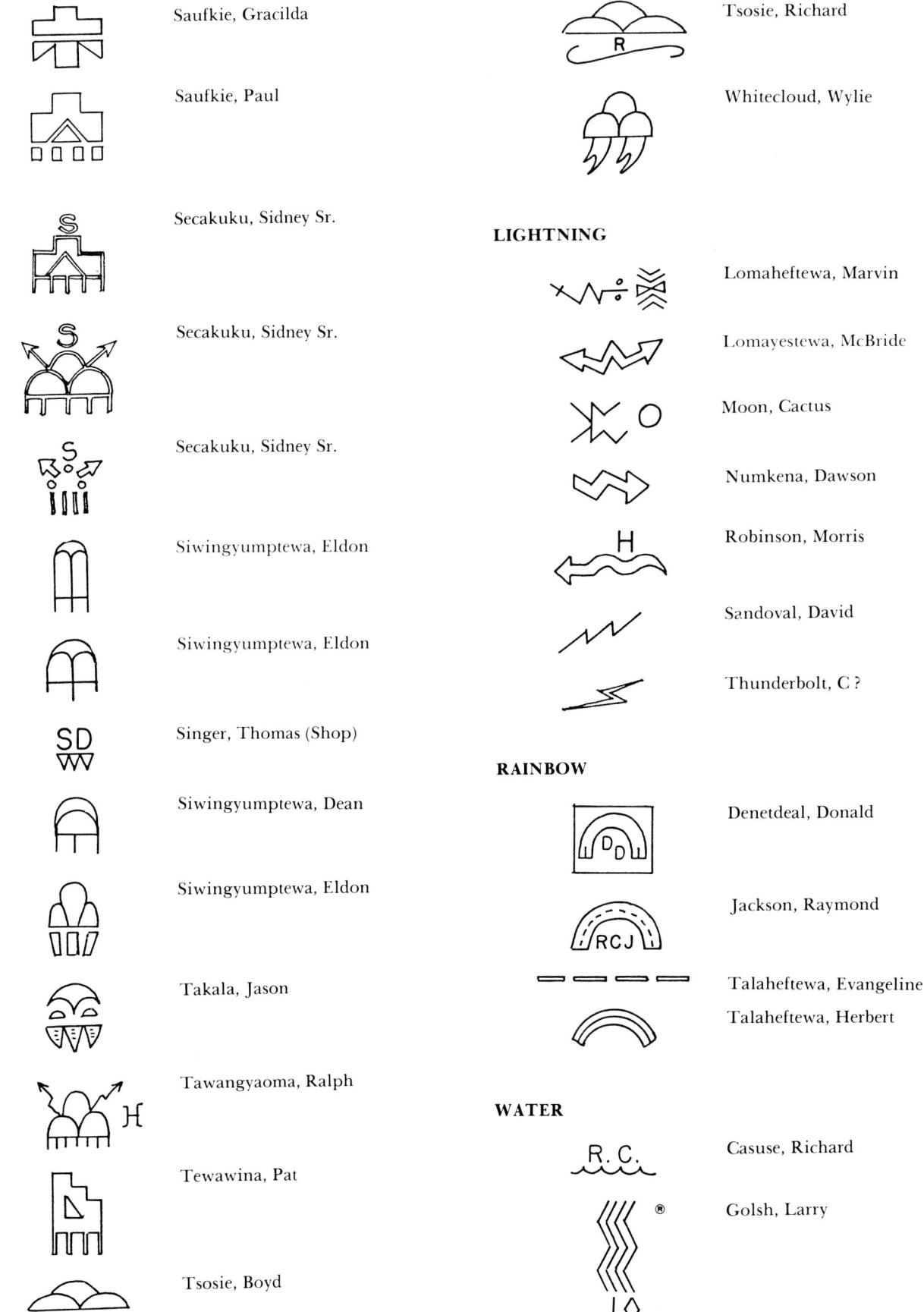

	Saufkie, Gracilda
	Saufkie, Paul
	Secakuku, Sidney Sr.
	Secakuku, Sidney Sr.
	Secakuku, Sidney Sr.
	Siwingyumptewa, Eldon
	Siwingyumptewa, Eldon
	Singer, Thomas (Shop)
	Siwingyumptewa, Dean
	Siwingyumptewa, Eldon
	Takala, Jason
	Tawangyaoma, Ralph
	Tewawina, Pat
	Tsosie, Boyd
	Tsosie, Richard
	Whitecloud, Wylie

LIGHTNING

	Lomaheftewa, Marvin
	Lomayestewa, McBride
	Moon, Cactus
	Numkena, Dawson
	Robinson, Morris
	Sandoval, David
	Thunderbolt, C ?

RAINBOW

	Denetdeal, Donald
	Jackson, Raymond
	Talaheftewa, Evangeline
	Talaheftewa, Herbert

WATER

	Casuse, Richard
	Golsh, Larry

SYMBOLS 191

Golsh, Larry

Golsh, Larry

Nutima, Jim

DIRECTIONS

Talaheftewa, Evangeline

WIND

Gasper, Raymond

Gasper, Raymond

Martin, Ray

Whirling Wind, Ray

MOUNTAINS

Anderson, Katie

Nava, Douglas

Tafoya, Ray

Tahe, ?

Thompson, Norman

Tsinnie, Orville

Tsinnie, Orville

Tsinnie, Orville

Wall, Steve

HOMES

Allesandro, Debby

Benally, Ernest

Cody, Sadie

Hill, Roger D.

Jackson, Dan

Jackson, Martha

Jim, Marie Le

Platero, Thompson

Three Hogans (Shop)

Tracey, Larry

White Hogan (Shop)

MUSICAL INSTRUMENTS

Koinva, Lauren

192 SYMBOLS

Lomakima, Charles T.

Lomayestewa, Marcus

Namingha, Floyd

BOWS AND ARROWS

Adakai, Glen

Anderson, Katherine

Armstrong, Raymond

Arviso, Lee

Atencio, Frank

Begay, T ?

Calavasa, Juan

Calavasa, Susie

Chee, Rose A.

Clah, Jessie

Fred, Nathan Jr.

Hanson, B ?

Koinva, Elliot

Lewis, Art

Lovato, Sam

Martinez, Eugene

Montano, Gibson

Natseway, Allen

Nez, Chester

Palmer, Keith

Peshlakai, Dalton

Peshlakai, Dalton
Peshlakai, Etta

Peshlakai, Etta

Peshlakai, Fred

Peshlakai, Fred

Romijo, Rosetta

Sandoval, Sherry

Scott, Rosco

Sekayumptewa, Willie

Smith, Bertha

Smith, Dennis

Smith, Dennis

Smith, Lorenzo

Smith, Lorenzo

Spencer, "Chaka"

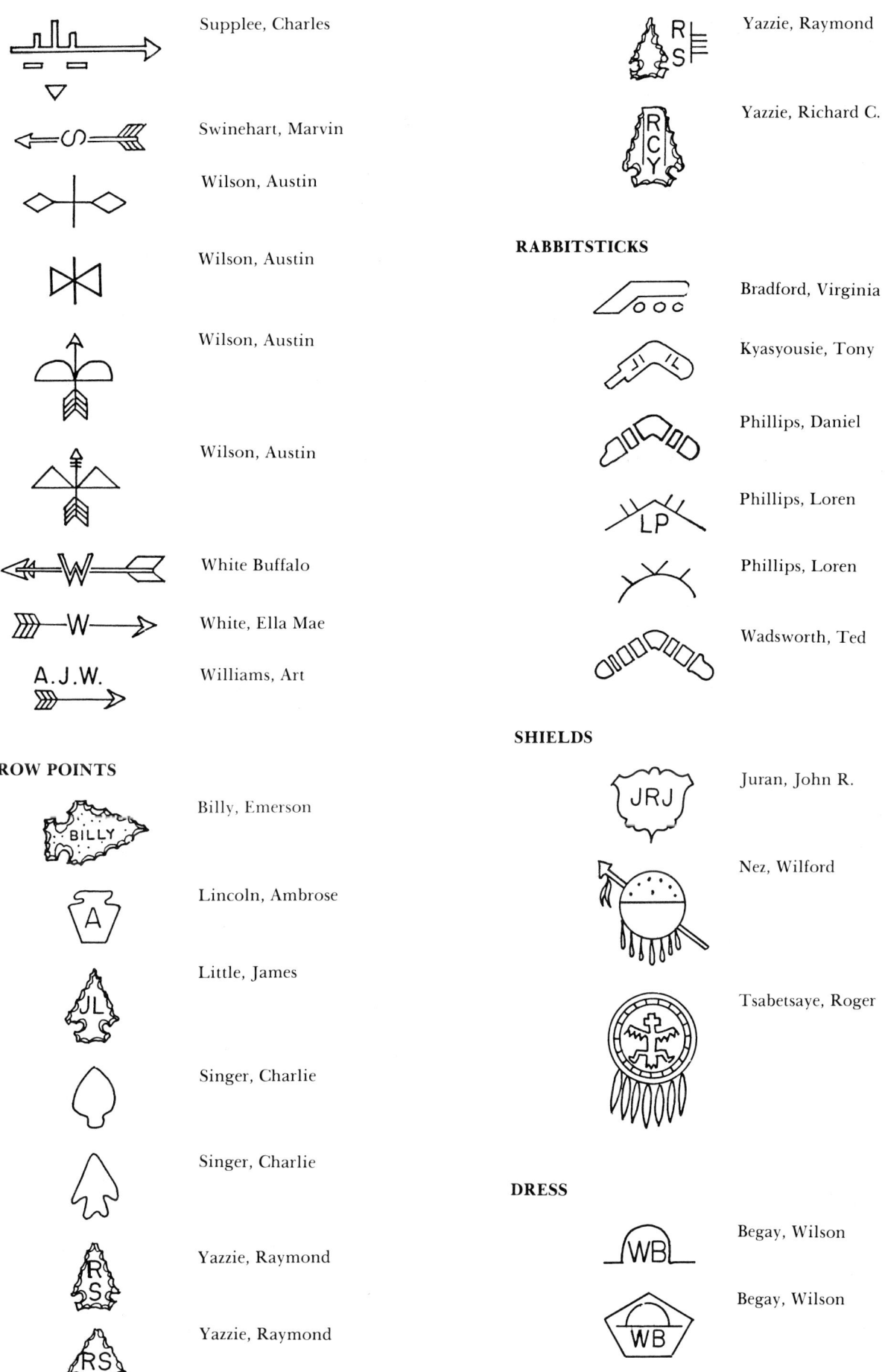

ARROW POINTS

RABBITSTICKS

SHIELDS

DRESS

194 SYMBOLS

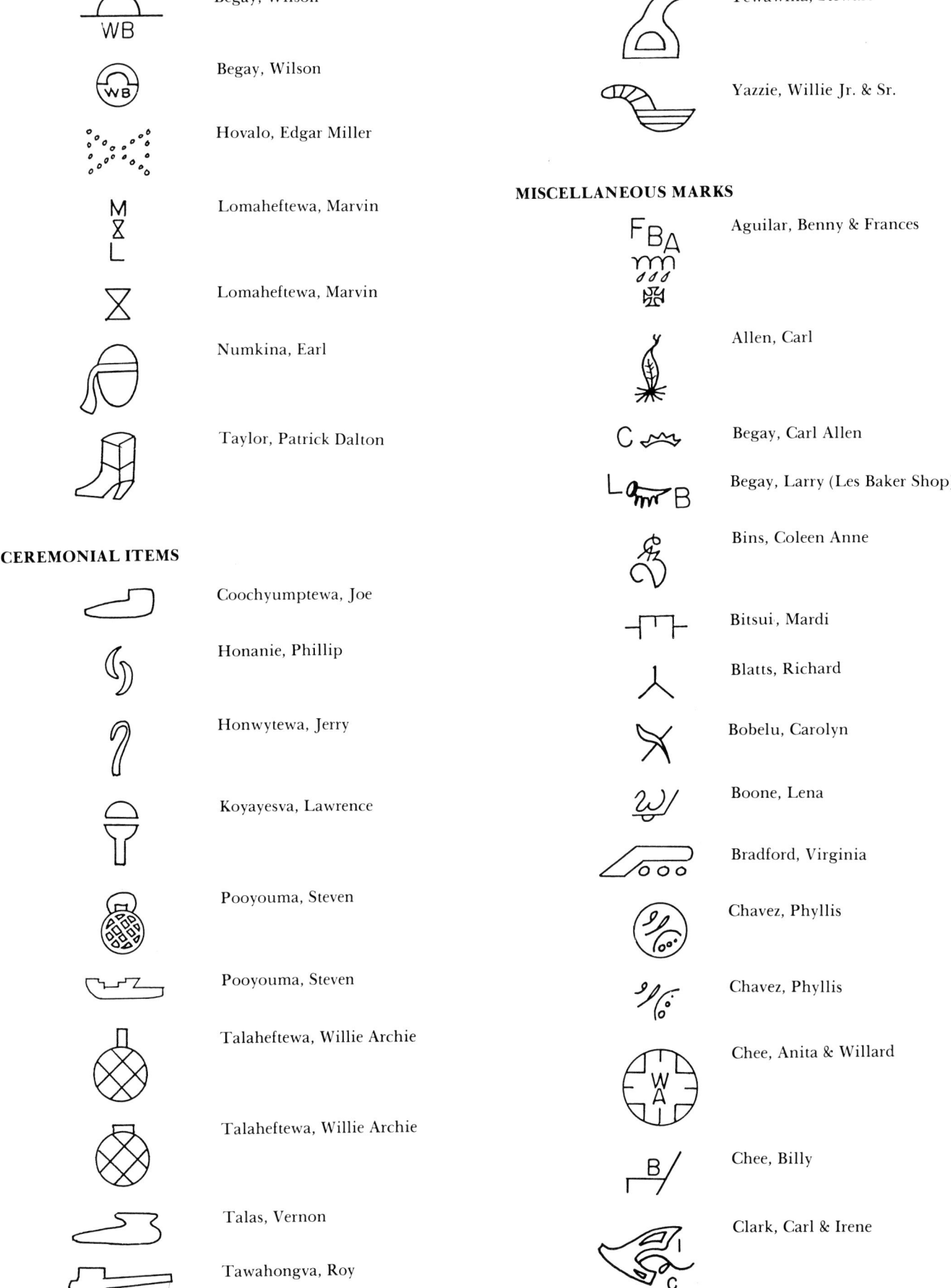

Begay, Wilson

Begay, Wilson

Hovalo, Edgar Miller

Lomaheftewa, Marvin

Lomaheftewa, Marvin

Numkina, Earl

Taylor, Patrick Dalton

CEREMONIAL ITEMS

Coochyumptewa, Joe

Honanie, Phillip

Honwytewa, Jerry

Koyayesva, Lawrence

Pooyouma, Steven

Pooyouma, Steven

Talaheftewa, Willie Archie

Talaheftewa, Willie Archie

Talas, Vernon

Tawahongva, Roy

Tewawina, Stewart

Yazzie, Willie Jr. & Sr.

MISCELLANEOUS MARKS

Aguilar, Benny & Frances

Allen, Carl

Begay, Carl Allen

Begay, Larry (Les Baker Shop)

Bins, Coleen Anne

Bitsui, Mardi

Blatts, Richard

Bobelu, Carolyn

Boone, Lena

Bradford, Virginia

Chavez, Phyllis

Chavez, Phyllis

Chee, Anita & Willard

Chee, Billy

Clark, Carl & Irene

SYMBOLS 195

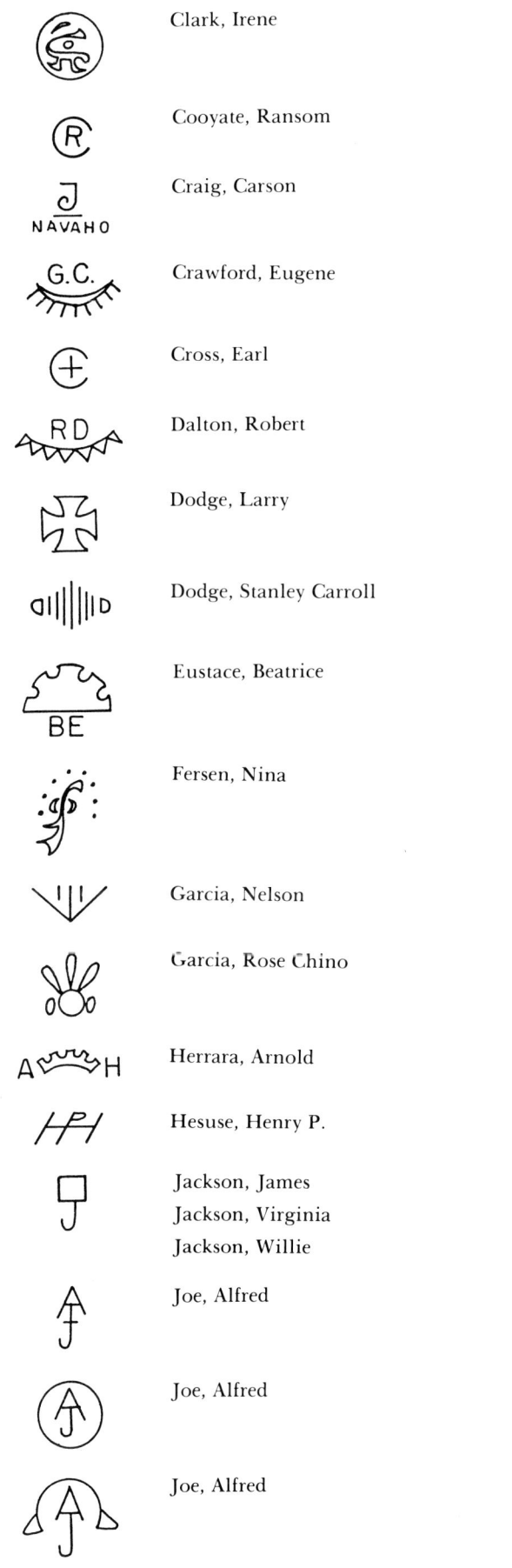

Clark, Irene
Cooyate, Ransom
Craig, Carson
Crawford, Eugene
Cross, Earl
Dalton, Robert
Dodge, Larry
Dodge, Stanley Carroll
Eustace, Beatrice
Fersen, Nina
Garcia, Nelson
Garcia, Rose Chino
Herrara, Arnold
Hesuse, Henry P.
Jackson, James
Jackson, Virginia
Jackson, Willie
Joe, Alfred
Joe, Alfred
Joe, Alfred

Komalestewa, Alton
Little, James
Long, Jimmie
Lonjose, Mabel C.
Lorretto, Phillip
Lorretto, Phillip
Martinez, Eugene
Moon, Cactus
Mowa, Tim
Parker, Lennie
Parker, Lennie
Tsosie, Harrison
Peshlakai, Norbert
Reagan, Gene
Reano, Percy
Sanchez, Tony
Sayesva

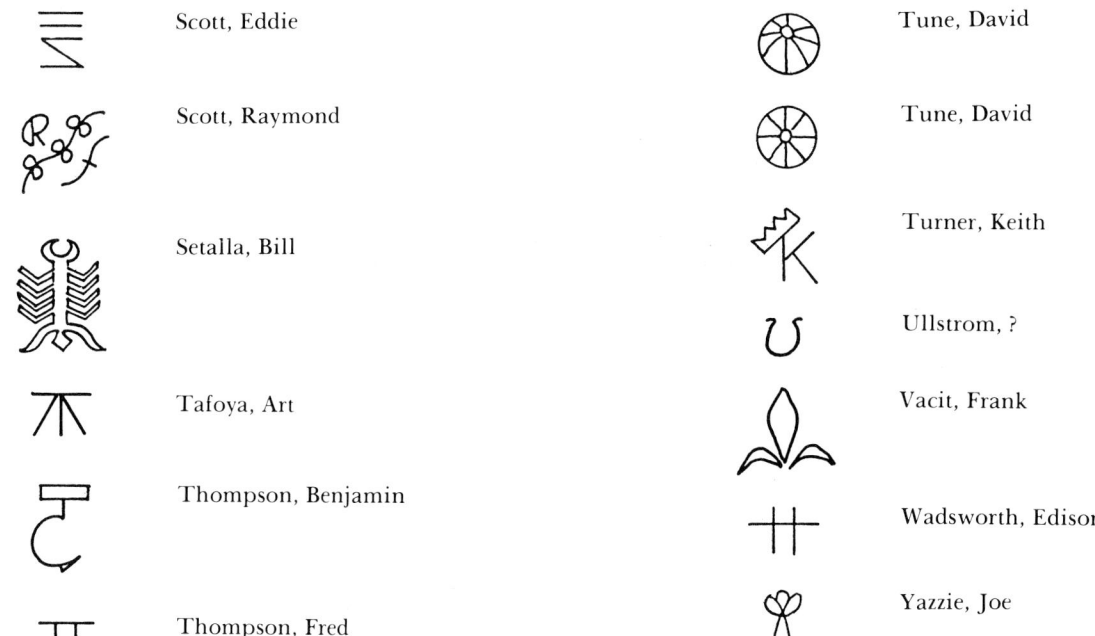

Index IV: Shop Marks

Atkinson Trading Company

Baker, Les

Baker, Les

Baker, Les

Shades of the West, A. Bischoff

Canyon Silver Company, B. Burnham

Canyon Silver Company, B. Burnham

Christies

Morning Star Enterprises

Grey Squirrel, Shop Manager

Hand Made Indian Jewelry, Ortega

Hill, Roger

Hopi Enterprises, Hopicrafts

Hopi Arts & Crafts Cooperative Guild, Hopi Silvercraft Guild

United States Department of the Interior-Indian Arts & Crafts Board

Iverson's Indian Arts & Crafts

Knowles, Mel

Kopavi International, R. Mehagian

Krazy Blonde Trading Post

Luthy, Carl

Luthy, Max

Navajo Arts & Crafts Enterprises

Gilbert Ortega's

198 SHOPMARKS

[mark]	Paquin's Arts & Crafts
FP	Thundbird Shops, Inc., F.Patania
[thunderbird with FP]	Patania's Indian Shop, F.Patania
JP	Navajo Silvercraft, J.Popovich
[rocking horse]	Rocking Horse Ranch, L.Randall
SD / VVV	Thomas Singer
S. L. I. J.	State Line Indian Jewelry
[sunburst]	Sunburst Traders
M [sunburst] SUNBURST	Sunburst Handcrafts, Inc., L.McKinney
Temè	Sunburst Handcrafts, Inc., L.McKinney
cTco	T & R Market
[3H mark]	Three Hogans, Bell
π	Tobe Turpen
UI△TA 22 / UITA 41	United Indian Traders Association
[hogan]	White Hogan, J.Bonnell
W / WIHMS/S	Woodard's Indian Arts
[line mark]	Zachary, Gertrude
ZCA	Zuni Craftsmen's Association
[figure mark]	Zuni Craftsmen Cooperative Association

Index V: Tribal Affiliations

ACOMA
Garcia, Rose Chino

ANGLO
Begay, Loren
Bradford, Virginia
Dube, J.P.
Durkee, Michael
Fersen, Nina
Foutz, John Allen
Hayden, Julian
Hornbeck, John
Juran, John R.
Knowles, Mel
Kraus, Adolf
Krepps, Don
McCrory, Jane
Meyer, Ruth A.
Morris, Dee
Nabers, Bill
Newman, Al
Patania, Frank
Patania, Frank Jr.
Ratzlaff, Karen
Robinson, Helen
Ross, Tommy
Sanchez, Tony
Seward, Charles W.
Shay, C.
Shay, G.
Spencer, Chaka
Sundt, Danny D.
Swinehart, Marvin
Thompson, Ben
Turner, Keith
Ullstrom, ?
Weigand, James
Wright, Donald
Zachary, Phillip

BLACK FEET
Long, Albert

CHEROKEE
Cone, Yonah
Munson, Thom
Wolf, John

Nighthorse, Ben

COCHITI
Herrera, Arnold
Loretto, Phillip C. (Jemez)
Lucero, Beverly
Quintana, Cipriano
Quintana, Jerry
Quintana, Joseph H.
Quintana, Terrecita
Taliman, Elizabeth

CHOCTAW
Brown, Darrell

COMANCHE
White Buffalo (Mike Perez)

HOPI
Albert, Ramon Jr.
Batala, Art
Benn, Shirley
Carl, Hattie
Casuse, Richard
Casuse, S?
Chapella, Grace
Cheedah, Zella
Cheekachi, Maria
Coin, Edgar
Coin, Willie
Collatetta, Sarah
Colton, Al (Qoyawaima)
Coochwikvia, Marcus
Coochwytewa, Ricky
Coochwytewa, Victor
Coochyumptewa, Joe
Coochyumptewa, John
Dalton, Sylvia
Dawahoya, Bernard
Dawahoya, Bueford
Day, Chalmers
Denet, Maryann
Dennis, Alec
Dennis, Philbert
Duran, Bernard
Earl, Vivian
Frank, Nathan Sr.
Fred, Nathan Jr.
Frederick, Bert
Gashwazra, Alfonso
Gashwazri, Bradley
Hamilton, Tonita

Harris, Everett
Hasting, Calvin
Hawee, Billy Rae
Holmes, Douglas
Holmes, Emery
Honanie, Phillip
Honanie, Watson
Honie, Agnes
Honie, Norman Jr.
Honie, Norman Sr.
Honwisioma, Randall
Honwytewa, Jerry
Honyaktewa, James
Honyaktewa, Neilson
Hooie, Daisy
Hooie, Norman Jr.
Hooie, Sidney
Hooie, Virginia
Hovalo, Edgar Miller
Hoyungwa, Manuel
Humeyestewa, Byron
Humeyestewa, Jay
Humeyestewa, Manuel
Humeyestewa, Tom
Humeyestewa, Winfield
Hunter, Harold
James, Eldon
Jenkins, Grant
Jenkins, Marshall
Joseyesva, Ross
Joshveama, Valjean
Josytewa, Jesse
Kabotie, Michael
Kagenvema, Bennett
Kagenvema, Richard
Kavena, Wilmer
Kaye, Wilmer
Kewanwytewa, Pierce
Kewanyama, Leroy
Koinva, Elliot
Koinva, Lauren
Komaletstewa, Alton
Komayouse, Herbert
Koruh, Harold
Koyayesva, Lawrence
Kuwanvayouma, Ken
Kyasyousie, Raymond
Kyasyousie, Tony
Laban, Samuel
Lamson, Shannon

Leslie, Rena
Loloma, Charles
Lomadapki, Robert
Lomaheftewa, Marvin C.
Lomaheftewa, Valjean
Lomahongva, Edward
Lomahukvu, Cortez
Lomakima, Charles T.
Lomakima, Lorna
Lomatewa, Lewis
Lomawaima, Kirkland
Lomawaima, Patrick
Lomawaima, Phillip
Lomayaktewa, Starlie
Lomayestewa, Arthur
Lomayestewa, Clarence
Lomayestewa, Dwayne
Lomayestewa, Jessica
Lomayestewa, Kendrick
Lomayestewa, Marcus
Lomayestewa, Mark
Lomayestewa, McBride
Lomayestewa, Nan
Lomayestewa, Stetson
Lomayesva, Lewis
Lucas, Glen
Lucas, Trinidad
Maktima, Duane (Laguna)
Monongye, Bessie
Mowa, David
Namingha, Floyd
Namingha, Franklin
Namingha, Raymie
Namingha, Warren
Naseyoma, Stephen Hyson
Navasie, Joy Ann
Navasie, Mary Ann
Navenma, Cedric
Nequatewa, Eddie
Nevayaktewa, Delbert
Numkina, Dawson
Numkina, Earl
Nutima, Jim
Nutumya, Sharold
Nuvayaoma, Arlo
Nuvayaoma, Willard
Onsae, Larson
Paqua
Pawiki, Grant
Pentewa, Lonnie
Phillips, Daniel
Phillips, Loren
Phillips, Roderick
Poleahla, Elaine
Polelonema, Tyler
Polelonema, Walter
Polequaptewa, Riley
Poleviyouma, Jacob
Poleyma, Ramona
Poleyviyouma, Jacob Jr.
Polingaisi, Riley
Polingyouma, Henry
Polingyouma, Philbert
Polivema, Larry
Pooyama, Allen
Pooyama, Lawrence
Pooyama, Steven
Poseyesva, Manuel
Poseyesva, Philbert
Puhuyestewa, Bert
Quanimptewa, Harvey Jr.
Quimayousie, Herbert
Qumyintewa, Alde
Ricky, Marcia Fritz
Robinson, Morris
Sakeva, Loren
Sakeva, Raymond
Sakyesva, Harry
Saufkie, Andrew
Saufkie, Elva
Saufkie, Gracilda
Saufkie, Lawrence
Saufkie, Paul
Saufkie, Wilmer
Scott, Courtney Amon
Scott, Eddie
Secakuku, Myron
Secakuku, Sydney Jr.
Secakuku, Sidney Sr.
Seckletstewa, Jackson
Sehongva, Doran
Sehongva, Elgene
Sekaquaptewa, Emory
Sekaquaptewa, Phillip
Sekaquaptewa, Wayne
Sekayumptewa, Wally
Selina, Weaver
Sequaptewa, Raymond
Setalla, Bill
Setalla, Pauline
Shupla, Hazel
Siewiyumptewa, Eldon
Siwingyumptewa, Dean
Siwingyumptewa, Eldon
Siwingyumptewa, Laverne
Sockyma, Michael
Sockyma, Mitchell
Sockyma, Steven
Sulu, Marietta
Supplee, Charles
Sumatzkuku, Dewan
Takala, Jason
Talaheftewa, Archie
Talaheftewa, Evangeline
Talaheftewa, Herbert
Talaheftewa, Ray
Talaheftewa, Willie Archie
Talas, Vernon
Talashie, Rosalie
Talayumptewa, Caroline
Talayumptewa, Orville
Tawahongva, Berra
Tawahongva, Roy
Tawangyaouma, Ralph
Taylor, Dalton
Taylor, Milson
Tewa, Bobby
Tewawina, Pat
Tewawina, Stewart
Thomas, Virgil
Tyma, Gilbert Andress
Wadsworth, Edison
Wadsworth, Ronald
Wadsworth, Ted
Wadsworth, Terry
Wadsworth, Elizabeth
Yaiva, Travis
Youvella, Ronald
Yowytewa, Arthur
Yowytewa, Hubert
Yoyokie, Elsie
Yoyokie, Gary

ISLETA
Abeita, Kathy
Baca, Lorenzo (Mescalero)
Calabaza, ?
Cayatineto, P.
Charveze, Ted (Mexican)
Jiron, Evelyn
Juancho, Joann Christine
Padilla, Paul (Sandia)
Velasquez, Mary

JEMEZ
Gachupin, Laura
Kohlmeyer, Royce J. (?)
Loretto, Phillip C. (Cochiti)
Toya, Maxine

KIOWA
Haungoah (Al Cody)

LAGUNA
Abeita, Eunice
Abeyta, H.
Carillo, Frank
Francisco, Lillian
Maktima, Duane (Hopi)
Natseway, Allen
Platero, Antoinette

MESCALERO APACHE
Baca, Lorenzo (Isleta)
Wall, Steve
White Eagle, Carlos

MEXICAN
Chizomana
Gambino, Nicolas
Maldonado, Gilbert
Monongye, Preston (Mission)
Terrazas, Richard
White Buffalo (Mike Perez)

MISSION
Golsh, Joseph
Golsh, Larry
Monongye, Preston (Mexican)

MOHAWK
Hill, Wendal J.

MORONGO
Cahuilla Margaret

NAVAJO
Abeita, Rita
Abeyta, Juan
Adakai, Fred
Adakai, Glen
Adakai, Jack
Adakai, Len-r
Adakai, Minnie
Adeky, Gilbert
Agoodie, Jerry
Ahasteen, Julius

Ahasteen, Tom
Alberta, Juan
Alessandro, Debbie
Alexius, Oscar
Allen, Carl
Allison, D.
Allison, L.
Anderson, Eddie
Anderson, Elizabeth
Anderson, Ella
Anderson, Evelyn
Anderson, Katherine
Anderson, Roy Jr.
Anderson, Wilbur
Anderson, William
Anselmo, Vincent
Apache, Morgan
Apache, Steven
Apachito, Archy
Apachito, Benny
Apachito, Clinton
Apachito, Genevieve
Apachito, Raymond
Apachito, Robert
Apachito, Velma
Armstrong, Raymond
Arviso, Floyd
Arviso, Kirk
Arviso, Leo
Arviso, Pontiac
Arviso, Wilbur Paul
Asheet, Fred
Ashley, Alice
Ashley, Cecil
Ashley, Fannie
Ashley, J.
Ashley, Monroe
Atsitty, Gilbert
Atsitty, Thomas
Attakai, P.
Avery, Mary Smith
Bahe, Fidel
Bahe, Louise
Bahe, S.
Bahe, Sam
Bahe, S.M.
Bahe, Tom
Bahi, Dini Tsai
Bahi, Joe
Bain, Nellie
Baloo, John
Barton, David
Bebo, Yvonne
Becenti, Annie
Becenti, Benjamin
Becenti, Eugene
Becenti, Robert
Beck, Victor
Bedall, Tim
Bedoni, John
Bedah, T.
Beedah, Tim
Begay, A.
Begay, Annie
Begay, Anthony
Begay, B.
Begay, Barbara
Begay, Bobby
Begay, Carl

Begay, Carl Allen
Begay, Carolyn
Begay, Charles
Begay, Clyde
Begay, D.M.
Begay, E.
Begay, Eddie
Begay, Edison
Begay, Ella Mae
Begay, Elouise
Begay, Elsie
Begay, F.M.
Begay, Frances
Begay, Francis M.
Begay, George
Begay, Harry H.
Begay, Harvey
Begay, Helen
Begay, Howard
Begay, Ida
Begay, J.M.
Begay, Jerome
Begay, Jimmy
Begay, Joe
Begay, Joe G.
Begay, John G.
Begay, Johnny Mike
Begay, John White
Begay, Kenneth
Begay, Keyonnie
Begay, L.
Begay, Larry
Begay, Leonard
Begay, Leroy
Begay, Manuel
Begay, Marie
Begay, Morris
Begay, Norma Jean
Begay, Pauline
Begay, R.H.
Begay, Richard C.
Begay, Richard T.
Begay, Robert
Begay, Roland
Begay, Roseanne
Begay, Sam
Begay, T.
Begay, T.
Begay, Tom H.
Begay, Victor Moses
Begay, W.
Begay, Wilson
Begay, Zearl
Begay, Sam C.
Bellson, Shirley
Benally, Alice
Benally, Betty
Benally, David
Benally, Edward Sr.
Benally, Emil
Benally, Ernest
Benally, Josephine
Benally, Kee Joe
Benally, L.
Benally, P.K.
Benally, Rita B.
Bennett, B.
Bennett, Betty
Bennett, Elizabeth

Bennett, Lee
Bennett, Raymond
Benton, Herman
Betony, B.
Bia, Sam
Bicenti, Raymond
Bickle, Esther
Bickle, L.
Bilagody, E.
Bill, Lorenzo
Billie
Billie, Betty Rose
Billie, Henry
Billie, J.
Billie, Joe C.
Billie, John Jim
Billie, J.K.
Billie, T.
Billison
Billy, Mary
Billy, Tom
Bini, Dine Tsosie
Bins, Coleen Anne
Bitsui. Jim
Bitsui, Maggie
Bitsui, Mardi
Blackgoat, Alice
Blackgoat, Arlene
Blackgoat, Ben
Blackgoat, Carson
Blackgoat, H.
Blackgoat, Jennie
Blackgoat, L.
Blatts, Richard
Bonny, Bernice
Bonny, Emma
Bowanna, Bertha
Bowie, Geraldine
Boyd, Delphine
Boyd, Gay
Boyd, H.
Boyd, James
Boyd, Julia
Boyd, Raymond
Boyd, Virgil
Brady, Wilber
Brown, Cea
Brown, Daisy
Brown, Gilbert
Brown, Marie
Burnham, Virginia
Burnside, Ann
Burnside, Frank
Burnside, John
Burnside, L.
Burnside, Milton
Burnside, Tom
Burris, D.
Byjoe, Phillip
Cadman, Julia
Cadman, L.
Cadman, M.
Calvin, Michael D.
Calvin, Sadie
Cambridge, Norman
Candelaria, Rama
Carroll, Michael
Carviso, E.
Carviso, Emma

Carviso, W. Jr.
Castillo, Bessie
Cating, Wesley
Chaco, Eddy
Chapo, Ben
Charley, J.
Charley, L.
Charley, Ric
Charley, Rose
Charley, Stanley
Charlie, H.
Charlie, John
Charlie, Tommie
Chatter, Delbert
Chatter, Jack B.
Chavez, Evelyn
Chavez, John
Chee, Anita
Chee, Betty Jean
Chee, Billy
Chee, D.
Chee, Donald
Chee, Howard
Chee, Irene
Chee, James
Chee, Louise
Claw, Eunice
Claw, Jessie
Claw, Mary
Claw, Paul Jr.
Clawson, Wayne
Cleveland, Frank
Cleveland, Fred
Cleveland, Ruby
Cly, Sarah
Coan, Frances
Coan, Jim
Cody, Sadie
Corn, John
Cowboy, Annie
Cowboy, D.
Cowboy, Ella
Cowboy, Jerry
Craig, Carson
Craig, Hyson
Craig, Marie
Craig, Wesley
Crawford, Eugene
Cresto, R.
Curley, M.
Curley, Nelson
Curley, Robert
Curley, Stanley
Curtis, Thomas
Curtis, Toni
Custer, B.
Custer, N.
Custer, Nancy
Damon, Gilbert
Dan, Frankie
David, Donald
David, E.J.
David, Frank
David, Tom
Davis, Caroline
Davis, Clyde
Davis, Mike
Davis, P.
Davis, R.

Daw, Lola
Dayea, Leroy
Dayea, Mary
Dedman, D.
Delgarito, B.
Delgarito, Roy Nez
Delvin, John
Denetclaw, Clarence Jr.
Denetdeal, Donald
Denetso, Tom
Dick, Johnny
Dickens, L.
Dickens, Sarah
Dickson, Benny
Dixon, Jean
Dixon, S.
Dodge, Lawrence
Dodge, Stanley Carrol
Draper, Lowell
Draper, Rose
Dubois, Alice
Dubois, Jake
Duboise, Ben
Duboise, Sarah
Eddie, Isabel
Edison, E.
Ellot, R.
Emerson, Bill
Emerson, Nelson
Endito, Ella
Endito, Randy
Etsate, Betty
Etsitty, E.
Etsitty, A.
Etsitty, Fred
Etsitty, Marie
Etsitty, N.
Etsitty, Nancy
Etsitty, Raymond
Etsitty, Richard
Etsitty, Tom
Etsitty, V.
Etsitty, Yazzie
Fernando, Lillian
Francis, Irma
Francisco, Helen
Francisco, Roger
Frank, J.
Frank, Jimmy
Frank, Johnny
Frank, Paul
Franklin, Jerome
Franklin, Nelson
Garcia, John C.
Gaussoin, Connie Tsosie
George, John
Gisnie, Roger
Goodluck, Teddy
Goruld, Joanne R.
Gould, J.B.
Gray, Joe Lee
Guerno, Frank
Guerro, Frank
Guerro, Fred
Guerro, Tony
Haley
Haley, Benjamin
Haley, Christine
Haley, J.

Haley, James M.
Haley, Julian
Haley, Paul
Haley, Presley
Haley, Robert
Haley, Willie
Hamilton, Alice
Hansen, Freda (Woodman)
Harrison, Douglas
Harrison, James
Harrison, Jim
Harvey, Herbert E.
Harvey, Henry
Henry, Arlene
Henry, Bernard J.
Henry, George
Henry, L.
Henry, Nusie
Henry, Wilford J.
Herald, Jimmy
Herald, Jimmy Jr.
Herrera, Katie
Hesuse, Henry P.
Hildreth, Bobby
Hildreth, Marguerita
Hill, C.V.
Holden, Les
Hotsoi, Ernest Sr.
Hoskie, Billy John
Hoskie, Ervin
Hoskie, Esther Coan
Hoskie, John
Hothan, Lani
Hurley, Ronnie
Ignacio, Irma
Jack, Rena P.
Jack, Rosa
Jackson, Dan
Jackson, D.A.
Jackson, E.
Jackson, Gene
Jackson, James
Jackson, Larry
Jackson, Martha
Jackson, Mary E.
Jackson, R.
Jackson, Raymond
Jackson, T.
Jackson, Virginia
Jackson, Willie
Jake, Harry
James
James, Alice
James, Bahe
James, Della
James, Dennis
James, Francis
James, L.
James, Leonard
James, Llewellyn
James, Marcella
James, R.W.
James, Ray Jr.
James, Rita
James, Virginia
Jameson, Don
Jamez, P
Jamez, S.
Jamez, Sarah

TRIBAL AFFILIATIONS 203

Jim, A.
Jim, D.A.
Jim, H.
Jim, I.
Jim, Irene
Jim, Marie Le
Jim, N.
Jim, Thomas
Jim, Wilson
Joe, Alfred
Joe, Anderson
Joe, Anson
Joe, Charlie
Joe, Corbet
Joe, Ella Mae
Joe, H.
Joe, Kee
Joe, Larry
Joe, Mary
Joe, Ted
Joe, Tom K.
Joe, Tony
John, Dennison
John, Kee
John, Kenny
Johnson, C.
Johnson, Don
Johnson, Etta
Johnson, Florence
Johnson, Freddie
Johnson, James
Johnson, Janice
Johnson, Jerry
Johnson, Joann
Johnson, Leonard
Johnson, M.
Johnson, M.J.
Johnson, Mary Ann
Johnson, Mary
Johnson, Morty
Johnson, Patterson
Johnson, Paul
Johnson, Tommy
Johnson, V.G. Johnson
Johnson, William G.
Johnson, Yazzie
Johnston, Mrs. H.R.
Jones, Francis
Jones, L.
Jones, Paul
Jones, Ray Jr.
Jordan, Billy
Joseph, D.
Juan, Don
Kahn, Chester
Kahn, Franklin
Kalisteo, Dennis
Keams, Chee
Kee
Kee, Allen
Kee, Anthony
Kee, Carol
Kee, E.
Kee, Ed
Kee, Elmer
Kee, Elizabeth
Kee, George
Kee, Harrison
Kee, I.
Kee, Inez
Kee, Irvin
Kee, Ivan
Kee, J.
Kee, Mabel
Kee, Marie
Kee, Richard
Kee, Samson
Kee, T.
Kee, Vee
Keeto, Larry
Kelly, Jerry G.
King, E.
King, Henry
King, Jim
King, Jimenez
King, Jimmy Jr.
King, Johnny
King, Rita
Kirk, Andrew
Kirk, Michael
Kiyoomie, Joe
Lante, Doris
Largo, B.
Largo, D.F.
Largo, Ern
Largo, Gilbert
Largo, Harrison
Largo, Mary
Largo, Max
Largo, Rita
Lary, Jinny
Lee, Allison
Lee, Angela
Lee, Annie
Lee, B.
Lee, Cecil
Lee, Clarence
Lee, Daniel
Lee, Doris
Lee, Ella Mae
Lee, George
Lee, Irene
Lee, Jameson
Lee, Louise
Lee, L.
Lee, S.
Lee, Samuel
Lee, Shirley
Lee, Stan
Lee, Timothy
Lee, Tom
Lee, Virginia
Lew, Mary S.
Lewis, Al
Lewis, Art
Lewis, Austin
Lewis, Charles
Lewis, Ervin
Lewis, J.C.
Lewis, J.J.
Lewis, James
Lewis, Jim
Lewis, Jimmie
Lewis, Manuel
Lewis, Roger A.
Lewis, T.A.
Lincoln, Ambrose
Lincoln, Benson
Lincoln, Elaine
Lincoln, Francis Thomas
Lincoln, Herman H.
Lincoln, Mary
Lincoln, Mary Marie
Lincoln, Randolph
Lincoln, Rose
Lister, D.K.
Lister, Ernest C.
Little, James
Livingston, B.
Livingston, Jacob I.
Livingston, Lorenzo
Livingston, Mary
Lizer, David
Long, Albert
Long, Alfred
Long, Alice
Long, Clarence
Long, Emerson
Long, Helen
Long, J.W.
Long, Jimmie
Long, Kee
Long, Mary
Long, Phillip
Long, R.
Long, Rose Haley
Long, Rowland
Long, Sammie
Long, Tom
Lowe, Joe Tom
Lynch, Ella
McCabe, Albert
McCabe, Allan
McCrea, Ernest
McGee, Bob
McHorse, Chris Nofchissey
McRae, Billy
Manuel, J.
Manygoats, B.
Manygoats, Jackie
Martin, Andrew
Martin, Benny
Martin, G.
Martin, Roy
Martin, Vicki
Martinez, Archie
Martinez, Benny
Martinez, Dorothy
Martinez, Ethel
Martinez, Leo
Mason, Edgar
Mason, James
Matt, Mary
Mexicano, Maryann Platero
Mike, Gloria
Mike, Dora
Mike, Lois
Monongye, Jessie
Montano, Gibson
Montoya, Kee
Morgan, Ben Billie
Morgan, Bertha
Morgan, Charley
Morgan, Herman K.
Morgan, Ida
Morgan, Louise
Morgan, Mary

Morgan, Ben Billie
Morgan, Bertha
Morgan, Charley
Morgan, Herman K.
Morgan, Ida
Morgan, Louise
Morgan, Mary
Morgan, Tom
Morris, Earl
Morris, Henry
Morris, Tom
Morris, Willie
Munson, H.
Murphy, Ben
Musket, W.J.
Myers, Grace
Navajohn, Leroy
Ned, Andrew Sr.
Nelson, Charlie
Nelson, Eddie
Nelson, J.L.
Nelson, Jerry
Nelson, John
Nelson, Matthew R.
Nelson, Ruth
Nelwoot, M.
Nez, Al
Nez, B.
Nez, Chester
Nez, Coolidge
Nez, Gibson
Nez, Henry
Nez, Hoskie
Nez, Jackson Jarrett
Nez, James
Nez, Julian
Nez, Lucy
Nez, Rosemary
Nez, Thomas
Nez, Wilford
Nezzie, Jimmie
Nezzie, Willie
Noble, E.
Notah, A.
Pablo, Johnnie
Pablo, Sam
Padilla, Bessie
Padilla, Wilson
Parker, Trudy
Patterson, Jimmie
Paul, Betty
Paul, Delores
Paul, Leo
Paul, Rita
Peshlakai, Dalton
Peshlakai, Etta
Peshlakai, Frank
Peshlakai, Fred
Peshlakai, Norbert
Peshlakai, Otis
Pete, Curtis
Peter, Ben
Peter, E.
Philnetto
Piaso, Cindy
Piaso, Virginia
Pino, Nellie
Pinto, Benny
Platero, Agnes

Platero, Albert
Platero, Alice
Platero, Betty
Platero, Carol
Platero, Don
Platero, F.C.
Platero, Fannie
Platero, Freddie
Platero, Herbert
Platero, Inez
Platero, Jeannette
Platero, Jerry
Platero, Joey
Platero, John
Platero, Johnson
Platero, Jonathan
Platero, Leonard
Platero, Louise/Lucille
Platero, Maria
Platero, Prewitt
Platero, Ramon
Platero, Robert
Platero, Sam
Platero, Scotty
Platero, Thompson
Platero, Tom
Platero, Veronica
Platers, Alice
Platers, John
Plummer, Harry
Popovich, Jane
Poston, James
Radcliffe, Sylvia Begay
Rafel, Tom
Randolph, Sadie
Ration, A.
Ration, Christine
Ration, E.
Reagan, Gene
Redwater
Reeves, H.
Reeves, L.
Roan, Jerry
Roanhorse, Ambrose
Roanhorse, Henry
Roanhorse, James
Roanhorse, Louise
Roanhorse, Sam
Robertson, L.
Rockbridge, Russ
Rogers, Kay
Ross, Edison
Salt
Salt, Larry L.
Sam, Alice
Sam, Benson
Sam, Betty
Sam, Jim
Sam, Junior L.
Sam, Margaret
Sam, Sadie
Sam, Tully
Sampson, Clyde
Sanders, Alice
Sanders, Cecil
Sandoval, Danny
Sandoval, Glenn
Sandoval, Irene
Sandoval, Larry

Sandoval, Leroy
Sandoval, Sherry
Schmallie, Leonard
Scott, Bennie Kee
Scott, David
Scott, Raymond
Scott, Rosco
Secatero, Rayna Platero
Secatero, Tommie
Secatero, Wilbert
Shabie, Lester D.
Shakey, R.
Shaw, Willie
Shay, James
Sheets, Irene
Shepherd, Lincoln
Shirley, Alice M.
Shirley, Annie
Silver, Marie
Silver, N.
Silver, Mary A.
Silvers, Wayne
Silversmith, Jimmie
Silversmith, Teddy
Singer, Charlie
Singer, Jackie
Singer, Juan
Singer, Tommy
Singer, William
Skeet, Roger
Skeets, Anderson
Skeets, Irene
Sleuth, Jerry
Slim, Billy
Slim, Grace
Slim, Helen
Slim, Michael L.
Slinkey, Herman
Sluein, Jerry
Smallcanyon, Doris
Smiley, Billy Ray
Smiley, Dan
Smiley, Lena Mae
Smiley, Martha
Smiley, Robert Lee
Smiley, Stella
Smith, Bertha
Smith, Dennis
Smith, Edison Sandy
Smith, Howard
Smith, Lorenzo
Smith, Marie
Smith, Mary B.
Smith, Oliver
Smith, P.
Smithy, Leonard
Sorrell, Robert
Spencer
Spencer, Dorothy
Spencer, E.
Spencer, H.
Spencer, J.J.
Spencer, John
Spencer, K.
Spencer, Kee Tso
Spencer, P.
Spencer, R.
Spencer, S.
Spencer, W.

Sperica, Betty
Sperica, Sam
Stago, Lula Mae
Sterling, F.W.
Tabaho, D.
Tabaho, S.
Tadytin, L.
Tahe, Verna
Taylor, Pat
Teller, D.
Thomas, Leroy
Thomas, Louise
Thomas, M.
Thomas, Richard
Thomas, T.
Thompson, Franklin
Thompson, Fred
Thompson, Hardy
Thompson, Jessie
Thompson, Leroy
Thompson, Marie
Thompson, Melvin
Thompson, Norman
Thompson, Phillip
Thompson, S.
Toadlena, J.
Toadlena, James
Todacheenie, Stella
Todacheeny, Johnson
Toledo, Curlene
Toledo, Mary
Toledo, Tony
Tolino, A.R.
Tom, Clarence B.
Tom, Duane
Tom, Elizabeth
Tom, H.L.
Tom, James
Tom, Joe
Tom, Larry Bill
Tooth, Duane
Tooth, Juan
Touchine, Benny
Touchine, Edward
Touchine, Grace
Tracey, Larry
Tracey, Ray
Trujillo, Harold
Trujillo, Velma
Tsinnie, Darlene
Tsinie, Orville
Tso, Billie
Tso, Dan
Tso, Nellie
Tso, Phillip
Tso, Raymond
Tso, Thomas
Tsodia, Delphine
Tsosie
Tsosie, Billie
Tsosie, Boyd
Tsosie, Dolly
Tsosie, Elie
Tsosie, Harrison
Tsosie, Irene
Tsosie, Julie
Tsosie, Kee
Tsosie, Lucie
Tsosie, Mary E.

Tsosie, Melvin
Tsosie, M.J.
Tsosie, Paul
Tsosie, Richard
Tsosie, Robertson T.
Tsosie, Wilson
Tsouhlarakis, George
Tsui, Leo S.
Tulley, Richard
Turner, Slim
Turquoise, Leroy
Upshaw, James
Vanderver, Anita
Vanderver, Anthony
Vandever, Lucy M.
Vandever, Roy
Vandever, William
Vaughn, Ted
Vincent, R.
Walker, Kent
Warner, Raymond
Watchman, Larry
Watchman, Lottie
Watson, G.
Watson, Jefferson
Watson, Major Joe
Watson, Sarah
Wauneka, Wilbur
Webster, C.
Wero, Freddie
Wesley, Lee
Whirling Wind, Ray
White, Alice
White, Ella Mae
White, F.
White, John
White, M.
White, Phillip
Whitegoat, Dennison
Whitegoat, James
Whitegoat, W.
Whitman, Elizabeth
Whitman, Tim Kee
Willeto, Martha
Willeto, Sargent
Willeto, Tom
Williams, Arthur J.
Williams, Billie Jr.
Williams, Guy K.
Williams, Laura
Williams, Remulda
Willie, Annie
Willie, Charles
Willie, Harrison
Willie, Laura
Willie, Lonnie
Willie, Robert
Wilson, Austin
Wilson, Lucy
Wilson, Chee
Wilson, Eunise J.
Wilson, Henry
Wood, Alice K.
Wood, Ernest
Woods, Joe E.
Woody, Clyde
Wylie, Ella Mae
Wylie, Eula
Wylie, Mary

Wylie, R.
Yazzie, A.
Yazzie, Alvin
Yazzie, Antonio
Yazzie, Benson
Yazzie, Bertha
Yazzie, Bessie
Yazzie, Charlene
Yazzie, Charlie Mike
Yazzie, David H.
Yazzie, Delores
Yazzie, Dick Mike
Yazzie, Don
Yazzie, Dudley
Yazzie, Eddie
Yazzie, Elsie
Yazzie, Eugene Jr.
Yazzie, Evelyn
Yazzie, Frances
Yazzie, H.D.
Yazzie, Harry
Yazzie, Helen
Yazzie, Henry A.
Yazzie, Irene
Yazzie, J.
Yazzie, Jason
Yazzie, Jimmy
Yazzie, Joe
Yazzie, Joe D.
Yazzie, Larry Lee
Yazzie, Lee
Yazzie, Leo Lando
Yazzie, Leroy
Yazzie, Leslie
Yazzie, Luke Billy
Yazzie, Marie
Yazzie, Mary Marie
Yazzie, Mary Chee
Yazzie, Nellie
Yazzie, Nelson
Yazzie, Pat
Yazzie, Raymond C.
Yazzie, Raymond E.
Yazzie, Richard C.
Yazzie, Richard Henry
Yazzie, Tim
Yazzie, W.
Yazzie, Wilber
Yazzie, Willie A. Jr.
Yazzie, Wilson
Yellowhair, Billy
Yellowhair, Marie
Yellowhair, Ann
Yellowhair, David

OSAGE
Lightfoot, Buddy (Edmundson)

PAIUTE
Benn, Virgil
Martinez, Eugene
Martinez, Huberta

PAPAGO
Fendenheim, James
Manuel, Rick
Noriega, Alton
Ranson, Roger

PICURIS
Duran, Tom

PIMA
Sosolda, Alvin

POTTOWOTOMIE
Shopteese, John (Sauk Fox)

SANDIA
Padilla, Paul (Isleta)
Velasquez, Mary (Isleta)

SAN CARLOS APACHE
Albert, Myra
Betoni, Ethel
Bohlen, Aurelia
Bush, Curley Jr.
Cassadore, Whitman Jr.
Edwards, Vergie
Ferreia, Jeanne
Fragua, Vera
Gilbert, Wilma
Halfmoon, Carlos
Hinton, Cornelia
Lukee, Rebecca
Kenton, Sandra
Mull, Margie
Pike, Snyder
Small, Serena
Stevens, Verna
Victor, Darrell

SAN FELIPE
Chavez, Mary
Ramone, Nellie
Velasquez, Mary (?)

SAN JUAN TEWA
Naranjo, Manuel
Tewa, Bobby

SANTA CLARA
Chavarria, Harvey
Lonewolf, Joseph
Tafoya, Richard

SANTO DOMINGO
Aguilar, Benny
Aguilar, Frances
Aguilar, Tony
Aguilar, Wayne
Aragon, Videl
Arragos, Virgil
Atencio, Frank
Benevidez, Jose
Bly, Jack
Boone
Boone, A.
Calabaza, Mitchell
Chavez, Alfred
Chavez, Luciano
Chavez, Trinnie
Coriz, Juanita
Coriz, Leo
Coriz, Raymond
Francisco, Nelson M.
Garcia, David F.
Garcia, Juan Pedro
Garcia, Nelson
Lovato, Charles
Lovato, Clara
Lovato, Dan
Lovato, Harold
Lovato, Homer
Lovato, Julian
Lovato, Manuelito Judy
Lovato, Marie
Lovato, Mary
Lovato, Mary C.
Lovato, Sam
Lovato, Sedalio F.
Moquino, Jim
Reano, Jerry
Reano, Joe
Reano, Percy
Reano, Terry
Rosetta, Dan
Rosetta, Johnnie
Rosetta, Marlene
Rosetta, Mary
Rosetta, Paul
Rosetta, Ray
Rosetta, Romijio
Sakewa, David
Tenorio, Joe
Tenorio, James
Tenorio, Mary
Tortalita, Joe
Tortalita, Lorenzo
Tortalita, Vickie

SAUK FOX
Christiansen, John
Shopteese, John (Pottowotomie)

SHOSHONI
Rogers, Michael (Paiute)

TAOS
Lujan, Arthur
Lujan, Bobby
Lujan, Jerry Orlando
Lujan, Jimmie
Lujan, Nettie
Lujan, Rick
Nava, Douglas
Schlosser, Mary Lou
Trujillo, Woody

TESUQUE
Stoddard, Mary

WALAPAI
Jackson, Murray

WESTERN TEWA
Adams, Sadie
Ami, Mary
Benn, Shirley (Tewa)
Carl, Sybil
Charley, Lena Chio
Carcia, Leah Nampeyo
Naha, Helen
Naha, Sylvia
Nash, Edith
Pavatea, Garnet
Polacca, Ellsworth Nampeyo
Polacca, Fannie Nampeyo
Polacca, Harold
Polacca, Tom
Quotskuyva, Camille
Quotskuyva, Dextra
Sahmie, Randolph
Shupla, Irene Gilbert

ZIA
Medina, E.

ZUNI
Acoya, Art
Acque, Evelyn
Acque, Gloria
Allapowa, Patsy
Allapowa, Thomas Jr.
Anderson, Paul
Anderson, Tom
Arviso, Paul
Banteah, Albert
Banteah, Dolly
Banteah, Gary
Banteah, Matilda
Banteah, Serena
Banteah, Valentino
Bassalente, Marie
Besselente, M.
Beyuka, Edward
Beyuka, Jonathan
Beyuka, Madeline
Bobelu, Carolyn
Bobelu, Owen
Bobelu, Rosalita
Boone, Alex
Boone, Lena
Boone, Paulinus
Boone, Perletta
Boone, Rigney
Booqua, A.
Booqua, Glendora
Booqua, Marlene
Booqua, Rickell
Bowannie, Adeline
Bowannie, Delia
Bowannie, Earlene
Bowannie, Fadrian
Bowannie, Fred
Bowannie, John Q.
Bowannie, Lula
Bowannie, Rosalie
Bowekaty, Agnes
Bowekaty, Bernard
Bowekaty, Hugh
Bowekaty, Lucille
Bowekaty, Samson
Bradley, Charlotte
Bradley, George
Bradley, Tom
Cachini, A.
Cachini, Fred
Cachini, Sybil
Calabaza, Olivia
Calabaza, Ronnie
Calabaza, Effie
Calavaza, Joan
Calavaza, Jose
Calavaza, Juan
Calavaza, Susie

TRIBAL AFFILIATIONS

Calavaza, Viola
Calavaza, Wayne
Caldito, Ray
Callaway, Mary L.
Celencio, L
Cellecion, Angela
Cellecion, LeIa
Cellecion, Oliver
Cellecion, Roger
Charlie, Darlene
Charlie, Dickie
Charlie, Felix
Charlie, Yvonne
Chavez, Eileen
Chavez, Felix
Chavez, Maryann
Chavez, Sabin M.
Chavez, Vidal
Cheama, Angelita
Cheama, C.
Cheama, Marvelyine
Cheama, Wayne
Chipito, Hilda
Clark, John D.
Cly, John
Cly, Raphina
Comer, Mary Jones
Cooche, Celestine
Cooche, Elizabeth
Coonsis, E.
Coonsis, Harlan
Coonsis, Rolanda
Cooyate, Ransom
Corey, Mary Jane
Couyancy, Clark
Delena, Lita
Dewa, Andrew
Dewa, Don C.
Dewa, Velma
Dewesee, Jeanette
Dickson, Larry
Dickson, Lorinda
Dishta, Charlene
Dishta, Duane
Dishta, Lena
Dishta, Robert
Dishta, V. Sr.
Edaakie, Dennis
Edaakie, Evangelita
Edaakie, Jennie
Edaakie, Mary Ann
Edaakie, Myron
Edaakie, Nancy
Edaakie, Theodore
Edaakie, Zeno
Edakie, Jack
Elliot, Chavis
Epaloos, Jennie
Eriacho, Christine
Eriacho, Daniel
Eriacho, Donald
Eriacho, Glenda
Eriacho, Kirk
Eriacho, Mary
Eriacho, Sefferino
Eriacho, Viola
Esalio, Howard
Escalio, Lawrence
Etsitty, Ann
Eustace, Beatrice
Eustace, Ben
Eustace, Charlotte
Eustace, Christine
Eustace, Felicita
Eustace, Joe
Eustace, Jolene
Eustace, Ken
Eustace, Linda
Eustace, Louvinda
Eustace, Nelson
Eustace, Roland
Eustace, Sensa
Eustis, Francis
Francis, James
Frank, Jerry
Gahate, Bart
Gahate, Dewey
Gahate, Janette
Garcia, Gloria Jean
Gasper, Annie
Gasper, Arlan
Gasper, Ashbarry
Gasper, Clara
Gasper, Elkus
Gasper, Filbert
Gasper, Joseph
Gasper, L.V.
Gasper, Raymond
Gasper, Rose
Gchachu, Ruby
Gchachu, Smoky
Gchachu, Terry
Gia, Ella
Gia, Wesley
Guardian, Esther
Guardian, Sammy
Haloo, Nancy
Haloo, Peter III
Haloo, Vivian
Hannaweeka, Alice
Hannaweeka, Charlie
Hannaweeka, Pauline
Hannaweeka, Thomas
Haskie, Florinda
Haskie, Norbert
Hattie
Hattie, Anita
Hattie, Bita
Hattie, Buddy
Hattie, Butch
Hattie, Derrick
Hattie, Harlan
Hattie, Ivan
Hattie, Naneen
Hattie, Vivian
Hawley, Johnnie
Hughte, Georgeann
Hughte, Rodney
Hustito, Alonzo
Hustito, Charles
Hustito, Sharon
Iule, Gary
Iule, Horace
Iule, Lupe
Iule, Phillip
Iule, W.
James, Rose Mary
Jamon, Cliff
Jamon, Cornelia
Jaramillo, Eddie
Jaramillo, Odelle
Johnson, Cecil Jr.
Johnson, Socorro
Johnson, Vincent
Kalestena, Jack
Kallestewa, Ben
Kallestewa, Dennis
Kallestewa, Farrel
Kallestewa, Harvey
Kallestewa, Janita
Kallestewa, John
Kallestewa, Lilly
Kallestewa, Lorrie
Kallestewa, Marcie
Kallestewa, Ralph
Kallestewa, Reyes
Kallestewa, Sibert
Kallestewa, Sue Ellen
Kalistewa, Quanita
Kanteena, Raybert
Kanteena, Rhoda
Kaskalla, Lebert
Kaskalla, Louise
Kaskalla, Roderick
Katsenih, Carrie
Kendy, Lorraine
King, Reyna
Kiyite, Alvin
Kiyite, Donna
Laahty, Andrew
Laahte, Morris
Laahte, Sadie
Laate, Larry
Laate, Lygatie
Lackey, Al
Laconsello, Nancy
Laconsello, Ruddell
Lahi, Julie O.
Lakela, Nick
Lalio, Evelyn
Lalio, Lavonne
Lalio, S.M.
Lamon, Sara
Lamy, Julalita
Lanyate, Hesser
Lasiloo, Milton
Laweka, Billie
Laweka, Lorraine
Laweka, Lucinda
Leconelle, Nancy
Leekela, Anson
Leekela, Deborah
Leekety, D.
Leekity, Bernice
Leekity, Corinne
Leekity, Curtis
Leekity, Edward
Leekity, Eva
Leekity, George
Leekity, Lupeta
Leekity, Mary
Leekity, Nancy
Leekity, Nora
Leekity, Olson
Leekity, Paul
Leekya, Robert
Leekya, Virgil

Lementine, Roland
Lementino, Elmer
Lementino, Evans
Lementino, Mary
Lemento, Julie
Lesansee, Blake
Lesansee, Velma
Lewis, Effie
Leyba, Rinnie
Lidase, Matthew
Lidase, Rosemary
Lonasee, Ellen
Lonasee, Lawrence
Lonasee, L.J.
Loncasion, Terry
Lonesee, Raynold
Lonjose, Andrew
Lonjose, Edith
Lonjose, Helen
Lonjose, Janta
Lonjose, Leonard
Lonjose, Mabel C.
Lowsayatee, Mary Helen
Lucio, Ervin
Lucio, John
Lucio, John B.
Lucio, Landy
Luhela, Nick
Luhela, Theresa
Luna, Vera
Luneo, Eunice
Lupe, Eddie
Mahooty, Chester B.
Mahooty, Dorothy
Mahooty, Eugene
Mahooty, G.
Mahooty, Jay W.
Mahooty, Pam
Mahooty, T.
Mahooty, Yvonne
Malamic, Lolita
Martinez, Betty
Martinez, George
Martinez, Huberta
Martinez, Joseph
Martinez, Juan
Martinez, Mark
Martza, Leonard
Massie, Dora
Massie, Jose
Mateya, Bruce
Mateya, Mamie
Mayes, Jobeth
Milani, Lolita
Moon, Cactus
Nacitacio, Lolita
Nakatewa, Elsie
Naranjo, Feline
Nastacio, Alvin
Nastacio, Amelio
Nastacio, Billy
Nastacio, Leroy
Nastacio, Myra
Nastacio, Raphael
Nastacio, Veronica
Natachu, Bernice
Natachu, Fred
Natachu, Gillerimo
Natachu, Lolita

Natewa, Bernall
Natewa, Neal
Natewa, Orlinda
Natewa, Pitkin
Natewa, Shirley
Natewa, Wanda
Natseway, James
Nieto, Annacita
Nieto, Davis
Nieto, Celia
Nieto, J.J.
Nieto, Ray
Nieto, Rosemary
Niiha, Darlene
Niiha, Ed
Niiha, Jeannette
Niiha, Jefferson
Niiha, Verdel
Ohmsatte, Berdie
Ohmsatte, Silas
Ondelacy, Alberta
Ondelacy, Fannie
Ondelacy, Sol
Othole, F.
Pablito, Anthony
Pablito, R.
Paquin, Isabelle
Paquin, Sherman
Paloma, Janice
Panteah, Alma
Panteah, Augustine
Panteah, Esther
Panteah, Florentine
Panteah, Gus
Panteah, Josie
Panteah, Lela
Panteah, Lorie
Panteah, Martin
Panteah, Paula
Panteah, Quincy
Panteah, Rosemary
Panteah, Wayne
Paquin, Alvin
Paquin, Isabelle
Paquin, Sherman
Parker, Lennie
Pasalente, Jane
Paylasi, Irene
Paywa, Jim
Peina, Bernard
Peina, Ethel
Peina, Sylvia
Peina, Zigmund
Pekytewa, Paul
Penketewa, A
Penketewa, Claudine
Penketewa, Dorothy
Pewa, Albert
Peyketewa, Carol
Peyketewa, Libert
Peynetsa, Amy
Peynetsa, Jane
Peynetsa, Mitzi
Peynetsa, Sarah
Peywa, Jean
Piaso, Sam
Pincio, Rose
Pinto, Arlinda Rose
Pinto, Augustine

Pinto, Rosalie
Platero, Lolita
Poblano, Mary
Poblano, S.
Poblano, Veronica
Poncho, Billy
Poncho, Charles
Poncho, Dan
Poncho, Don
Poncho, Mary Ann
Qualo, Effie
Qualo, Elliot
Qualo, June
Qualo, Myra
Quam, Alice
Quam, Andrew
Quam, Bonnie
Quam, Duane
Quam, Elsie
Quam, Francine
Quam, Gerlinda
Quam, John
Quam, Raymond
Quam, Shirley
Quam, Virginia
Quam, Wayne
Quandelacy, Amy
Quandelacy, Dickie
Quandelacy, Ellen
Romancito, Emma
Romancito, Joyce
Salvador, Jennie
Salvador, Lloyd
Salvio
Sampson, Lucy
Sanchez, Angelita
Sanchez, Horace
Sanchez, Morenda
Sanchez, Willard
Seciwa, Charlotte
Seotewa, Irma
Seotewa, Octavius
Seotewa, Odelle
Shack, Bobby
Shack, Corraine
Sheeche, Arden
Sheeche, Melinda
Shelendewa, Linda
Shetima, L.L.
Sheyka, Ann
Sheyka, Corinne
Sheyka, Porfilio
Sice, Bernice
Sice, Norman
Simplicio, Carmelita
Simplicio, Lena
Simplicio, Mike
Simplicio, Sarah
Siow, Lorene
Siow, Thomas
Siutza, Avis
Siutza, Herbert
Siutza, Louise
Siutza, Stephen
Solomon, Judson
Soseah, Gloria
Tekala, Annie Lee
Tekala, Bernice
Tekala, Lawrence

Tekala, Roosevelt
Terrazas, Geneva
Todlena, Gordon
Tsabutie, Lloyd
Tsabetsaye, D.
Tsabetsaye, Edith
Tsabetsaye, Evangeline
Tsabetsaye, Griffin
Tsabetsaye, J.
Tsabetsaye, Joe
Tsabetsaye, Roger
Tsadiase
Tsadiase, Mary Ann
Tsadiase, Percy J.
Tsalate, Joanita
Tsalate, Linda
Tsethlikai, Doris
Tsethlikai, Ivan J.
Tsethlikai, Vivian
Tsethlikia, Lena
Tsethlakia, Patrick
Tsikewa, David
Tucson, Lee
Tucson, Myra
Tulley, Edison
Tulley, Elsie
Tzunie, Benjamin Jr.
Uhastine, Tom
Ukastine, Alma
Ukestine, Clarissa
Ukestine, Danny
Ukestine, Jason
Ukestine, Lebeck
Ukestine, Pearl
Unkestine, Irma
Vacit, Frank
Veronica
Waatsa, Bryant Jr.
Waatsa, Erma
Waatsa, Evans
Waatsa, Lorraine
Walela, Edison
Walela, Shirley
Wallace, Anselm
Wallace, Judy
Wallace, Regina
Wallace, Rosita
Wallace, Vernon
Waseta, Helen
Waseta, Louie
Watasilo, Edward
Watson, Mabel
Weahkee, Tom
Weebothee, Beverly
Weebothee, Lee
Weebothee, Leonard
Weebothee, Lula
Weebothee, Mary
Weebothee, Mike
Weebothee, Taft
Weeka, Eleanor
Weeka, W.D.
Weekoty, Fred
Weekoty, Jack
Westika, Nancy
Westika, Sheldon
Wyaco, Bernie
Wyaco, Elanda
Wyaco, Evangeline

Wyaco, Kerry
Wyaco, Ray
Yamutewa, Benny
Yamutewa, Irma
Yamutewa, Roger
Yamutewa, Victoria
Yatsattie, Ann
Yatsattie, Polly
Yatsayte, Josephine
Yawakia, Adeline
Yawakia, Henry
Yawakia, Lila
Yesslith
Yuselen, Gilbert
Yuselew, Nita
Zunie, Charlene
Zunie, Clybert
Zunie, Ernest
Zunie, Geneva
Zunie, Helen
Zuni, Joe
Zunie, Lincoln
Zunie, Michael
Zunie, William

UNKNOWN TRIBE
Adams, Del
Alcott, Michael
Anderson, Dorothy
Andler, R.
Apodaca, Linda
Arviso, Susie
Baca, Henry
Barber, Henry
Barber, Linda
Barton, Bernard
Batte, B.
Blancarte, Juan
Bowie
Brown, Benjamin
Cadman, Delores
Candman, L.
Carusetta, Thomas
Casuse, Mary
Chama, Felix
Chambers, Mary Jane
Chavez, Ben
Chavez, C
Chavez, Christopher
Chavez, H.E.
Chavez, Jimmie
Chavez, Phillip
Chavez, Phyllis
Chavez, Ramos
Cheromiah, Ethel
Christie, Tom
Comosona, Chino
Concha, Pablita
Cord
Crawford, Yvonne
Cross, Earl
Cunejo, Joaquin
Curtis, Max
Dale, Karen
Dalton, Robert
Dennison, Lester
DeSoto, Joe
Dixon, Don
Dodson, W.

Douglas, Wm.
Eaglestar, Dennis
Eldred, Steve
Elthe, L.
Emmanuel, James
Enrico, F.
Feliciano
Felix, Duffy
Fredenburg, Dennis
Garcia, Cathy
Garcia, Tony
Garnett, James
Garrett, Donald
Garrison, Jerry
Gordon, D.
Graham, Midge
Grijalva, David
Guerro, Amy
Guerroy, J.J.
Gurule, Presiliano
Hansen, Bo
Harmsen, William
Harugy, Herbert
Harvey, L.
Hatch, Paul
Henry, J. P.
Horace Emerson
Horse, K.
Hosler, Bob
Howarter, Terri
Hubbard, George
Itaiko, Lee
Iverson, Elmer
James, Jefferson
Jansen, D.
Jensen, D.
Jogar
Kelly, Robert
King, Anna
Kirk, John
Klimaj, Stephen J.
Johnson, L.
Laroche, Rose
Leonard, Sandra
Leota
Lightfoot, Melody
Linkin, Tully
Loma, K.
Long, Roland
Loretto, G.
McKinstry
Madrid, Joseph
Montana, M.
Morgan, Jack
Motse, Nora Naranjo
Muehler, David
Myrtle, Ellen
Najdowski, Mike
Olguin, J.
Ortiz, L.
Ortiz, Raymond
Othole, Adrian A.
Padilla, J.
Palmer, Keith
Paquin, Geraldine
Paquin, Leonard
Parker, D.
Peone, Les
Peterman

Pino, Dave
Pino, Gilbert
Pino, Harog
Pino, Harvey
Pino, Ida
Pino, Ira
Pino, Jackson
Pino, Katherine
Pino, Marie
Pino, Offina
Pino, Rita G.
Prince, Lee
Quraishi, Masallah
Raincloud, Harry
Rainstar
Ramone, Annie
Ramone, Frank
Ramone, Geneva
Ramone, L.
Ramone, Sally
Ray, Silver
Redbird, D.
Romero, Cipriano
Romero, Adelaido
Salisteo, D.
Sanchez, Larry
Sandoval, Ben
Sandoval, David
Sayeswa
Schendel, Gene
Schmaltz, Mike
Seago, Eunice
Seibert, Don
Smith, Ed
Spurgeon, Richard
Strain, Clyde B.
Strong, John B.
Tafoya, Art
Tafoya, Ray
Thunderbolt, C.
Thunderfoot, C.
Toledo, Eva
Toledo, H.
Toledo, Russell
Tracy, Stan
Trueba, Jim
Trujillo, Charles
Trujillo, Ernest
Tune, David
Walley, N.
Wanikia, Tommy
Weatherford, David
White Cloud, Wylie
White Wolf
Willeto, Joe
Wolf, Christin
Wood, Jasper

Index VI: Unidentified Marks

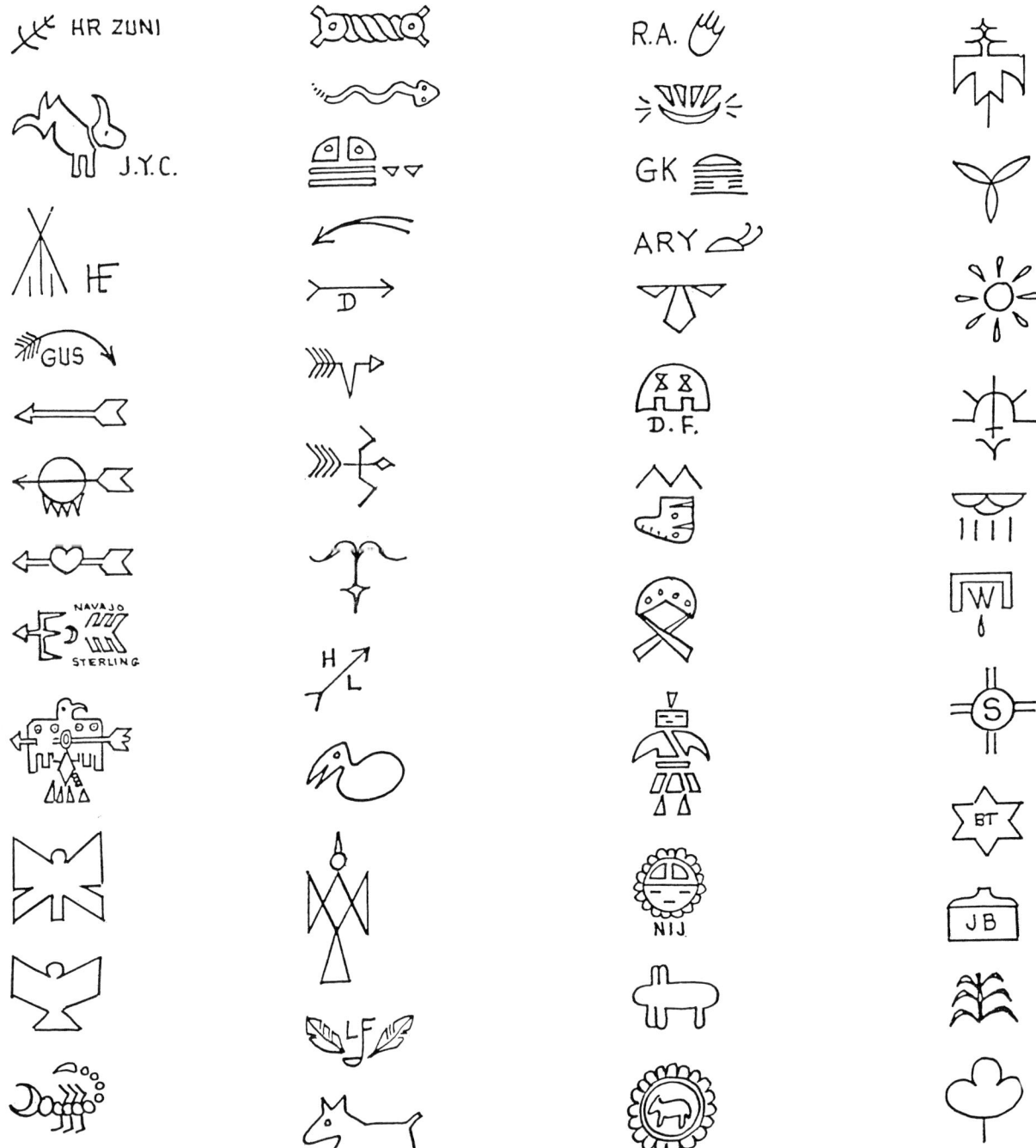

212 UNIDENTIFIED MARKS

用B	IK
AG, A_G	LR
ALH	L^S
AZKP	~4
BK (crossed)	M
BE	J
BK	MK
DF	MNT
DHL	N
DJB	N (script)
DJN	NJ ZIJ
E^L R	NK
EM	NSR
EM (monogram)	P7
F|	P.T.B.
FNG	>R
F_Y^M	RH
G	RHC
GG	B
Gao.JN	(RM)
GN	Ry
Ho	S.B.
HD	SG
HGS	Ş
IH	S_D^V
IN	T (circled)
J.H.	<T
L.H. ZUNI	TN
JMB, [JMB]	TR
LAN	TSH
L.B.TOM	TTM
[LH]	V3

References

Adair, John *The Navajo and Pueblo Silversmiths*. University of Oklahoma Press. Norman, OK. 1946.

Bell, Ed and Barbara. *Zuni, the Art and the People*. Vol. 1. Taylor Publ. Co. Dallas, TX. 1975.

Bell, Ed and Barbara. *Zuni, the Art and the People*. Vol. 2. Taylor Publ. Co. Dallas, TX. 1976.

Bell, Ed and Barbara. *Zuni, the Art and the People*. Vol. 3. Taylor Publ. Co. Dallas, TX. 1977.

King, Dale Stuart. *Indian Silverwork of the Southwest*. Vol. 2. D.S. King Publ. Tucson, AZ. 1976.

Levy, Gordon. *Whos Who in Zuni Jewelry.Western* Arts Publ. Co. Denver, CO. 1980.

Wright, Margaret Nickelson. *Hopi Silver*. Northland Press. Flagstaff, AZ. 1982.